HTML *Goodies*

HTML Color Codes

Aliceblue F0F8FF	Antiquewhite FAEBD7	Aqua 00FFFF	Aquamarine 7FFFD4
Azure F0FFFF	Beige F5F5DC	Bisque FFE4C4	Black 000000
Blanchedalmond FFEBCD	Blue 0000FF	Blueviolet 8A2BE2	Brown A52A2A
Burlywood DEB887	Cadetblue 5F9EA0	Chartreuse 7FFF00	Chocolate D2691E
Coral FF7F50	Cornflowerblue 6495ED	Cornsilk FFF8DC	Crimson DC143C
Cyan 00FFFF	Darkblue 00008B	Darkcyan 008B8B	Darkgoldenrod B8860B
Darkgray A9A9A9	Darkgreen 006400	Darkkhaki BDB76B	Darkmagenta 8B008B
Darkolivegreen 556B2F	Darkorange FF8C00	Darkorchid 9932CC	Darkred 8B0000
Darksalmon E9967A	Darkseagreen 8FBC8F	Darkslateblue 483D8B	Darkslategray 2F4F4F
Darkturquoise 00CED1	Darkviolet 9400D3	Deeppink FF1493	Deepskyblue 00BFFF
Dimgray 696969	Dodgerblue 1E90FF	Firebrick B22222	Floralwhite FFFAF0
Forestgreen 228B22	Fuchsia FF00FF	Gainsboro DCDCDC	Ghostwhite F8F8FF
Gold FFD700	Goldenrod DAA520	Gray 808080	Green 008000
Greenyellow ADFF2F	Honeydew F0FFF0	Hotpink FF69B4	Indianred CD5C5C
Indigo 4B0082	Ivory FFFFF0	Khaki F0E68C	Lavendar E6E6FA
Lavenderblush FFF0F5	Lawngreen 7CFC00	Lemonchiffon FFFACD	Lightblue ADD8E6
Lightcoral F08080	Lightcyan E0FFFF	Lightgoldenrodyellow FAFAD2	Lightgreen 90EE90
Lightgrey D3D3D3	Lightpink FFB6C1	Lightsalmon FFA07A	Lightseagreen 20B2AA
Lightskyblue 87CEFA	Lightslategray 778899	Lightsteelblue B0C4DE	Lightyellow FFFFE0
Lime 00FF00	Limegreen 32CD32	Linen FAF0E6	Magenta FF00FF
Maroon 800000	Mediumauqamarine 66CDAA	Mediumblue 0000CD	Mediumorchid BA55D3

HTML Color Codes (Continued)

Mediumpurple 9370D8	Mediumseagreen 3CB371	Mediumslateblue 7B68EE	Mediumspringgreen 00FA9A
Mediumturquoise 48D1CC	Mediumvioletred C71585	Midnightblue 191970	Mintcream F5FFFA
Mistyrose FFE4E1	Moccasin FFE4B5	Navajowhite FFDEAD	Navy 000080
Oldlace FDF5E6	Olive 808000	Olivedrab 688E23	Orange FFA500
Orangered FF4500	Orchid DA70D6	Palegoldenrod EEE8AA	Palegreen 98FB98
Paleturquoise AFEEEE	Palevioletred D87093	Papayawhip FFEFD5	Peachpuff FFDAB9
Peru CD853F	Pink FFC0CB	Plum DDA0DD	Powderblue B0E0E6
Purple 800080	Red FF0000	Rosybrown BC8F8F	Royalblue 4169E1
Saddlebrown 8B4513	Salmon FA8072	Sandybrown F4A460	Seagreen 2E8B57
Seashell FFF5EE	Sienna A0522D	Silver C0C0C0	Skyblue 87CEEB
Slateblue 6A5ACD	Slategray 708090	Snow FFFAFA	Springgreen 00FF7F
Steelblue 4682B4	Tan D2B48C	Teal 008080	Thistle D8BFD8
Tomato FF6347	Turquoise 40E0D0	Violet EE82EE	Wheat F5DEB3
White FFFFFF	Whitesmoke F5F5F5	Yellow FFFF00	YellowGreen 9ACD32

HTML Ampersand (&) Commands

® ®	± ±	µ µ	¶ ¶	· ·	¢ ¢
£ £	¥ ¥	¼ ¼	½ ½	¾ ¾	¹ ¹
² ²	³ ³	¿ ¿	° °	¦ ¦	§ §
< <	> >	& &	" "	(A Space)	&Ccdil; Ç
ç ç	Ñ Ñ	ñ ñ	Þ Þ	þ þ	Ý Ý
ý ý	ÿ ÿ	ß ß	Æ Æ	Á Á	Â Â
À À	Å Å	Ã Ã	Ä Ä	æ æ	á á
â â	à à	å å	ã ã	ä ä	Ð Ð
É É	Ê Ê	È È	Ë Ë	ð ð	é é
ê ê	è è	ë ë	Í Í	Î Î	Ì Ì

Ï Ï	í í	î î	ì ì	ï ï	Ó Ó
Ô Ô	Ò Ò	Ø Ø	Õ Õ	Ö Ö	ó ó
ô ô	ò ò	ø ø	õ õ	ö ö	Ú Ú
Û Û	Ù Ù	Ü Ü	ú ú	û û	ù ù
ü ü	« «	» »			

Praise for Author Joe Burns' HTML Goodies Web Site

From the Web Site Visitors

"Thanks for the beautiful pieces of work. I salute you."
—*John J. Lacombe II; <jlacombe@cpcug.org>; Organization: Capital PC Users Group*

"This is not only a first-rate page, but is also a huge help to me, and, my guess is, many, MANY people like me. These tutorials have helped me create my own page. Once again, thank you. You're terrific."
—*Rose Dewitt Bukater; <renatab@webspan.net>*

"Wow! Either I'm not as dumb as I thought or you are a very good teacher! I think it's the latter."
—*Greville Hulse; <hulsegrevgeh@access1.net>*

"You probably get dozens of thank you notes each day, but I just wanted to add my own to the lot. Since I'm a just starting out in the HTML world, I've been visiting your tutorials a lot. Just wanted you to know I've learned more from your site than from any of the books I've bought!"
—*Dawn C. Lindley; <lindley@usa.net>*

"Dear Mr. Really Smart cool-happening dude, I would like to thank you because I have made the transition from FrontPage 98 to HTML all because of you. I spent months trying to learn HTML before I learned of your site, and at age 14 I fully understand the ins and outs of HTML 4. My page is in the works and I owe it all to you. =)"
—*Taylor Ackley; <ackleyx@hotmail.com>*

"I just wanted to let you know that you are doing an amazing service to all of us weekend Web masters. Thanks a million! P.S. My Web page looks and feels a thousand times better since I have been following your tutorials."
—*Aaron Joel Chettle; <ajchettl@learn.senecac.on.ca>; Organization: Seneca College Engineering*

"WOW!!!!...I was always interested in setting up a Web page, but was afraid that it would be too difficult for me to comprehend...So my first introduction to HTML were actually YOUR primers...and WOW!!!!!!! I went through ALL of them this very morning with my mouth hanging wide open...I am still so surprised that I cannot gather any words to describe to you how I feel at this moment."
—*Ludwin L. Statie; <ludwinl.statie@curinfo.an>*

"I'm an old dog learning new tricks. I will be taking a Web publishing college course come August. I used your primer as a jump start. I really enjoyed your primer and thought it would...help me. I now feel prepared for the college course and not so afraid to 'run with the big dogs.'"
—*Patricia Cuthbertson; <desertratpat@thegrid.net>*

From the Media

"If you are just learning, or already know HTML, this site is the only place you'll need. Expert tutorials make learning Web design quick and easy. Definitely check this site out."
—*HTML Design Association*

"Dr. Joe Burns offers help at all levels—from novice to the expert."
—*Signal Magazine*

"Great stuff. Probably the best overall site reviewed here."
—*NetUser Magazine*

"If you're looking for information on HTML, you'll find it here."
—*USA Today Hot Site*

"His is a technical site that appeals to an exploding piece of the Internet pie—people building their own Web site."
—*PCNovice Guide to Building Web Sites*

"We would like permission to use your Web pages [HTML Goodies] to help teach [building] Web sites."
—*San Antonio Electronic Commerce Resource Center*

From Teachers

"If everyone wrote 'how to' pages and books as well as you, boy life would be simpler."
—*Deb Spearing Ph.D.; University Registrar, Ohio State University*

"I am going to use your Goodies [to teach with] this summer! Awesome!"
—*Cynthia Lanius; Rice University*

"I hope your own students and colleagues appreciate the importance and magnitude of the service you provide to the discipline of communication technology via the Internet. In just a short time, Joe Burns has become a legend on the Internet among those who teach in this field."
—*Raymond E. Schroeder; Professor of Communication Springfield University*

"The English classes at Union Alternative High School [are] using Dr. Joe Burns' Web site HTML Goodies as an online text book. Students now have Web pages they are proud of. They have learned to teach themselves unfamiliar subject matter. There is new excitement in the class, self-esteem is up. In a nutshell: We have succeeded. Thank you for helping, Dr. Burns."
—*Aaron Wills; English teacher, Union School District, Union, MO*

Readers Praise HTML Goodies

CONGRATULATIONS ON YOUR FIRST BOOK!!!

I feel I must express my gratitude for all your work and dedication towards good and useful Web education. I am one of the silent users and readers that greatly benefit from and stand in awe of your resourcefulness. Your "insightful" comments and humor are always very refreshing (how do you do that?). I wish I could be attending one of your classes.
Keep smiling. You deserve it.
Xuan Brandes; <xuanb@ibm.net>

Just wanted to write and let you know that your book is the best! I have been messing around with HTML for about 3 years and by far this book is the easiest and most down to earth one I have read!
Kelly L Valqui, Senior Web Developer, R & K Web Publishing Inc.;
<kelly@rnkwebpublishing.com>

Congrats on your book!

I have to tell you, and I am sure that you have heard it a hundred times, your site and its content is AWESOME, without a doubt. I am a professional Web developer and also a computer instructor; in one of my Internet classes I refer to your site all the time.
Al Williams; <Ertlshots@aol.com>

With all the information crammed into this book, how can you not become a Webmaster (guru) by just reading it and following the demonstrations?! I just received this book this morning (approx. 5 hours ago) and all I've done since is skim thru it in amazement.
Matt Lewis; <impyrator_@hotmail.com>

Reviews from barnesandnoble.com

HTML Goodies was voted one of the top eight computer book titles of 1998 by `barnesandnoble.com`.

I Like Joe's Style (5 stars)

Easy to follow and understand. Great for beginners. He has humour which makes me want to go on. Better than *HTML for Dummies* any time. I would recommend it to someone who has no knowledge of HTML and is rather wary of diving into it.
Kim L. Chang, an environmentalist from East Asia; <kimota@bigplanet.com>

Great Book (5 stars)

I would recommend this book to any beginner. It is easy to read and understand. Joe Burns starts you out with a serving of HTML goodies that you can digest.
A reviewer; <buthd2@hotbot.com>

Outstanding Book! The best HTML book you can get! (5 stars)

I use this book all the time in designing my Web pages and, in my opinion, it is the most outstanding HTML book there is. Joe Burns explains everything in detail and takes the fear out of learning HTML by giving clear and concise examples. His Web site at htmlgoodies.com helps you see his examples in action. I recommend anyone who is currently a Web page addict like myself or someone who is just starting out designing Web pages to obtain a copy of this book. You will certainly get your money's worth by what you get out of it.
Robyn Barnette; <barnette@fnmail.com>

This is the BEST HTML Book (5 stars)

You all have to get this book.... Thanks sooo much, Mr. Burns!
Joel McLaughlin, a 13 year-old from Arizona; <joel@g-brooks.com>

TOTALLY BUILT WITH JOE'S HELP (5 stars)

I built my Web site using Joe's on-line *HTML Goodies*—it's the undisputed BEST among all the on-line tutorials out there. Now I got his book, and I know my pages will become even better. The book makes everything FUN FUN FUN—get excellent pages without killing yourself in the process. HIGHLY RECOMMENDED.
Beverly Claire, a 21-year-old law school student in Japan; <BeverlyClaire@looksmart.com>

The blind man sees! (5 stars)

Many thanks Joe. I have had a nightmare over the last two years trying to understand CGI. At last it is making sense. This and so much more! I have a long way to go but think I will now make it.
Simon Spencer, over 60 and going strong!; <compusit@dircon.co.uk>

Possibly the best book on the WEB (5 stars)

I recommend that anyone who is the Webmaster for the most sophisticated Web page or even the modest page get this book. It is very easy to understand and without this book your page will not excel.
Kents Web Design, a 15 Web page Designer; <kmacka@aol.com>

HTML Goodies

by Joe Burns

Macmillan Publishing
201 West 103rd Street   Indianapolis, Indiana   46290

HTML Goodies

Copyright © 1999 by Que

International Standard Book Number: 0-7897-1823-5

Library of Congress Catalog Card Number: 98-87277

Printed in the United States of America

First Printing: October 1998

00 99   5

Trademarks

Warning and Disclaimer

Executive Editor
Tim Ryan

Managing Editor
Patrick Kanouse

Project Editor
Andrew Cupp

Copy Editor
Tonya Maddox

Indexer
Heather Goens

Proofreader
Kim Cofer

Technical Editor
Bill Bruns

Software Development Specialist
Craig Atkins

Interior Design
Louisa Klucznik

Cover Design
Aren Howell

Layout Technician
Marcia Deboy

About the Author

Joe Burns, Ph.D., began writing HTML tutorials in 1994 in order to be able to remember complex commands while teaching. Less than a month after his first five HTML Goodies tutorials were available, they were the most visited pages on the university Web site. At one point, the tutorials were taken down for a short while because the volume of visitors was putting too much of a strain on the server. The site exploded into millions of visitors in 1996 when 7 HTML primers and 10 new tutorials were added to the first five to create HTMLGoodies.com. HTML Goodies is now the largest HTML help site on the Web, sporting over 120 tutorials, hundreds of free images, and numerous bad jokes. The site serves up close to four million page views a month from a mind boggling number of users. The site has won over 130 awards, been reviewed favorably in national newspapers and magazines, and continues to grow. HTML Goodies author Joe Burns holds a Ph.D. in communications from Bowling Green State University. He's currently a professor of communications at Susquehanna University in Pennsylvania, where he lives with his wife and two cats, Phydeaux and Chloe.

EarthWeb Press

EarthWeb Press is a co-publishing partnership between EarthWeb and Macmillan Computer Publishing. Our mission is to serve Web developers, programmers, and IT professionals by giving them the technical information they need to build tomorrow's systems.

EarthWeb is the leading provider of information resources for the worldwide professional IT community. We provide timely information through both EarthWeb Press books and Web sites. Our most popular site, developer.com, represents the largest collection of technical information in the world. All told, more than 14,000 technology resources can now be found in developer.com, as well as the full text of several hundred technical publications, hourly-updated news and information, practical development tutorials, in-depth explorations of the newest technologies, and a thriving community area.

Macmillan Computer Publishing (MCP) is the world's largest computer book publisher. The books published in our two leading imprints, Que and Sams, help computer users deal with the complexities of new technologies, such as the Internet. Macmillan Publishing is much more than a print publisher. We are a multimedia content provider. Our information is available not only as bound books, but also as multimedia software products and online interactive Web sites.

Already MCP has one of the top sites on the World Wide Web—the Macmillan Information SuperLibrary.

Contents at a Glance

Contents

xiii

10   Adding Sound and Video   265

11   Java Applets and JavaScript   281

12 Common Gateway Interface (CGI)   329

Preface

So you're reading the preface, huh? Good for you. I usually skip over them. It's so hard to pass up jumping right to chapter one. I actually do end up reading the preface, but only after I finish the book itself. Strange yes, but that's what I do.

Hopefully you're not following my out-of-order lead and are reading this first. It will help you a great deal in understanding how this book was put together, why I did all this, and how you can use it to start putting yourself on the Cyberspace road map.

A Little History...

Around 1992, when the World Wide Web was still something most people had never heard about, a new browser called Netscape 1.0 had come out and I started studying for a Ph.D. in Communications at a large university in Ohio. During the first couple of weeks of the semester, everyone wanted to get hooked up to the school's Internet server so they could send email around. I was the first to successfully attach. It was more dumb luck than skill.

Of course, that also meant I was the first to be called when someone else couldn't seem to make their connection. After helping three or four people, somehow I was given the moniker of Computer Wizard. It was a totally groundless title, but one I wasn't willing to give up by telling the truth.

Word spread to the computer science department of this great computer guru housed within the Communications building. They needed someone to teach a section of basic computers. I nervously accepted. Luckily it was getting to be Christmas break which meant a month's free time. I had to teach myself the computer. I traded a guy the use of his computer for a month in exchange for taking care of his cats. When I got started, however, I found I did have a knack for these fancy thinkin' boxes. I began to become consumed by what they could do.

When school started again, the Webmaster asked if I wanted some World Wide Web space on their server. At this stage in my computer learning curve, he might as well have been speaking Lebanese. But it was free. I took it. `Http://www.cs.bgsu.edu/~jburns` was created that afternoon.

I began asking anyone that seemed to have any form of computer knowledge how to go about making a Web page. Very few were willing to offer any help. It seemed that if I was going to learn this HTML language that I was going to have to teach myself.

My first and only home page to this point existed only on a computer disc. It had clean lines and looked good. Later in the same day the page was finished, I got into a conversation with the head of the computer department who asked what I had been up to lately. I showed her my page. She asked if I would be willing to teach the HTML summer class.

Sure.

Once again, I had accepted a position I was completely unqualified to perform. I started looking at the source codes of World Wide Web pages, collecting, categorizing, and sub-categorizing the commands and what they did. There wasn't a chance on earth that I was going to remember all this, so I wrote seven tutorials covering seven basic HTML areas. The purpose was to help me remember the required commands while lecturing.

I also collected a handful of images that all looked like little pieces of candy, what my father use to call *goodies*. The name stuck. The first HTML Goodies page went up in June of 1994.

I figured it couldn't hurt to register the tutorials with Webcrawler and Yahoo!. I had a hard enough time learning this myself. If I could make someone else's life a little easier, all the better.

A month went by and I received a letter from the Webmaster who had offered me the space in the first place. He was yelling, as much as one can yell in an email letter, that so many people were using my site that it was putting a strain on the server. It seemed that I had built the better mousetrap. People were coming in droves.

The email poured in. People wrote long, emotion-filled, thank you letters, telling me they were happy to have found a site that showed them HTML in a language they could understand. No one had yet taken the time to explain the language in simple English, let alone offer it on the World Wide Web. Others wrote with questions. I started answering them. Within three months of posting the pages, I was answering 20 questions a day and servicing some 50,000 people a month. And they keep coming...

In November of 1996, the domain name `htmlgoodies.com` was born.

HTML Goodies now sports over 100 tutorials and services over a million people a month. And yes, I still attempt to answer every email question personally. This book is the culmination of four years of research, hard work, and an untold number of questions from readers.

What I Believe

The purpose of this book is to allow you to teach yourself to write HTML. Some may suggest that actually learning HTML code is no longer required now that software applications that will build the pages for you are available.

Resist. Learn the language.

I believe HTML is an art. My pages are my creations, my art. Learning to build Web pages by clicking buttons in a helper program is not creating.

A Goodies visitor once told me that she created almost her entire site using a software application that did 90% of the work.

However, she saved one page for herself. She placed every command and worried over the modification of every shape and structure. It's her favorite page. She called it her "child" because she sees all of her hard work every time she looks at it.

Don't allow yourself to miss that feeling.

Dedication

This book is dedicated to my wife, Tammy, who always seems to have more faith in me than I ever seem to have in myself.

Acknowledgments

My very special thanks to Dr. Bruce Klopfenstein for making me buy my first modem, Dr. Ann Marie Lancaster for allowing me to teach HTML for the first time, Ben Amerman for setting up the first HTMLGoodies.com, everyone at Wolverine Web Productions (now Go Beyond Media) for helping me create the HTML Goodies hierarchy format, Murray, Jen, Mike (Joe, how the heck are ya?), John, and Brian at EarthWeb for the use of their huge powerful servers and being there just before I gave it all up for good; and my editor, Tim Ryan, for putting up with my rants.

On a personal side, thanks to my mother for being the inspiration for my writing style. I knew if I could write so she understood the concept, I was at the right level. And to my father who instilled in me that a thank you is enough payment for doing something nice for someone else.

Thank you to all the people who would *not* help me learn HTML when I first got started. It was because of you I promised myself that if I ever learned this language, I would do my best to make it so others wouldn't have such a hard time.

And of course, thanks to everyone who ever visited or wrote an email letter to me over the last six years. It has all been taken to heart to create what you read today.

...and Gus

Tell Us What You Think!

As the reader of this book, *you* are our most important critic and commentator. We value your opinion and want to know what we're doing right, what we could do better, what areas you'd like to see us publish in, and any other words of wisdom you're willing to pass our way.

As the Executive Editor for the Web development team at Macmillan Computer Publishing, I welcome your comments. You can fax, email, or write me directly to let me know what you did or didn't like about this book—as well as what we can do to make our books stronger.

Please note that I cannot help you with technical problems related to the topic of this book, and that due to the high volume of mail I receive, I might not be able to reply to every message.

When you write, please be sure to include this book's title and author as well as your name and phone or fax number. I will carefully review your comments and share them with the author and editors who worked on the book.

Fax: 317-817-7070

Email: java@mcp.com

Mail: Executive Editor
Web Development
Macmillan Computer Publishing
201 West 103rd Street
Indianapolis, IN 46290 USA

Introduction

About This Book

Have you ever embarked on a new project and found it difficult to get all the information you need? Sometimes it gets to the point where you throw up your hands and scream, "I wish someone would just explain this to me!"

Me too. I had a hard time finding anyone who would just simply tell me how HTML was done, let alone explain it in a language I could understand.

That's why I built the HTML Goodies site and wrote this book. I promised myself that if I ever learned this language, I would do my best to make it easier for the next person. It makes me very happy to say that my HTML Goodies site gets over 4 million page hits a day from lots of people like you.

This book is a series of self-contained tutorials written in a very friendly, conversational way. Everything needed is contained in the lesson. There's no need to keep checking in the previous chapters for information. If that meant I had to offer the same command in three or four different tutorials, I did. And the great thing is that my HTML Goodies Web site has a wealth of code, graphics, JavaScript, and other stuff that you can use for free.

 This icon gives you the address on a specific page of the HTML Goodies Web site where you can download stuff and see exactly how the examples in the book work!

I tried to put together the most complete book possible. HTML is covered from the ground up. But even more, I go into what you need to do with the pages you write, what makes a good home page, how to get people to visit you, how to get a domain and sell advertising, and what concerns you should have about copyright. All the color codes and ASCII and ampersand commands are contained, as well as a full list of all available HTML commands for quick reference. There's even a glossary for some of those more interesting acronyms computer people love to throw around.

You're going to have questions. I know—I answer around 150 a day from the HTML Goodies Web site. I've tried to anticipate your queries and have put them in the sidebars that show up throughout the book. On the Web we call these types of questions *FAQs* (Frequently Asked Questions). The FAQs are all true readers' questions taken straight from the Goodies email box. I bet you see your own questions asked and answered in one or more of these sidebars.

My Thoughts on Building a Home Page

We'll start with the most asked questions I receive: "What should my home page look like?" Up until now I thought it would be a bit bold to state my views on home page building because I believe that HTML is an art and telling you how to create your art would be a bit egotistical on my part. But there was nothing good on television this weekend, so here goes.

The suggestions are my own thoughts; they are by no means laws or rules. If you want to disregard everything I write, do it. Goodness know I've been wrong before.

If you are brand new to HTML, some of the suggestions might not make sense right off. But read it through—when you get to the tutorial that explains that part in more detail, you'll already have an idea on how to use it.

The Four Basic Rules

Above all else, I believe this:

- Offer something worthwhile—If the reader leaves your page asking herself, "Why did I come here?" the mission has not been accomplished. You have been given this small bit of space with which to post what is important to you. Home pages have become the business cards of the 21st Century. Tell me about yourself, post your poetry, write a story, show me your cats, tell me a good joke, show me your son or daughter, tell me what makes you, you. Give me something in return for my time with you. Allow me to leave your site a little more enriched than when I came.

- Make it easy on me—Don't make me have to search for the items on your page. Don't fill up with 20 JavaScripts, 15 applets, 12 scrolling words, flashing lights, and polar opposite colors. Make it so the links are obvious. Use words like Click Here for This. And put the links up high! Let me see them immediately when I come to the page. If the page does scroll, give me a quick way to get to the section I want.

- Answer me—I get letters telling me that it was amazing that I wrote back. If someone writes to you, that is a form of communication. They want you to respond. You have posted this page. You gave people a way to contact you. Talk back.

- Change is good—Work on your page. Update it. Add to it. Fix it when there's a problem. Show me that you are taking as great an interest in your page as you want me to take. Static pages die slow. People just stop coming.

Was that too preachy?

The Home Page

This is your welcome mat. There's a commercial that states that you never get another chance to make a first impression. Here it is. This page should be representative of you and your site and should immediately guide the viewer. Big graphics aren't needed. Style, page layout, and guidance are what work best.

Make your home page small and simple. It should never be longer than two screens. Get it all onto one if you can. There's nothing wrong with offering a ton of good information. Just don't attempt to offer it all on the home page. In fact, offer none of it. Use the home page as a map to all the great information. Multiple pages are much easier to surf that one big page that melds into a useless block of text the more you attempt to read. Think of your home page as the body of a spider. Everything comes out from and is attached to it.

Here are the things that bug me most on home pages:

- A home page that is just a logo, corporate or otherwise.

- The logo is active and you're suppose to click it to go further. Why? Don't get me started.

- A home page that asks if you want frames or no frames. That drives me nuts. Pick one!

- A home page with more than two advertising banners. I like Bannermania, the Internet Link Exchange, and money too, but it just takes too long to load.

- A home page with only text telling me how great the following is going to be. It changes for me or asks me to click to continue to the real home page. This should be outlawed or at least severely punished.

- Ditto with JavaScripts telling the same. The silly thing comes up every time I return to the home page.

- No more double windows please! Just one window is fine, thanks. I don't need the main window and then a second smaller window with other links that bring up other windows.

Images

Let's be honest. The WWW is what it is today because of images. The ability to place pictures is just the greatest part of this pup. Don't get me wrong, I love images. But there are limits.

When to use:

- GIF—GIF is a format of little colored dots. After the image is created, there is no compression when it is stored. (There is when the file is created, but not afterwards.) What is transferred is what is displayed. GIF is good for pictures with great detail or lines. Faces show up best with GIF. GIFs can also be saved at 256, or all the way down to two colors, and still look crisp. I think black and white images look best in GIF.

- JPEG—JPEG is a compressed format. That means it is sort of squashed together when it's put away. JPEG is best for pictures with bold colors and not much detail. Detail fades fast on a JPEG. JPEG is also good when you do offer large images. They take less time to load.

In terms of images:

- Go with as few as possible to cut down on load time. I know they look great, but waiting for them to load is dull. Learn the value of understatement.

- Always denote every image's height and width. Not a question—do this.

- If at all possible, combine images that sit next to each other into one big image. That helps a lot with load time. If the images need to be different links, make the image an imagemap.

- Use GIF as often as possible. The format is just more computer friendly in terms of memory. JPEG should be reserved for large images.

- As often as possible, offer people the choice of whether to look at the image. Your photos from the last family reunion may be great, but no one outside of your immediate family will sit through 20 50K JPEGs loading into their browser window. Offer links to the pics and explain them. Let people decide whether to view them.

- Easy on the animation and applet motion. I speak the truth here: One good animation is far better than nine pretty good ones.

- Lose the blue border on active links images. Maybe this is just personal opinion here, but that blue border is annoying, especially on imagemaps. Lose it by placing BORDER="0" into the image command between the IMG and the SRC.

- Use ALT commands. Be nice to those who surf without images.

- There is no replacement for content. If what you are offering is dull or not worth someone's time, no amount of graphic support will do the trick.

Backgrounds

I love a good background image, no doubt. But remember that it slows the completion of the page. If you are going to use a background image, ask yourself these questions:

- What does it do for the page? If it visually helps it, great—keep it. Just try to make it as small as possible to cut down on load time.
- Does it disrupt the text? If the text is at all hard to read, lose the background or do something to the text.

Colors

Love 'em! I think the use of color in a Web page is wonderful. The main reason I like color commands is that they are part of the HTML document and they don't tax the server any more than they have to. Just watch a few things:

- Pick complementary colors—Your mother taught you how to dress. You know a gross combination when you see one.
- No white text—I'm begging. I'm pleading! Maybe on a black background, but no other time. Please?! Unless there is some really good reason, text is black. I speak for the masses here.
- If when you stare at the page, the text appears to be moving around—bad color combination. Enough said.
- Bright primary colors tend to tire the eye. Pastels and calm color combinations work better.
- Try to use color to draw the eye. Get attention through the use of one bright color. If everything on the page is turned up to 11, nothing stands out.
- Just because colors are available doesn't mean you have to use them.

Text

I mean what you write here. This is where I really can't say much. It's your page and you have every right to write what you want, topics or otherwise. I just have one simple rule:

Brevity is the heart of wit.

Say what you are going to say quickly, with as few words as possible. Looking back over the size of this section, it seems even I have trouble following that rule.

Hopefully, you can take something from this. I truly don't mean to be high and mighty here, but I thought this might be helpful. Even so, feel free to ignore it all. It is your page, after all, and I respect that a great deal.

No matter what you do, I still think these four main points apply:

- Offer something worthwhile
- Make it easy on me
- Answer me
- Change is good

Here's to writing great Web pages.

Enjoy!

Part 1

How to Build a Web Site in 7 Steps

What You Need to Get Started

Welcome to HTML!

This is Primer 1 in a series of seven that calmly introduces you to the very basics of HTML (Hypertext Markup Language). I suggest you read the primers one at a time over seven days. By the end of the week, you'll easily know enough to create your own HTML home page. No, really you will.

I say that because many people scoff at the notion that they can actually learn this new Internet language. I'm still amazed that one of the best-selling line of computer books calls its readers "dummies." People seem to revel in that title. Some of the smartest people I know love to proclaim themselves "dummies" regarding every aspect of computers. Strange. I think you'll do a whole lot better at your next cocktail party by handing out your home page address rather than laughing about how dumb you are regarding the Internet.

You can do this!

 Visit this tutorial online at `http://www.htmlgoodies.com/primer_1.html.`

What Do I Need to Create a Web Page?

I'm assuming at the beginning of this tutorial that you know nothing about HTML. However, I am assuming some computer knowledge. You wouldn't be looking at this page without having some knowledge. To continue with these primers, you will need

1. A computer (obviously).

2. A browser like Netscape, Microsoft Explorer, Chameleon, Opera, or Mosaic. You probably have one if you've purchased this book.

3. A word processor. If you have access to Window's Notepad program or the Macintosh Simple Text program, use that to get started.

That's all you need to create a Web site, but you'll need a few more things, which are mentioned in Primer 7, to make that site available on the Internet so people can see it. Now here are a few questions you probably have:

FAQs from the HTML Goodies Web Site

Q. I have a Macintosh (or IBM). Will this work on my computer?

A. Yes. HTML does not use any specific platform; it works with simple text. More on that in a moment.

Q. Must I be logged on to the Internet to do this? More specifically, will learning this throw my cost for online way up?

A. No—to both. You will write HTML offline.

Q. Do I need some sort of expensive program to help me write this?

A. No. You will write using what I outlined earlier. You can buy those programs if you'd like, but they are not essential. I have never used one.

Q. Is this going to require that I learn a whole new computer language, like Basic or Fortran, or some other cryptic, silly-looking, gothic, extreme gobbledygook?

A. Touchy, aren't we? No is your answer. HTML is not a traditional computer language. There is no programming involved. Allow me to repeat that...HTML is not some complicated computer language!

What Is HTML?

HTML stands for Hypertext Markup Language. Computer people love acronyms—you'll be talking acronyms ASAP. Let me break it down for you:

- *Hyper* is the opposite of linear. Computer programs in the past had to move in a linear fashion. This before this, this before this, and so on. HTML does not hold to that and allows the person viewing the World Wide Web page to go anywhere, anytime they want.

- *Text* is what you will use—real, honest-to-goodness English letters.

- *Markup* is what you will do. You will write in plain English and then mark up what you wrote. More to come on that in the next primer.
- *Language* because the creators needed something that started with *L* to finish HTML, and Hypertext Markup Louie didn't flow correctly. (Because it's a language, really.)

HTML is the language you use to write your Web pages. HTML tells the browser how you want your text and graphics to be arranged. HTML denotes that something will be bold, or that something will be underlined. HTML is also used to insert images and make words act as links to other pages. It's easy. You can do this.

Some More Information Before We Write

You will actually begin to write HTML in Primer 2. For now I just want to tell you how you will go about creating a Web page with HTML.

You will write the HTML document with your word processor, with Notepad, or with Simple Text. When you are finished, you will then read the document in the browser (such as Netscape). Those who are schooled in HTML are going to immediately jump up and down and yell that you should be using an HTML assistant program (like HotDog or FrontPage) because it makes it easier. Perhaps, but it also makes it harder to learn HTML because the program does half the work for you. Take my word for it: Use the word processor for a week, and then go to the assistant if you want to. (I'll even tell you later how to get one.) You'll be far better off for the effort.

Creating HTML Documents with a Word Processor

If you write with the word processor (this does not apply to Notepad or Simple Text), you need to follow a few steps. Here they are:

1. Write the page as you would any other document.
2. When you go to save the document (here's the trick), always choose **Save As**.
3. When the Save As box pops up, you need to save the page in a specific format. Look at the box when you get into the word processor; there will be a place where you can change the file format.
4. If you have an IBM-compatible computer, save your document as ASCII text DOS or just text format.

   If you have a Macintosh, save your document as text format.

Please remember that it is very important to choose Save As every time you save your document. If you don't, your program may not save as text, but as its default format. In layman's terms, use Save As or you'll mess up your document.

You should note that notepad and Simple Text save your work as text without being prompted, so all the preceding steps need not be followed. It's almost as if the programs were made to write HTML documents. In fact, I still use Notepad to write some of my pieces.

How to Name Your HTML Document

You must name your document and add a suffix to it. What you name your document is very important. That's the way everything works in HTML. Follow these steps to name your document:

1. Give it a name. If you have an IBM that's not running Windows 95, you are limited to eight letters.
2. Add a suffix. For all HTML documents, you will add .htm or .html—.htm for PCs with Windows 3.1 and .html for Macintoshes and PCs running Windows 95 or 98.

Here's an example: I am naming a document I just wrote on an IBM machine. I want to name the document *fred*. I'm using an IBM, so the name of the document must be fred.htm. If it were a Macintosh I would name it fred.html. Please notice the dot (.) before .htm and .html!

Uhhhhhh...Why Do I Do That?

Glad you asked. It's a thing called *association*. It's how computers tell different things apart. .html tells the computer that this file thing is an HTML document. When you get into graphics, the suffix will be different. All files will be *name.suffix*—always.

Why .htm for Some and .html for Others?

Older operating systems like Windows 3.1 can only handle what's known as an 8.3 filename, which means the file can only have an eight-letter name and a three-letter suffix. Macintoshes and PCs with Windows 95 or 98 allow four—or more!—letter suffixes. Your browser can read all files, whether they have three- or four-letter suffixes. I would stick with three letters, in case you want to transfer your files to a PC with an older operating system. That's just a suggestion. Feel free to ignore it.

Why Do I Save It as Text or ASCII Text DOS?

You're just full of questions! HTML browsers can only read text. Look at your keyboard. See the letters and numbers and little signs like % and @ and *? That's all considered text. That's what the browser reads.

If you do not save as text or ASCII text DOS, you are saving a lot more than just the text. You are saving your margin settings, your tab setting, bold, italics, and so on, and so forth. With a browser, you don't want all of that—*just the text*! All that other stuff will confuse your browser and make your Web site look like a mess.

Remember that if you are using Notepad or Simple Text, the document will be saved as text with no extra prompting. Just choose Save.

Opening Your HTML Document in a Browser

Once you have your HTML document on the floppy disc, you need to open it in the browser:

1. Under the **File** menu (top-left of this screen), you will find Open, Open Page, Open File, or other words to that effect.

    Click those words. In some browsers a dialog box immediately opens. Explorer users, and users of later Netscape versions, need to click the **Browse** or **Choose File** button to get to the dialog box. When you get there, switch to the A:\ drive (or the floppy disk for Macintosh users) and open your document.

    The browser will do the rest.

FAQs from the HTML Goodies Web Site

Q. I opened my document in the browser and saw all the code I wrote instead of the Web page. What gives?

A. Ten bucks says you saved the file with a .txt extension rather than an .htm or .html extension.

One More Thing

You now easily have enough to keep you occupied for the first day. Don't worry, the primers get less wordy after this.

If you are going to do this, I suggest you make a point of learning to look at other people's HTML pages. You say you're already doing that, right? Maybe. What I mean is for you to look at the HTML document that presents the page you are looking at. Don't look at the pretty page; look behind it at the document.

Why Would I Do That?

Let's say you run into a page that has a really neat layout, or a fancy text pattern, or a strange grouping of pictures. You'd like to know how to do it. I'm not telling you to steal anything, but let's be honest—if you see some landscaping you like, you're going to use the idea. If you see a room layout you like, you will use the idea. That's the point of looking at another page's HTML document.

Here, I'll give you an Internet URL (that's computerspeak for a Universal Resource Locator. We non-computer people call it a Web address). The page is located on my site. You can go into the page and look at the HTML I used to make it. The instructions on how to do this are printed right on the Web page.

And by the way, please feel free to look at the HTML code of any of the pages posted on HTML Goodies. Then go ahead and use the code yourself. I want you to. That's what Goodies is for!

 To find out how to view the HTML code behind any Web page, go to http:// www.htmlgoodies.com/book/firstpage.html.

The following steps tell you how to view the HTML that was used to create a Web page. (This doesn't work for AOL, but keep reading.)

1. When you find a page you like, open the **View** menu on your browser. You'll find it way at the top of the browser screen.

2. Choose **Document Source** from the menu.

3. The HTML document will appear on the screen as it was written.

It's going to look like chicken-scratch right now, but by the end of the week, it will look readable and you'll be able to find exactly how a certain HTML presentation was performed.

Those of you who use AOL can see the source code by right-clicking the page. You'll get a little window that offers you the ability to see the code.

That's the primer for today. Get ready to dive in and write your first HTML document. See you tomorrow...or whenever you turn the page.

FAQs from the HTML Goodies Web Site

Q. Should I really use someone else's code? Isn't that against copyright?

A. I didn't tell you to steal code straight away and paste it to your page (except from HTML Goodies; I gave you permission to do that). Besides, what fun would that be? You are new to HTML. You should take the time to view pages that are already finished and try picking out commands you already know. In addition, seeing how someone else set code will help you build your own pages. That said, don't just copy and paste someone else's code.

Flags and Commands

Hello and welcome to Primer 2. No doubt you've attempted to write a small document on your word processor and save it in the appropriate text format. You also remembered to save the document with the .htm or .html suffix, I'm sure. Good. Now let's move on to today's lesson, for today you write!

 Visit this tutorial online at `http://www.htmlgoodies.com/primer_2.html`.

What Are Flags?

HTML works in a very simple and very logical format. It reads like you do—left to right, top to bottom. That's important to remember. HTML is written with text—English text. You use a series of *flags* to set all this text apart as bigger, smaller, bold, underlined, and so on.

Think of flags as commands. Let's say you want a line of text to be bold. You put a flag at the exact point you want the bold lettering to start and another flag where you want the bold lettering to stop. If you want just a word to be italicized, you place a start italic flag at the beginning of the word and an end italic flag at the end of the word. Is this making sense so far?

All flag formats are the same. They begin with a less than sign (<) and end with a greater than sign (>)—no exceptions. The command goes inside the < and >. When you learn HTML, you are learning the code to perform whatever manipulation you want. The HTML flag for bold lettering is <B>. That makes sense. Here's what the flags that turn the word *Joe* bold look like:

```
<B>Joe</B>
```

Let's look closer at what's happening:

1. `<B>` is the beginning bold flag. It turns bold on.
2. `Joe` is the word being affected by the `<B>` flag.
3. `</B>` is the end bold flag. It turns bold off. Notice that the end bold flag is exactly the same as the beginning flag, except there is a slash in front of the `B`.

FAQs from the HTML Goodies Web Site

Q. Is the end flag for other commands simply the begin flag with the added slash?

A. Yup.

Q. Will the flags show up on my page?

A. No. As long as your commands are inside the < and > marks, they perform the command, but are hidden from the viewer.

Q. Your bold flag uses a capital *B*. Do all HTML flags use a capital letter?

A. The browser doesn't care. In terms of flags, upper- and lowercase letters are equal, but it is a very good idea for you to make a habit of writing your flags in uppercase letters because it sets them apart from the normal text.

Q. Must everything have a flag to show up on the page?

A. No. Text with no flags will show up, but the text will not have any special look.

Q. What if I forget to add the end flag or forget to add the slash to the end flag command?

A. That's trouble, but easy-to-fix trouble. It will be obvious if you've not placed an end flag when you look at the document in your browser. All the text that follows the unended command will be affected.

Q. Do all HTML flags require both a begin and end flag?

A. No. There are exceptions to the rule, but let's stay on those that do require both flags to work.

Open and Close Flags

The majority of HTML flags do require both an open and a close flag (a begin and end flag). Table P2.1 shows a few flags and what they do to text.

Table P2.1 A Few HTML Flags

Effect	Flags	How It Looks
Bold	`<B>Bold</B>`	**Bold**
Italic	`<I>Italic</I>`	*Italic*
Typewriter	`<TT>Typewriter</TT>`	`Typewriter`

Can I Use Two Flags at Once?

Yes! One of the neat things about HTML is that you can combine flags to make different effects. Just make sure to begin and end both sets of flags, like so:

`<B><I>Bold and Italic</I></B>` gives you ***Bold and Italic***

`<B><TT>Typewriter and Bold</TT></B>` gives you `Typewriter and Bold`

FAQs from the HTML Goodies Web Site

Q. If I use two types of flags, (like bold and italic), does it matter what order they are used?

A. You should try to keep the tags in order. If the bold command is closest to the affected word on the left, it should be closest on the right. If italic is second closest on the left, it should be second closest on the right.

Single Flags

The open and close flags format dominates the majority of the available HTML flags, but there are flags that stand alone. Table P2.2 shows the three most commonly used single flags, and Figure P2.1 shows how they look on a Web page.

Table P2.2 Most Commonly Used Single Flags

Flag	What It Does
`<HR>`	This command gives you a line across the page. (`HR` stands for horizontal reference.)
` `	This breaks the text and starts it again on the next line. Remember that you saved your document as text, so where you hit Enter to jump to the next line was not saved. In an HTML document, you need to denote where you want every carriage return with a ` `.
`<P>`	This stands for paragraph. It does the exact same thing as the ` ` except that this flag skips a line. ` ` just jumps to the next line. `<P>` skip a line before starting the text again.

Figure P2.1

The <HR>, <BR>, and <P> flags.

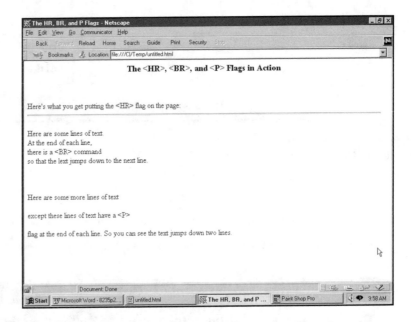

Writing Your First Web Page

So here we go. You're going to write your first HTML page using what you have learned, in addition to two other items. These two items are important to every page you will ever write. Why? Because they will be on every page you ever write.

1. You start every page with this: <HTML>. That makes sense. You are denoting that this is an HTML document.

2. Your next command is always this: <TITLE> and </TITLE>. Look at the very top of your browser next time you have it open. See the blue line way up top? What you write between these <TITLE> commands will appear in the blue line.

3. Finally, you end every page you write with this: </HTML>. Get it? You started the page with <HTML> and you will end the page with </HTML>. That makes sense again.

So Here We Go!

I want you to play around with these commands. Just remember that HTML reads like you do—top to bottom, left to right. It will respond where you place the start command and stop where you place the end command. Just make sure your commands are within < and >.

Here's a sample page to show you what I want you to do tonight:

```
<HTML>
<TITLE> My first HTML page </TITLE>
<B>This is my first HTML page!</B><P>
```

```
I can write in <I>Italic</I> or <B>Bold</B><BR>
<HR>
<B><I>Or I can write in both</I></B><BR>
<HR>
<TT>...and that's all</TT>
</HTML>
```

Notice that I only used the flags I showed you on this page. Yes, it's a simple page, but you're just starting out. Notice the <HTML> and </HTML> at the beginning and end of the page. Notice <TITLE> and </TITLE>. See how there's a begin and end flag and that the <P> and <BR> commands are used to go to new lines?

Figure P2.2 shows you what all this will look like run through a browser.

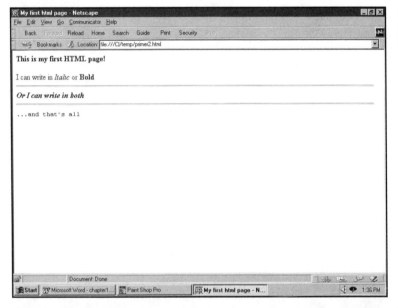

Figure P2.2
How your first Web page looks in a browser.

Look at the program and then at what it produced. See how the HTML flags denote where text was affected? Good! I knew you would. Now go! Go into the world—or at least to your word processor and create. Follow the instructions in HTML Primer 1 to help you save and then display your first HTML page.

You can do this!

Manipulating Text

How did it go with your first HTML page? I'll assume it went well. If I don't assume as much, I can't go on, and I want to go on. Now you know the basics about placing flags and manipulating text in terms of bold, italic, and typewriter font. That's good, and along with the <HR>, <BR>, and <P> commands, you'll be able to play with text placement. Now we'll talk about changing text size.

 Visit this tutorial online at http://www.htmlgoodies.com/primer_3.html.

Heading Flags

Heading flags are used extensively on HTML documents to—you guessed it—create headings! How novel.

There are six heading flags: <H1> through <H6>. <H1> is the largest and <H6> is the smallest. Headings need begin and end flags, as shown in Figure P3.1.

Heading commands create nice bold text, as shown in the figure, and are quite easy to use. It's a simple <H#> and </H#> command. However, they do have one other annoying trait: They like to be alone. When you use a heading command, the text is set alone by default. It's like the heading commands carry a <P> command with them. It's hard to get other text to sit next to it. It's as if it wants to be, dare I say, a heading. Try a few for yourself.

Figure P3.1
The six heading flags.

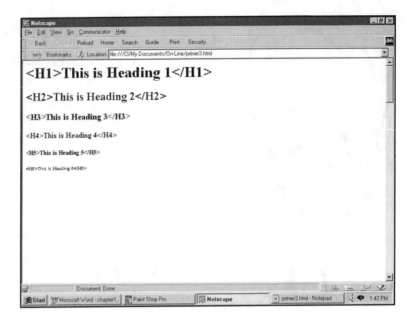

Font Size Commands

Maybe you'd like a little more control over your text size. Well, here it is: the <FONT SIZE> flags. Heading commands are great for text at the top of the page, and they're also good for separating your Web page into logical sections of text.

There are twelve font size flags available to you: +6 through +1 and –1 through –6. As you probably guessed, +6 is the largest. It's huge. The smallest one is –6. It's a little small. Figure P3.2 shows a few in action. Follow this pattern to place one on your page:

```
<FONT SIZE="##">
```

The ## can be anything from +6 to –6.

Notice that the first flag is actually doing two things:

1. It's asking for a new font size.
2. It's offering a number with which to denote the font size.

This is what's referred to as a *command inside of a command,* or just a *subcommand.* When you have that, you denote the subcommand with an equal (=) sign and enclose it within quotation marks. Look at the preceding code. See the equal sign, and the plus or minus number in quotation marks? That's the subcommand:.

Also notice in Figure P3.2 that the end command for a <FONT SIZE> flag only requires </FONT>.

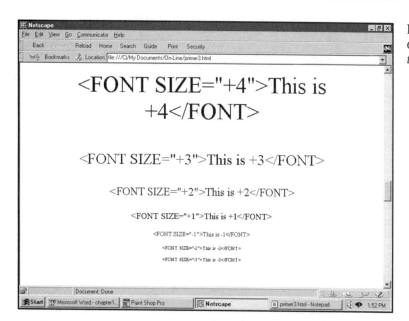

Figure P3.2
Changing font sizes with the <FONT SIZE> *flag.*

FAQs from the HTML Goodies Web Site

Q. Every so often I come to these pages that have really great text. It's like the letters are made out of steel or blood or other stuff. How do I do that?

A. I think if you look at the source code, you'll learn that the text is really an image or series of images rather than a different font. In Primer 5 we'll get into how to place images on your page.

Centering Text and Aligning It to the Right

Since you've already created a few Web pages, you no doubt noticed that the text always starts at the left of the screen. That's the default; it just happens without you doing anything. What if you want your text centered, or aligned with the right side of the screen? Can you do that? Yes! (and Figure P3.3 shows you some examples).

You center text by surrounding it with simple <CENTER> and </CENTER> commands. Here's what it looks like:

```
<CENTER>All text in here will be centered</CENTER>
```

Getting text to align on the right is a little trickier. You need to set the text aside as a paragraph unto itself. Here's the format:

```
<P ALIGN="right">text that will go to the right</P>
```

Figure P3.3
Left-aligned, centered, and right-aligned text.

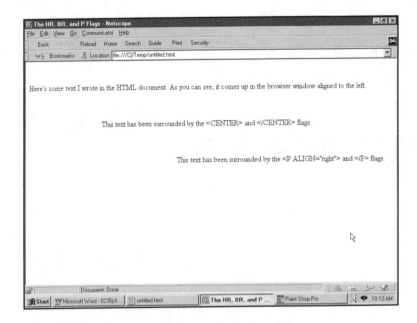

You probably remember that `<P>` command from Primer 2. Here again is the concept of a command inside of a command. You are setting an attribute of the `<P>` flag. That alignment command is what pushes to the right. Remember this: When you use a subcommand in the `<P>` flag, you need to end with a `</P>` flag.

Want to see a live example of text that is centered, right-aligned, and in different font sizes and headings? Point your browser to `http://www.htmlgoodies.com/book/textexample.html`.

FAQs from the HTML Goodies Web Site

Q. You say on your site that you should use quotation marks around subcommands, but when I look at the code for other people's pages, the quotation marks aren't there. Should I use them or not?

A. I'm a traditionalist in terms of HTML. If you want my opinion, yes, use them. The marks have become required less often with the coming of later-version browsers. I still use them because I think they serve the purpose of setting the commands apart from the rest of the page, if only for my eyes. Just remember that if you use them, use them all the time. Using them now and again easily leads to forgetting to add a closing quotation mark on a subcommand. That will cause problems.

And Primer 3 comes to an end. Notice that they're getting shorter? Now go and incorporate a few of these `<H>`, `<FONT SIZE>`, and `<CENTER>` commands into a page. To do is to learn. A brilliant man once said that...I think he had a beard, too.

Making a Link to Someone Else

Linking to Other Web Sites

Welcome to your fourth day. Today you learn only one thing—how to create a link to another page. It's a basic format like any of the others you have seen so far.

 Visit this tutorial online at `http://www.htmlgoodies.com/primer_4.html`.

Once you learn the format, you can make as many links as you want to any other page you want. The following line of HTML creates a link to the HTML Goodies home page. Figure P4.1 shows how this link looks on a Web page.

```
<A HREF="http://www.htmlgoodies.com">Click Here To Go To HTML Goodies</A>
```

Here's what's happening:

- `A` stands for Anchor. It begins the attachment to another page.
- `HREF` stands for hypertext reference. That's a nice, short way of saying, "This is where the link is going to go."
- `="http://www.htmlgoodies.com"` is the *full address* of the site you want to link to. Always use the full address in the link. Also notice that the address has an equal sign in front of it and is enclosed in quotation marks. Why? Because it's a subcommand. Remember that from yesterday?
- Where it reads `Click Here To Go To HTML Goodies` is where you insert what will appear on your Web page for the viewer to click. Write some text that describes the link.
- `</A>` ends the entire link command.

Figure P4.1
A link on a Web page.

Go ahead and place a link on your page. Now, without clicking, simply lay your pointer on the blue words. You'll see the address of the link you created come up along the bottom of the browser window, where it usually reads "Document Done."

FAQs from the HTML Goodies Web Site

Q. Can I link to any site on the Net?

A. Yes, as long as you have the correct address (URL) in the command. I will say this, though: In very rare instances people have been asked to take their links down, and since the people requesting that the link be taken down own the copyright to their page, they can say who links to it and who doesn't. Here's an example: A link was made to HTML Goodies, and the owner wrote to tell me all about it. When I went to see the site, it was all dirty pictures. My HTML Goodies banner was sitting above pictures no one should see! I used my copyright abilities to tell him to take the link down.

Q. I made a link to another site and I keep getting a box that tells me the page doesn't exist. I know it exists!

A. First I would suggest checking your spelling. If you're positive that's right, you may have corrupted the link by allowing the address to break over two lines. Make sure the address appears on one line in your HTML code. The HTML code can go on two lines, but the address should all run together. You see, if you have a line break in there, the browser may add a space. That puts a space in the address—then you've created a Web address that doesn't exist. Just like the browser told you.

 Here's a page with a series of links on it and a link that allows you to write to me. You can look at the source code to see how I did it. Go to `http://www.htmlgoodies.com/book/links.html`.

Allowing People to Email You from Your Page

You can make it easy for people to send you email from your Web site by using what's known as a `mailto:` command. It follows the same formula as the preceding link. The command places blue wording on the screen that people can click in order to send you a piece of email. Here's the pattern:

```
<A HREF="mailto:jburns@htmlgoodies.com">Click Here To Write Me</A>
```

Notice it's the same format as a link, except that in a link you put in an address to jump to. This example sends email to me. To set it up to send email to you, simply delete `jburns@htmlgoodies.com` and substitute your own email address.

The `mailto:` portion of the code calls on the email program contained in your visitor's browser. The browser does most of the work—you are just setting the "trigger" to make it work. Now, if you run this command and it doesn't do what I've described, you may not have the email preferences in your browser set up. If you use Netscape, you'll find the Preferences under the Edit menu at the top of the browser. If you use Explorer, you'll find your Options under the View menu. In there you'll find a place to put in your email address, your real name, and a few other items. Make sure that's all filled in and you'll be good to go for setting up `mailto:` links.

Figure P4.2 shows what happens when a visitor to your Web site clicks the `mailto:` link.

Now put one on your page. Go ahead, click it; I know you're dying to. You'll get an email page addressed to me, or whomever you address the link to.

FAQs from the HTML Goodies Web Site

Q. I did the link command exactly like you said to. Now everything on the page is blue!! AAAAUUUGH!?

A. If everything on the page is blue, you probably either forgot the `</A>` flag or are missing the slash before the `A` in the end flag. The computer doesn't know when to stop the link, so it makes everything a link (which makes everything blue).

Figure P4.2
Results of clicking a
mailto: link.

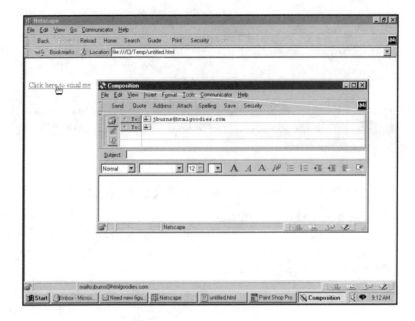

And that wraps up Primer #4. The next primer gets into the fun part of the World Wide Web—little pictures.

Placing an Image on Your Page

By now you know enough to write a very nice text-based home page, but it is the World Wide Web's capability to provide pictures that made it so popular. In this primer you learn how to place a picture on your page as well as how to turn a picture into a link to another page.

 Visit this tutorial online at `http://www.htmlgoodies.com/primer_5.html`.

Inserting the Image

The flag you use to place an image is constant—you will use the same format every time. When you are writing your pages, wherever you place the image tag is where the image will appear in relation to the items on your page (including text).

It is not necessary, but it is a good idea to store your HTML files and your image files in the same directory on your hard drive. There's more on that coming up in Primer 7.

Here's how to insert an image on your Web page:

```
<IMG SRC="image.gif">
```

Replacing the example name *image.gif* with the name of an actual image I have, joe.gif, gives you the results shown in Figure P5.1. No doubt about it—I'm a handsome man!

Here's what's happening:

- IMG stands for image. It basically states that an image will go here.

- SRC stands for source. It's telling the browser where to go to find the image. Again, it's best for you to place the image you want to use in the same directory on your hard drive as the HTML page that uses the image. More on that in Primer 7.

- *image*.gif is the name of the image. Notice it's following the same type of file format that your HTML documents follow. There is a name (*image*), a dot, and then a suffix (gif).

Figure P5.1

Inserting a picture of me on your Web site.

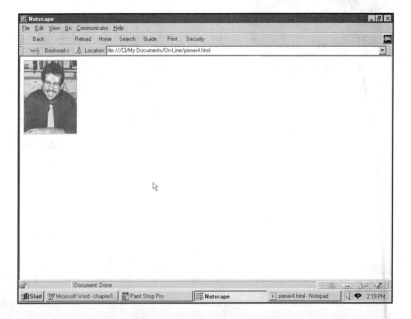

Image Formats

There are three basic graphics file formats you can use on your Web pages. Each is denoted to the browser by a different suffix:

- .gif (pronounced *jif*). This is an acronym for Graphics Interchange Format. The format was invented by CompuServe and is by far the most popular image format on the World Wide Web. The reason is that it's a simple format. It's a series of colored picture elements (*pixels*) that line up to make a picture. Browsers can handle this format quite easily.

○ .jpeg or .jpg (pronounced *j-peg*). There are two names to denote this format because Macintoshes and Windows 95/98 allow four letters after the dot. jpeg is an acronym for Joint Photographic Equipment Group, the organization that invented the format. The format is unique in that it's a *compressed format*. That's fancy computer talk that means that when the computer is not using a jpeg image, it folds it up and puts it away. For example, if the picture is 10KB when displayed, it may be only 4KB when stored. Nice trick, huh? It saves on hard drive space, but also tends to require a lot of memory on your part to unfold the image.

○ .bmp (pronounced *bimp* or *bump*). This is a bitmap. The BMP format was invented by Microsoft for use in Windows. Microsoft Explorer allows you to display bitmaps by simply using the same image format as described earlier, but I wouldn't do it. AOL and Netscape people won't see the image.

FAQs from the HTML Goodies Web Site

Q. My image won't show up! All I get is a red X (or a broken image).

A. This is by far the most asked question of the Goodies primers. There are many reasons the image may not be showing up. Here are the most common:

1. You have made an error in the code. Look for misspellings (SRC is the biggest one people mess up), or a missing quotation mark.

2. You have not used the correct image name. Remember, the image name you call for must be the file's exact name of the image. Even the capitalization must be the same.

3. You have included a path in the command like a:\ or c:\. If so, lose it. Call for the image by name only.

Where Do I Get My Images?

You can draw them with a paint program or create them with a scanner. In addition, pre-made images are available almost everywhere. The HTML Goodies home page allows you access to over 700 images—for free—and there are other sites out there that offer just as many.

 Go to http://www.htmlgoodies.com/images.html *to grab a few free images for yourself.*

Since you've been surfing, you've seen hundreds of images already. If you see something on someone's page that you really like, ask to use it.

Don't just take it. It may be against the law because you may be using something protected by copyright. Ask before you use. I have found most people on the Internet are very giving. Some aren't. If you ask and they say no, just find another image to use.

FAQs from the HTML Goodies Web Site

Q. I found that if I put in the entire address to an image on another site, I can get that image to show up on my site. Woohoo!

A. Woohoo indeed. You might be breaking copyright law. Yes, you can put in a full address and run images off other sites, but did you get permission to do so?

 To see a page with a few images and image links on it, see `http://www.htmlgoodies.com/book/imagelinks.html.` *Be sure to look at the source code!*

Creating a Clickable Image

Okay, this gets a little fancy. In the previous primer I showed you how to create a hypertext link. It created blue words on your page that someone could click and then jump to another site. Well, now you're going to set it up so an image becomes clickable (or *active*). The viewer clicks the image instead of the blue words to make the jump. I'll make a link to my HTML Goodies home page using the preceding image. Here's the format:

```
<A HREF="http://www.htmlgoodies.com"><IMG SRC="joe.gif"></A>
```

Look at it again. See what happened? I placed a basic image command where I would have placed wording. Put one on your page. Lay your pointer on it, but don't click. You'll see that the entire image is active. Figure P5.2 shows what you should get.

When you click the image, your browser will take you to the Web address you listed (in this case, my HTML Goodies site). Neat, huh? But what's with that blue line around the image? That's what happens when you activate an image. The browser attempts to turn the link blue like the wording it's replacing, so it places what's known as a *border* around the image. Some people like it. I don't, and I know how to get rid of it.

This is a nice way to end this primer because it gives you a hint of what's to come tomorrow. To make the border disappear, you must add a subcommand inside the image flag.

To rid yourself of the blue border, make this the image command in this format:

```
<IMG BORDER="0" SRC="joe.gif">
```

See what I did? I added a command that denoted that the border should be 0. You can go the other way, too, if you'd like. Make it BORDER="55" if you want; you'll have a huge border.

Note that the number 0 is in quotation marks. Figure P5.3 shows what you get using
BORDER="0".

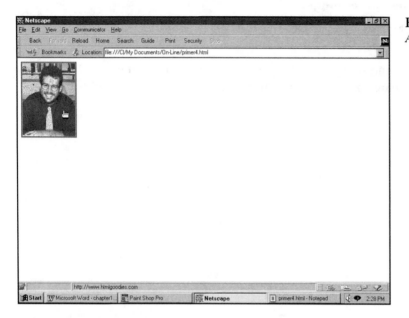

Figure P5.2
A clickable image.

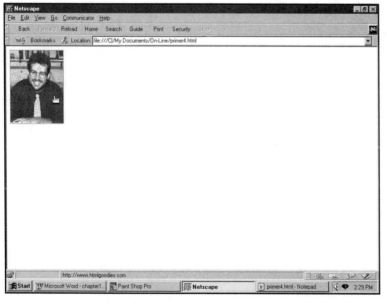

Figure P5.3
A clickable image with
BORDER="0".

Again, put one on your page. Lay your pointer on the image without clicking. You'll see that
it is active but doesn't carry that annoying blue border.

FAQs from the HTML Goodies Web Site

Q. How do I make the border bigger?

A. Instead of BORDER="0", try 2, or 4, or 700. That will be a big border.

That brings us to a close. Tomorrow you deal almost exclusively with commands inside of commands, which manipulate your images. You'll truly impress your friends with this one.

Manipulating Images

Just as I believe a primer, Primer 3, was required to explain manipulating text, I also think a primer is needed to explain manipulating images. Believe it or not, manipulating images is easier than manipulating text. Here we go.

 For some more examples of manipulating images, see `http://www.htmlgoodies.com/book/ manipulatingimages.html`.

Placement on the Page

First let's look at placing the image somewhere on the page. The default is left. If you simply place an image command on a page, the image will pop up hard left. There's nothing to it. If you want to have an image placed in the center of the page, simply surround the image command with <CENTER> and </CENTER> flags, like this:

```
<CENTER><IMG ALIGN="right" SRC="image.gif"></CENTER>
```

But to get the image to the right of the page, you need to add an ALIGN subcommand. Figure P6.1 shows what you get using this command.

```
<IMG ALIGN="right" SRC="image.gif">
```

Figure P6.1
An image aligned on the right side of the page.

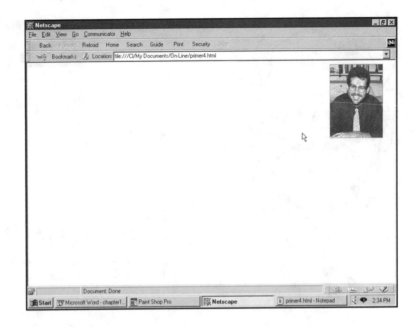

Aligning Text with Images

Images don't always stand alone. You will often want text alongside of them. To set that up, you simply insert an ALIGN subcommand with top, middle, or bottom depending on where you want the text. Figure P6.2 shows what these examples produce on your page.

```
<IMG ALIGN="top" SRC="htmlgdds.gif"> Text at the top
<IMG ALIGN="middle" SRC="htmlgdds.gif"> Text in the middle
<IMG ALIGN="bottom" SRC="htmlgdds.gif"> Text at the bottom
```

FAQs from the HTML Goodies Web Site

Q. When I use the ALIGN commands, the text jumps down to under the image after the text reaches the end of the line. I want it to wrap around the image. How do I do that?

A. Use ALIGN="left". Yes, I know the image automatically aligns to the left. Trust me.

Changing Image Size

To begin this little section, remember that images on a computer are not like a photograph. Computer images are made up of a lot of little colored dots all mushed right up alongside each other. The little colored dots are known as *picture elements*, or *pixels*. Just remember that during this part of the primer: Numbers refer to pixels rather than inches, centimeters, or the like.

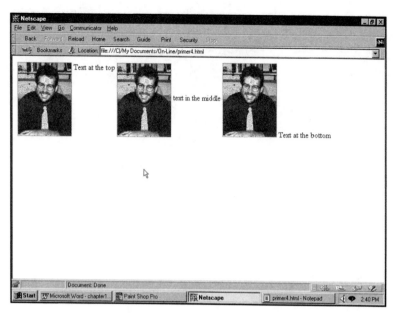

Every image is made up of pixels. This means that you can also measure the size of an image by its number of pixels. For example, the joe.gif image is 154 pixels high by 116 pixels wide. How do I know that? I have a graphics program that tells me so. How would you know? Without a specific program, you might have to play around with the numbers in these commands a little bit, but it's easy to do.

Here's what you do. Denote to the image command how many pixels high by how many pixels wide you want. The joe.gif image is 50×100 pixels. If I want the image to appear smaller, I will ask for the pixels to be smaller, say 25×50. If I want it bigger, I would set the pixels larger, say 100×200. If I want to totally distort the picture, I can.

Here's the format:

```
<IMG HEIGHT="" WIDTH="##" SRC="image.gif">
```

Notice the HEIGHT and WIDTH commands nestled right where the U command went before. (Yes, you can also use an ALIGN command when using the HEIGHT and WIDTH commands.) You will replace the ## with a number of pixels for height and width. Figure P6.3 shows three examples.

Figure P6.3
The same image with different HEIGHT *and* WIDTH *commands applied to it.*

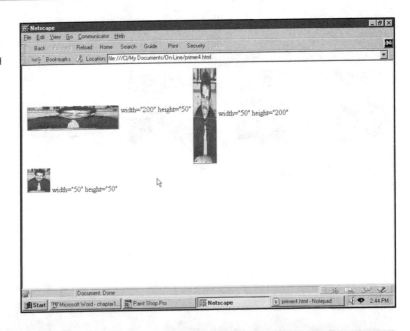

FAQs from the HTML Goodies Web Site

Q. Should I use the HEIGHT and WIDTH commands even when I don't want to change image size?

A. Yes! You should use the HEIGHT and WIDTH commands every time you place an image. When you want to place an image and not distort its size, enter its actual height and width. That allows the text on your page to load while leaving a space just big enough for the image to load later. Your users will thank you for it.

Making Horizontal Lines of Different Lengths

That WIDTH command also works on the <HR> flag, except you use percentages to indicate the size. Just put the WIDTH command right after the <HR>, like this: <HR WIDTH="##%">. Replace the ## with a number from 1 to 100. The following commands produce the page shown in Figure P6.4. Notice that if you want a full-length HR, you can just use the <HR> flag—you don't have to put <HR WIDTH="100%"> even though that will also work.

```
<HR>
<HR WIDTH="80%">
<HR WIDTH="50%">
<HR WIDTH="30%">
<HR WIDTH="10%">
```

You get the idea of how to combine all these flags and commands, yes?

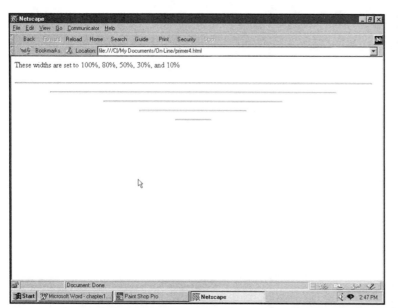

Figure P6.4
Making lines of different length with HR and WIDTH.

FAQs from the HTML Goodies Web Site

Q. Will the HEIGHT command work in the HR command too?

A. Yes, but you can only set it to 1 through 6; 6 is the largest.

That wraps it up. Try these in the comfort of your own home under the supervision of an adult. If you are an adult, find a kid who can program the VCR to help you along.

Graduation Day

Congratulations! You have beaten through six days of HTML and struggled with all those silly flags.

Here's your diploma:

You Passed!

May all your HTML dreams come true.
--Joe Burns

So you know it all, huh? Well, not quite. It's literally impossible to know everything. I don't come close. HTML is a growing and ever-evolving art. You have the basics. Now you can go on to the major tutorials located in the chapters of this book; you will understand them now. First let's talk about how to get your new Web pages on the Web.

How Do I Get an Internet Service Provider?

Now you need to find a place to post the page you wrote for the World Wide Web. Where should it go? Choose any one of a million places. ISPs (Internet service providers) are popping up everywhere—just graze through your Sunday paper. You should be able to choose from a bunch.

How Much Should I Pay?

Depending on what you want, you could pay a great deal or a little bit. I hold an entire domain, htmlgoodies.com. I pay a good bit. You shouldn't pay more than between $20 and $30 a month. Here are a few things you should get for your money:

1. You should pay a flat fee for your time on the Net. Do not pay for every second you're using your computer.

2. You should be able to dial a local number to connect.

3. You should get free connection software.

4. The connection should be a SLIP, PPP, or another TCP/IP connection that allows you to use a browser on your computer. Ask for one of these specifically. Even if you don't know what the terms mean, just know you need one of them.

5. You should get at least one megabyte of space on a server for placing your own HTML documents.

6. You should get email, Telnet, FTP, and newsgroup access. Again, even if you don't now know what the terms mean, ask for them.

7. You should have access to help, where you talk to a person, not just make contact via email or a help line answering machine.

I cannot recommend or downplay any provider. I think getting a connection to the Net should be a personal choice. Make a point of getting these things listed here, as you can get it all fairly easily.

How Do I Get My Pages on the WWW?

In order for all the world to see your Web page creations, you are going to have to get those HTML and image files from your computer to your ISP's server. When you get an account with an ISP, he or she will give you your own Web address and tell you what directories on the server you can use to store and display your Web pages. Once you have this information, you can begin putting your pages on the Web. This primer tells you how to do it, and discusses a few things to watch out for.

 This FTP tutorial can be found online at http://www.htmlgoodies.com/ftp.html.

Using FTP Software

FTP stands for File Transfer Protocol. It's the concept of moving a file from the hard drive on your local computer to the remote Internet server (probably owned by your ISP), where others can look at it. The process of transferring files from your computer to the server is called *uploading*. Being able to upload files is a basic skill needed to build a Web site. It's easy to do, but sometimes people get confused about why files can sometimes be corrupted when transferring. This primer helps you make sure your files arrive at the server in one piece.

How FTP Works

FTP is actually very basic. There are about a million different FTP programs you can take from the Internet as shareware or commercial software. I use a shareware program called FTP2000. Figure P7.1 shows what it looks like.

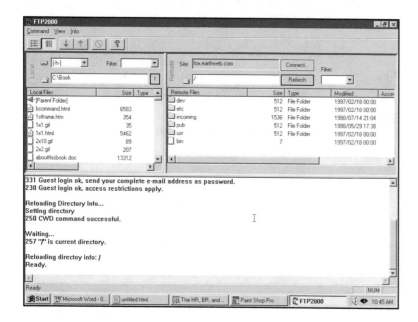

Figure P7.1
The FTP2000 software.

My guess is that you have your own FTP program already. Your ISP should have given you one that is compatible with your server. You should have also gotten full instructions on installing and using it. If not, head to Dave Central's FTP page (`http://www.davecentral.com/ftp.html`) and grab a few programs for yourself. You'll find FTP2000 there, as well as another favorite, called CuteFTP.

Figure P7.2 shows an illustration of the interface for a generic FTP program. Yours is something like this. The bold ASCII and BINARY at the top are buttons that change the file transfer type.

The column on the left that says Files On Your Hard Drive is where a directory that lists all the files on your computer appears. Sometimes this area is labeled `local` files.

The column on the right that says Files On Your Server is where a directory appears that lists all the files found on the part of your ISP's server that you have access to. This is where you place all your Web page files so others can see them.

Figure P7.2

A simplified illustration of what FTP software looks like.

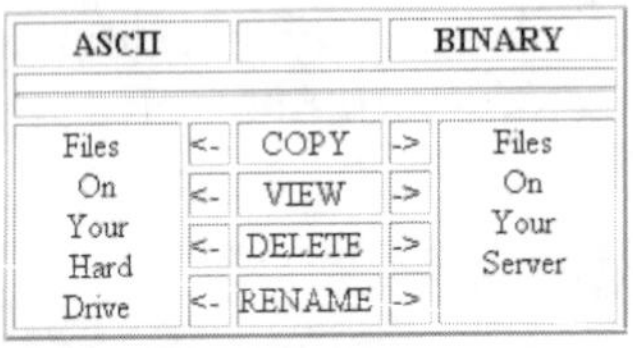

The center column of buttons allows you to click either side of the command to transfer the file between your computer and the server. Sometimes, as with the FTP2000 program, there are not buttons. Instead, you drag and drop from your side to the other; the upload is performed for you.

ASCII Versus Binary

This issue is the main reason for this tutorial. I get letters all the time asking why images (or applets, or JavaScripts) don't work. My answer is usually that the person corrupted or broke the object in the FTP. That usually confounds the problem further. The following sections hold a more in-depth explanation.

ASCII Sometimes Called TEXT or TEXT DOS

ASCII stands for American Standard Code for Information Interchange. It is text, short and simple. It is text that is standardized, so that all computers everywhere understand it. Look at your keyboard. See all those things, those letters and characters? There are actually 128 of them in all (counting upper- and lowercase as two).

Now it gets loopy...

Computers deal with numbers. Period. You see little letters, but the computer doesn't. It sees numbers—1s and 0s to be exact. Each 1 or 0 is called a *bit*, which is short for *binary* digit. ASCII is a series of seven 1 and 0 number combinations representing letters and characters. (Some computers now use an Extended ASCII, which uses eight numbers.) An extra digit is often added as a check to see if the other seven are correct. It's called a *parity digit* or a *check bit* and it checks to see if the numbers are correct via a mathematical equation involving the other seven numbers. Here's what some ASCII code looks like:

```
Symbol ASCII Code Symbol ASCII Code A 01000000 a 01100001 ! 00100001
➥ $ 00100100 Z 01011010 z 01111010 ...etc, etc, etc up to 128
```

Notice that there are only two numbers involved, 1 and 0. This is what's known as *binary*, two items. What's the difference between the two, you ask? I told you this gets loopy. ASCII code is code for text alone. Those 128 groupings of 1s and 0s represent text, period.

In terms of FTP: If you are FTPing something that only has text, like an HTML document, use your application's ASCII mode. More on why in a moment.

FAQs from the HTML Goodies Web Site

Q. Does my FTP program choose ASCII or binary for me?

A. Your program chooses for you. Mine does too, but it's still a good idea to force the FTP program's hand and decide for it. There are times when it will choose incorrectly.

Binary—Sometimes Called Raw Data *or* All Files

Binary is best explained in comparison to ASCII. Binary also uses the seven (sometimes eight) digit 1s and 0s combinations, but it sees the characters in a different light.

Let's say you are FTPing an image. Yes, it is text, 1s and 0s, but with one major exception— all characters are not equal. If you look at your image (in a text editor), it looks like text. Remember that the computer sees numbers only, and characters are a good representation of those numbers. You see, the computer doesn't require that you see what happens to work. Text is there just so you can get a representation of what it is doing.

A binary transfer differs from ASCII in how it treats the characters used. An image needs to not only retain the same characters when it transfers, but it also needs to retain the form. It has to be equally as wide and tall when it arrives at its destination as it was when it left. If it is not, it's corrupted and won't work.

An example: When you create an HTML document, you may have noticed that adding a ton of spaces between words did not translate into a ton of spaces in the browser window. In addition, hitting Enter to jump to the next line didn't mean diddley when you posted it. The line broke when it wanted (unless you put in a <BR> command).

The reason for this is because you saved the document as text of one form or another. That only saved the letters, nothing else. Hitting Enter didn't matter. Your margin settings weren't saved—only the text was saved. This is why you have to put in flags to make the text do what you want. Only the text goes when you transfer the file over as ASCII, because that's all that is required. Its form is immaterial. You could write your HTML document as one really, really long line. The computer doesn't care. It changes the text off the flags, not by the form it was sent. How pretty you make your HTML document doesn't matter.

Imagine you just finished creating an image. Yes, it's 1s and 0s, but the text is more than just a bunch of numbers; it is in a certain format. Some of the text represents commands for the computer, and some represents text that will appear on the screen. Still other text represents a jump to the next line. That format must be retained. If you send the image as ASCII, the transfer literally changes the image into a long line of characters—it basically makes it text alone. The different types of commands have lost their meaning. All is now equal. It is corrupted. It will not work.

Rule of Thumb

This goes for both FTP uploading and downloading!

- Use ASCII only for transferring HTML documents.
- Everything else goes binary (or raw data or all files, depending on your program).

Why Not Send and Save Everything as Binary?

You can. It's just that sending an HTML document as binary tends to mess it up a bit. More than just text is being sent; form is now involved and it may alter what you want. Make a point of sending in two forms, binary and ASCII.

Finally!

The things I said go for both FTP and downloading! Text is text. Images are quite different.

If you download or transfer something and it fails to work, the smart money is that you corrupted it through one or many of your transfers.

Thanks for stopping by...now go FTP something. And enjoy your FTP software!

Speaking of software, what about those HTML assistants I mentioned in Primer 1?

I knew you'd ask me that.

What Do Those HTML Assistants Do?

They do a good bit, actually. The Help programs are usually set up like a word processor with a whole lot of little buttons to push. Those buttons give you the flags. For instance, you'd click the B button and get the begin and end flags to make something bold. They also save the files in the text format required. I use HTMLPad. It's an IBM program that only gets as involved as you allow. You can use the buttons or not. I've also been told HoTMeTaL is good as is Hot Dog. Each is available as shareware on the Internet. There are links to these and other HTML assistant programs in Appendix C, "Valuable Links."

Assistants are helpful, but don't get too involved in using one. Remember, this is your page—you do the writing. What fun is using a program that does half the work for you?

Where Do I Go Now?

You've put your foot in the water, so now it's time to dive right into Chapter 1, "Playing with Text," and start learning all the fun details of HTML.

You have the technology. You have the power. Heck, you have this book (and a Web site to go with it). Use my other tutorials and create your own little corner of the World Wide Web.

Go get 'em!

Part 2

Everything You Need to Know About Text and Graphics

Chapter 1

Playing with Text

Text Codes

I get letters from new users all the time asking if there are any commands for manipulating text other than `<B>` and `<I>`. I usually tell them no and go on.

I'm kidding, of course! The following 40 HTML flags can be used to manipulate text. I thought I'd throw this little deal together so you could see all those commands in one place.

Please understand that a few of these commands basically do the same thing. For instance, the `<STRONG>` command produces basically the same effect as `<BOLD>`. I'm sure that there's a very, very specific difference between the two, but in five years of writing over 5,000 pages, I've never needed `<STRONG>`.

Each of the tags described here is useful, but this is the only place you'll see many of them in this book. They're just not popular or complex enough to warrant their own tutorial.

So play with these. Put them on your page and "Oooooh" and "Aaaah" at what they do. Use the ones you like and dismiss the ones you don't. These are your pages you're creating.

In each of the following examples, I used the words *The Altered Text* as the text that the flags affect.

 If you want to see all these in action, point your browser to `http://www.htmlgoodies.com/` `textcodes.html`.

51

Abbreviation: <ABBR>

This is a new command in HTML 4.0. Your browser may not support it yet. It tells browsers and search engines that the text is not a word, but an abbreviation. It also produces a ToolTip—a rollover effect that brings up a small text box when the mouse rolls over.

```
<ABBR>The Altered Text</ABBR>
```

Acronym: <ACRONYM>

This is a new command in HTML 4.0. Your browser may not yet support it. The purpose of the command is almost exactly like the <ABBR> flag, except that this flag specifically denotes the text as an acronym.

```
<ACRONYM>The Altered Text</ACRONYM>
```

Address: <ADDRESS>

This sets text apart as an address and makes the text italicized.

```
<ADDRESS>The Altered Text</ADDRESS>
```

Bold: <B>

This one simply bolds the text.

```
<B>The Altered Text</B>
```

Base Font: <BASEFONT>

This works like the more popular font commands, except the basefont command also accepts style sheet commands, such as COLOR. It's another command that will be used more extensively when HTML 4.0 becomes the norm.

```
<BASEFONT COLOR="red">The Altered Text</BASEFONT>
```

BDO: <BDO>

This is a new command in HTML 4.0. Your browser may not support it yet. The BDO command denotes direction. See the following DIR command? RTL means right to left; LTR means the opposite. This comes into play if you are using a language, such as Hebrew, that has text going the opposite of English's left-to-right format.

```
<BDO DIR="rtl">The Altered Text</BDO>
```

Big: **<BIG>**

This is a great command. This bolds the text and bumps its size up a few pixels.

```
<BIG>The Altered Text</BIG>
```

Blink: **<BLINK>**

This command is only supported by Netscape. Hopefully, they'll drop it soon. It makes the text blink on and off, and on and off, and on and off...until you go crazy.

```
<BLINK>The Altered Text</BLINK>
```

Block Quote: **<BLOCKQUOTE>**

This command can surround a large chunk of text and indent it as a whole.

```
<BLOCKQUOTE>The Altered Text</BLOCKQUOTE>
```

Cite: **<CITE>**

This works just like the italics command. It sets the text aside in the browser's mind as a being a reference to another written piece. You remember, like in high school, when you wrote all those papers?

```
<CITE>The Altered Text</CITE>
```

Code: **<CODE>**

This sets text aside as code that is to be displayed. The text is placed in a monospace font, which is a bit more blocked (or square) than the normal font. The effect is similar to the <PRE> flag. <PRE> is a simple display, whereas <CODE> sets text aside in the browser's mind to display it as code, rather than just displaying it.

```
<CODE>The Altered Text</CODE>
```

Comment: **<COMMENT>**

Nothing appears on the page when you use this flag. You see, this flag marks text as a comment. Comments are good ways to make notes to yourself while writing HTML, and to make sure those notes don't appear on your Web site. Surrounding text with the <!-- and --> commands achieves the same effect.

```
<COMMENT>The Altered Text</COMMENT>
```

Delete: `<DEL>`

This is a new command in HTML 4.0. Your browser may not support it yet. It stands for deleted text. You text you mark with the `<DEL>` tags should get a strikethrough effect.

```
<DEL>The Altered Text</DEL>
```

Definition: `<DFN>`

DFN stands for definition. It is more for the browsers and search engines than it is for your eyes. Let's say you were searching for the definition of a word via an online search engine. If the pages you were searching through used this command, your search could be limited to definitions. It would produce a much better search than hitting everything.

```
<DFN>The Altered Text</DFN>
```

Division: `<DIV>`

DIV sets apart a section of the page so that it can be altered—usually with style sheet commands. You should also take a look Chapter 8, "Cascading Style Sheets and Layers," for more exciting exploits of the `<DIV>` flag; the chapter also holds the class, ID, and layering tutorials. It makes great bedtime reading.

```
<DIV>The Altered Text</DIV>
```

Emphasis: `<EM>`

EM makes the text stand out by making it italic. (I know it seems at this point like many commands do the same thing. They do. Critics of HTML have been pointing this out for a while.) I always use italics rather than emphasis, but to each his own. Some tell me they use both because it helps them keep things straight in their code.

```
<EM>The Altered Text</EM>
```

Font Color: `<FONT COLOR>`

You've seen this before. Read over Primer 3 on manipulating text for a refresher course.

```
<FONT COLOR="red">The Altered Text</FONT>
```

Font Size: `<FONT SIZE>`

Ditto. For more, see Primer 4. Hey! That rhymes!

```
<FONT SIZE="+1">The Altered Text</FONT>
```

Font Face: `<FONT FACE>`

This changes the text's font face. For more, see the text font tutorial in the next section of this chapter. That doesn't rhyme.

```
<FONT FACE="arial">The Altered Text</FONT>
```

Heading: `<H#>`

You can create six levels of headings by replacing the # sign with any of the numerals 1–6. For more information, see Primer 4.

```
<H#>The Altered Text</H#>
```

Italics: `<I>`

This makes the text italic.

```
<I>The Altered Text</I>
```

Inserted: `<INS>`

This is a new command in HTML 4.0. Your browser may not support it yet. This tag indicates inserted text. You should get an underline effect with it.

```
<INS>The Altered Text</INS>
```

Keyboard: `<KBD>`

KBD makes the text look like text typed out on an old typewriter.

```
<KBD>The Altered Text</KBD>
```

Listing: `<LISTING>`

I wouldn't slap this on a brain cell just yet. When HTML 4.0 becomes standard, this will be a dead command. Use `<PRE>` instead.

```
<LISTING>The Altered Text</LISTING>
```

Multiple Columns: `<MULTICOL>`

This sets text apart in multiple columns in Navigator only. For a full example, see the full tutorial in this chapter.

```
<MULTICOL>The Altered Text</MULTICOL> No example
```

No Break: **<NOBR>**

When you surround text with the <NOBR> flag, it does not wrap at the end of the line, but keeps rolling right off the right side of the screen.

```
<NOBR>The Altered Text</NOBR>
```

Plain Text: **<PLAINTEXT>**

No need to know this one cold, either. When HTML 4.0 becomes standard, this will be a dead command. Use <PRE> instead.

```
<PLAINTEXT>The Altered Text</PLAINTEXT>
```

Preformatted: **<PRE>**

Use <PRE> to keep text in the same format and shape it appears in when you type it into your Web site. Imagine you've just finished writing a paper that contains a few tables with lines of data. You could go in and add the commands to make an HTML table with the data—or you could just put the <PRE> command before and after the table—it will display as you wrote it. In fact, you could post the entire paper by using the <PRE> commands.

I don't usually use the commands; I go into the paper and format the text. I think it looks better. When you use the <PRE> command, you get text that looks a little weak compared to other HTML text. Go ahead and place text in <PRE> commands next to straight text in an HTML document—you'll see the difference. All in all, I think formatting the text looks better, but using the <PRE> command sure is fast.

```
<PRE>The Altered Text</PRE>
```

Quote: **<Q>**

This is a new command in HTML 4.0. Your browser may not support it yet. It is a replacement for the <BLOCKQUOTE> flag. It will also have the same properties available that the new Span command has.

```
<Q>The Altered Text</Q>
```

Strikethrough: **<S>**

The <S> flag causes text to be marked with a line through it.

```
<S>The Altered Text</S>
```

Sample: <SAMP>

SAMP creates very block-style text that is set to equal widths. It sets up nice, straight columns of text if you use it with tables.

```
<SAMP>The Altered Text</SAMP>
```

Small: <SMALL>

This renders text one size smaller than the browser's default setting.

```
<SMALL>The Altered Text</SMALL>
```

Span: <SPAN>

The SPAN command works a lot like the <DIV> command. You can set all sorts of parameters with it. For instance, if you are using a version 4.0 browser, you can lay your mouse pointer on the altered text and get a little box with text to pop up—a ToolTip. See the HTML 4.0 tutorial for more information.

```
<SPAN>The Altered Text</SPAN>
```

Strong: <STRONG>

This makes the text bold. This, again, is an instance of two commands producing the same effect. I use the <BOLD> flag for all places where I want text to be made stronger.

```
<STRONG>The Altered Text</STRONG>
```

Subscript: <SUB>

This sets text apart as subscript. The 2 in H_2O is an example.

```
<SUB>Altered</SUB>
```

Superscript: <SUP>

This flag sets the text to superscript, like the 8 in 10^8.

```
<SUP>Altered<SUP>
```

Typewriter Text: <TT>

The <TT> flag sets text in the a typewriter-style font. Typewriter font makes old-fashioned, bland, blocky text.

```
<TT>The Altered Text</TT>
```

Underline: <U>

This underlines the text.

```
<U>The Altered Text</U>
```

Variable: <VAR>

Text marked with the <VAR> flag is set in a small, fixed-width font.

```
<VAR>The Altered Text</VAR>
```

Wrapping Break: <WBR>

Placing the <WBR> allows no-break text to wrap at the indicated point if it needs to.

```
<NOBR>The Altered<WBR>Text</NOBR>
```

XMP: <XMP>

This is also a dead command when HTML 4.0 comes to pass. You should use the <PRE> command instead.

```
<XMP>The Altered Text</XMP>
```

Changing Text Colors

You need two things in order to change text colors:

- A color code. These come in either hex or word form.
- A command to change the text color.

I'll get to the commands in a moment. First, grab yourself a color hex code and a color word code. There are a slew of them in Appendix B, "Useful Charts." Any one will do.

Waiting...waiting...waiting...

If you don't feel like flipping through the pages, here's a favorite: *blue* (word form), which is the same as #0000FF (hex code).

 To see the text color tutorial online, head to http://www.htmlgoodies.com/backgrnd.html.

Changing the Color of all the Words on the Page

You have the ability to change full-page text colors over four levels:

`<TEXT="######">`   Denotes the full-page text color.

`<LINK="######">`   Denotes the color of the links on your page.

`<ALINK="######">`   Denotes the color the link will flash when clicked upon.

`<VLINK="######">`   Denotes the colors of the links after they have been visited.

These commands are placed inside the `<BODY>` container tag. Again, in that position they affect everything on the page. You also need to place them all together inside the same command, along with any background commands you might be using. Something like this:

```
<BODY BGCOLOR="######" TEXT="######" LINK="######" VLINK="######">
```

Here's an example of a `<BODY>` command in which the background is yellow, the text is black, the links are blue, the visited links are green, and the active links are purple. I have used color commands in both word and hex code form. You can combine them, like I do here:

```
<BODY BGCOLOR="yellow" TEXT="#000000" LINK="blue" VLINK="green" ALINK="#800080">
```

 Check out `http://www.htmlgoodies.com/book/bgexample.html` *to see these commands used. Be sure to look at the HTML source code.*

FAQs from the HTML Goodies Web Site

Q. I see that you use a pound sign (#) before your hex codes. Do I have to use them?

A. It depends on if you're a stickler, like me. Later browsers don't require their use, but I use them anyway, just in case someone out there is still using version 1.0 of a certain browser. You should never forbid the browser-challenged from enjoying your page.

Q. I found a great way to use color codes: I set the background color and the color of the visited links to the same color. Then, after the person clicks, the link disappears.

A. Clever. Good tip—if you don't ever want someone to use the same link twice.

 If you want to see the disappearing link in action, go to `http://www.htmlgoodies.com/book/disappear.html`*.*

Changing Color of One Word at a Time

But I only want to change one word's color! (Or maybe just a paragraph's color.) Once again, you use a color code, either hex or word, to do the trick. Follow this formula:

```
<FONT COLOR="######">text text text text text</FONT>
```

It's a pain in the you-know-where, but it gets the job done. It also works with all H and text-size commands. Basically, if it's text, it will work.

FAQs from the HTML Goodies Web Site

Q. I used three or four different `<FONT COLOR>` commands, but only the first one seems to be working.

A. I'll bet you only have one `</FONT>` command. Remember, every time you use a `<FONT>` command, you need a `</FONT>` command.

Q. I want to use both the `<FONT COLOR>` and `<FONT SIZE>` commands together. Do I need to have two whole font commands?

A. No. Just put both the SIZE and COLOR subcommands in the same `<FONT>` command, like so: `<FONT SIZE="+" COLOR="######">`. Then you only need one `</FONT>` command.

 See some examples of using hex and word color codes to change text color at `http://www.htmlgoodies.com/book/textcolor.html`.

What About Specific Link Colors?

You saw earlier that you could affect the color of every link on the page using the `<LINK="####">` flag. You then saw one word affected through `<FONT COLOR="####">`. It would seem to follow, then, that you could use either, or both, to affect the color of only one link. But it ain't necessarily so.

At the time of this writing, only the Netscape Navigator and Microsoft Internet Explorer browsers versions 4.0 or later support the altering of one link's color through the use of `<FONT COLOR="####">`.

Changing Text Fonts

I have been asked time and time again how to get the font face to change. I'm assuming you already know you can change font size through the use of H and FONT number commands. If what I just said is Greek to you, see Primer 3.

 See this text font tutorial online at `http://www.htmlgoodies.com/textfont.html`.

Figure 1.1 shows what I'm talking about. I have listed a few font face commands that you can use. I simply wrote this tutorial using Word 7.0 and entered all the font faces available with the little TT next to them (that TT stands for truetype, by the way). Here are the ones that worked. Follow the format for your page.

Just remember that older browsers will not process these commands and the text will appear unchanged. Even if the user has a new browser, she must also have all the fonts that you use already installed on her own computer. Changing fonts like this is fun, but not the most reliable thing you can do. The safest fonts to use (because they are the most common on Windows machines) are Arial, Times New Roman, Courier New, and Comic Sans.

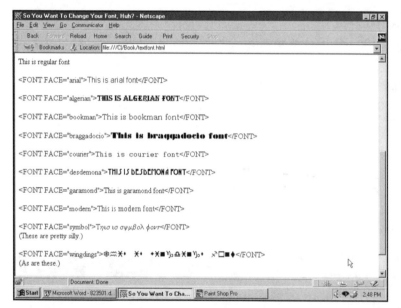

Figure 1.1
You can display some fonts on your Web site.

FAQs from the HTML Goodies Web Site

Q. Hey! I tried using your <FONT FACE> flag and it didn't work. I saw the font, but my friend didn't. Is it because we were using two different browsers?

A. Could be, but I doubt it. You see, these font commands will only work if the computer reading the page has that specific font loaded onto its hard drive. If it doesn't, you'll get straight text like your friend did. Just be sure to choose more common fonts in the future.

Good luck with other fonts. Just remember that not all computers are built the same. What displayed perfectly on your computer might not on someone else's. In fact, Murphy's law suggests it won't.

Go to `http://www.htmlgoodies.com/book/testfonts.html` *to see if these common fonts will display on your computer.*

Indents and Lists

I have received a good many letters asking how I indent paragraphs and bullet lists. Here's a quick rundown of the how's and why's.

This tutorial is online at `http://www.htmlgoodies.com/lists.html`.

Indenting a Paragraph

I simply indent by adding blank spaces. "But my browser ignores my spaces!" you say.

Mine does, too. I can put in 50 spaces, and only one of those spaces will display. But I know the way around it. I use this small code to create each of my spaces:

That thing is an ampersand command, which creates a space as if you pushed the Spacebar. I have a whole tutorial, "& Commands," in Appendix A if you would like to see more.

This is what I use when I indent five spaces:

```
     
```

See the five spaces? That's what I do. Look at the View Source of any of my tutorials if you don't believe me. There may be another method, but I like this one.

FAQs from the HTML Goodies Web Site

Q. Can you send me the little black dot image you are using for those lists of yours? I can't find it anywhere.

A. The little bullets aren't images. They are placed there with HTML commands. In fact, the entire list format can be created through commands. I'll show you how in the next section.

Bulleted Lists

Bulleted lists are nice. Here's why I like them:

- They present information in an easy fashion.
- The bullets look cool.
- They make me happy.

Sorry about that last one. I just needed another item to make a three-item list. Figure 1.2 shows these bullets on a Web site. Here's how I did it:

```
<UL>
<LI>They present information in an easy fashion.
<LI>The bullets look cool.
<LI>They make me happy.
</UL>
```

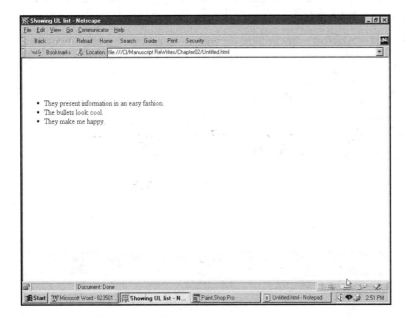

Figure 1.2
Making a bulleted list.

Don't be put off by the commands; there are actually only two commands being used again and again. Here's what's happening:

- ⬤ <UL> stands for unordered list. That means bullets will be used rather than numbers.

- ⬤ <LI> stands for list item. It denotes the next thing that will receive a bullet. Please note that no </LI> is required. The text will stay within a confined space and remain indented from the left without your doing anything.

- ⬤ The <LI> does all that good stuff for you, like make the little black dot. </UL> ends the entire list.

Using a center command before these commands doesn't center the entire list, it centers each item. That messes up the look of the list. If you would like to move the list closer to the center of the page, simply add more <UL> commands. Just remember that if you use three <UL> commands, you need to offer three </UL> commands. Like this:

```
<UL><UL><UL>
<LI> list item
</UL></UL></UL>
```

Please note though that using multiple <UL> flags will create different-looking bullets. The first <UL> level is a solid dot, the second is a circle, and the third is a square. The preceding example would create a square bullet. It's not quite the same with multiple <OL> flags. Multiple <OL> lists will not change the text of the numbers or the letters. If you set the TYPE to I, however, it will indent each list level.

For more precise control over the spacing you can add an   to bump the text over a little more.

I Don't Like Round Bullets—I Want Squares!!!

Easy there, fellah. You can have your list and squares too. Simply add the command TYPE="square" into your UL command. Figure 1.3 shows what your list bullets will look like.

```
<UL TYPE="square">    Note: Square must be in lower case letter
<LI>List Item 1
<LI>List Item 2
<LI>List Item 3
</UL>
```

Figure 1.3
Square bullets on your Web page.

FAQs from the HTML Goodies Web Site

Q. I saw this page that had a bull's-eye where the little black dots should be in a list of items. What's that command?

A. There ain't one. I'll bet if you look at the source code, you'll find those bull's-eyes are images. You can use images for a lot of things on a Web site—don't forget that!

Numbered Lists

If you would like to create a list that numbers the items rather than just bulleting them, HTML can do that for you, too. Yeah, you could just number the things yourself, but that's no fun. It's also time-consuming. Dig this and then look at Figure 1.4:

```
<OL>
<LI>List Item 1
<LI>List Item 2
<LI>List Item 3
</OL>
```

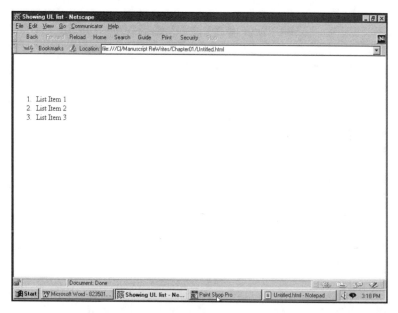

Figure 1.4
A numbered list.

Notice it's the same format the other list, except <OL> is where <UL> used to be. Nothing to it. The browser will continue to count up as long as you keep putting <LI> items after the <OL>. By the way, OL stands for ordered list.

FAQs from the HTML Goodies Web Site

Q. How can I get the list to start at a specific number? I need the list to start at 3.

A. Add the subcommand START="3" to the <OL> flag, so that you get this: <OL START="3">. Keep in mind that is a fairly new command and might not work across all browsers.

But I Want Roman Numerals!!!

Arabic isn't good enough for you, huh? Well, simply place a TYPE="I" inside the <OL> flag. Notice that is a capital I, not the number 1. You can see the list in Figure 1.5. Here's how you do it:

```
<OL TYPE="I">
<LI>List Item 1
<LI>List Item 2
<LI>List Item 3
</OL>
```

Figure 1.5
Numbered lists with Roman numerals.

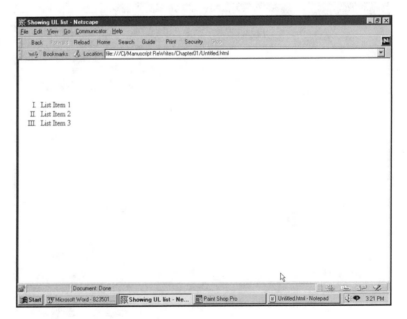

Can I Combine Types of Lists?

Yes—just remember to close each one. You could make an <OL> list and put in a small <UL> under each <LI> command for the <OL>. The following code produces what you see in Figure 1.6:

```
<OL>
<LI>Main Heading
  <UL>
    <LI>List item 1
    <LI>List item 2
  </UL>
<LI>Secondary Heading
  <UL>
    <LI>List item 1
    <LI>List item 2
  </UL>
</OL>
```

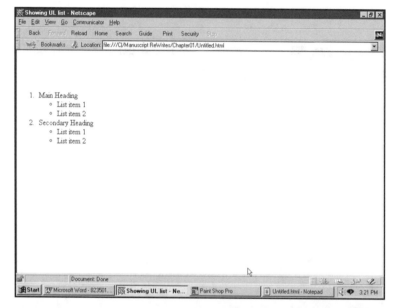

Figure 1.6
Combining types of lists.

FAQs from the HTML Goodies Web Site

Q. I see sites where some of the bullets (little dots) are just circles. How do I do that?

A. My guess is that those little circles were created because the person is using a <UL> list under another <UL> list (as is shown earlier). That produces different types of bullets at each level.

You can check out multiple lists under lists and see the kind of bullets produced by going to http://www.htmlgoodies.com/book/diffbullets.html.

The Definition List

There's one more set of list commands that manipulates the text for you. The previous ones are all single-item lists; each <LI> flag makes one list item. Here's what the HTML looks like (see Figure 1.7):

```
<H4>Here's What's For Dinner</H4>
<DL>
<DT>Salad
<DD>Green stuff and dressing
<DT>The Meal
<DD>Mystery meat and mashed yams
<DT>Dessert
<DD>A mint
</DL>
```

Figure 1.7
A definition list.

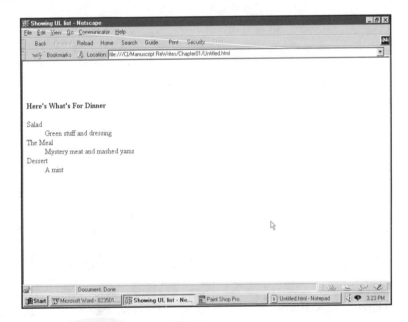

Here's what's happening: I used an <H4> command to create a heading.

- <DL> stands for definition list. It tells the browser that a double-tier list is coming up.
- <DT> stands for definition term. It's the first tier.
- <DD> stands for definition description. It's indented and describes the definition term.

It's a nice look, although I haven't run into any place to use it quite yet. I usually go with multiple <UL> lists, one under the other.

Well, that's all I have. You can play with the text all you want inside of these list commands. Bold, italic, and any other text command you want will work. Use the list commands to present information to your readers in a fashion smoother than writing long, drawn-out paragraphs with a lot of detail. I use these lists all the time. Enjoy, and happy listing.

Newspaper Columns

Look at Figure 1.8!

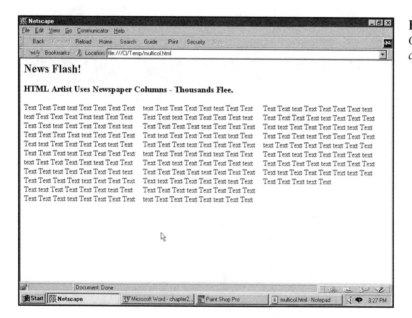

Figure 1.8

Creating newspaper-style columns.

Sorry for the drama, but it had to appear newspaper-like. Now onto the matter at hand—how did I get these three nice columns? (Please note that the techniques in this section work in Netscape browsers only!) I used a command that looks more like an afterthought than something the HTML know-it-alls created for everyday use.

I used this to get the effect shown in Figure 1.8:

```
<MULTICOL COLS="3" GUTTER="10" WIDTH="90%">
text text text text text, etc., etc.
</MULTICOL>
```

To do this, simply surround a block of text with the commands <MULTICOL> and </MULTICOL>—you're off and running.

There are three other subcommands that go with MULTICOL. They all go inside the first MULTICOL as subcommands and affect everything in between:

- ○ Use COLS="#" to denote how many columns your page will have. I chose three. I just felt like a trio at the time.

- ○ Use GUTTER="#" to denote the width, in pixels, between the columns of text. I chose the number 25 for this lovely tutorial.

- ○ Use WIDTH="#" to denote the overall width of the columns combined. All the commands that manipulate text shape, like CENTER and ALIGN, will work inside the column. If you center something, it will center inside the column. But you knew that.

 To see an example of these commands being used, go to http://www.htmlgoodies.com/ book/multicol.html.

FAQs from the HTML Goodies Web Site

Q. How do I make sure that both Netscape and Explorer users can see my newspaper columns, since the <MULTICOL> flag only works in Netscape?

A. Don't use the <MULTICOL> flag. There's no way you can "make" a browser use a command if it doesn't understand it. You need to create this effect via table cells; see Chapter 5, "All About Tables." That's the only way to ensure it's working across browsers.

Speaking of commands that don't work in certain browsers:

Q. What happens if I use a command that Internet Explorer understands, but Navigator does not? Does the code show up, cause problems, or what?

A. None of the above. The one really nice thing about all the browsers out there right now is that they are very adept at ignoring commands they don't understand. If you have commands that produce something in Internet Explorer, but not in Netscape, go ahead and use them. The Explorer users will get to see the effect and the Netscape users will never know the commands were there to begin with. Just don't make the commands that work in one browser or the other a crucial part of your page.

I think the <MULTICOL> flag is a bit of an afterthought because there isn't a command that jumps you to the beginning of the next column to start a new story or heading. The flag simply takes text and breaks it into columns. The only real downfall is that you have to keep scrolling the browser window up and down to read the silly thing.

Oh, and in case you were wondering if there is a <MULTIROW> command, the answer is yes. It's called paragraphs. Ha! I kill me!

Enjoy!

Chapter 2

Making Links

Setting Up a Site

Answering a ton of email every day allows me to keep an eye on when the new batch of HTML writers come into the fold. The questions I receive always become more and more difficult, and then all of a sudden they become much simpler. The latest group of people have arrived. With that in mind, I offer this—it's a popular topic with beginning writers.

 This tutorial is online at `http://www.htmlgoodies.com/sitelinks.html`.

Putting a Site Together

Okay, you write some pages. Let's say you create a home page. We'll call it `homepage.html`.

You then create three more pages:

- `links.html`   A page of your favorite links
- `photos.html`   A page of your favorite photos
- `story.html`   A page with one of your best stories

At the moment they are just sitting on your hard drive or floppy disk; `homepage.html` offers links to the three other pages. That is your first site—good start. How do you hook them all together?

The HREF *Links*

First, I'm assuming you already have a place to post these pages. If you don't, read over Primer 7 for help finding and choosing an Internet service provider (ISP).

Now you have a place for your files. This "place" you have been given is actually a small section of a hard drive on a server somewhere. In computer lingo, you have a directory where you can place your files. Think of this directory as an equal to a floppy disk or a directory on your own hard drive. It's a contained area where the pages (and all the images that go on those pages) are housed.

This is important to remember when you're writing the links that connect these four pages.

FAQs from the HTML Goodies Web Site

Q. I made links like you said, but they don't work. I checked for spelling, but that's all correct. What's wrong?

A. If the spelling and capitalization are correct in reference to the file you're calling for, I would think the problem might be between .htm and .html. Servers see them as two different files. If the file you are calling for is .htm and you call for .html, the link won't work. Check that.

In-Site Versus Off-Site Links

You've probably already read through Primer 4. If not, give it a once-over pretty soon. It gives you the basic format of a link.

First attach to a page outside of your site. Here's the basic format:

```
<A HREF="http://www.htmlgoodies.com">Click Here</A>
```

Note that the address is a full URL (Universal Resource Locator). It starts with that http thing and ends with that .com deal.

The format is simple. The A stands for anchor and the HREF stands for hypertext reference. It's a reference to another page, thus the address http://www.htmlgoodies.com.

Now let's look at what I call an *internal link*. This is a link that stays within your own site. One of your pages is calling for another one of your pages. We'll say this is a link from homepage.html to links.html. Remember those two from earlier? Here's the format:

```
<A HREF="links.html">Click Here</A>
```

Notice I'm only calling for the page without the full address attached? Why? Because I don't need it. To make the point a little stronger, look at the directory structure of Web addresses.

Directory Structure

For the sake of continuing this discussion, and because I love to hear myself talk, let's take this little fantasy of mine a bit further. You purchase an account on a server called www.joeserver.com. You choose the login schmoe when you sign up for your account. This means that your email address will most likely be schmoe@joeserver.com and your Web site address will be http://www.joeserver.com/~schmoe. The little squiggly line (~) is called a tilde. It tells the server, "There is one directory on this server called schmoe—find it."

When you use your file transfer protocol (FTP) program to upload files to your new server, you upload into the directory that was set aside for you; in this case, schmoe.

You upload your homepage.html page into your directory. The address of that page is now http://www.joeserver.com/~schmoe/homepage.html.

See the slash I added and the name? I do that because the homepage.html page is now inside your schmoe directory.

Think of a directory structure as one item being inside a larger item. For example, a word is inside a sentence, is inside a paragraph, is inside a page, is inside a chapter, is inside a book. If this were written in directory structure format, it would look like this:

```
Book/chapter/page/paragraph/sentence/word
```

Notice that the bigger ones are to the left. The items get smaller as you move to the right. Take this URL for example:

```
http://www.server.com/users/pages/ohio/joe.html
```

The page joe.html is inside a directory called ohio, is inside a directory called pages, is inside a directory called users, is on a server called server.com.

That's why the page homepage.html is at the end of the address. Make sense?

Internal Links

Now we put together a site in your own directory. Once again you have a home page called homepage.html and three sub-pages that you want to link to from homepage.html— links.html, photos.html, and story.html. First off you need to FTP all four pages to your directory. Here's the first link on homepage.html; it calls up your links.html page:

```
<A HREF="links.html">Click Here</A>
```

Notice I am only calling for the page by its name. I am not using the full address.

I could use the full address; there's no reason why I couldn't. If you followed along with the earlier discussion, you'll remember that since the file was uploaded into the schmoe directory, its full address would be http://www.joeserver.com/~schmoe/links.html. Why not use it?

To Use the Full URL, or Not to Use the Full URL

If you are linking to a page on your site, you must use the full URL because you are leaving your own directory. In fact, the chances are really good that you are leaving your server altogether. Because of that, you need to offer your HREF attribute the full address to the new site.

When you're staying within your own site you need only call for the page name. You see, your directory is a closed home for all of your pages. If you only call for a page or an image through its name (minus the full address), the server looks for the page or the image inside the same home that houses the page that called for it. In other words, servers search a page's home directory by default. That's good to know when you create your links. It means you only have to use the page's name minus the full URL.

FAQs from the HTML Goodies Web Site

Q. I've written my pages using the full URL every time. Would you suggest going in and changing them?

A. If the site is working up to your expectations, I wouldn't go to the trouble.

What if I Do Use the Full URL?

You're always playing the rebel. The answer is that your internal links might run slower. If you use the full address, a full search process begins when your user clicks a link. First the server is located, next the directory is located, and then the page is located. If you use only the name, the search is already at its destination. The server simply searches itself. Slick, huh?

Are there exceptions to this? Oh, sure. If you use form buttons on your page, you'll want to use the full URL because of its structure. I cover form buttons in Chapter 7, "Adding Link Buttons and Forms."

The Home Page Links

What is written onto `homepage.html` that links the pages together? This:

```
<A HREF="links.html">Click Here for My Favorite Links</A>
<A HREF="photos.html">Click Here for My Photos</A>
<A HREF="story.html">Click Here for My Best Story</A>
```

Now you're all linked. Hey! You made more than a couple of pages. You linked them all together. You made a site.

 I have this exact example set up at `http://www.htmlgoodies.com/book/site.html.`

Page Jumps

I get letters about how to do these internal page jumps all the time. They are a great way to allow people to move quickly inside a long page. I have them all over my HTML Goodies tutorials. Stop into any of them; at the top and bottom there are hypertext links that send you to whatever sections you choose. They are great for helping people navigate big pages—and I have big pages. I just can't shut up when I get rolling.

 This tutorial is online at `http://www.htmlgoodies.com/pagejump.html`.

Here's How You Do It

You need to place two items on each page:

- A basic link command pointing to another section of the page
- The point where the page will jump

Here's the basic link command:

```
<A HREF="#codeword">Blue Words, Blue Words</A>
```

This command then denotes where the link scrolls the page:

```
<A NAME="codeword">
```

You place this command at the very top of the browser screen. I usually put some space on the page before the code word by using `<BR>` flags so that I don't cut any words off. But that's just a suggestion.

It's a great look when you offer these jumps. Netscape Navigator just jumps right to the spot; Internet Explorer actually does a quick scroll.

Here's What's Happening

Take a look at this quick rundown:

- The A HREF command is the same as a basic link except the link is to a code word rather than to an URL.
- Please notice that there is a # sign in front of the code word. You need that to denote its being an internal link. Without the # sign, the browser looks for something outside the page named after your code word. And it isn't going be there.
- Your "code word" can be just about anything you want. I try my best to keep it short and make it represent what it is jumping to.
- The point where the page jumps follows the same general format, except you replace the word HREF with the word NAME.

- Please also notice that there is no # sign in the NAME command.
- Where you place the <A NAME="---"> page jump target is the section of the HTML page that appears at the top of the browser window after the page jump occurs.

FAQs from the HTML Goodies Web Site

Q. Is there a limit to the number of letters a code word can have?

A. There might be a limit to the number of letters you can use, but I haven't found it yet.

Q. Can I have spaces in my code word?

A. No. Just run the text all together or use underscores (_) between words. No spaces allowed.

Q. Do I have to use a different code word for every page jump on my site?

A. You mean completely? No—just on the same page. You can use the same code word on different pages. I do it all the time.

Jumping from Another Page

Let's say you have a tutorial—much the same as this one but online—and that you will be jumping from page to page. It would make things a lot easier if, when you jump between pages, you could have the jumped-to page load at a specific point rather than loading at the top each time. Well, you can.

Jumping to a Specific Page Section

Okay, let's say you want to jump to a page at a certain point. You will do so using a basic A HREF command that denotes both the page and the NAME target.

Pretend I used <A NAME="welcomeback"> as the code word jump point for a section about halfway down this page: http://www.htmlgoodies.com/pagejump.html.

The Link Form

Take a look at the following code:

```
<A HREF="http://www.htmlgoodies.com/pagejump.html#welcomeback"> Blue Words, Blue
Words</A>
```

See what's happening? I did a simple A HREF link back to the page—but I added the # sign and then the code word! No slashes or dots; just run it all together.

When the user clicks that link she'll go to the page and right to that section.

Use page jumps often. I think they're great. Your visitors will thank you, too.

 I have a page for you to try out these page jumps; see `http://www.htmlgoodies.com/book/pagejumps.html`.

Active Images (Images That Act Like Links)

This is a topic covered in the Primers section of HTML Goodies, but it deserves its own short section here. As the new wave of HTML artists are trying their hands at the craft, this is the question they ask most:

How Do I Make an Image Act as a Link to Another Page?

 This tutorial is online at `http://www.htmlgoodies.com/imagelink.html`.

Remember the basic text link format:

```
<A HREF="http://www.htmlgoodies.com">Click here for HTML Goodies</A>
```

`Click Here for HTML Goodies` shows up on the Web page, and it shows up in blue. Figure 2.1 shows an image whose name is `cool_computer.gif`. I will use it as a link to the HTML Goodies page.

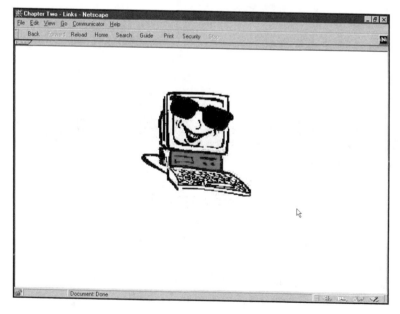

Figure 2.1
Hello, my name is
`cool_computer.gif`.

You can make an image a link by simply replacing the text that explains the link (in my example that's `Click here for HTML Goodies`) and substitute the HTML code for inserting an image.

```
<A HREF="http://www.htmlgoodies.com"><IMG SRC="cool_computer.gif"></A>
```

Figure 2.2 shows you what you get.

Figure 2.2
The image is now a link. (Notice the mouse pointer has turned into a hand, which indicates a link.)

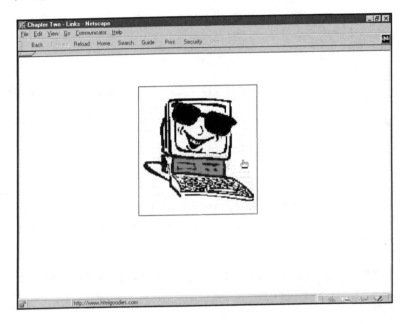

When you place your pointer over the image, you'll see it's active and points to the HTML Goodies home page. You're done. Almost.

FAQs from the HTML Goodies Web Site

Q. Can I use a JPEG image as a link?

A. Yes; just follow the same format I do with my GIF image.

Removing the Blue Border Around the Link Image

Look again at the image in Figure 2.2. See the border? That happens when you make an image active. Remember that linked text is blue? That's what happens here. If you like it, great. You're done. I think it looks unprofessional. I get rid of it. Here's how:

```
<A HREF="http://www.htmlgoodies.com"><IMG BORDER="0" SRC="cool_computer.gif"></A>
```

All I did was add the command BORDER="0" inside the image command, right between IMG and SRC. That sets the blue border around the active image to 0. You can see the borderless image in Figure 2.3. If you'd like, you can do the opposite and write in BORDER="50". That will give you a huge blue border.

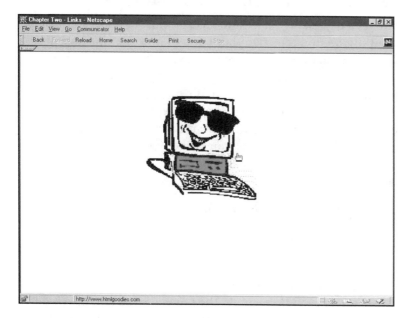

Figure 2.3
The border around the link image is gone!

Lay your pointer on the image. It's still active, but no blue. That looks much more crisp.

FAQs from the HTML Goodies Web Site

Q. I found that I can set the link color to the same color as the background and the border will disappear. That also allows me to make the border a lot bigger and give the image some room.

A. Yup, that'll do it. You might want to think about also setting space apart for your image by using table commands to surround the image with a table cell and then using the cellpadding command to set space. (Read about tables in Chapter 5, "All About Tables.") By the way, make sure you set the VLINK color to the same shade as the background; otherwise the border shows up after someone has visited the linked page. You might also run into a few problems if the user has his own background colors set rather than using what you send them.

That's about it. Just allow me to remind you that all images should have HEIGHT, WIDTH, and ALT commands attached to them in order to make the transfer of pages much faster and easier to understand. To learn more, go to Chapter 3, "Adding Images and Backgrounds."

You can see a couple of active images demonstrating these sections at `http://www.htmlgoodies.com/book/active.html.`

Creating Links That Open a New Browser Window

I used to receive at least one letter a day asking for information on how to make a link open a new browser window, so I put this section together—but I don't know that the benefits outweigh the extra memory and computational power required to do it. Opening a new browser window can help when navigating through frame pages, keeping one set open while you browse another. It is also good when you want to download out of frames pages. It also helps when you have a MIDI sound file on a page that you want to have continue playing through many pages, and this is a good way to show another page quickly and have your pages remain open. Remember, however, that the more pages you open through more browser windows, the more you are taxing the user's computer. You will slow the process a bit and might crash computers with less memory capacity.

 This tutorial is online at `http://www.htmlgoodies.com/new_win.html.`

You will have two windows open at the same time when you use these commands. Keep this in mind:

- You can get back to the original browser screen by closing the top level window. In Windows 3.*x*, choose **Close** under the **File** menu in the browser's top left. In Windows 95/98, select the button in the upper-right corner. Macintosh users can find the button in the upper-left corner. Of course, you can always toggle between the two new open windows.

- If you choose **Exit**, you'll close the browser altogether. You don't want to do that.

Here's the basic HTML code for creating a link that opens a new browser window:

```
<A HREF="http://www.site.com/page.html" TARGET="resource window">
Text Text Text</A>
```

See that `TARGET="resource window"`? That's what does it.

How Do I Stop It from Happening?

I also get letters stating that a client-side imagemap or a frames page is causing a new window. Some people want rid of it. Try this:

```
<A HREF="http://www.site.com/page.html" TARGET=="_top">
Text Text Text</A>
```

Notice that I targeted the link to the top of the page. This is the default in HTML. Not putting it in has always resulted in an A HREF link jumping to the top of the same browser window. You need to force the browser's hand in order to stop the new window from popping up to display the page the A HREF link is pointing to. Please notice the underline mark (underscore) before the word top. This doesn't always work, but is often successful.

FAQs from the HTML Goodies Web Site

Q. I have found that closing the browser and opening it again also solves the problem.

A. I've heard that, too. I have also heard that holding the Shift button and selecting reload often solves the problem.

Now go and use the commands for good, not evil. They are yours to exploit at your own will.

My suggestion is to use this sparingly. You're taking up precious memory running two or more windows.

 See new windows galore at http://www.htmlgoodies.com/book/new_windows.html.

How to Create a Dynamic Page

If you see this tutorial online, you are treated to a slide show of sorts. Without your doing anything, the pages change every three seconds. That's the purpose of these commands, to perform a redirect with no user input.

 This tutorial is available online at http://www.htmlgoodies.com/dynamic1.html.

No, this tutorial has nothing to do with Dynamic HTML (DHTML). You'll find that in lucky Chapter 13, "Internet Explorer Tutorials and DHTML." I use the term *dynamic* here because the process occurs on its own. Plus, I was calling these commands dynamic long before DHTML was even a twinkle in the Internet eye. I like to think of myself as progressive and ahead of the curve. My wife just says I'm lucky.

If you'd like to sound intelligent at your next cocktail party, the commands' actual name is *meta-refresh*.

Before we get started, wait—this page uses things called *meta* commands. What you learn here is a small part of what meta commands can do. See "Using Meta Commands with Search Engines" in Chapter 15, "Other Stuff You Should Really Know," for gobs more.

Getting a Page to Change

This is a great effect that offers your readers some surprises. I've seen this used to take people on guided tours, to tell jokes, and almost talk to the viewer, which is just what I do with this tutorial online. You should be able to find an equally good use.

Here are the commands I placed on my HTML document to get the page-changing effect:

```
<META HTTP-EQUIV="refresh"
CONTENT="5;URL=http://www.page.com/page.html">
```

I placed it right after the <HTML> (and <HEAD> if you're using one) command and just before the <TITLE> and </TITLE> commands.

Here's What You Are Telling the Computer to Do

Here's a list of the code broken down:

- META HTTP-EQUIV tells the computer that after the page is loaded it is to find an HTTP equivalent item—another Web page in other words.

- REFRESH tells the computer that it's supposed to refresh the page. It reloads the page, but because we are offering a different URL, it loads that new page rather than refreshing itself.

- CONTENT is a strange word in this case. It denotes the number of seconds before the meta-refresh is to occur. I have this one set at 5. You can set it at whatever you want.

- URL is the address it's supposed to load after the five seconds (or however many you denote).

FAQs from the HTML Goodies Web Site

Q. How can I make this change almost instantaneous?

A. Set the content to 0.

The CONTENT command includes the URL command, so there is no quotation mark after the 5 or before the URL. Make a point of copying exactly what is noted in the preceding code. It won't work otherwise.

How to Add Sound

Those of you who saw this tutorial online should have gotten a little "ta da" sound when you logged in. That's another thing you can do with this META format. I had it set up that after the page loaded, your browser should have played a little .au file called tada.au (clever name, eh?).

Here's the command that did the job:

```
<META HTTP-EQUIV="refresh" CONTENT="1; URL=http://www.page.com/tada.au">
```

I simply replaced the URL with a sound file address.

There are a few assumptions you make using these dynamic commands:

- You are assuming the viewer has a browser level 1.1 or higher. If your viewer is using 1.0 or a browser with text-only capabilities (yes, they do still exist, contrary to the growth of the WWW), the dynamic page that is supposed to change just sits there. Then the viewer waits...and waits...and nothing happens. He or she swears at you and moves on.

- By using a sound file, you assume the viewer can play what you have offered. That's a tough call because there are many different filenames. I suggest trying .au first (my opinion).

- Finally, and most annoyingly, you assume that people care to see the little page change or hear that "ta da" every time they log on—a very big assumption.

You can read a great deal more about incorporating sounds into your Web pages in Chapter 10, "Adding Sound and Video."

FAQs from the HTML Goodies Web Site

Q. Can I set it so that the sound only plays once?

A. I did that by creating only one page that has the sound on it. Past that, every link back to the page that has the sound goes to a copy of that page—the one without the sound file on it. The effect is that the page loads without playing the sound. Of course, it doesn't work if the user hits the Back button.

My suggestion is to use these pups sparingly and offer those less browserly-endowed a way around the effect. Put something on the page that is supposed to change but allows users to click and join in the merriment of your page.

 Go to `http://www.htmlgoodies.com/book/metarefresh.html` *to see this in action.*

So You Don't Want Links Underlined?

Please note that taking the underline away from links requires that your browser recognize style commands. That generally means Netscape Navigator browsers 3.0 or later or Internet Explorer–style browsers. Take a look at the links in Figure 2.4.

This tutorial is online at `http://www.htmlgoodies.com/nounderlineonlinks.html.`

Figure 2.4
Links with no underlines.

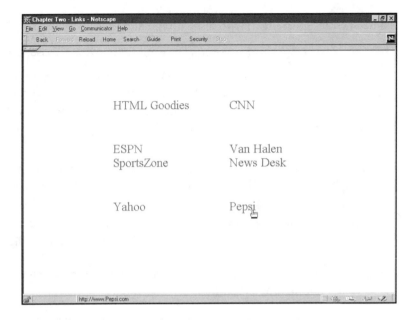

Notice anything about them? They are not underlined, yet they're still active. See that the pointer is a hand over top of the Pepsi link?

By the way, if you followed this tutorial and your links are still underlined, you might not have a browser level high enough to run this command. You can still use the commands, though; others will have the correct browser!

For a good while, people wrote to me and asked how to rid the links on their page of the awful underline. I always wrote back that you could always get rid of it—just go into your browser's preferences and set it so the links are not underlined. Done.

But I knew what they wanted. They wanted the links to be without underlines on all browsers, not just theirs. Here's how you do it:

```
<STYLE>
<!--
A{text-decoration:none}
-->
</STYLE>
```

You place that STYLE block statement inside the HEAD commands on your HTML document. In that position, it affects all the links and makes them plain, like you see here. The links retain their coloring, but lose their underline.

Affecting Just One Link

There is a way to make just one link lose its underline. Do this:

```
<A HREF="wherever" STYLE="text-decoration: none">Huh</a>
```

I added the style commands right into the A HREF link itself rather than putting it up in the <HEAD> commands. This works great if you'd like some links underlined and others not. I've seen non-underlined links in blocks of text, and those that stood alone underlined. It did make the page easier to read.

Pretty slick.

 See a few links that aren't underlined at http://www.htmlgoodies.com/book/ nounderline.html.

Chapter 3

Adding Images and Backgrounds

Images

Images are a big part of what makes the Web so great. Learning how to manipulate images on your Web pages is key to building a great site.

Grabbing Images Off the Web

Let me state up front that just because you have the ability to grab an image does not mean that you always can...legally. Copyright laws, contrary to what some people believe, apply to the Internet. I have a whole slew of copyright questions and answers in the back of the book. For now, a good rule of thumb is to always ask permission to use the images you want unless the person is specifically offering the image for downloading. Just to be more of a party-pooper, if you know the image being offered is copyrighted, don't use it. You are just as guilty posting the image as the person offering it.

As a fine Ohio Trooper once told me, ignorance of the law is no excuse, young man. Then he gave me a $70 ticket.

If you'd like to brush up on how copyright laws work in regards to the Internet before pushing on, see the copyright reference piece in Chapter 15, "Other Stuff You Should Really Know."

 This tutorial is available online at `http://www.htmlgoodies.com/howto.html`.

FAQs from the HTML Goodies Web Site

Q. **If I download an image as GIF, but I want it JPG, can I just change out the last three letters of the name?**

A. No, you'll mess it up doing that. You need to download in the format the image currently uses. You then need to use a graphics program to save it in a different format.

Always make a point, when downloading images and placing them on your own server, to run them. Don't make an HREF link to other people's servers run the image. By doing that, you are unnecessarily taxing the other person's server, and might be breaking the copyright law. Plus, if the image is on your server, you will get it to load to your page much faster.

How It's Done

After the image comes up on the screen, place your pointer on it. Figure 3.1 shows an image of a basketball for demonstration.

Figure 3.1
A pointer on top of the image.

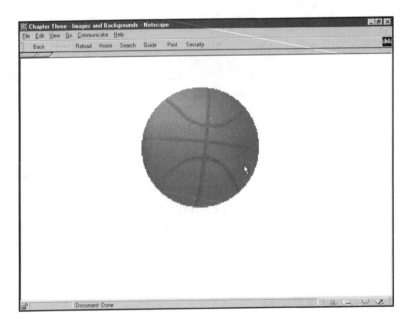

When your pointer is on the image, click the right mouse button. Macintosh users should push the mouse button and hold it. A menu appears, as shown in Figure 3.2.

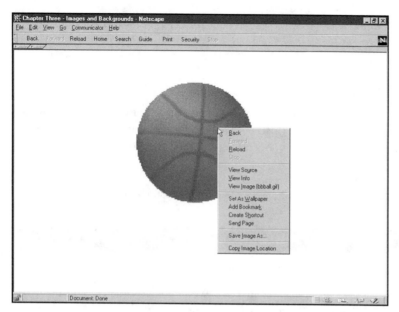

Figure 3.2
The menu that appears with a right-click.

Now choose to save the image, as shown in Figure 3.3.

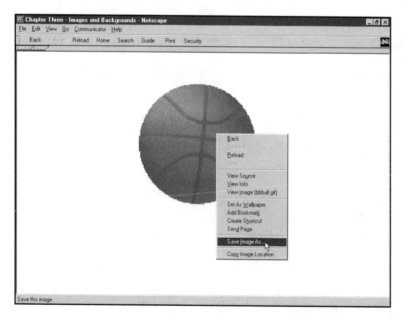

Figure 3.3
Choose Save Image As from the menu.

Once you choose to save the image, your computer's Save As dialog box pops up. There you tell it where to save the image on your computer's hard drive or to floppy disk.

Enjoy!

You can try to download an image (with the instructions printed right underneath) from http://www.htmlgoodies.com/book/trydownload.html.

Aligning Text with Images

People ask all the time how to get images onto pages. If you aren't sure how yet, take a look at Primer 5. Once people do get those images onto a page, they start asking how to get text to align or wrap around the images they have placed there. That's the purpose of this tutorial—to tell you how to get the text to wrap.

 You can get to this tutorial online at http://www.htmlgoodies.com/align.html.

FAQs from the HTML Goodies Web Site

Q. How do I get images right next to each other?

A. You mean so they look like one larger image? Just use two image commands and place them next to each other—on the same line. Placing one below the other might create a space between them. Also, if the images are active, make sure to use BORDER="0", or they'll never butt against each other.

Getting Text to Wrap

One of the more popular questions I receive is how to get text to wrap around a left- or right-aligned image. Figure 3.4 shows an example of what I mean.

Figure 3.4
Text wrapping around left- and right-justified images.

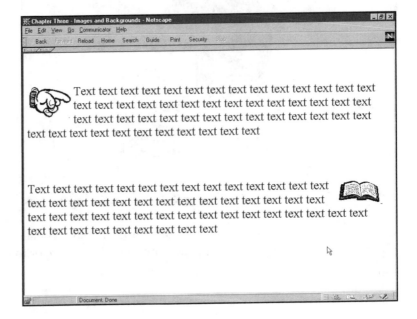

Notice that the two images, the hand and the book, are sitting far left and then far right and the text just wraps around them. It's done by adding one command to the image itself. Here's the code for the pointing finger:

```
<IMG SRC="finger.gif" ALIGN="left">
```

Notice that all I did was add the ALIGN="left" command inside a basic image command and between the IMG and the SRC. "But wait!" you say, "The image was already aligned to the left before you added the ALIGN command." Yes, I know. The ALIGN command caused the wrap of the text. Without it, you wouldn't get the effect.

As for how I got the image to move to the right and the text to wrap, here's the code:

```
<IMG SRC="book.gif" ALIGN="right">
```

This is the same format except I told the image to align to the right. In this instance, the image was moved and the text wrapped around it. I use the commands all the time; they are very useful. Now let's get a bit fancier.

Image in the Center

Figure 3.5 shows an example of text wrapping on either side of an image. Isn't that a neat trick, getting the image in the middle of flowing text? It actually isn't much of a trick. It's a three-celled table with half the text in one side and half in the other.

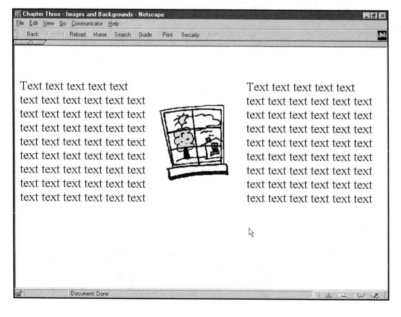

Figure 3.5
An image in the middle of text.

To do it, I wrote the text I wanted and split into the two parts. I made sure to write enough text so that the image height was equaled. I then put it all into this table format:

```
<TABLE BORDER="0" CELLPADDING="3" CELLSPACING="3">
<TR>
<TD> First Half of Text</TD>
<TD> Image</TD>
<TD> Second Half of Text</TD>
</TR>
</TABLE>
```

FAQs from the HTML Goodies Web Site

Q. Why can't I use `ALIGN="center"` so that text wraps around both sides?

A. Because the command doesn't work that way; that's the best reason I can give. Go with table cells.

If you're following through the book in order, you probably haven't gotten around to tables yet. I cover them in mind-numbing detail in Chapter 5, "All About Tables." For now, look over the format I offer here and understand what this does. It offers a jump-start.

Speaking of Tables...

Will the `ALIGN="###"` command work when you are using tables? Sure will. Just make a point of adding `ALIGN="left"` or `ALIGN="right"` inside the main `TABLE` command. Like so:

```
<TABLE BORDER="3" CELLPADDING="3" CELLSPACING="3" ALIGN="left">
<TR>
<TD>Table Cell</TD>
<TD>Table Cell</TD>
</TR><TR>
<TD>Table Cell</TD>
<TD>Table Cell</TD>
</TR>
</TABLE>
```

Figure 3.6 shows a table aligned to the left of the text.

Of course, you can also align the table to the right of the screen by changing the command to `ALIGN="right"`, just like in the earlier image commands.

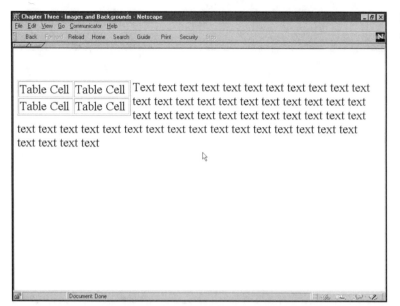

Figure 3.6
A table to the left of text.

FAQs from the HTML Goodies Web Site

Q. Can I wrap a list around an image?

A. Yes. Just follow the ALIGN="###" format and put the UL or OL list where you would regular text. (If lists are also new to you, you can read about them in Chapter 1, "Playing with Text.")

Align One Line of Text

If you want to align one line of text (a title, for instance) with a picture, use one of three commands in the ALIGN flag: top, middle, or bottom (see Figure 3.7).

Remember that the top, middle, and bottom ALIGN commands refer to the text only. They do not place the image. The only real downfall is that you cannot use two ALIGN commands in the same image. For instance, you can align the image left and then the text top just by putting in two ALIGN commands, but you can't get the effect. You need to align the text inside the image command, and then align the image through the <P> command. I'll cover that in a little bit.

Note that headings won't align; H heading commands want to be alone. To get bigger text next to the image, use <FONT SIZE> commands.

Figure 3.7

Lines of text aligned with images.

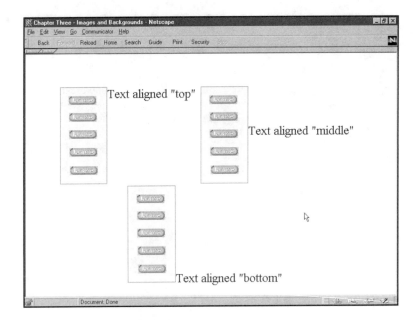

Aligning Two Lines of Text Around an Image

If you've tried the top, middle, and bottom commands, you know that after you run out of browser screen and get more than one line of text the second line jumps under the picture. The following code shows you what to do if you'd like to get that one-line effect but denote exactly where the line breaks and jumps under the image, or if you'd like only a small amount of text to wrap around the image and then jump below the image:

```
<IMG ALIGN="left" SRC="image.gif">Text text text text text text
<BR CLEAR="all">
text text text text.
```

That little <BR CLEAR="all"> doodad clears the remainder of the picture wrap and starts you on the next line under the picture (see Figure 3.8).

Some may say they want the text to start down the picture a bit. They want the same effect as the ALIGN="middle" or ALIGN="bottom" commands. Easy to do—add blank lines.

"But," you say, "I have tried adding 50 <P> commands and I never get more than one line." That's true. That's because you never put anything on the line after the <P> command. Try this:

```
<P> <P>
```

This little deal adds a couple blank lines. Why? Because the   is a space. You've put something on the line so the next <P> can act. The space is invisible, so no one sees it and you get two blank lines. Slick, huh? Use a few to "bump" your text down the image face. You can also do it by adding a slew of <BR> commands, but I have found this creates more space quicker.

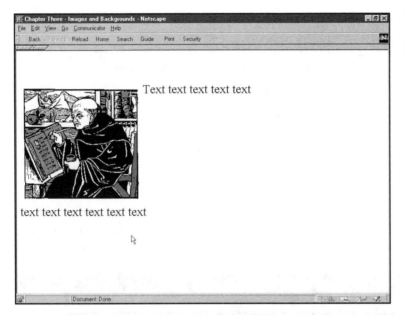

Figure 3.8
Text wraps and then jumps under an image.

FAQs from the HTML Goodies Web Site

Q. Why do you add blank spaces to get text to the top? Why not use the VALIGN="top" command to do the trick?

A. Because VALIGN is a newer command and my method works across all browsers at all levels. If you want to use the command, and the text being at the top isn't terribly needed, use it.

Using HEIGHT, WIDTH, and ALT Commands to Load Your Images Faster

Have you ever gone into someone's site and sat there waiting, looking at a blank page? You know the page is loading because the little numbers across the bottom are rolling, but there's nothing. My pages don't do that. When you log onto HTML Goodies, the entire page loads right away—all the text is there. The images are not there yet, but there are little boxes that appear to be pressed into the page, just waiting for the image to arrive. Sometimes there's even text telling you what's going to go in the box. Neat trick, huh?

Actually, it's not all that tough to do. Make a point of denoting every image on the page with HEIGHT, WIDTH, and ALT commands.

Here's an example of how to use the HEIGHT and WIDTH commands:

```
<IMG HEIGHT="45" WIDTH="22" SRC="image.gif">
```

The new commands are denoting the image's height and width in pixels. *Pixels* are little colored dots. If you put enough of them close together, they form a picture.

The word *pixels* actually is a smooshing together of two other words, *picture* and *element*.

Those of you with vivid imaginations know that the HEIGHT and WIDTH commands can be used to change an image's shape. If the image is really 50×50 and you put in HEIGHT and WIDTH commands of 150 and 10, you distort the picture pretty well. For an example, see Primer 6.

A better way to use the commands is to denote an image's exact height and width. I know that seems a bit silly on the surface, but if you do it for all the images on your page, the page and its text load completely, leaving open spaces for the pictures to load later. Your viewer is reading and surfing your site immediately, rather than waiting for the whole page to load.

FAQs from the HTML Goodies Web Site

Q. Should the HEIGHT and WIDTH numbers be exactly the same as the image, or maybe a little bigger?

A. No, go with the exact size.

How Do I Find Each Image's Size?

The best way is to grab a graphics editor either by buying one or by downloading one of the shareware versions off the Web. I'm partial to Paint Shop Pro for my shareware download.

If you have Netscape Navigator, you can open the image alone in the browser window and the pixels will display across the title bar.

Now, most of you are saying "Aaaaaauuuugh!" Why didn't I know about this earlier? My pages are written! Aaaaaugh!

(AAAAAAUGH! was first seen in Peanuts sometimes in the mid '60s when Lucy first pulled the ball out from Charlie Brown as he tried to kick it. We thank Charles Shultz for it. Where would we be today without the word "Aaaaaaugh"?)

Easy there, big fellah. It's not a concern. Changing it by hand is not that tough if you are using Netscape Navigator. What you do is load your page; then systematically go from image to image with your pointer. When your pointer is on an image, right-click. (Macintosh users click the button and hold it down.)

A window pops up. Choose the item that reads **View This Image**. Poof. It pops up for you. Write down the pixels and press the Back key to reload the page totally. Later browsers have eliminated this feature, so if yours doesn't do it surf the Web for a shareware graphics program. They're plentiful and help you find the height and width. If you are goofy into this like I am, you'll spend the time playing with numbers until you get it.

There are numerous ways to have the browser window and a text editor open at the same time so you just zip, zip, zip down the page.

 To try getting an image by itself on the screen in order to get the height and width, go to http://www.htmlgoodies.com/book/hw.html.

FAQs from the HTML Goodies Web Site

Q. You talk about HEIGHT and WIDTH, but you never tell how I can make it so that one image loads before another one.

A. I don't talk about it because you can't do it. The images load in the order they are on the page, or at least try to come in that order (as long as Net congestion doesn't hinder their working).

The ALT *Command*

I get letters from people saying they want the commands that place text in those little boxes, or they want the commands that make the little yellow boxes pop up when a mouse pointer is placed on an image. Here you go: the ALT command.

FAQs from the HTML Goodies Web Site

Q. You should let your users know that they need to use the ALT command every time they place an image. That ALT command is read by computers used by the blind and tells them what the image is.

A. Glad you wrote. I'll let them know.

ALT is short for alternative. It's the text that pops up as an alternative to the actual image (see Figure 3.9). It also sits inside the box and pops up in the yellow box, officially known as a ToolTip. All that from one little command. It's a great world, ain't it?

The text following the ALT commands is used to tell the viewer what's coming. Other text could be entered so that more information about a picture is given as the person lays the mouse pointer over it. Here's the format.:

```
<IMG HEIGHT="45" WIDTH="22" ALT="Good Picture" SRC="image.gif">
```

Figure 3.9 is an example of the ToolTip box popping up.

Figure 3.9

The ALT command creates a ToolTip window that pops up when you place your cursor on an image.

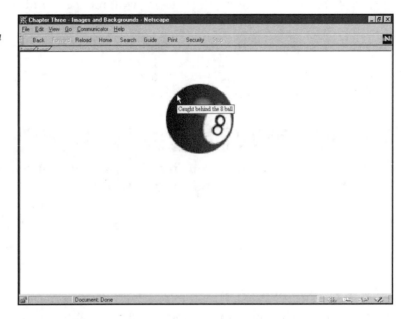

And that's that. Use these commands to help your viewers understand and move through your pages faster.

Enjoy!

 To see an ALT command in action, go to http://www.htmlgoodies.com/book/ alttest.html. *Watch it as the page loads; you'll see the text in the box.*

Making Lines with Images

Here is a great trick that helps you create nice, straight, colorful lines on your page without overly taxing or slowing your server. Look at this series of horizontal lines in Figure 3.10.

Every line you see was created using the same image. You can see the image if you look very hard: It's the dot right at the tip of the mouse pointer. That's what has become known as the 1×1 image. It's only one pixel tall and one pixel wide, but it can do some great things by playing with the image's height and width.

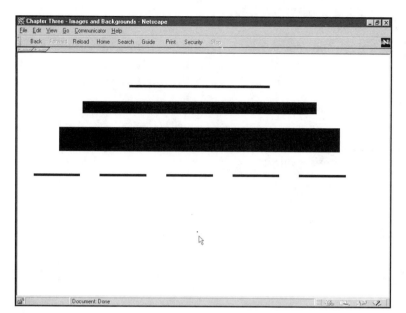

Figure 3.10
Here are multiple black lines created with images.

 To see this tutorial online, go to `http://www.htmlgoodies.com/1x1.html.`

The Image

No way around it, you need to be able to make an image—a 1×1 pixel image. I use Paint Shop Pro; it's shareware and available at a number of different sites. At the time of this writing, `http://www.shareware.com` has it.

That done, use the image program to create a 1×1 image. Some programs won't allow you to make anything smaller than 2×2. That's fine; do it.

How to Use the Image

Easy as pie. Once you have the little image, you can play around with its size through HEIGHT and WIDTH commands. See that thick black line up there in the figure? Here's the code I used to make it:

```
<IMG WIDTH="500" HEIGHT="25" SRC="1x1.gif">
```

It's just a little image named `1x1.gif` made far larger than it really is through the use of HEIGHT and WIDTH commands. Since the little image is all one color, the line is a solid color the whole way across. It's a great effect.

Why on Earth Would I Do This?

Speed—pure and simple. Remember that a server has to transfer every image that must be placed on a page. The smaller the image, the faster the image travels across phone lines, and the faster the image loads. Let's take a look at relative sizes for the different size line in Table 3.1.

Table 3.1   Image Sizes

Line Size	Bytes Required
300×2 (thin line)	256 bytes
500×25 (thick line)	3,001 bytes
1×1 (small image)	8 bytes

You can see that the 1-byte image loads and displays far faster than creating the images in different sizes. In addition, one image does all the lines rather than the server being asked for three different lines.

You can add some color into the deal if you go with a 2×2 or larger image. I once made a 6×6 image and changed the color of every pixel in my graphics editor. It made a very ugly line, but it was only 16 bytes.

If you make a multiple-pixel image, you can set different lines or columns of pixels to different colors and make some beautiful multicolored lines.

It's all about making your page come in faster. Try a few of these for yourself and see if you don't like them. They add crisp lines and blocks of color to your page without the need for large byte-filled images.

Enjoy.

 You can download a few different 1×1 images from `http://www.htmlgoodies.com/book/` `1x1images.html`. *Don't worry, they're much larger than the dot, so they'll be easier to download.*

Creating Thumbnail Images

If you've ever gone into a page that loads a bunch of large pictures, you know that it can get annoying. The pictures often are loading way off the browser window and it's difficult to see it all in a glance. Here's where thumbnail images come in handy (see Figure 3.11). You offer very small versions of the pictures for viewers to click, so they can see the larger version. It makes for smaller, more easily viewed pages. Plus, it allows the viewer to be in charge of what she wants to see.

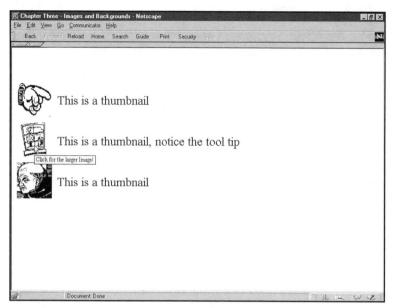

Figure 3.11
Three thumbnail examples.

To see this tutorial online, go to http://www.htmlgoodies.com/thmbnail.html.

If you have a photo gallery of favorite pictures you want people to see, I suggest you offer them one of three ways:

- Offer text links to images—This makes for the fastest load. Simply offer text descriptions of the pictures with a link directly to the image. I do that with my image pages. Most people won't like this suggestion because it doesn't create very fancy pages.

- Offer two images—You offer a smaller version of the picture, or a detail of the picture, for people to click in order to see the larger second image.

- Offer one image—This method has the image acting as its own thumbnail. I explain each method later.

FAQs from the HTML Goodies Web Site

Q. When should I use thumbnails?

A. There's a funny statement I like that says, nothing is less exciting to me than your kids or your vacation. Use that rule. If the image is needed for the page, use it. If it's something you're offering because you're being nice, use one of the thumbnail formats mentioned here so the user can decide whether he wants to sit through the load time.

continues

101

Q. When I make thumbnail images so that people can click them to see the bigger picture, do I have to have that big picture on its own page?

A. No, your browser has the capability to display just a picture. It doesn't have to be on an HTML document; just make the HREF link point directly to the picture.

Offering Text Links to Images

This is the first method of offering images to users. I think it's the way to go because you speed your pages along by only offering text. The text should be in the format of a hypertext link that points right at the image. Let's say I have an image of my last vacation to Las Vegas. I call it lv.gif. Here's a possible link format:

```
< A HREF="http://www.htmlgoodies.com/lv.gif">
See me and my wife in Vegas!  We just lost it all!</A>
```

Notice it's a simple link format with the text pointing right at the image. The image shows up in the browser screen's top-left corner. If you want to place the image more specifically, point the link to an HTML document that contains the image and the coding to place it. I prefer that it only point to the image. That way only one item has to load the image, rather than two (the page and the image).

Offering Two Images

This is the way I see most thumbnail images set up. One smaller image acts as the thumbnail that is attached to the larger. Like so:

```
<A HREF="http://www.htmlgoodies.com/thumb.gif">
<IMG SRC="bigimage.gif"></A>
```

Notice this is a simple A HREF link with an IMG command in place of the link words. See Primer 5 for more on making images links. The smaller image just links to the larger. You can also get rid of the blue border that appears around the link image by entering BORDER="0" inside the IMG command and just before the SRC portion.

This method's downfall is that it requires two images to load. The first is the thumbnail image and the second is the larger image. This takes time...and hard drive space.

On the up side, you can offer a detail, a smaller section, of the image.

If I were to suggest choosing either a detail or a smaller version of the picture, I advise using the detail. If the image is a landscape, you could use just a section of the trees; if the image is a photo of a person, you could use just the eyes. It can be quite alluring. By offering a detail of the picture, not only do you give a good thumbnail, but you keep some of the image hidden. It may draw the user to click.

By offering the full picture, oftentimes you've made it so small, maybe 50×100 pixels, that detail is lost and the image really doesn't give a good representation.

Offering One Image

What you do here is offer the same image as both the thumbnail and the larger image. This is done via the same link format as described earlier, but here you make the link to the same image that is being offered as the thumbnail. The thumbnail version is created through the use of HEIGHT and WIDTH commands. It looks like this:

```
<A HREF="http://www.htmlgoodies.com/bigimage.gif">
<IMG HEIGHT=50 WIDTH=50 SRC="bigimage.gif"></A>
```

Remember that you are denoting pixels per inch, not a percentage, when resizing an image using the HEIGHT and WIDTH commands. There are no hard or fast rules to this; you may have to simply play around with numbers until you get the size you want.

You'll notice how much faster the one-image method loads when the user clicks the thumbnail. That's because the image that the viewer receives is already loaded into the browser's cache. The cache is a small section of the hard drive where browsers keep images and pages while they display them. The image appears much quicker because you are not bringing up a whole new picture—you're just offering the same picture at the normal size. It just pops up onto the screen.

The trade-off is that the page that contains the thumbnail does not load very fast. Even though the image is small due to the HEIGHT and WIDTH commands, it is still full size in terms of bytes to be downloaded.

FAQs from the HTML Goodies Web Site

Q. My thumbnails look bad, all out of shape.

A. Remember that you need to keep the same general parameters if you are making a smaller version of the original. If the original is a rectangle and you make it a square in the thumbnail, you're going to get less-than-pleasing thumbnails. Keep the same general dimensions.

A Final Thought on Offering Images and Thumbnails

Images are great, no doubt, but remember that the majority of people surfing the Net are still dial-up users. Pages load only as fast as your server gives and the modem accepts. Here are a few tips:

- Be kind. Offering a 100K image in JPEG format takes upwards of a minute to load at 28.8. Go as small as you can.

- Use GIF format for smaller images such as icons, JPEG for the larger images. That helps with load time.

- Go for content, not flash. A page with 30 images is impressive, but so is the ability to put three billiard balls in your mouth at the same time. Both get old after a while.

Enjoy!

 I'll show you some examples of using the thumbnail methods at `http://www.htmlgoodies.com/book/thumbs.html`.

Loading a Low-Res Version of an Image First

This tutorial only works with Netscape Navigator! Internet Explorer does not yet support the command.

Figure 3.12 shows an example of a LOWSRC command at work. There are actually two images working. One is a very low-byte version of the main color version. Notice that there are two images? One is black and white line art, just an outline of the other, and the other is color. The image above is static. The online effect is that the image that is mostly line art pops up first, and then the more intricate color version is loaded over top. The images are the same, except the black and white line art takes up far fewer bytes. I tell the browser to load it first so that the viewer isn't looking at a blank box while waiting for the pretty color one to load.

Figure 3.12
An example of the LOWSRC *command.*

Okay, I'll level with you: This doesn't translate to book very well. You should see it online. Go to http://www.htmlgoodies.com/lowsrc.html.

It is a very helpful image command that moves your page along if you are determined to use large, byte-filled graphics. Here's the command that made the image in Figure 3.12:

```
<IMG HEIGHT="212" WIDTH="300" ALT="Phydueaux the Cat" SRC="cat.gif"
  LOWSRC="bwcat.gif">
```

This is all one image command that produces the picture...or two pictures in this the case. Here's what's happening:

- IMG starts it all off like any other image command.
- HEIGHT and WIDTH denote the size of the image.
- ALT ditto always using this.
- SRC is the large color picture that came in over the top of the black and white image. The color image name is cat.gif.
- LOWSRC is the key to this tutorial. It is the black and white image of the cat face that comes in first. The LOWSRC image's name is bwcat.gif.

Why Would I Do This?

Because it helps your viewer a great deal. Plus it looks cool. You see, if you have a huge image that is going to come in, that takes time. The color picture in Figure 3.12 is 56,000 bytes.

However, the black and white line art picture is only 3,000 bytes. It loads in a heartbeat. The color image is just wiped over top of it. Using the HEIGHT and WIDTH commands creates a box where the picture will go, and the ALT command informs the viewer what is going in. By using this LOWSRC command, however, a smaller byte version of the picture zips right in, giving an example of what is to come. Neat, huh?

When Would I Use This?

There's no reason you couldn't use this all the time, but remember that it does make each picture two hits of the server. That slows the page a bit. I would reserve it for really large images. Smaller images will do just fine with the HEIGHT, WIDTH, and ALT commands discussed earlier in this chapter.

FAQs from the HTML Goodies Web Site

Q. Can I use two different pictures in the LOWSRC command or must they be a different version of the same shot?

A. No, use two totally different shots. Just make sure they are the same size.

How Do I Make the LOWSRC *Picture?*

If you haven't taken this from what I wrote earlier, the purpose of the LOWSRC command is to quickly put up a picture that underlies a larger picture. Make whatever picture you use for the LOWSRC as low on the bytes as possible. Otherwise, the whole process is loopy.

I made the black and white line art image by opening the original color picture in my Paint Shop Pro graphics program and reducing the color level to two colors, black and white. That immediately dropped the amount of bytes from 56K to 3K. Nice drop. I then used one of Paint Shop Pro's image filters to change it to line art. You can do the same. Get your copy of Paint Shop Pro at http://www.shareware.com.

That's about all for that. I'm off to play with other little commands and waste more time till dinner...or lunch...or whatever other meal is eaten around the time you are reading this. Midnight snack might work too, I guess.

Enjoy!

 Go to the main tutorial to see the example in Figure 3.12, but head to http:// www.htmlgoodies.com/book/lowsrc.html *if you'd like to see the example with two different pictures. Try reloading the page again and again to get the full effect.*

Transparent Images

I get letters all the time asking how to make parts of an image invisible or transparent. So many times someone puts an image on their page and it looks great until the background comes in—then the little icon reveals itself as square rather than round. Oh, the humanity!

On some pages, you can see right through the image to see the background. I used to think the person went in with an image program and simply cut holes with the crop command. Don't laugh; it seems plausible.

 This tutorial is online at http://www.htmgoodies.com/transpar.html.

What Is Actually Happening

There is no cropping going on at all. The person who provides a transparent image has simply run the GIF (yes, it has to be a GIF) through a transparency program, highlighted the color that she wanted made transparent, and saved the image again in a special format called GIF89a.

It's named *GIF89a* because the GIF format was standardized in 1989. The transparency was the second part of the list of standards, thus the *a*.

Where Do I Get a Transparency Program?

There are a good many of them available for free on the Net. There is a link for Yahoo!'s Transparent Image Page in the "Net Notes" section of this tutorial. There you can surf for a program.

I'm sure all the programs that come up are good, and I can't attempt to explain here how they all work, so I'll only go over the one I use: LView Pro. "Net Notes" gives you links to get the program. Whatever program you choose, read over the instruction provided either on the downloading page or in the Help section of the program itself. I believe you'll find the process to be very close to what is explained here.

FAQs from the HTML Goodies Web Site

Q. I have an image that I want to give a transparent background, but I keep getting speckles of color when I run it through the LView Pro program. What's wrong?

A. For the background to be completely transparent, it must be one color so it is acted upon equally. If your background has more than one color, not all of it will be blanked out and you'll get those speckles.

Q. My friend says he uses totally transparent images. Why would he do that?

A. For spacing. He knows the image is *x* pixels wide so that it will stretch everything around it (like text and table cells) to that width. The image does the work by setting the size but doesn't show up on the page. It's pretty clever, actually.

Making Transparencies with LView Pro

To create a transparent GIF with LView Pro, simply follow these steps.

1. Open the program; you get something that looks like Figure 3.13.
2. Open the GIF. This is the GIF that you alter in order to have one part be transparent. When it opens, it looks something like Figure 3.14.
3. Choose to **Alter a Background Color**. You find the command under the **Retouch** menu. If your image is small like this one, you find it under the R header (see Figure 3.15).

Figure 3.13
The LView program.

Figure 3.14
*The LView program with
image opened.*

Figure 3.15
*The background menu
opened.*

4. Choose the Color to Make Transparent. I'm choosing white. A color pallet pops up and
   now I only have three colors in this image. Your images will have many more. You
   have to choose the color you want. It can be confusing at times. See where it says to
   Mask Selection Using? You know you've chosen the correct color on the pallet because
   the part of the image you want transparent blackens (or whitens), as shown in Figure
   3.16.

Figure 3.16
The color to be made transparent is chosen.

5. Save it correctly. Now that you've denoted a color to make transparent, choose **Save**—not **Save As**. You get the dialog box shown in Figure 3.17.

Figure 3.17
Save as Gif89a?

6. Choose **Yes**. You're done; now the image comes up with that portion of color you highlighted transparent. The image that I used has every part of what was white now transparent. Figure 3.18 shows the image placed on a gray background so that you can see that all the white parts are now transparent.

So go and make your own transparent GIFs...you have the power.

Enjoy!

 To see a couple of before and after transparencies, go to http://www.htmlgoodies.com/ book/tranparent.html.

Net Notes

Yahoo!'s Transparent Image Page: http://www.yahoo.com/Arts/Design_Arts/Graphic_Design/ Web_Page_Design_and_Layout/Graphics/Transparent_Images/

Download LView Pro: http://www.lview.com/

Figure 3.18

The image is now transparent—the gray background shows through. It's that simple....

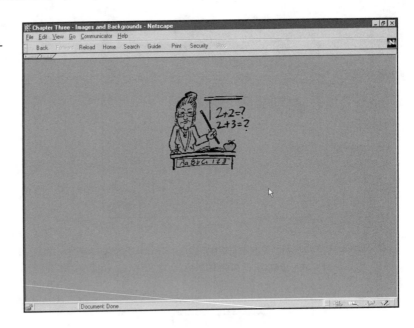

Creating Animated GIFs

Ah, the animated GIF. Or as I call it, the "anti-java." The image in Figure 3.19 is an animated GIF. On this page it's obviously not moving. If this were on the HTML Goodies site, that little arrow would be whizzing around the dial at breakneck speed. Thank goodness you're here where it's safe.

 You really need to see the image online. It's just spinning around and around. Go to `http://www.htmlgoodies.com/animate.html`.

My testing shows that animated GIFs will run on all browsers. They can because of the way the animation is created. This is not something created by Java or a JavaScript. What is actually happening is that the browser is placing one GIF after another into that same space. A little series of counting numbers called a *SMPTE Code* (Society of Motion Picture and Television Engineers Code) is embedded in the image, sort of counting one-hundredths of seconds and telling the image when to post the next cell. Your eye just perceives it as a fluid movement, kind of like a movie.

The problem with showing you how to create an animated image, be it here or online, is that the method I show isn't the only way of doing it. There are a great number of programs that assist you in creating your animated GIFs. What I show here is only one method. However, I chose this particular program because it is easy to understand and gives a general idea of the process. In the "Net Notes" section there are links to pages that offer other programs to animated GIFs. Whatever you choose, either follow the instructions included on the download page or those found in the program's Help section. No matter which program you choose, I can safely say that the process will be very close to what I outline here.

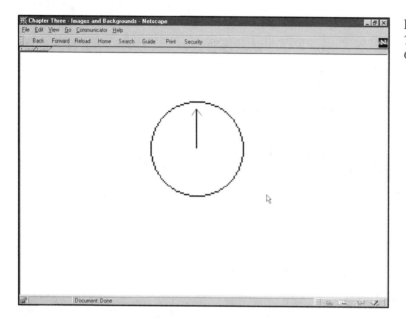

Figure 3.19
This clock is an animated GIF.

FAQs from the HTML Goodies Web Site

Q. I often see animation on other sites that runs once and then stops. Why?

A. The author could have wanted it that way. It may also be that you're using an Explorer browser. For some strange reason they do that now and again. Having your cache set to 0 would also do it.

Before we go any further, you must first get a program. To follow this tutorial specifically, you need the GIF Construction Set for Windows and W95 and—if you can find it—MAC, by Alchemy Mindworks, Inc. It is at the time of this writing a shareware program. That means it's free, but if you like it, you are requested to send in a few bucks. Go get it and install it on your computer. You can download it from http://www.mindworkshop.com/alchemy/gifcon.html.

Making the GIFs for Your Animation

Did you go and get the GIF Construction Set yet? Did you install it on your computer? Okay, good. Now on to the hard part. No, not the creation of the animation, but rather the pictures that you will animate.

I know you've seen a flip book. It's one of the books that have a little picture up in the right corner of each page and if you flip the pages quickly enough it appears as if the little pictures are moving. It's the same principle as a movie or video tape—a bunch of still pictures rolling past rather quickly and your eye perceiving it as movement.

Where do you get the pictures? You make them!! You could go out into the world of cyberspace and find them, but what fun would that be?

If you don't have a paint program with which to make GIFs, either go to a site called Shareware.Com, or head to Yahoo! and search for one. Use the keywords "graphic program." It's pretty easy to use and makes really nice images out of nothing.

FAQs from the HTML Goodies Web Site

Q. I got some shareware programs, but every time I use them this box keeps popping up asking me to pay $20 to the author. How do I get rid of that?

A. Pay the $20. It's only fair—you're using the program, aren't you?

Q. I found a program you can use to crack the code so the nagging shareware window asking for money doesn't pop up. Want it?

A. No. What you are doing is illegal.

You need to follow a few guidelines when you create the GIFs. These aren't my guidelines, either. These are the specs the GIF Construction program requires:

- You must save the images in GIF (CompuServe) format.
- You must save the image at the 256 color level.
- All the images you use must be the same size.

Why? The easy answer is that the GIF Construction program requires it. The actual reason is that you are literally creating a little movie frame by frame. All the frames must be the same size, they must all be in the same format, and all at the same color level.

Here are a few tips:

1. Create a template for your images. Remember the clock animation I did? I created a white square using my graphic program. I then drew a circle in the middle of the square and saved it, at the 256 color level, as clock.gif. I was then able to bring that template up, draw a line to 1:00 and save it under another name. Ditto for 2:00, 3:00, 4:00, and so on, until I went the whole way around the dial. That way I was sure the circle would remain stable through the complete animation. With me still?

2. Place each animation, and the images that make it up, on its own disk. You'll thank me for this later.

3. Make your GIFs as small as you can.

4. Make your GIFs with the fewest number of bits as possible.

The reasoning for numbers 3 and 4 is obvious. Remember that the browser loads one GIF after another, giving the impression of movement. If the GIFs are huge, it's slow. They load faster and look better if they are small.

If you don't have any GIF images to use in your animation, I'll give you four from my collection. They are four arrows, all the same size, all saved at the 256 color level. You will make a four-panel animation of an arrow spinning to the right, round and round.

Download all four and place them in a directory. Do not change the names of the images. Also, don't worry that the numbers appear to be out of order. I'll fix that when we make the animation. My suggestion is to place all the images in an empty directory on your hard drive or on a blank floppy disk. It will make your first one easier. Follow these four links to get your arrows:

Left Arrow: `http://www.htmlgoodies.com/arrow1.gif`

Right Arrow: `http://www.htmlgoodies.com/arrow2.gif`

Up Arrow: `http://www.htmlgoodies.com/arrow3.gif`

Down Arrow: `http://www.htmlgoodies.com/arrow4.gif`

When you follow the link, the image appears in the upper-left corner of the browser, all by its lonesome. Once it's there, follow these steps:

1. Place your mouse pointer on the image.

2. PC users should right-click. Macintosh users hold the button down for three seconds; a menu pops up.

3. The name of the GIF and a menu item allowing you to save the image are on that menu. Choose to save the image.

4. A dialog box allows you to save the image on your computer.

5. You could change the name to anything you want at this point, but for this tutorial, keep them the same as I use.

6. After you have chosen where the image will save to, click **OK**.

Making the Animated GIF

Now that you have some GIF images to work with, make the animation. Follow these instructions straight away:

1. Close your browser. Open the GIF Construction program you downloaded and installed.

2. A box with some buttons along the top opens. The buttons read **View**, **Insert**, **Edit**, **Delete**, and so on. It looks like Figure 3.20. If what you have is close to this, you're ready to go.

Figure 3.20
The GIF Construction Set interface.

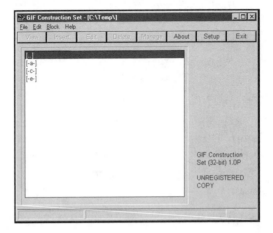

3. Go under the File menu at the top and choose New.

4. A highlighted line appears and states HEADER GIF89a SCREEN 640×480; 640×480 deals with the image's number of pixels high and wide. Remember that this is a computer image; it is made up of little dots of color.

5. 640×480 is not the correct size of the arrow images you downloaded. They are only 30×30 pixels. Click the highlighted **HEADER GIF89a** line twice.

6. A box should pop up, where you again see the numbers 640 and 480. It looks like Figure 3.21. Change those numbers to 30 and 30 and click **OK**.

Figure 3.21
This dialog box deals with image size.

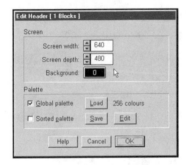

7. You're back to the original screen and the line should now read 30×30. Does it? If not, try again to change the numbers.

8. You must now tell the system what you want to happen regarding the movement of the GIFs. For now we are going to *loop* the animation, meaning the pictures will

114

continue to go one after the other at all times. There are other formats that are covered in the program's Help section.

9. Click the **Insert** button; a box that looks like Figure 3.22 pops up. Choose **Loop**. It should now say LOOP under the HEADER line.

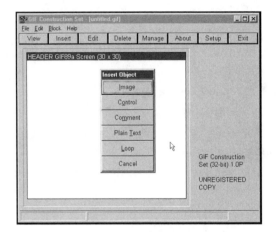

Figure 3.22
The LOOP-choosing menu.

10. Now it's time to start placing images. Remember this: All images must have a CONTROL command before them. Always. No exceptions. That code embeds the SMPTE command I told you about earlier.

11. Click Insert and choose **CONTROL**. CONTROL should now be on the screen.

12. Click the highlighted **CONTROL** that just popped up. Another box should appear, and it looks like Figure 3.23.

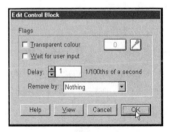

Figure 3.23
The Construction Set's Edit Control Block dialog box.

13. You can do more in this box, like set transparent colors, but for now I am only concerned with speed. The other items are explained in the program's Help section. See in the box where it says 1/100ths of a second? That's the time span between the current GIF and when the next one will load. More one-hundredths make it slower, fewer make it faster. For now, insert 15 for 1/100ths of a second. Choose **OK**.

14. Click **Insert** again and choose **IMAGE**.

15. Another box pops up and gives you the ability to find and choose the images you downloaded from me. Find `arrow1.gif` and choose it. It should appear on the screen.

16. Choose **Insert** again and select **CONTROL**.

17. Click twice on the line and again change the 100ths of a second to 15. Click **OK**.

18. Choose **Insert** again and choose **IMAGE**.

19. When the box pops up, find arrow3.gif and select it.

20. Follow the format again and place another CONTROL, changing it to 15 1/100ths of a second.

21. Again choose **Insert** and **IMAGE** and place `arrow2.gif`.

22. Place another CONTROL, changing the 1/100ths of a second to 15 again.

23. Place the last image—`arrow4.gif`. See how you're doing the same thing again and again: control, image, control, image, control, image, and so on.

24. After you place all four images, this is what should be written in front of you:

```
HEADER GIF89a SCREEN 40x40
LOOP
CONTROL
IMAGE ARROW1.GIF 30X30,256
CONTROL
IMAGE ARROW3.GIF 30X30,256
CONTROL
IMAGE ARROW2.GIF 30X30,256
CONTROL
IMAGE ARROW4.GIF 30X30,256
```

25. You're not quite finished yet, but you can see it run at this point. Click **View**. The screen goes black and the arrow spins around.

26. To get back, press the Esc key.

27. Save the image animation by choosing **Save As** under the **File** menu.

28. If you have any problems, you now get a warning and what needs to be fixed. If you don't get a warning, good job. Save it under a name you can remember.

The program will undergo a long list of movements for your entertainment while it compiles your animation.

FAQs from the HTML Goodies Web Site

Q. I ran my animated GIF through the LView transparency program and now it won't work. Why?

A. Because you broke it. Remember that this animation is a series of images, not just the one. The best way to do it is to transparent the cells, and then build them into an animation. Many programs allow you to do that along the way of building your animation.

Q. I am using the GIF Construction Set and every time I put in an image it tells me that I need to pick a color pallet. What in the world is that?

A. You are not using the correct 256 color level—otherwise you wouldn't get that message. The program doesn't understand your image because you are using more than the expected 256 colors. Choose the option to use local pallet and go on.

Placing an Animated GIF on Your Page

Place the animation using the last name you gave it just as you would any image: via the image command format:

```
<IMG SRC="animation.gif">
```

Don't try changing the pixel size. Let it remain just as you saved it.

In case you're wondering, the animated GIF is totally self-contained. It runs on its own. The images you used to make up the animation are no longer needed.

FAQs from the HTML Goodies Web Site

Q. Do I have to upload the images that I used to create the animation along with the animation?

A. No, but if you do it won't hurt anything. In fact, if you have the space it's a good way to keep the images safe in case you need them later.

You can discard them, but I wouldn't. I always keep them, and the animation I made with them, all on one disk. You can always reopen the animation inside the GIF Construction Set and change it around—speed it up, slow it down. If you don't have all the parts saved, you're out of luck.

What if it's not working on your page? Strange, huh? Did it work when you clicked the View button? I have found that, too. Try uploading the animation onto your server and looking at it. I'll bet it works. Go figure.

These things are real touchy. I have found my 486 Netscape 1.1 will only run them when they are loaded on the server. 2.02b will run it off the hard drive. My W95 computer will run it all straight away. Weird, huh?

I hope this helps. It really is easier than it may seem at first. After you roll through your first one, you'll wonder what you thought was so hard. You will also want to make a point of reading the banner creation primers in Chapter 14, "Building Web Site Banners." They get into this much deeper than what's here.

Enjoy!

Net Notes

Download the GIF Construction Set by Alchemy MindWorks:

Windows 3.*x* version: `http://www.coast.net/cgi-bin/coast/dwn?win3/graphics/gcs16n.zip`

Windows 95 version: `ftp://ftp.rose.com/pub/alchemy/gifcon32.exe`

If you have trouble using these links try Alchemy MindWorks:

`http://www.mindworkshop.com/alchemy/gifcon.html`

For Macintosh versions and a long list other GIF compilers:

`http://www.agag.com/makeown.html`

`Shareware.Com http://www.shareware.com`

Some of these programs may come as zip files. To unzip them, go to the WinZip home page:

`http://www.winzip.com`

Go to `http://www.htmlgoodies.com/book/animation.html` *for a few animation examples and the images that make them up. You can even download them if you want.*

Creating Image Links That Don't Turn Your Cursor into a Hand

I am getting a ton of mail from people who want active images on their site that do not produce a hand cursor when you go over it with the mouse. Please understand that this only works on Netscape Navigator browsers 3.0 and later. If, when you try this and get a hand, you may need a different or higher-level browser. Figure 3.24 shows an example of an image that is a link and a mouse pointer that does not turn into a hand. This tutorial is online at `http://www.htmlgoodies.com/nohand.html.`

The image in Figure 3.24 is active. If you could click it, you would be sent to the Goodies home page. Yet, when your mouse is on it, there's nothing to indicate that it is an active image. Here's the code I used to make it:

```
<FORM METHOD="LINK" ACTION="http://www.htmlgoodies.com">
<INPUT TYPE="image" SRC="banner.gif" "WIDTH="500" HEIGHT="100"
 BORDER="0" ALT="To Goodies">
</FORM>
```

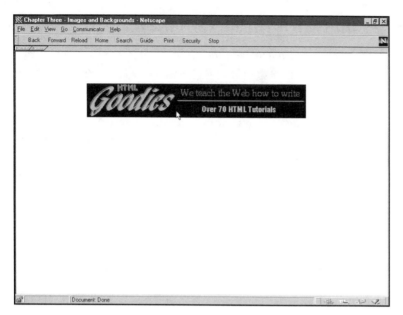

Figure 3.24
HTML Goodies active banner with no hand.

Here's what's happening: The format is almost identical to the link button format. The difference is that you insert an image where you would configure the button.

- ⬤ FORM starts the process.
- ⬤ METHOD="LINK" tells the computer this image will link with another page.
- ⬤ ACTION="###" is the link's URL.
- ⬤ INPUT TYPE is an image.

From there on out, it follows an image's format using the SRC, HEIGHT, WIDTH, and ALT commands to define the size and alternative text. You can set the border to any number you want, but 0 loses any blue border. I'd always set the border to 0 or the look will be ruined.

Enjoy!

FAQs from the HTML Goodies Web Site

Q. I don't want a hand or a pointer. I want the cursor to change into something totally different when I pass over a link. How do I do that?

A. As soon as you find out, tell me. I have never gotten it to work no matter what I do with cursor files and such.

Go see some examples of the no-hand active images at http://www.htmlgoodies.com/book/cursor.html.

119

Creating Horizontal Lines with the HR *Command*

I want to shake the hand of whomever came up with this <HR> line. It is a great and simple way to break up your page. I use them to death. Here I'll try to get into the more subtle sections of the <HR> line. This one is online at http://www.htmlgoodies.com/hr.html.

You probably already know that you can place a line simply by typing <HR> on the page. *HR* stands for horizontal rule, by the way. It makes a nice line, with a little bit of shading all the way across the screen. And it's centered. Coolness. But all those lines looking the same tends to get dull. Let's change it a bit.

Changing the Rule's Width

You change the width of the line by adding a subcommand to <HR>. I do this with all my lines. I think the line going all the way across the page is a bit much. I only have mine go 60 or 80% of the page. I just added different percentages to a series of HR commands. Here's the format:

```
<HR WIDTH="60%">
```

Figure 3.25 shows horizontal rules with widths set to 20, 40, 60, 80, and 100% (and back down again), respectively.

Figure 3.25
Horizontal rules set to widths of 20, 40, 60, 80, and 100%.

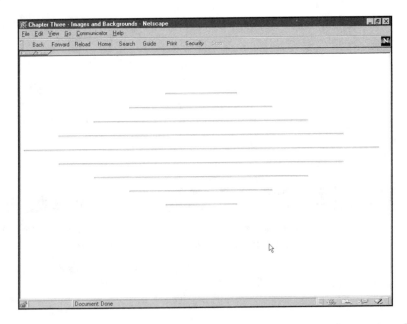

Notice it's done with an HR command with WIDTH="- -%" added. You can set the width to any percentage you want. There's no need to stay with round numbers. If you really want a line that only goes 17%, that's fine. Just remember to include the percentage sign! You can also lose the percentage sign if you'd like and go with pixels. That lets you get quite precise.

FAQs from the HTML Goodies Web Site

Q. How do I get the HR line to appear like it's coming out of the page rather than going in?

A. You can't, though if you stare at it long enough it gives that appearance.

Changing the Rule's Height

Do you want a thicker horizontal rule? You can do that, too. Just look at Figure 3.26. Here's the format:

```
<HR SIZE="6">
```

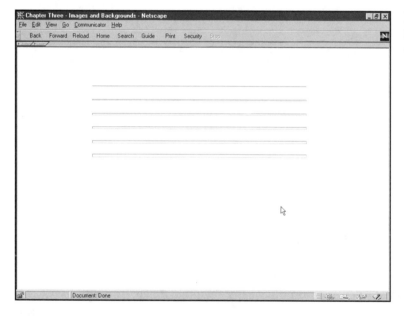

Figure 3.26
HR *lines showing thickness levels 1 through 6.*

Think of the size command as an equal to the H commands in that there are six of them, numbered 1 through 6—1 being the most narrow. You might also notice that the lines are only 60% width. I just used both commands inside the same <HR> command—nothing to it.

Aligning Horizontal Rules

You can use our old friend the ALIGN command on horizontal rules, too (see Figure 3.27). It works just the way you think it would. I added ALIGN="###" inside the command. Here's what made the four lines shown in Figure 3.27:

```
<HR WIDTH="60%" ALIGN="LEFT">
<HR WIDTH="60%" ALIGN="RIGHT">
<HR WIDTH="60%" ALIGN="LEFT">
<HR WIDTH="60%" ALIGN="RIGHT">
```

You can also state ALIGN="CENTER", but that's a bit of overkill, as the line centers for you anyway. Notice also that I used the WIDTH command in there.

Figure 3.27
HR lines aligned left and right.

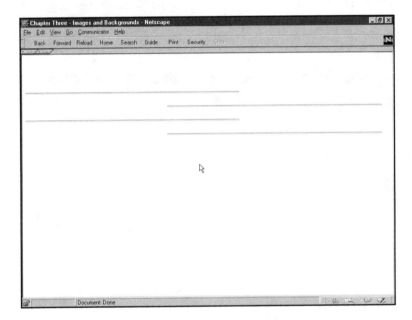

Horizontal Rules without Shading

You can also create horizontal rules that don't have any shading (see Figure 3.28). Here's how you do it:

```
<HR WIDTH="60%" NOSHADE>
```

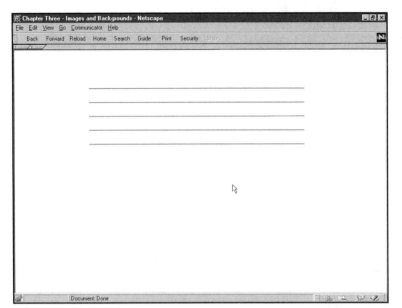

Figure 3.28
HR lines with no shading.

FAQs from the HTML Goodies Web Site

Q. I want to put an image in the HR line. Can I?

A. No, not yet. What you can do is open your image with a paint program and draw a horizontal rule in your image. This gives you the effect you're looking for.

Backgrounds

This is one of the staples to building a great-looking Web page. A nice background, be it color or an image, can really make a page stand out. I think a good background is the difference between a pretty good page and a great page.

Changing the Background Color

You need two things to change the background color of your page: a command that alerts the browser that the color is going to be changed and a color code.

1. The command for changing any background is located in the <BODY> command immediately following the </HEAD> command. To change just the background color, enter this:

```
<BODY BGCOLOR="##">
```

2. Now you need a color code. This code tells the browser what color to use. The six-digit code goes in place of the "##" in the command. The technical term for these little puppies is a *hex code*.

The codes are not very user friendly and you need a chart to let you know what code makes what color. I've created a page showing some basic color codes, 140 in all. It's in Appendix B, "Useful Charts." There are actually about 16 million hex codes producing every imaginable shade of red, or yellow, or whatever color you like. You'll see what I mean. Look over the page, write down a couple of codes, and come on back to finish the tutorial.

Waiting....waiting...waiting...

Welcome back. No doubt you looked around and saw a couple of colors. Neat, huh? Hopefully you brought back a color or hex code you'd like to use.

If not, no matter. I have one: #FFFFFF. That code produces pure white. Why #FFFFFF? I told you the codes weren't too nice. There is a reason #FFFFFF creates pure white. It has to do with the red, green, and blue hues used to create the color. I attempt to explain it in Appendix B. However, I would save that bit of reading for a time when you're a little more awake. And wait at least 30 minutes after eating.

FAQs from the HTML Goodies Web Site

Q. I want my background to become a rainbow of colors, dark to light. How do I put in the hex commands?

A. No dice. You need to use an image to do that. The backgrounds achieved through hex codes go for one color.

Q. I am getting this awful background made up of a ton of little dots when I look at my page. What's that all about? I'm using a basic hex code.

A. You are witnessing a wonderful fact of computer life called *dithering*. You see, your computer screen is incapable of producing the color you are asking for so it is doing its best through those little dots. You can solve it two ways: You can get a color that doesn't dither (see the non-dithering chart in Appendix B), or you can bump your computer's screen resolution up to 16 million colors. Remember, however, that just because it looks good on your screen doesn't mean others will see it the same. I suggest you go with the non-dithering color.

Please note that when you write these codes, you write them with a # (pound sign) in front of the code. Be sure to enclose it all inside of quotation marks. Now that I know the code of the background I want to create, I insert the code into the command and place the command on the HTML page.

Background Wallpaper

The name is a bit misleading. When you see an HTML page with *wallpaper*, or backgrounds, it is most often not one continuous GIF or JPEG—it is instead one small GIF or JPEG repeated, and it is equally as simple as the colors described earlier.

Before someone tells me—yes, you can create a background with one image that is large enough to cover the entire screen. The problem with that is that the image would have to be so large that it would take forever to load into the browser window. The viewer could have lunch before your page comes in. Try it if you want, but bring a newspaper to pass the time. First you need a background image. I make most of mine. I'll get to making a background in a second.

FAQs from the HTML Goodies Web Site

Q. This guy had a page where the background was one large sunset. How did he do that?

A. With one huge image. Did the page take a long time to load? I'll bet he also took great pains to make sure that the text on the page was not larger than the image or it would have started to double up and display again. You just weren't allowed to see it. Clever move, since it appears from your letter he pulled it off.

Since you need a scanner to make backgrounds, and I know not everyone has one of these at their fingertips, the best way to use a background is to grab one off the Internet. There are a few good background repositories around. See the "Net Notes" at the end of this tutorial for links.

Now that you have a GIF or JPEG for your background, you will want to put it in the same directory in which you place all your other images. Again, all background commands come right after the </HEAD> command inside the <BODY>. The format is this:

```
<BODY BACKGROUND="image.gif">
```

Sometimes browsers allow you to use the commands together. You offer a color and then an image. The background changes color and is then wiped over by the image. It looks nice, but some higher-level browsers aren't too fond of it. Here's the format for your records:

```
<BODY BGCOLOR="#FFFFFF" BACKGROUND="image.gif">
```

Might work, might not.

Make Your Own Wallpaper

There are no hard or fast rules to this except that you need to have access to an image scanner. Most copy places have them. A local college or university might be helpful, too.

Easy Wallpapers

Just follow these steps:

1. Find a piece of paper, other than white, that already has text on it. That way you know that when you use it as a background, your text will show up.

   Paper that works well for this includes diplomas, citations, stationary, and fancy copy paper.

2. Simply scan the paper and crop a perfect square. Make it kind of small—1×1 works really well.

3. Use it as a background. Most of the wallpapers here were made this way.

Harder Wallpapers

Now it gets a little tougher:

1. Find a geometric image to scan. Bricks work well, as does lined paper.

2. Scan the picture.

3. Using a graphics program, crop the picture so that the items on the ends and top are cut exactly in half. That way they line up when posted as wallpaper.

4. This is tough. Try doing one on lined paper first, for practice.

If you have access to an image program, try this. It works a lot better than you might think.

1. Scan any picture you want as a background and crop it small.

2. Use your image program to do an offset of 50%. This turns the picture in on itself by half.

3. Use the program to touch up any lines that don't come together at the midpoint of the graphic.

4. Save it. Doing this guarantees that the graphic you just created will line up perfectly as a background. It works, trust me. Have I steered you wrong yet?

FAQs from the HTML Goodies Web Site

Q. I went to a page and the background didn't scroll along with the text. Cool! How do I do that?

A. You must be using the Explorer browser; the command only works with that browser. Add this BGPROPERTIES="fixed" and that's that.

One More Thing...

These background commands are great, but let me warn you that any image you add to a page will slow its completion. Keep your background images small or avoid using them at all. Load time is important. A page that doesn't load doesn't get read.

Enjoy!

 I have a series of background examples and a bunch of backgrounds for you to download at http://www.htmlgoodies.com/book/background.html.

Net Notes

Yahoo!'s Background Image Page: http://www.yahoo.com/Arts/Design_Arts/Graphic_Design/Web_Page_Design_and_Layout/Graphics/Backgrounds/

You will get more background images that you could possibly use from this site.

Sideline Backgrounds

This is currently a very popular Web page design element. *Sideline backgrounds* are a stripe of color or an image down the left side of the page. On that stripe you put icons and text that deal with the larger section of the browser window. It's a solid, clean look. Figure 3.29 shows an example of what I'm talking about from the HTML Goodies Web site.

 You can see this one online at http://www.htmlgoodies.com/sideline.html.

How You Do It

First off, you need a program that creates graphics for you. Create an image that is long and thin; the thickness, or how tall the image is, is up to you. I keep it fairly small to cut down on bytes and load time. The width is set. It has to be long enough to span the entire screen. Go with something at least 1,200 pixels wide. You see, when an image is defined as 650×10 (or something comparable), it fails to address 800×600 and 1024×768 monitor resolutions. A width of 1,200 covers all. The image I'm using on this page is 5×1,200 pixels. That's pretty long and thin.

Using the graphics program again, make the left side a different color. I made mine lime green. That's an eye-catcher, don't you think? How much of the left side of the image you color will determine how thick your sideline stripe will be. When you use the thin strip image as a background, the color lines up and you have a stripe.

Figure 3.29
An example of a sideline background on HTML Goodies.

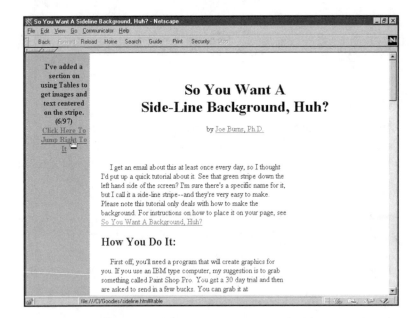

You could try making a much taller image if you want a look other than straight up and down. Figure 3.30 gives you a look at the sideline background used on the HTML Goodies Web site that uses a more textured stripe.

Figure 3.30
An HTML Goodies site background stripe.

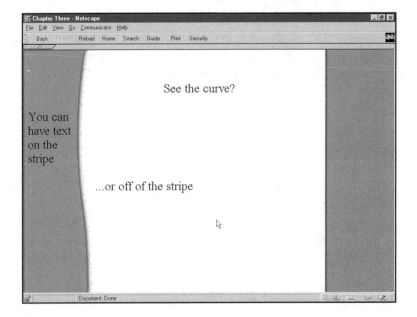

The sideline stripe is done via a very tall image that completes one full curve. When the image doubles up, the ends meet perfectly. The stripe on the right is also part of the background image.

You have to be careful using this kind of background to get the text exactly where you want it—on or off the stripe. I'll tell you how in a moment.

Do I Have to Use Just Color?

No. If you'd like to place an image on the side rather than a color, do it. Just remember that it's going to occur again and again. Some football sites use what appears to be yard markers, some sites make the side of the page look like a loose leaf notebook, and so on.

What About Text?

Yeah! What about text?! Oh, you're asking me. There are a couple of ways of dealing with this. The easiest is if you own and use Microsoft Internet Explorer. Just add this command in your `<BODY>` command at the top of your page:

```
LEFTMARGIN="---"
```

The numbers are relative. One is bigger than two, two is bigger than three, and so on. You have to play with the numbers to get just the right indentation, one that does not cover your stripe. But remember that not everyone uses Explorer.

But I Don't Have Explorer; I Use Netscape Navigator!

That's what I said. Here's how I indent. Please remember, this is only to get text off the stripe. Stay tuned for how to have items on the stripe. Now, someone is going to go bonkers about me saying this isn't right and that there's a better way of doing it. All that aside, if all you want is the text off the stripe, this is how I do it—and it works: I add `<OL>` commands at the top. I don't add any `<LI>` commands, list items, or `</OL>`. You'll find that every `<OL>` pushes all the text in just a little bit. Just keep adding `OL` until the text bumps over far enough for you. Let's remember I taught myself HTML. I use what works no matter how strange it seems. I think that's a good way of learning.

Placing Items on the Stripe

This is a bit involved because it involves using a table. If you haven't already, you can read about tables in Chapter 5, "All About Tables." First you create the sideline stripe background; then you create a large table with two cells that house everything that appears on the page. That table will have one cell not wider than the stripe and another cell not wider than the open space. Imagine Figure 3.31 being the table's format.

Figure 3.31

An example of sideline background with table borders showing.

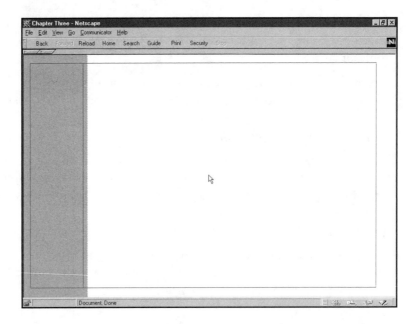

Constructing the table is not the hard part. As you can see, the table in Figure 3.31 is just two cells. Here's the code that made it:

```
<TABLE BORDER="0" CELLSPACING="5"
CELLPADDING="5">
<TD ALIGN="----" WIDTH="###">
<TD ALIGN="----" WIDTH="###">
</TABLE>
```

You place everything that will go in the left column (on the stripe) after the first <TD> and everything that will go on the other side under the second <TD>. The BORDER="0" command makes the table borders invisible.

Now the Trick

You need to play with this a bit. Notice in the code that the <TD> commands have a WIDTH="###" subcommand—that's the key here. You need to make the width of the left cell a bit smaller than the width of the stripe and make the width of the right cell just a bit bigger than the open space.

The CELLSPACING and CELLPADDING commands leave the gutter between the two. Make it a large number, 5 or larger. I always use pixels to do this; percentages aren't as exact. It seems like you should be able to find out the pixel width of the stripe, knock off a few, and make it work. It has never yet worked for me. I always have to play with the numbers a little to get it straight.

130

I have also found that setting the BORDER to 1 helps find the pixel numbers. You can always go back in and set it to 0 after you're done.

FAQs from the HTML Goodies Web Site

Q. I read your tutorial on sideline backgrounds. You suggest making a table that goes over the sideline. If that works, why not just make that table the background and color the one cell a different color?

A. Because it wouldn't look right. The table wouldn't conform to all screen settings nor would it go to the edges of the browser window. It would look like a large table instead of a background.

Q. I saw this page where the sideline stripe had links on it and when you clicked on the links, the right section changed. Is the page just reloading a new table every time?

A. Nope. You're seeing this same effect being done with frames. It's a bit more complicated (and is explained in Chapter 6, "Using Frames").

Can I Get a Right-Side Border?

Yes. Just make your left sideline very wide. It appears to be a right sideline. Play with it; you'll get the look you want.

Enjoy!

 You have to see this in action to fully appreciate what I'm saying here. Go to http://www.htmlgoodies.com/book/sideline.html *for a good look around.*

Chapter 4

Creating Imagemaps

You've seen how you can turn any image into a link. Imagemaps enable you to turn one image into many links. You can make different areas of the same image lead to different HTML pages, sounds, other images, or whatever you want.

This thing is called an *imagemap* because it is the map the computer uses, not the image. The image is simply there for the user to see and use as a guide. It's the map that the computer uses to make the links.

When you create an imagemap you've laid a point graph—a map—over an image. One is lying on top of the other. The GIF is just there for the visual. It is the map and its coordinates that are lying on top of it that the computer uses; thus the name imagemap.

There are two types of imagemaps: server side and client side. Server-side imagemaps are older and more complex, but they work on virtually every browser. Client-side imagemaps are easier to create, but only work on newer browsers. I'll show you both in this chapter (as well as a way to make fake imagemaps), but I suggest that you consider building client-side imagemaps.

Server-Side Imagemaps

This is the beauty of an imagemap. One image is divided into sections, each assigned a different URL. The success of an imagemap, I believe, is how well the image leads the viewer. Unless the image is fairly blatant about what each link will do, it's better to go with simple blue text hypertext links.

The original version of this tutorial is on the HTML Goodies site at http://www.htmlgoodies.com/imagemap.html. *This was also the first of the HTML Goodies tutorial to win an award. You should head here so you can try out an imagemap:* http://www.htmlgoodies.com/book/gbook.html.

Note

This tutorial refers to the use of a CGI, a Common Gateway Interface. You need to attach to a CGI to make this work. Chances are your server has one, but you have to ask your techie or ISP exactly where it is.

A CGI is a small program, usually in the Perl or C++ computer language that does some of the work for you.

Again, ask the people who take your money each month if they have one available to you. I assume they do if you're on a server of any size.

I have no doubt you can create the items needed for an imagemap. What I am concerned with is whether your server will allow you to use this type of imagemap. You see, an imagemap in this format must be connected to a little ditty called a CGI.

"No problem!" you say. There are imagemaps all over the Web. "I'll just connect to one and use it." Hmmm. If people were always that generous with their CGIs.

You may be searching for a long while before you find a public domain imagemap CGI.

My suggestion: Talk to your Webmaster and ask her if your server supports imagemaps. If so, make sure to ask for the path to the imagemap CGI! That bit of Greek will make sense in a moment.

The picture in Figure 4.1 is an imagemap. It's just one large image, even the text. You can click each cat's face to go to a different page devoted to that cat. One image sends you to three different pages.

Does that image do the trick? Is it blatant enough that someone will know what to do? I think so. You see the three cats, it tells you to click. I think it gets the job done.

The Imagemap Command

Following is the basic code to insert an imagemap. Please don't be thrown because the IMG command went to the next line. This all goes together. I just put the IMG on the next line because the entire command is just too long to fit across the page.

```
<A HREF="http://www.htmlgoodies.com/cgi-bin/imagemap/~jburns/imap.map">
<IMG SRC="imap.gif" ISMAP></A>
```

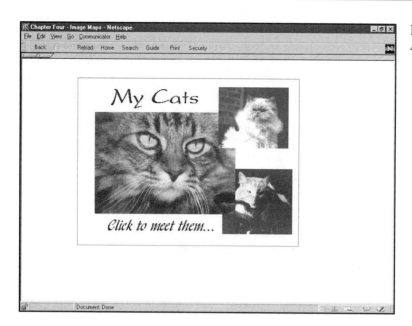

Figure 4.1
A CGI-driven imagemap.

Notice there are three parts to an imagemap. There's the CGI, a map, and a GIF. The map in the command is titled `imap.map`.

All three of these items must be grouped together in the format of a hypertext link. Notice the `<A HREF>` and `</A>` at the front and back of the command. A link's format makes it active and clickable. Let's take the three items in order of appearance. Please remember that this command format works on my server.

You must configure the command so it works on your server. I'll get into how in a moment.

The CGI

The very first thing the preceding command does is tell the computer where to get the CGI. This is known as the *path* to the CGI. The path is as follows (notice this follows the `A HREF`):

```
http://www.htmlgoodies.com/cgi-bin/imagemap
```

This beginning portion tells the computer where to find the CGI. Sometimes the CGI is in a "bin" (`bin`) like it is here. Computer people will tell you that *bin* stands for binary, which in turn has to do with the UNIX-type format the CGI is using, and on and on. Unless you're actually thinking of writing your own CGIs in UNIX, bin probably should mean little more than a place where there's a lot of stuff, like a trash bin. Get it? `imagemap` is the actual CGI name we are using.

You'll notice the CGI does not have an extension. Depending on how your server is configured, it may not. However, it may; .pl is a common extension for CGI programs if the CGI script is written in the Perl programming language.

Again, please don't try to connect to this CGI. It won't work. You have to be on this server for it to react favorably. Go to your Webmaster or technical people and ask for your own server's specific path to the imagemap CGI.

The Map

Now that you have told the computer where the CGI is, you will tell the computer where the map that the CGI is going to read is. Once again (shake head here), you have told the computer the CGI's location. That CGI reads the map for you but it needs to know where the map is. The second part of the command is the *path to the map*. The preceding path is as follows:

```
~jburns/imap.map
```

Here's the tricky part. Notice that the path to the map just follows right along after the path to the CGI. Here's why: You probably know that when you have a/lot/of/names/ inside slashes—those are directories. They are inside one another from right to left. In the preceding path, `imap.map` is inside `~jburns`.

But is the path to the map inside the CGI? No. When you put them together you tell that specific CGI the path it should take to find the map it is supposed to read. You are giving it directions.

Notice that I only wrote the server's URL (`http://www.htmlgoodies.com`) once. It would seem the path to the map would need it again. You can write it all out again if you'd like, but it is not needed. The computer understands that the path to the map is on the same server as the path to the CGI. These plastic thinking boxes are so smart.

Making the Map

Hey! I need a map, right? Where do I get a map? Good question. You have to make it. You can't just go somewhere and download a map for your GIF. The map you use has to be custom made for your purposes. What does a map look like? It looks like this:

```
default http://www.htmlgoodies.com
circle http://www.htmlgoodies.com/fido.html 433,67 478,108
rect http://www. htmlgoodies.com/stimpy.html 107,18 372,75
poly http://www. htmlgoodies.com/chloe.html 3,108 103,63
103,76 123,78 33,126
```

Neat, huh? It's kind of a grid with points denoted for each URL—a grid of points that the CGI reads. A certain URL is sent for when the mouse is on a certain area on the map grid.

There are a ton of shareware programs that enable you to make a map. I could not even begin to explain each one here. You must go out, find one you like, and use its instructions to make your map. That said, my favorite program for Windows is MapEdit. It is wonderfully easy. Others have told me that Map This is also good. The best program for Macintosh is MAC-Image-Map.

Once you have created your map, you can place it in any directory you want as long as the path to the map is correct. I always place my map and the GIF that goes along with it in the same place. It makes things a little easier.

The Image

No matter what map creation software you choose, you are asked to create your map using an image. This image will, of course, be the one that appears on the page as your imagemap. For instance, the preceding map was created over top of the GIF you see. It's just the way the programs work. They display the GIF you choose and then you section the GIF off and assign URLs. But I'm rambling.

This is the command for placing the image:

```
<IMG SRC="imap.gif" ISMAP>
```

Notice that it is just a normal image command with the addition of ISMAP. The computer displays this image for people to click. It will be, for all purposes, your imagemap.

So pick a nice one.

You place the ISMAP inside the image command to alert the computer to avoid activating the image, and instead read the map that is lying on top of it.

Please note that I allowed the blue border to remain in the preceding example and in Figure 4.1. In an imagemap setting you should really lose it by adding the command BORDER="0" in the image command between IMG and SRC. The border is too distracting.

FAQs from the HTML Goodies Web Site

Q. How small can I make the section of an imagemap? I want to make the alphabet and each letter a different section.

A. It can be made as small as four pixels square. Just be nice to your users and don't go so small that they have a hard time getting it to run.

Putting It All Together

Here's the basic format of an imagemap:

```
<A HREF="PATH TO CGI / PATH TO MAP"><IMG SRC="image.gif" ISMAP></A>
```

It is difficult for me to tell you exactly what the paths are for your server. I have no idea where on the server your Webmaster has placed the imagemap CGI, if there is one at all. My guess is that there is one. You just have to follow the instructions and path structure to connect them all.

FAQs from the HTML Goodies Web Site

Q. I can't get this map program thing to work. Can't I just guess at the points and make the map myself?

A. Sure, if the image is geometrical, you can probably take an educated guess as to where the points are. You need to know how many pixels across and how many down, then guess away. Just make sure you save the map with the .MAP extension.

Q. I copied exactly what you had on the page for my imagemap and it didn't work.

A. It didn't work because you are not on my server. You need to contact your own server people and ask them if they offer an imagemap CGI and if so, what the paths to attach to it are.

I want to make one more point about using an imagemap. Many people surf with their inline images turned off. That means they don't see any pictures when they surf, just text. It happens more often than you think. It also happens that people get tired of waiting for a large imagemap image to load; they want to get moving.

Because of all that, I would suggest that you always offer links to the items linked to your imagemaps. You could also offer a link to a text-based version of your page. Try to be helpful to your users—all your users.

Hopefully this has helped a bit. I understand it all may seem a bit boggling at the moment, but try to muddle through it. Once you do your first map, you'll wonder what you thought was so hard.

Enjoy!

Net Notes

Here are some URLs worth checking out:

Grab MapEdit: `http://www.boutell.com/mapedit`

Grab MAC-Image-Map: `http://weyl.zib-berlin.de/imagemap/Mac-ImageMap.html`

Yahoo!'s imagemap links: `http://www.yahoo.com/Computers_and_Internet/ Internet/World_Wide_Web/Imagemaps/`

Client-Side Imagemaps

A *client-side imagemap* is run by the browser rather than a CGI. What happens is that you provide all the information required to run the map in your HTML document. That's why it's called a client-side map. The map's functions are provided on the client's end of things rather than by a CGI on your server's side.

 This tutorial can be found online at `http://www.htmlgoodies.com/cs_imap.html`. *Go and see how it works.*

Figure 4.2 is a client-side imagemap. Do you like the graphic? I got it by scanning a clip art book. You should get one. Or six. They're great. All the images are in crisp black and white and scan wonderfully. Better yet, all the images are out from under copyright. You can use them to your heart's content.

The image is a drawing of a monk that I used to create links to some medieval sites for a friend's Web page. The image in Figure 4.2 is sitting alone. On this Web page it was surrounded by strange gothic images. Oooooh, scary.

Figure 4.2
A client-side imagemap.

In this tutorial I used the same image but have links to more popular pages. I'd like to point out that the image was allowed to keep its blue border for demonstration purposes only. When using an imagemap, you should really add `BORDER="0"` to the image command to lose the border altogether.

Remember the last time you ran your pointer over a basic CGI-run imagemap? Hopefully it was the previous online tutorial. The map's coordinates fly by in the online example. That's because the pointer was reading the map. Here, the pointer is still reading the coordinates; it's putting up the URL associated with the coordinates.

Let's Make a Map!

You can make a map by hand if you have a paint program that displays your images' coordinates. Otherwise, you need to go and get a map-making program. There are only a million different programs out there that will do the trick for you. I could not even begin to explain each one here. You must go out, find one you like, and use its instructions to make your map.

See the previous tutorial on CGI-driven imagemaps for more on how to make a map.

The difference between the last imagemap tutorial and this one is that with a CGI-driven imagemap, you actually use the map you make. In this tutorial, you are creating the map just so you can find the points on the grid. You then transfer those points right to the HTML document.

Putting the Image on the Page

Once you have the map finished and know the points, you need to place them and the image they support on the page. We'll do the image first. Here's the command I used to place the monk image in Figure 4.2:

```
<A HREF="monk.map"><IMG SRC="monk.gif" ISMAP USEMAP="#monkareas"></A>
```

Neat, huh? Look at what's happening:

- A HREF= denotes the link to the map. You must place the name of the map you created after the HREF. This is the map you created using the map program you downloaded.
- IMG SRC= is your basic image command.
- ISMAP stands alone. It tells the browser that this is an imagemap. The browser is basically being told that the image is active, but to read the map instead of activating the image.
- USEMAP= tells the browser where to find the map coordinates. Notice that the format is that of a page jump. The browser is being told where on the page to look for the map coordinates. In this case the coordinates are on a section of the HTML document marked monkareas. Please notice the preceding # mark! You need that.
- The </A> command ends it all.

The Coordinates

Okay, okay, you have the image up there. Where do you put the map's coordinates? Glad you asked. You place them on your HTML page. "Won't the coordinates show up on the page?" you ask, perplexed. "No," I answer brazenly. You set it aside as commands rather than straight text.

Here are the coordinates for the map. Remember what the map looked like? Well, here are those same coordinates in client-side imagemap format:

```
<map NAME="monkareas">
<area SHAPE=RECT COORDS="91,30 186,98" HREF="http://www.nfl.com"
 ALT="NFL Home Page">
<area SHAPE=CIRCLE COORDS="25,72 28,97" HREF="http://www.cnn.com"
 ALT="CNN Home Page">
<area SHAPE=CIRCLE COORDS="107,158 132,162" HREF="http://www.cbs.com"
 ALT="CBS Home Page">
<area SHAPE=POLY COORDS="9,115 86,79 98,116 69,131 86,175 48,206"
 HREF="http://www.cnn.com" ALT="USA TODAY Home Page">
<area SHAPE=default HREF="http://www.htmlgoodies.com">
</MAP>
```

FAQs from the HTML Goodies Web Site

Q. Where do I put the coordinate text on the HTML document?

A. Pretty much anywhere, but rule of thumb is beneath the map image, which is usually way down at the bottom of the page. That's where I put it.

Here's How You Do It

You first denote that these are the coordinates for the map. You do that with MAP NAME=. See that? You place the name you used after the # mark—just don't use the # mark here. The browser jumps to this part of your page to read coordinates rather than going to a CGI.

It's then a matter of following the format again and again.

- AREA denotes that this is a new section of the map.
- SHAPE denotes the shape you used. The map program tells you all this.
- HREF denotes the URL this section points to.
- ALT tells users who have their inline images turned off that this is an imagemap.
- DEFAULT follows the previous format. It denotes an URL for every part of the map not set aside by an imagemap set of coordinates.
- </MAP> wraps up the whole deal.

That's it. Follow all of this and you should have a client-side imagemap. People will soon be clicking like crazy.

Once again, allow me to proclaim that not everyone surfs with their images turned on and many people surf with text-only browsers. If you offer an imagemap, it's always best to also offer hypertext links too, or offer one link a text-based version of your page. Be nice to all your visitors.

Enjoy!

 I made another map for you to look at. Make sure you view the source code. Go to `http://www.htmlgoodies.com/book/anothermap.html`.

Fake Imagemap

Figure 4.3 looks like all the other imagemaps we've seen so far, right? If you were to run your mouse over it and keep an eye on the status bar at the bottom of the browser window, you'd see it acts like an imagemap. If you click the section you want, it would work; you'll go to the page. The trick is that this thing isn't an imagemap. In fact, it isn't an image at all. It's six images. Stay with me here...

Figure 4.3
A fake imagemap.

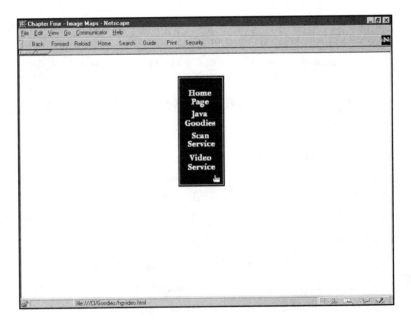

 This is another tutorial you have to see to believe. It's so easy, but looks great. Head to `http://www.htmlgoodies.com/fakemap.html`.

This is a fake imagemap. Figure 4.4 shows what that fake map looks like in what intellectuals call an *exploded view*.

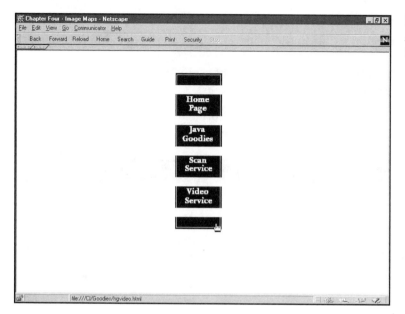

Figure 4.4
A fake imagemap exploded view.

See what I did? I took one image, cropped it into six and made each one active. Here's the code that I used to put the fake map together:

```
<center>
<A HREF="index.html"><img src="mapo2.gif" width="100" height="25"
 border="0"></A><BR>
<A HREF="index.html"><img src="cellone.gif" width="100" height="45"
 border="0"></A><BR>
<A HREF="/javagoodies/index.html"><img src="celltwo.gif" width="100"
 height="45" border="0"></A><BR>
<A HREF="scan.html"><img src="cellthree.gif" width="100" height="45"
 border="0"></A><BR>
<A HREF="hgvideo.html"><img src="cellfour.gif" width="100" height="45"
 border="0"></A><BR>
<A HREF="hgvideo.html"><img src="mapo3.gif" width="100" height="25"
 border="0"></A><BR>
</center>
```

I included the <CENTER> commands in the code because they do play a pretty big part. You can also add ALT commands to each image, but I don't do so when I am making a fake imagemap; I think it kills the illusion. But if you want to, go for it—it's your page.

The Image(s)

You can do this one of two ways:

1. Create one image and cut it up.
2. Create a template image. Add words to the image and keep saving in a different name.

I used the first method. Both methods work, but I thought it was easiest to cut the image up. You'll need an image editing program to do this.

Once you have the images and are sure they will line up correctly, simply build the map. Make sure the images load in order, top to bottom, left to right.

FAQs from the HTML Goodies Web Site

Q. You said that the fake imagemaps had to be one picture cut up. Well, I did it with five pictures lined up along the top of the page.

A. Wonderful. I'll bet it looks great. Good thinking. There are no rules to any of this. If it looks right, it probably is right.

Getting It All to Line Up

This is the tricky part. You know each image is active. That means you need to use the BORDER="0" command to eliminate the blue border that would normally form.

First, make sure all of your images are of equal width and height, so they line up and form a perfect second image. It kills the entire effect without it.

FAQs from the HTML Goodies Web Site

Q. I made a fake map but it keeps getting messed up. There are five images left to right and the last one keeps jumping down to the next line. How do I stop that?

A. Make the images smaller. If five are going across the top, knock them down a bit. You can set it so that the page scrolls right by surrounding the images with <NOBR> and </NOBR>. That disallows the break. A page that scrolls to the right is not really a good idea. People want it all on their screen in one shot. Go with smaller graphics.

The use of a line or smaller image that moves through the multiple images gives a greater perception that the image is solid rather than a sum of parts. See the white box I have running through the image? This takes a little practice.

Keep all the commands tight together. If there is a space between the image and </A>, that space will show up and kill the effect.

Run it all together. If you have two images that sit next to each other on the same line, do not skip the second image's commands to the next line. That works on some browsers, but on others (earlier versions in particular) you see that you're going to the next line as a space.

Part 3

Getting More Control Over the Layout of Your Web Pages

Chapter 5

All About Tables

Simple Tables

You want a table? Okay. Figure 5.1 shows a table of the Brady family. Feel free to sing.

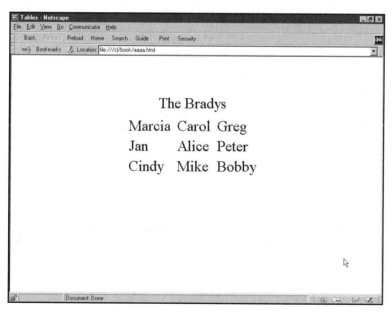

Figure 5.1
A simple table of the Brady clan.

Hey! That's Not What I Wanted!

Yes it is. You asked for a table. That thing was made using the <TABLE> </TABLE> commands. That's a table because...Oh, wait. I'll bet Figure 5.2 is the thing you were looking for.

Figure 5.2
A much better table of the Brady kids.

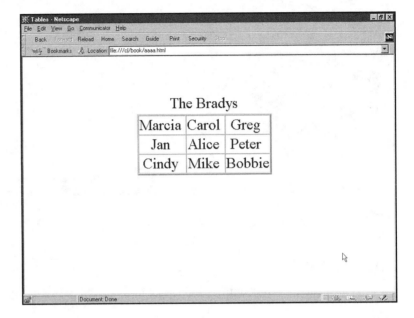

Am I right? You wanted those fancy frame lines so that it looks like a graph or, dare I say, a table?

The Simple Table Flags

First things first. Let me explain the table I showed you in Figure 5.1—the one you didn't want. It will make explaining the framed table a whole lot easier. Here's the little program I wrote to give me the Brady family table:

```
<TABLE>
  <CAPTION>The Bradys</CAPTION>
  <TR>
    <TD>Marcia</TD>
    <TD>Carol</TD>
    <TD>Greg</TD>
  </TR>
  <TR>
    <TD>Jan</TD>
    <TD>Alice</TD>
    <TD>Peter</TD>
```

```
    </TR>
    <TR>
      <TD>Cindy</TD>
      <TD>Mike</TD>
      <TD>Bobby</TD>
    </TR>

  </TABLE>
```

Now, don't be put off by this little ditty. At first glance it looks rough, but look again. There are really only four commands being used again and again. Here are the commands:

- <TABLE> and </TABLE> start and end the entire thing. I think that makes perfect sense. This is a table, after all.

- <CAPTION> and </CAPTION> place a caption over your table. In my example the caption is The Bradys. These flags also bold your caption text and center it across your table cells.

- <TD> denotes table data. You put this in front of every piece of information you want in a cell. You need a </TD> at the end of each data cell.

- <TR> is used when you want a new table row to begin. Again, make sure you close each row with a </TR>.

Table flags create a series of cells. Each cell's data is denoted by the <TD> flag. Please note that even though the preceding program has each cell (or <TD>) flag on a new line, the cells keep going to the right until you tell the computer that a new row of cells will start; you do that by using the <TR>, or table row, command.

Think of it as constructing a Tic Tac Toe board. You'll need nine cells for the board, right? Three across in three rows. Use the <TD> command to make three cells across and use <TR> to jump to the next row. Keep going until you have nine cells in three rows of three. Nothing to it.

Remember that whatever follows the <TD> command will appear in the cell. The width of each column is determined by the widest cell in each column. One column could possibly be three times as wide as the other columns. Just because one column is a certain width doesn't mean the others will be the same. Biggest wins, in other words. In life as in HTML.

FAQs from the HTML Goodies Web Site

Q. Where's my table? I copied everything from your page and it's not showing up!

A. I'll bet you forgot to get the end table flag: </TABLE>. If you miss that, nothing shows up.

Q. I made a table, but the first row isn't in cells. It's just text.

A. You may have missed an end quotation mark somewhere before the table started. I have done this a few times. The next quote the browser sees was after the first table row, so it ignored the first few <TD> flags until it got to an end quote. That finished the command before the table started. Check your code carefully.

Q. You say in your table tutorial that I need a </TD> and a </TR> for every <TD> and <TR> I write. I've been told that you really only need one </TD> and one </TR> at the very end of the table. Who's right?

A. I have seen tables done both ways. In fact, I have seen many tables done without any end flag. I used to make my tables that way when I started, but the traditional format is an end flag for every flag you open. If you follow that format, you won't run into any trouble.

Really Fancy Table Stuff

Now on to making the fancy lines between cells. Figure 5.3 is the same table you saw before.

Figure 5.3
A simple table with borders.

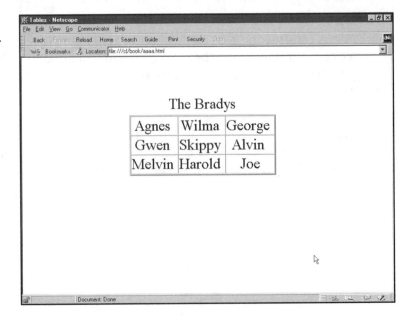

Okay, so I changed the Bradys' names, but you get the idea. The following code is the program I used to create this table. Please note that the flags are the same as the first table you looked at! I just added a few more commands inside the table flags, but you already know about them.

```
<TABLE BORDER="3" CELLSPACING="1" CELLPADDING="1">
<CAPTION>The Bradys</CAPTION>
<TR>
<TD ALIGN = "center"> Agnes</TD>
<TD ALIGN = "center"> Wilma </TD>
<TD ALIGN = "center"> George </TD>
</TR>
<TR>
<TD ALIGN = "center"> Gwen </TD>
<TD ALIGN = "center"> Skippy</TD>
<TD ALIGN = "center"> Alvin </TD>
</TR>
<TR>
<TD ALIGN = "center"> Melvin </TD>
<TD ALIGN = "center"> Harold </TD>
<TD ALIGN = "center"> Joe</TD>
</TR>
</TABLE>
```

If it looks to you like all the work is done in the <TABLE> flag, you're right. You are using three commands to do the work for you:

● BORDER tells the table how large the border should be. This is all relative. Three is larger than two, two is larger than one, and so on. Try different numbers. I happen to like the look of BORDER="3". BORDER="0" gets rid of the lines altogether.

● CELLSPACING tells how much space you'd like between cells. I'd keep this kind of small. Large spacing tends to defeat the purpose.

● CELLPADDING tells how much padding is required between the text and the walls of the cell. Note that the cell walls tend to fill out. A higher number fills out more. Try a few different numbers. Sometimes bigger is better.

How about that new ALIGN command in the <TD> flag? See it? I have told the <TD> flag that I want the data that follows centered within the cell walls outlined in the table command. Remember that using an ALIGN command inside a <TD> only affects the data in that one cell. You need to add an ALIGN command to the other <TD> cells if you also want them affected. Can you do other ALIGN types? Sure. Try ALIGN=left and ALIGN=right. Use them in combination. Save them, trade them!

Activating Cells for Links

Wouldn't it be great if you could make a table with words and the words in the table were active, so you could click them? You can do just that. Take a look at Figure 5.4.

Figure 5.4
This is a table showing four links in four cells.

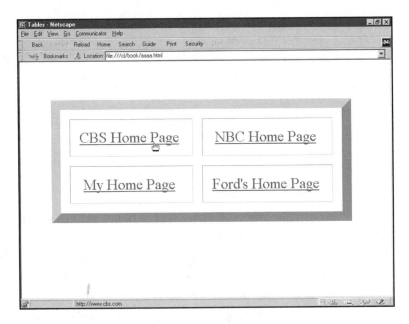

The flags are the same for this table except that you place a link command after the `<TD>` flag. Here's what the tag for the upper-left cell looks like:

```
<TD align="center"><A HREF="http://www.cbs.com">CBS Home Page</A> </TD>
```

By the way, the BORDER, CELLSPACING, and CELLPADDING flags are all set at 20 in Figure 5.4's table, which gives you an example of some larger numbers.

of the page and then set the border to 0 so that the table borders disappear, but the formatting remains.

A. That's correct. In fact, I do that all the time. The entire HTML Goodies home page is one big table. Good thinking. Thanks for writing.

Images in Cells

Can you put images in each of the cells? You bet. Here ya go—just take a look at Figure 5.5.

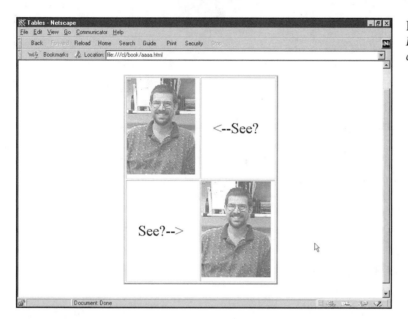

Figure 5.5
Images placed in a table cell.

All you have done is followed the <TD> flag with an image flag. This command creates the upper -left cell:

```
<TD ALIGN="center"><IMG SRC="joeburns.gif"></TD>
```

Framing Images

I am asked at least once a week how to frame an image. What you have done until now is framed two images. A frame around one image is nothing more than a one-celled table. Figure 5.6 shows a framed image.

Figure 5.6

A framed image.

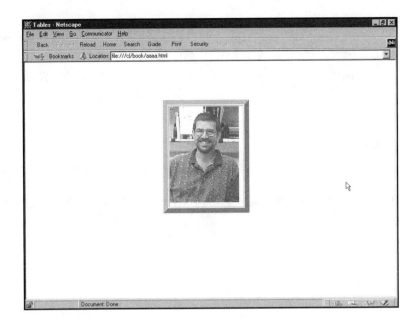

The commands for doing this are much simpler than the earlier ones. There's only one cell to deal with, so there's no need to tell the table any type of CELLPADDING or CELLSPACING. You can if you'd like, but there's really no need. Here are the commands that placed the preceding image in a frame:

```
<TABLE BORDER="10">
<TR>
<TD ALIGN="center"><IMG SRC="joeburns.gif">
</TD>
</TR>
</TABLE>
```

Centering the Image

Here's one more quick hint: See how the images in the cells are pushed into the upper-left corner (see Figure 5.5)? They're not quite in the center. There's some space on the right and bottom of the image. Here's a quick trick to fix that. Check out Figure 5.7.

Add a <TR> tag before the <TD> that holds the image, then close both tags with </TR> and the </TD>. Here's the trick! Make sure the </TR> and the </TD> are on the same line as the <TD> and <TR>, like so:

```
<TABLE BORDER="10">
<TR><TD ALIGN="center"><IMG SRC="joeburns.gif"> </TD></TR>
</TABLE>
```

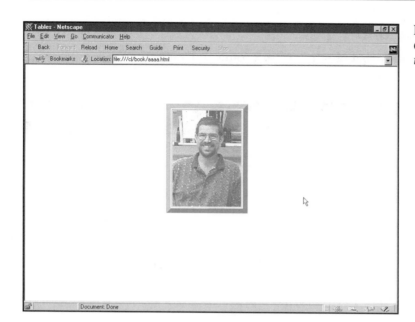

Figure 5.7
Centering an image inside a table cell.

Again, notice that the end flags are on the same line as the start commands. The effect is lost if you move the end commands to the next line. By the way, technically it isn't supposed to work like this—no matter what line an HTML flag is on, it should always work the same. I've found, however, that when it comes to centering things, where you put your flags often makes a big difference.

Finally...

Just about anything will go inside a table. The table flags just surround the items with a frame. Try putting a few of your page's items within a frame or a table; it looks professional. Just don't go overboard with it. If you do, it starts to take on the not-so-nice look of too many lawn ornaments.

Enjoy!

 I have a couple of larger tables for you to look at online at http://www.htmlgoodies.com/ book/bigtables.html. *Make sure to look at the source code.*

Advanced Table Commands

This tutorial only deals with three commands. Some advanced tutorial, huh? Actually, these three commands are great when you want more control over the spacing of your table cells. I strongly suggest that you read over the first part of this chapter before beginning. Otherwise, this stuff will be way over your head. Then you'll call me a name. Then you'll bring my mother into it, and nobody wants that.

The COLSPAN *Command*

Figure 5.8 shows a simple table that uses the COLSPAN command to create a single table cell that spans the entire width of the table.

Figure 5.8
A table with the COLSPAN *command.*

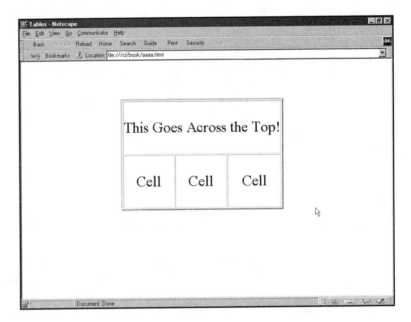

See how the top row spans across three columns? That's what the COLSPAN command does. It really isn't that tough to do; the problem comes in figuring out where the <TR> flag goes. If you place a <TR> in the wrong place, you can mess up the table's complete configuration. Here's the program that created the table:

```
<TABLE BORDER="3" CELLPSACING="3" CELLPADDING="3">
<TR>
<TD ALIGN="center" COLSPAN="3">This Goes Across the Top!</TD>
</TR>
<TR>
<TD ALIGN="center">Cell</TD>
<TD ALIGN="center">Cell</TD>
<TD ALIGN="center">Cell</TD>
</TR>
</TABLE>
```

Notice the first <TD> line. See how it contains the ALIGN command plus that COLSPAN thing I talked about? Here's the deal: A table is a series of columns (the up and down sections) and rows (the left to right sections). I wanted the first <TD> cell to span across three columns, so I added the command COLSPAN and told the span to go across three columns. Note that there are three cells (columns) that are being spanned by that command.

If I had written COLSPAN="2", the span would have been only two columns. Note where the first <TR> flag fell—it is immediately after the row that spanned three columns. If I had spanned only two, I would have had to place another <TD> cell before the first <TR> flag.

It is best to draw out your table before writing your HTML code. That helps you see where the table rows must break to keep within the square that is the table.

FAQs from the HTML Goodies Web Site

Q. You may want to add the command VALIGN="top" to your advanced table tutorial.

A. I will. VALIGN stands for vertical align. Using the top command like you did sets all text right to the top of the cell.

The ROWSPAN *Command*

I would think that you can guess what is going to happen here—basically the same thing that just happened, but this command spans rows rather than columns. Figure 5.9 shows an example.

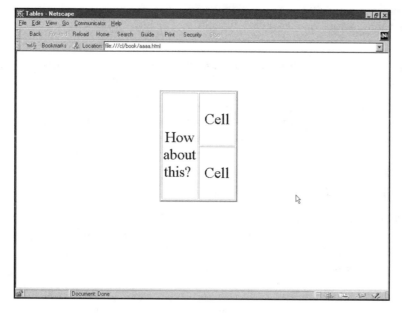

Figure 5.9
A table with the ROWSPAN *command.*

Here's the HTML code that made it:

```
<TABLE BORDER="3" CELLPSACING="3" CELLPADDING="3">
<TR>
<TD ROWSPAN="2" ALIGN="center" WIDTH="75">How about this?</TD>
<TD ALIGN="center" WIDTH="75">Cell</TD>
</TR>
<TR>
<TD ALIGN="center" WIDTH="75">Cell</TD>
</TR>
</TABLE>
```

See what happened? I simply told the column to span over two rows. I think it's a bit confusing too. You tell columns to span rows and you tell rows to span columns. It confuses me every so often.

Again, the best thing to do is draw out the table before you attempt to create it with HTML commands. Getting the span is never the difficult thing; the problem is where to place the <TR> command to keep this information inside the four corners.

FAQs from the HTML Goodies Web Site

Q. Can I set a separate CELLPADDING for each cell?

A. No. A table will always stay four-sided. If you leave the <TD> blank, you won't get the cell (coming up in the next tutorial), but you still have to put those <TD> flags in there to stay four-sided. Setting an individual CELLPADDING will affect all the other cells, anyway.

Q. I want to make an L shape in a table that goes across a couple of columns and a row. How do I do it?

A. You can't through HTML alone, but you could create the table, turn it into an image through a screen capture (discussed later in the book), and then erase the one horizontal bar. It's a bit of trouble, but it gets the effect you want.

What's That WIDTH="nn" Deal?

Yeah, I did just pop that up out of nowhere, didn't I? That command denotes the width of the cell. When you use numbers, like I did earlier, it is defining the width in pixels. If you use percentages, like WIDTH="20%", it denotes the width of the cell in relationship to the screen. The percentage sign is required.

This helps a lot in defining the space your tables will take up on the page. Using percentages helps keep the cells somewhat equal between browsers and differing screen settings.

FAQs from the HTML Goodies Web Site

Q. Can I set a separate width for each cell?

A. To a point. You can make some cells wider than others by using the COLSPAN and ROWSPAN commands, but it must all stay within four sides. (No row can stick out farther than other rows, and no column can stick out farther than other columns.)

I have an example of a very intricate table created using the COLSPAN *and* ROWSPAN *commands. Try to figure out the code yourself before you look. Go to* http://www.htmlgoodies.com/book/fancytable.html.

Can I Use COLSPAN *and* ROWSPAN *Commands Together?*

Yes. As a matter of fact, the HTML Goodies master page (at http://www.htmlgoodies.com/master.html) is little more than a giant table using both ROWSPAN and COLSPAN commands. Bop over, take a look, and feel free to look at the view-source to see the commands.

Good luck with these two new commands. Take my word for it—these will give you more headaches than you'll want. You may be sorry you saw this tutorial. So go look at another...

Enjoy!

A Table Within a Table

I've pointed out many times that you can combine different HTML flags to create new effects. Figure 5.10 shows a good example of that—a table within a table.

There's an online example of a table inside a table inside a table. Go to http://www.htmlgoodies.com/book/tableintableintable.html.

Here is the code that created the table in Figure 5.10. The outer table's commands are regular text and the inner table's commands are italicized so you can quickly tell them apart.

```
<TABLE BORDER="3" CELLPADDING="10" CELLSPACING="10">
  <TR>
    <TD>
      <TABLE BORDER="3" CELLPADDING="3" CELLSPACING="3">
      <TR>
        <TD>2nd Table</TD>
        <TD>2nd Table</TD>
      <TR>
        <TD>2nd Table</TD>
        <TD>2nd Table</TD>
      </TR>
```

```
        </TABLE>
      </TD>
      <TD> The cell next to this one has a smaller table inside of it,
  a table inside a table.</TD>
    </TR>
  </TABLE>
```

Figure 5.10
A table within a table.

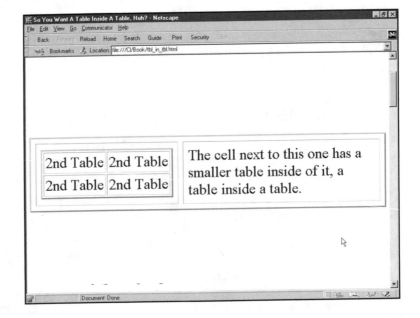

For those of you already up-to-speed on tables, you can probably pick up from the code how it's done; you make a point of ending every line with an end command. It can get confusing, but each <TD> and <TR> must be closed as soon as it ends.

Tip

When I do a table in a table, I tend to get a little confused about what goes with what. What I do is create all the tables separately, making sure every section has its own end command. I create the tables that go in the cells first. The last thing I make is the larger table. That way I can create the large table and when I need to fill in the <TD> with a smaller table, I just cut and paste it in. It also helps me remember to follow the smaller table with a </TD> for the larger table's benefit.

It's super easy to forget one and doing so messes up the whole table scheme.

FAQs from the HTML Goodies Web Site

Q. I tried to create a table in a table, but all I get are the horizontal lines, no verticals.

A. You are missing some </TD> and </TR> commands. Remember, every <TD> or <TR> you write needs an end command when doing a table within a table.

Using Tables to Make an HTML Calendar

Why didn't I think of this sooner?! That's why I read the email from viewers—you give the best ideas. I should have seen this coming, but I didn't. Instead, I received 50 requests to make an HTML calendar. So I made one; take a look at Figure 5.11.

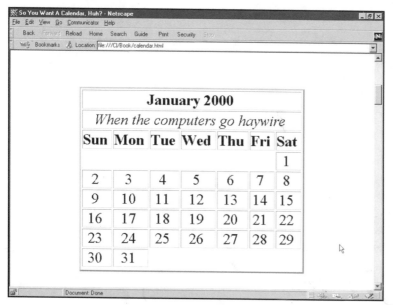

Figure 5.11
A calendar created with tables.

Isn't that neat? And it's not that rough to do. It's actually just a simple table with a couple of additions. Here's the really long-winded code I used the create the calendar:

```
<TABLE BORDER=3 CELLSPACING=3 CELLPADDING=3>
<TR>
<TD COLSPAN="7" ALIGN=center><B>January 2000</B>
</TR>
<TR>
<TD COLSPAN="7" ALIGN=center><I>When the computers go haywire</I></TR>
```

```
</TR>
<TR>

<TD ALIGN=center>Sun</TR>
<TD ALIGN=center>Mon</TR>
<TD ALIGN=center>Tue</TR>
<TD ALIGN=center>Wed</TR>
<TD ALIGN=center>Thu</TR>
<TD ALIGN=center>Fru</TR>
<TD ALIGN=center>Sat</TR>
</TR>
<TR>

<TD ALIGN=center></TR>
<TD ALIGN=center></TR>
<TD ALIGN=center></TR>
<TD ALIGN=center></TR>
<TD ALIGN=center></TR>
<TD ALIGN=center></TR>
<TD ALIGN=center>1</TR>
</TR>
<TR>

<TD ALIGN=center>2</TR>
<TD ALIGN=center>3</TR>
<TD ALIGN=center>4</TR>
<TD ALIGN=center>5</TR>
<TD ALIGN=center>6</TR>
<TD ALIGN=center>7</TR>
<TD ALIGN=center>8</TR>
</TR>
<TR>

<TD ALIGN=center>9</TR>
<TD ALIGN=center>10</TR>
<TD ALIGN=center>11</TR>
<TD ALIGN=center>12</TR>
<TD ALIGN=center>13</TR>
<TD ALIGN=center>14</TR>
<TD ALIGN=center>15</TR>
</TR>
<TR>

<TD ALIGN=center>16</TR>
<TD ALIGN=center>17</TR>
```

```
<TD ALIGN=center>18</TR>
<TD ALIGN=center>19</TR>
<TD ALIGN=center>20</TR>
<TD ALIGN=center>21</TR>
<TD ALIGN=center>22</TR>
</TR>
<TR>
<TD ALIGN=center>23</TR>
<TD ALIGN=center>24</TR>
<TD ALIGN=center>25</TR>
<TD ALIGN=center>26</TR>
<TD ALIGN=center>27</TR>
<TD ALIGN=center>28</TR>
<TD ALIGN=center>29</TR>
</TR>
<TR>

<TD ALIGN=center>30</TR>
<TD ALIGN=center>31</TR>
<TD ALIGN=center></TR>
<TD ALIGN=center></TR>
<TD ALIGN=center></TR>
<TD ALIGN=center></TR>
<TD ALIGN=center></TR>
</TR>
</TR>

</TABLE>
```

You can just simply copy this code, write it to your page, and get the calendar shown in Figure 5.11. Again, this is a lot easier if you understand tables. The two headers were created by entering a COLSPAN command that tells the top to span across all seven columns.

Each cell was created by simply entering a number for the day. The trick is making sure each day gets the correct numbers. Notice that each little grouping is seven items that represent each week.

You can activate each cell simply by putting an HREF command and activating the number to be clicked:

```
<TD ALIGN=center><A HREF="http://www.page.com">22</A>
```

The raised look, where there are no days, is created by offering a <TD> command but giving no data. You must offer the <TD> to keep the format square, just don't offer any information.

FAQs from the HTML Goodies Web Site

Q. **You tell me how to make it so that no cells appear in a calendar. I would like cells like on a regular calendar, but I want the cells to be empty. I have tried putting a ton of spaces after the <TD> because it has to be blank, but no luck. How do you do it?**

A. You're on the right track. You do need a space, but the space needs to be a space other then one created by hitting the Spacebar. Use the   command discussed in Chapter 1, "Playing with Text." Place the command right after the <TD> (without using the quotation marks), and you'll get your cell walls.

Enjoy!

 There's a full-year calendar online at `http://www.htmlgoodies.com/book/fullyear.html`*. I did it by creating twelve tables inside a larger table, but I made the outer table's border equal to* `0`*, so it is only acting as a layout template. Think about how you would write the code for a full year before looking.*

Adding Color to Your Tables

I receive letters all the time asking me how to put different colors in table cells. According to my research, you have to be using at least Netscape or Explorer 3.0 for these commands to take effect. I should point out that this tutorial does not get into the creation of the table itself, only changing the background and text color.

 This stunning color table tutorial can be found online at `http://www.htmlgoodies.com/` `colortbl.html`*.*

Changing Cell Colors

Figure 5.12 shows a table with different colored cells.

Here's the HTML code that created that multicolored table in Figure 5.12:

```
<TABLE BORDER=4 CELLSPACING=4 CELLPADDING=4>
</TR>
<TD BGCOLOR="#ffff00">Yellow Stars</TD>
<TD BGCOLOR="#00ff00">Green Clovers</TD>
</TR>
<TR>
<TD BGCOLOR="#ff00ff">Purple Moons</TD>
<TD BGCOLOR="#00ffff">Blue something or other... </TD>
</TR>
</TABLE>
```

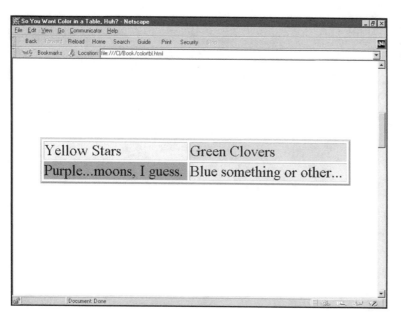

Figure 5.12
A table with multicolored cells.

Notice it's just a basic table with a `BGCOLOR=` command stuck in now and again for good measure. Insert either the hex code or the word code for the color you like and you're off and running. There is a long list of color words and hex codes in Appendix B, "Useful Charts."

FAQs from the HTML Goodies Web Site

Q. Does it matter if I use hex codes or word codes for my tables' colors?

A. Nope. In fact, you can use them both, although I suggest that you use very basic colors that won't dither (see the non-dithering color chart in the back of the book). If your table, full of intricate color, shows up on a computer that can't handle it, it will look like a mess.

Changing Text Colors

You can also change the color of text in your tables. It's really easy—you just have to make sure you don't make some combination of text and cell colors that makes everything too hard to read. Figure 5.13 shows some interesting color combinations.

The HTML code for one of the cell's in Figure 5.13's table follows. You can see how the cell and text color commands are combined:

```
<TD BGCOLOR="#ffff00"><FONT COLOR="#800517">Something Old</FONT> </TD>
```

Figure 5.13
A table with multicolored text and cells.

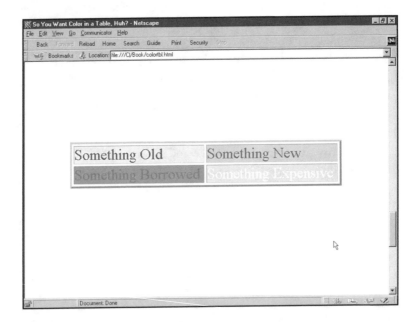

Notice that it's the same commands for the table; I just used the font color commands to change the text color. Put it all together and you can create some pretty awful-looking tables (and some gorgeous ones).

FAQs from the HTML Goodies Web Site

Q. Color is nice, but can I get an image as a background in a table cell?

A. Sure, but only in later browsers like versions 3 and 4. You would handle it the same way you handle a background image in the `<BODY>` flag. You add `BACKGROUND="`*`image.jpg`*`"` inside the `<TD>` and exchange *`image.jpg`* with the name of your image. It's a neat effect, but keep load time in mind. The more images you include, the slower your page loads.

I've created the Purina checkerboard pattern (nine red and white alternating cells) online at `http://www.htmlgoodies.com/book/checkerboard.html`. *Think about how you would do it, then go see it.*

Changing Table Border Colors

Whomever decided that tables should have color capabilities shall be brought before me for a good lashing! As soon as people learn that they can put color in table cells, the next volley of questions includes how to put color into the table borders. Many people out there are creating color test patterns to make sure their new Trinitron monitor can actually handle 16 million colors. Wow!

But I digress. Let's try out a few different angles, for those using the newfangled browsers and those who still dig the earlier versions. I still surf with 1.1 every so often. I figure it's a good page if I can still see all the important parts using the earlier browsers.

But I digress again...

 Point your browser to `http://www.htmlgoodies.com/bordercl.html` *to see this tutorial in action.*

Take a look at Figure 5.14; see the text in the second table? Can you tell me what song that's from?

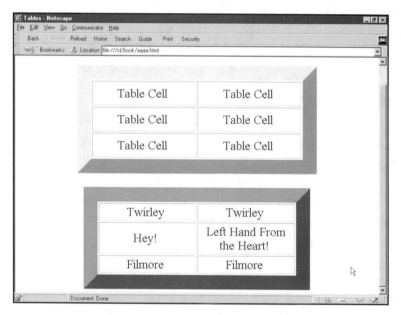

Figure 5.14
A table with multicolored borders.

You are using a higher-level browser if you go to the Web site (or type in the following HTML code) and the two tables in Figure 5.14 are green and then purple. You can run some table border commands. If both of them are purple, stay with me and I'll explain that stuff later. First: the HTML commands.

```
<TABLE BORDER="30" CELLPADDING="10"
CELLSPACING="3" BORDERCOLOR="00FF00">
```

I am only showing the main TABLE command because there's nothing new with the rest of the table.

169

As you can see, I made a point of making the borders quite large (30 in fact). That's to see the colors more than anything required for the border color itself. The border around the table is green because I entered this in the <TABLE> flag:

```
BORDERCOLOR="00FF00"
```

Those of you who still use hex codes know that little ditty, 00FF00, as green. Those of you who are now using word color commands should type in "green". You'll get the same effect.

FAQs from the HTML Goodies Web Site

Q. How can I make the borders around just one table cell a different color?

A. You are on a quest to make the ugliest table ever, huh? There is a way, but it only works on Explorer browsers. Use the command BORDERCOLOR= to get the effect. The command BORDERCOLOR="00FF00"gives you a green border around the cell. In fact, Explorer offers a bunch of other commands to play with that Navigator doesn't; see Chapter 13, "Internet Explorer Tutorials and DHTML," for the entire list.

Some Extra Play with Colors

This is where I get into some fancy stuff. This info, despite being fancy, is best for those without the newer browsers. This is the way I get color into my table borders before the BORDERCOLOR command was created.

This page may appear to only be using the <BODY BGCOLOR="FFFFFF"> command. It doesn't appear that there is any background image being used. That is wrong; I am using one. It's pure white. Here's the BODY command from this page:

```
<BODY BACKGROUND="clbg.gif" BGCOLOR="800080">
```

Notice I am using both a BGCOLOR and a BACKGROUND command. The BACKGROUND command is simply posting graphics (called *clbg.gif*) that have a pure white background. It looks like I did it with a BGCOLOR command. I didn't; it's an image. I then used a BGCOLOR command set to "#800080" (purple).

Now I know what you're thinking: How do I get images into my table borders? Sorry, but you can't. But why, Joe, why?! Table borders don't accept images or patterns right now. That may all change soon, but at the moment it doesn't work.

Oh, and by the way: The lyrics came from "Billy the Mountain" by Frank Zappa.

 I have a table online that uses absolutely every color command available to tables. It looks like a box of Crayolas exploded, so go take a look at http://www.htmlgoodies.com/book/uglytable.html/.

Chapter 6

Using Frames

Introduction to Frames

Frames were a massive hit when they first came out, and they are in widespread use today. I'll tell you every trick to using them, but keep in mind that using frames means loading multiple pages into the same browser window. That can take a while and can bore your readers. Consider whether you really need them before using them. If you do decide to use them, make the pages mostly text and go easy on the big images. Be good to your readers and they'll be good to you. At least they won't write you nasty email letters.

 This tutorial can be found online at http://www.htmlgoodies.com/frame1.html.

Frames are a little different than anything you've done in HTML. Frame commands allow you to display more than one page at the same time in the same browser screen. What goes in the frame cells? I'm glad you asked. Other pages go in the frame cells. Those pages can contain anything a normal page does: text, graphics, images, and so on.

I went on a short surfing trip with my Internet Explorer browser to find a few good examples of sites using frames. I thought these were particularly nice; the page layout was attractive and it was pretty easy to navigate through the site.

Figure 6.1 shows the main page from Film.com (http://www.film.com/Default.htm), a site all about current movies and the movie business.

Figure 6.1

Film.com makes good use of frames by putting a menu of links at the bottom of the page.

Notice the links are along the bottom. They stay on the page, while the larger frame window at the top changes when you click. Figure 6.2 shows another good example of frames being used by the Internet Yellow Pages (http://www.the-yellowpages.com/index.html). Same basic idea, in a slightly different layout.

Figure 6.2

Good use of frames on the Internet Yellow Pages.

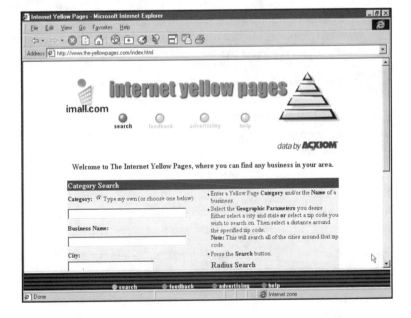

Finally, just to prove that not everyone loves using frames on their home page, here's the Campaign Against Frames home page (see Figure 6.3). The page is called "So You Like Frames?" (http://hem.passagen.se/ceel/frames/frames.htm). The page is truly a bad example of using too many frames.

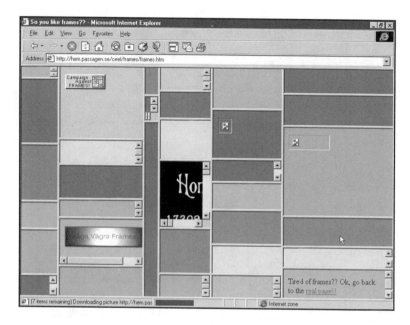

Figure 6.3
A reminder that it is possible to overuse frames.

Now we get into how you make your own frames. Hopefully you'll do better than the layout in Figure 6.3.

Simple Frames

Figure 6.4 shows a rather involved frame page. The browser screen has been broken up into six different frames. Remember that each frame window is displaying a full HTML document, so this frame setup needs to load seven pages to work properly—the six pages that show up in the frame windows plus the page that has the frame commands.

In case you're wondering, this is the code that created those six frames:

```
<FRAMESET ROWS="20%,45%,35%">
  <FRAMESET COLS="100%">
    <FRAME  SCROLLING="no" SRC="page01.html">
  <FRAMESET COLS="50%,25%,25%">
    <FRAME SCROLLING="no" SRC="page02.html">
    <FRAME SRC="page03.html">
    <FRAME SRC="page04.html">
  </FRAMESET>
```

```
<FRAMESET COLS="30%,70%">
  <FRAME NORESIZE="YES" SRC="page05.html">
  <FRAME SRC="page06.html">
</FRAMESET>
</FRAMESET>
```

Figure 6.4

A Web page with six frames.

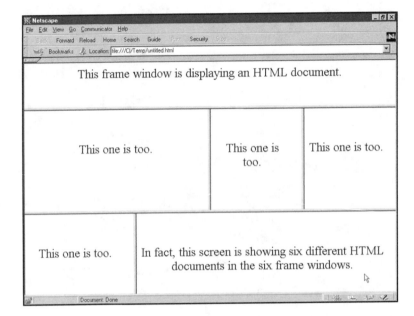

Don't be put off by it just yet. By the end of this tutorial you'll understand everything you see and be able to create frames with the best of 'em.

FAQs from the HTML Goodies Web Site

Q. Where do I put the text that appears in the two frame windows? After the `<BODY>` command?

A. Nowhere, actually. This is the question I get most often from people starting to work with frames. The text that appears in the frame windows are actually full HTML documents in themselves. Look again at the code in the first frame tutorial. See how the `FRAME SRC` command is calling for a whole other page? You need to create full documents to fit into those frame windows.

Q. Do I really need a `<BODY>` flag on the HTML page that holds the frame template?

A. No. My frame template pages contain only a `TITLE` and the frame commands.

Q. Do I have to put a title on the pages that go into the frame windows? It doesn't appear anywhere.

A. Technically no, but I suggest you do it anyway. Many people will want to break the pages out of their frame window and see them full-screen. In that case it is nice to have a title.

Creating Frame Columns

Figure 6.5 shows a very simplified version of a Web page with two frames. The frames break up the browser screen into two sections: Page_A.htm and Page_B.htm.

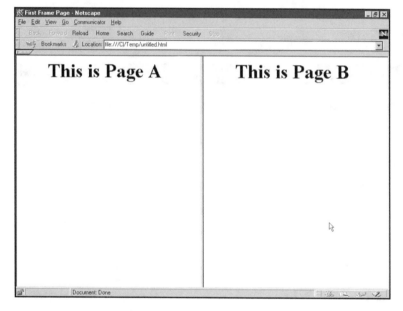

Figure 6.5
A Web page with two frames in columns.

The frame commands that create the Web page in Figure 6.5 look like this:

```
<HTML>
<TITLE>First Frame Page</TITLE>
<FRAMESET COLS="50%,50%">
<FRAME SRC="PAGE_A.htm">
<FRAME SRC="PAGE_B.htm">
</FRAMESET>
</HTML>
```

Neat, huh? I wanted to display two pages at the same time, so I simply split the screen into two parts and placed a different page in each part. Please note that there is a hypertext link on each page that will send you back to the tutorial. I'll get into those in a moment. Look again at the small HTML frames in the previous code. Here's what the commands are doing:

- ◗ <FRAMESET> starts any frame page. It alerts the browser that frames are going to be used.

- ◗ COLS denotes that I want columns. In this case I want two, each 50% of the screen. You can do other percentages; go nuts if you want. Make sure you separate the percentages by commas and get it to add up to 99% or 100%. 99%?! Yes.

  You see, 33%, 33%, 33% adds up to 99% and splits the screen three ways. The browser just distributes the final 1% over the three spaces.

- ◗ FRAME SRC denotes the source of the frame. Frames read like you do, left to right. The first offered source is hard left. I only have two frame sections, so I need only two sources.

- ◗ </FRAMESET> ends the whole deal. You need one of these for every <FRAMESET> you use. More on that in a moment.

FAQs from the HTML Goodies Web Site

Q: Do I have to write pages skinny enough to fit in only one half of the page frame?

A: Nope. The browser will cram it all in there, but it tends to look smooshy. (How about that word?) I'll offer an example in a moment.

Q: What if my page is taller than the screen? How do I put in a vertical scrollbar?

A: Don't concern yourself with it; the browser will do it for you. Write for content, not frame.

Adding Frame Rows to the Mix

Do you want two frames in rows (left to right) instead of columns? Simply use the command ROWS rather than COLS. In fact, if you take the previous example and replace the command COLS with ROWS, you get something that looks like Figure 6.6. The frame you define first goes on the top (PAGE_A.htm in this case).

```
<HTML>
<TITLE>First Frame Page</TITLE>
<FRAMESET ROWS="50%,50%">
<FRAME SRC="PAGE_A.htm">
<FRAME SRC="PAGE_B.htm">
</FRAMESET>
</HTML>
```

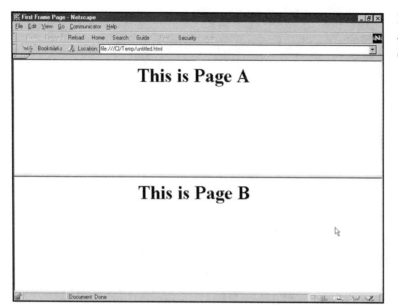

Figure 6.6
A Web page with two frames in rows.

Combining Frame Columns and Rows

Now it starts to get a little goofy. You can make really complex and creative Web pages by combining frame rows and columns. Just remember what I said before: The more frames you have, the longer it takes to load your Web pages. Figure 6.7 shows a Web page with a combination of frame columns and rows.

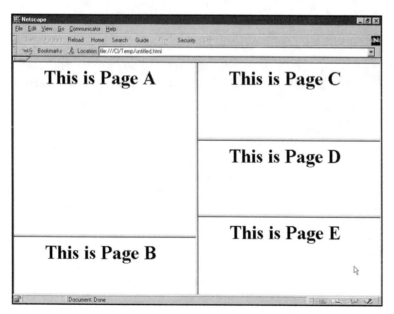

Figure 6.7
A combination of frame columns and rows.

Here are the frame commands I used to create the rows and tables shown in Figure 6.7:

```
<FRAMESET COLS="50%,50%">
  <FRAMESET ROWS="75%,25%">
    <FRAME SRC="PAGE_A.htm">
    <FRAME SRC="PAGE_B.htm">
  </FRAMESET>
  <FRAMESET ROWS="33%,33%,33%">
    <FRAME SRC="PAGE_C.htm">
    <FRAME SRC="PAGE_D.htm">
    <FRAME SRC="PAGE_E.htm">
  </FRAMESET>
</FRAMESET>
```

Let's look at what's happening here. Remember that frames read left to right. I told the computer I wanted frames by using the `<FRAMESET>` flag. I then broke up the page vertically, just as before.

Here's where the rows come in. I added a new `<FRAMESET>` flag denoting ROWS. I asked for 75%, 25%. That breaks up the first column into two rows. I then offered two sources for the first column's two sections. The first frame that's offered a source is always the top one. I then put in a `</FRAMESET>` to denote I was done with breaking up the first column. Still with me? Good...let's go on.

Note that I did another `<FRAMESET>` flag denoting ROWS, but this time I set the rows at 33%, 33%, 33%. I then denoted SOURCES for those three rows in column two. I then added a `</FRAMESET>` to end those rows and another `</FRAMESET>` still to end the whole deal. Please note that I am going to show five different pages on the same browser screen. Still with me? Good.

FAQs from the HTML Goodies Web Site

Q. I get nothing! My frame pages are blank and I'm ready to throw this computer down the stairs.

A. Make sure everyone's out of the house before you go crazy. If the page comes up blank, it is probably one of two things: You either have a piece of code other than the `<TITLE>` commands before the `<FRAMESET>` command, or you are missing a `</FRAMESET>` command or two. You need one for every `<FRAMESET>` you open. You could also have misspelled something, but at this point I would assume you have checked that fully.

Q. The exact frame code works perfectly in Internet Explorer but loads a blank page in Navigator. Am I going nuts?

A. Yes, you are going nuts. Actually, you're getting caught in another of those wonderful differences between browsers. You will find that Navigator is far less forgiving than Internet Explorer. You have missed a </FRAMESET> command. Explorer didn't mind; Netscape decided to punish you.

Why Use Frames?

Good question, because frames have a few downfalls. First, they take longer to load than single pages, and they're a little hard to write. On the up side, they are fantastic for presenting information.

I'm not saying you need to use frames on every page, but if some of your pages are to show comparisons between items, frames are the way to go. They break up the page in attractive geometric patterns and offer nice page layouts. In addition, a frame page allows for some fun interaction between your viewer and your page. Imagine a list of links in a left frame that functions as a menu. Each time a user clicks an item in the left frame, what he or she requested comes up in the right frame. That's a good layout with good-looking interaction.

Here's how to get that interaction on your page...

Dynamics of Frames, Names, and Targets

The question now is how to control page changes in your frames. There are three basic methods of changing data within frames:

1. Click a link in a frame—just that frame changes pages.
2. Click a link in a frame—another frame on the screen receives the information.
3. Click a link in a frame—the frames go away and you get a full page.

Click a Link in a Frame—Just That Frame Changes Pages

This is the default. It happens without you doing a darn thing. If that's all you want, do nothing more than what you already know. Browsers are programmed to handle frame clicks just that way. The other two methods require a little more work.

Click a Link in a Frame—Another Frame on the Screen Receives the Information

Now we get into that useful effect I talked about before: Your user clicks an item in a menu frame and the page she requested shows up in another frame. Not only does it look good, but the effect is quite functional. The links are always visible, and you're only loading one new page rather than several through a whole new frames page.

Setting this up is basically a two-step process. First you have to create and name each frame. Then you create the HTML pages that appear in the frames. The links between the frames that cause the menu effect are on those HTML pages.

In this example you place a link in the page in frame A. When you click that link it loads a new page into frame C (see Figure 6.8). Now it's time to talk about two new commands: NAME and TARGET.

Figure 6.8

A three-frame page, before clicking the link in frame A.

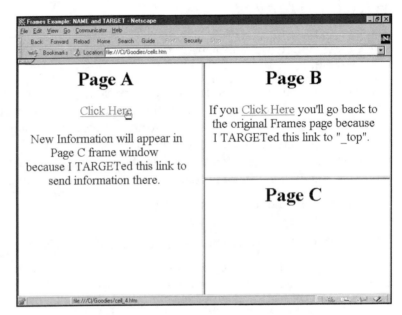

Here's the code that builds those three frames:

```
<FRAMESET COLS="50%, 50%">
  <FRAME NAME="A" SRC="PAGE_A.htm">
  <FRAMESET ROWS="50%, 50%">
    <FRAME NAME="B" SRC="PAGE_B.htm">
    <FRAME NAME="C" SRC="PAGE_C.htm">
  </FRAMESET>
</FRAMESET>
```

The frames must have names in order to send data from one frame to another. "Ah, ha!" you say, "That's the NAME deal." Bingo. Name them whatever you want, but I suggest you keep it simple, like capital letters. (I named mine A, B, and C.)

The second step is inserting the link in frame A's HTML page that will cause frame C to change. Here's the link code that must be inserted in cell_1.htm:

```
<A HREF="PAGE_D.htm" TARGET="C">Click Here</A>
```

See how the code is a normal hypertext link except the command `TARGET` is added to direct the output of the link? When you click this link on the page in frame A, it tells frame C to load `PAGE_D.htm` (see Figure 6.9).

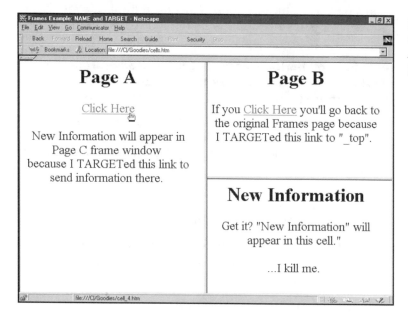

Figure 6.9
Clicking the page in frame A changes the page in frame C.

 If you like to try out target hypertext links and such firsthand, I've put together an extra tutorial for you at `http://www.htmlgoodies.com/book/frames.html`.

Completely Leaving a Frames Page

Now you can send information from one frame to another. One limitation to this approach is that you're ending up in a frame page—and some of the larger pages are squished inside a frame. Say you want to have someone click a link in a frame and have it go to a page that pops up in a full browser window. You have to tell it to do that. Remember: The default has the information stay in the same frame.

You need to `TARGET` the hypertext link to be its own page. Just follow the format discussed in the previous section, but make `TARGET="_Top"`. Note the underscore before the word *Top*. The code looks like this:

```
<A HREF="http://www.cbs.com" TARGET="_Top">
```

FAQs from the HTML Goodies Web Site

Q. I can't get that "_Top" target to work.

A. Netscape Navigator version 4 (or later) is the picky one. Is that the browser you're using? Even though HTML is not case sensitive, capitalizing the *T* in *Top* will fix the problem.

Q. I want people to be able to bookmark my page, but it has frames. How can I set it up so that even if the person goes three or four pages deep in the frames, it will always go to those pages?

A. You really can't because the page that is being bookmarked is the frame template page and it only calls for the pages that are on its code—the first two pages. It can be done, but you need to set it up so that a new frame template loads each time. It's not so bad, I've done it before.

What About People Who Don't Have Frame-Ready Browsers?

That's a problem. The browserly-challenged will get an error code if they attempt to log onto a page with frames; either that or they will receive a blank page. There are a couple of ways around it:

1. Don't do frames. (You could have guessed that one, I know.)

2. Write a page without any frames and offer a choice: Go to a framed page or go to a non-framed page. That means you have to write two sets of pages. Bummer.

3. Use <NOFRAMES> and </NOFRAMES> commands.

Tell me more about the <NOFRAMES> flag, you say? Well, it's simple. You write a basic frame page like any of the three listed previously, but immediately following the first <FRAMESET> flag you put in a <NOFRAMES> command and write a message to the browserly-challenged. Like so:

```
<FRAMESET COLS="50%,50%">
<NOFRAMES>

Greetings Browserly-Challenged. The page you are attempting to enter has frames,
and if you're reading this message—you don't have the ability to see it.
I suggest you go <A HREF="page.html">To my non-Frame version</A> of this page.
</NOFRAMES>

<FRAME SRC="PAGE_A.htm">
<FRAME SRC="PAGE_B.htm">
</FRAMESET>
</HTML>
```

The person who can't see frames gets the message and the person who can read frames gets the frame page. I should say here that you might also want to put an entire page's text between the <NOFRAME> flags. That way the page displays and the user doesn't have to click to go to a page he can read. I do it as it's shown earlier because I also like to offer links to browser home pages so people can download a frame-ready browser and get in on all the fun. Isn't technology wonderful?

I guess that wraps up the tutorial on frames. There are other commands you can use when creating frames; they create different margin sizes and such, but this tutorial was becoming a monolith. If you'd like to gather more information about frames, head to my advanced frames tutorial; it's next in line. It contains a few more tricks and bits of knowledge. Plus it's sugar free and low in fat.

Enjoy!

Advanced Frame Commands

So far we've only touched the surface of what you can accomplish with frames. This section tells you about some more sophisticated uses and shows you how to hide frames to make your Web page more visually appealing.

 For interactive examples of how frames work, check out `http://www.htmlgoodies.com/` `ad_frame.html`*. I have the tutorial set up so that one page fills all the cells (see Figure 6.10). I'll explain it all here in this book, along with a bunch of advanced commands. Seeing it in action might be easier for you than reading it here.*

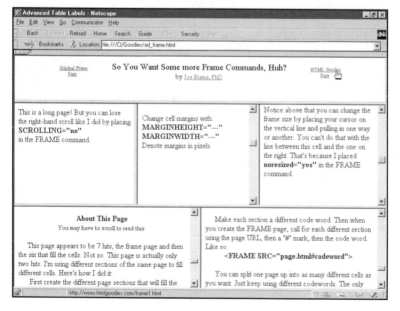

Figure 6.10
An interactive frames tutorial for this book.

Let's get started. To demonstrate these commands, I wrote a very simple frames code that simply splits the browser screen in half. Figure 6.11 displays the results of the code.

```
<FRAMESET COLS="50%,50%">
<FRAME SRC="PAGE_ONE.html">
<FRAME SRC="PAGE_TWO.html">
</FRAMESET>
```

Figure 6.11

A simple page with two frames.

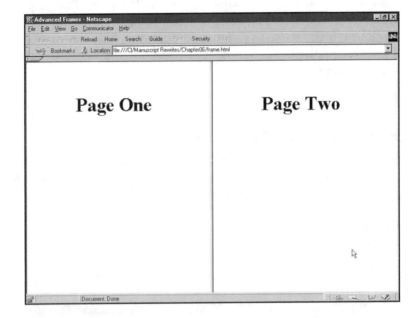

Resizing Frame Window Borders: BORDER="###"

Now you'll play with the frame window border itself. The frame window border in Figure 6.11 is the gray stripe down the center that splits the page. To adjust the size of the border, you use the BORDER="###" command, which goes inside the <FRAMESET> command:

```
<FRAMESET COLS="50%,50%" BORDER="50">
```

It affects each of the borders denoted by that particular <FRAMESET> command. If you have more than one <FRAMESET>, you can set the borders to different sizes. The preceding code sets the border to 50—that's huge (see Figure 6.12).

Changing the Space Between Frames

This command allows you to set a specific number of pixels between the frame windows. I find it acts a lot like the border command. Again, you can use it every time you use a new <FRAMESET> command.

```
FRAMESPACING="###"
```

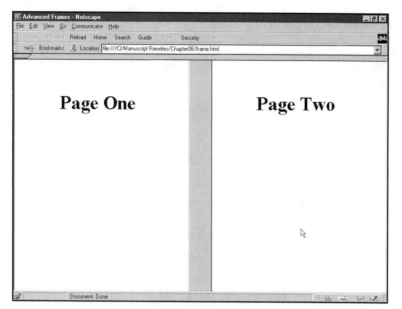

Figure 6.12
A frame border set to 50.

Figure 6.13 has the FRAMESPACING set to 700 pixels. Why? Because I can, that's why! Here's the code I used to get it:

```
<FRAMESET COLS="50%,50%" FRAMESPACING="700">
```

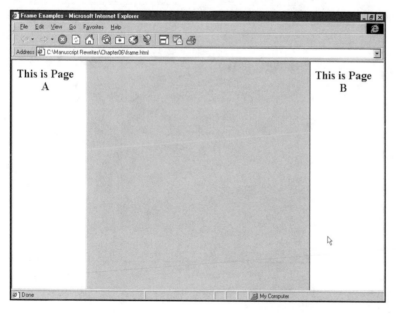

Figure 6.13
Using FRAMESPACING *to add space between frames.*

Changing Frame Window Margins

You can also change how much space surrounds the text on the top and bottom of your frames. It's a good way to add whitespace to the frames so that the text doesn't butt up against the border. Here are the commands you use:

- ● MARGINHEIGHT="###" sets the space above and below the text.
- ● MARGINWIDTH="###" sets the space on either side.

Both commands go inside the <FRAMESET> flag. Here's a <FRAMESET> using the two commands:

```
<FRAMESET COLS="50%,50%" MARGINHEIGHT="200" MARGINWIDTH="200">
```

That will set some pretty wide margins around the text. Remember that the numbers are in pixels. Again, you can set new margins each time you use a new <FRAMESET> flag.

Keeping Your Frame Window Borders in Place

Anyone visiting your Web site can put her mouse cursor on one of your frame borders and adjust its size by dragging the frame one way or another (see Figure 6.14).

Figure 6.14
Anyone can change your frame sizes by dragging them.

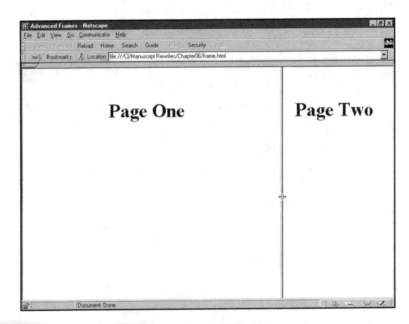

You can stop people from changing your frame sizes by placing a RESIZE="no" command in your FRAME flag. The <FRAMESET> will look like this:

```
<FRAMESET COLS="50%,50%" RESIZE="no">
```

This disallows the user from pulling your frame window borders. You can use this command every time you use a new <FRAMESET> command. You can also use this command inside the <FRAME SRC> command to disallow certain frame window borders from being altered.

To Offer or Not to Offer...A Scrollbar

You probably already know that you get a scrollbar when your page is longer than the browser screen is tall. It just happens without your asking for it. Browsers are nice that way.

Now we want to be in control. The layout of frames can be greatly disturbed if you have a scrollbar popping up in every other frame window. Here's the command that gives us the power:

```
SCROLLING="###"
```

This command can either be placed in the <FRAMESET> command where it affects everything under that command's umbrella, or in individual <FRAME SRC> commands where it affects just that frame window.

There are three settings for this command: "yes", "no", and "auto". You can guess what each one does.

"yes" provides a scrollbar whether you need one or not; "no" denies your use of a scrollbar whether you need one or not; "auto" gives you one when you need it. I actually see no need for the "auto" command. That's the same effect you get by using "no".

I've slightly changed the familiar example I've been using in this chapter to show how this one works. I have made page A very long by adding Blah..... The page is longer than the screen, but as you can see in Figure 6.15, there's no scrollbar; I set the left frame window to SCROLLING="no". The command looks like this:

```
<FRAME SRC="PAGE_A.html" SCROLLING="no">
```

Again, please note that I placed the command in <FRAME SRC>, not in <FRAMESET>. Figure 6.15 shows the result.

I often set my frames to disallow all scrollbars because I think a scrollbar popping up in the middle of a frames page looks bad. If you set the scroll to "no", you have to be very careful: Avoid creating pages that scroll farther than the size of the screen, and remember that many people have smaller screens than you do.

A Tip for Filling Multiple Frame Windows with One Page

Take a look at Figure 6.16. It appears to be seven different pages—the page that contains the frame code, and then the six individual frames. Not so. It is actually only two pages. I'm using different sections of the same page to fill in the different frames.

Figure 6.15
Eliminating scrollbars from your page.

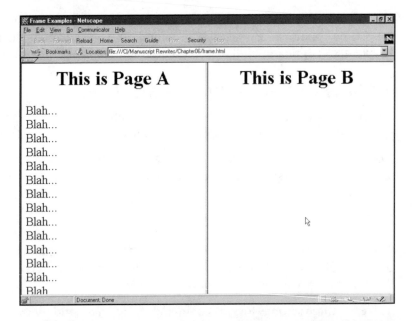

Figure 6.16
There are only two different HTML pages in this picture.

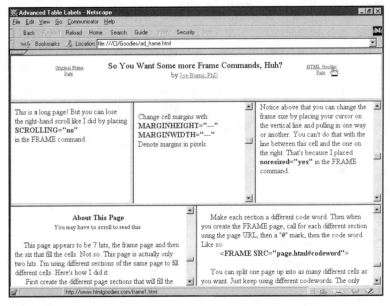

To do this, create the one single HTML page that contains all the text and graphics that you want inserted in the frames. Divide that page into the sections that you want displayed in the frames by marking each new section with this:

```
<A NAME="codeword">
```

Make each section a different *code word*. When you create the frame page, call for each different section using the page's URL, a pound sign (#), and then the code word. Like so:

```
<FRAME SRC="page.html#codeword">
```

You can split one page into as many different cells as you want; just keep using different code words. The only downfalls I've found are that you always get a scrollbar, and sometimes deleting the scrollbar eliminates the text. Try it for yourself and see what happens.

I put about 10 of these between each page section:

```
<P>
 
<P>
```

That little combination puts spaces between sections so that words don't bleed over from cell to cell.

Enjoy!

FAQs from the HTML Goodies Web Site

Q. I tried your trick of using one page to fill all of the frame windows, but now none of the hypertext links work. They keep loading in other frames and look terrible.

A. Remember that it's one page doing all the work, so you really can't change one frame window without changing all the others. My trick is best for displaying a lot of information in frames very quickly without loading seven different pages. I said it was cool, not the end all.

There's an example of a frame pages using all these commands. Try it out at http://www.htmlgoodes.com/book/advframes.html.

Seamless Frames

People have been writing and asking me how this is done for a while now. These seamless frames give a great look to the page. In addition, they also make a great sideline background, left or right. I'll give examples of each use, but first let's look into how it's done. Figure 6.17 shows you what I'm talking about.

This tutorial is online at http://www.htmlgoodies.com/seamless_frames.html.

Figure 6.17

Two seamless frames.

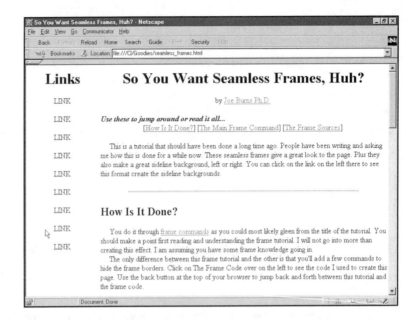

It's a nice clean look, with links on one side and the full screen on the other. The links in the left frame control the main window. It's a solid presentation.

You achieve it through frame commands, as you most likely gleaned from the title of the tutorial. You should make a point to first read and understand this chapter's first frame tutorial. I will not go into more than creating this effect; I am assuming you have some frame knowledge going in.

The only difference between this frame tutorial and the other is that with this one you add a few commands to hide the frame borders.

The Main Frame Command

I'll cover the remainder of the frame code in a moment. Right now I want to focus on the main <FRAMESET> flag. It looks like this:

```
<FRAMESET COLS="15%,*" FRAMEBORDER="0" FRAMESPACING="0" BORDER="0">
```

Notice I have done little more than add three commands—FRAMEBORDER, FRAMESPACING, and BORDER—and set them all to 0. It goes the other way, too. You can set the command to 50 to get really, really wide borders. We want seamless frames here, however.

There are two pages being displayed in the preceding example. The seamless effect is achieved because I have set the background color of the two source pages to white [#FFFFFF]. If I were to set the colors otherwise, the effect would be more of a sideline background; the seam would then be visible. Here's the exact same frame code as was just used. The only change I made was setting the background color of the page that loads in the left frame to blue (see Figure 6.18).

Figure 6.18
Two seamless frames showing pages with different background colors.

One other new thing—here's the main FRAMESET command from before:

```
<FRAMESET COLS="15%,*" FRAMEBORDER="0" FRAMESPACING="0" BORDER="0">
```

See the COLS="15%,*" in there, right after FRAMESET? That asterisk is a nice way to speed up your math skills: Put the asterisk in the second position. It does the 100% math for you. You can also use it for a right frame just by flipping it around: COLS="*,15%".

I have seen a great use of this format at the Van Halen News Desk (http://www.vhnd.com), where the colors appear to go from light to dark into the frame (see Figure 6.19).

I liked the band better when David Lee Roth was the lead singer. Moving along...

The Frame Sources

These are the commands that fill the frame windows:

```
<FRAME NAME="left" SRC="left.html" MARGINWIDTH="3" MARGINHEIGHT="10"
SCROLLING="no">
<FRAME NAME="main" SRC="mainwindow.html" MARGINWIDTH="3" MARGINHEIGHT="10">
```

The frame sources are the same as you have used in the past. Each is given a target name so that the links in the left side targets the information to the larger, right window. See the

191

original frame tutorial at the beginning of this chapter for more on how to target frame HREF links. Just as a quick refresher, the format for targeting a link in this frame setup would be as follows:

```
<A HREF="newpage.html" TARGET="main">Click Here</A>
```

Figure 6.19
Great seamless frames and blended background colors.

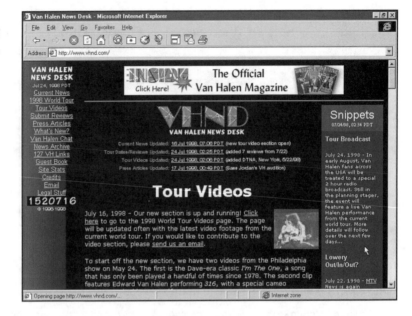

In the previous example I set the MARGINHEIGHT and MARGINWIDTH to my liking. You can play with the sizes to get the text closer or further from the actual seam. Any text centering is done on the source page itself by surrounding text with <CENTER> </CENTER>.

Notice also that a SCROLLING="no" command was added to the left frame to eliminate the scrollbar, should a visitor have his screen settings lower than you had hoped. A scrollbar would kill the entire effect.

FAQs from the HTML Goodies Web Site

Q. You said to not have a scrollbar on the left frame window, but on some screens the links I have go off the bottom and people cannot get to them. What should I do?

A. I know you would like me to say to use the scrollbar, but I won't. That kills the effect and two scrollbars is not good page design. My suggestion is to lessen your links—either make them smaller or make fewer of them so that they do fit on the small-screen browsers.

As long as all of your links are on your site you have control in terms of background color, text size, and image width, but if an outside page comes through one of your links and has a different background (or the like), the effect dies. I'd be rather picky about what links will be used in this format. I would make the link to anything you don't have control over open a new browser window or target the output of the HREF link to "_top"; that way the page opens in a full browser screen with no frames.

That should do it. The effect can be compounded by adding more frames to the mix. You could create many seamless connections. The problem comes when you shift the pages or link to a new page—that pesky scrollbar shows up and it's all defeated. I would stick with the lowest number of frames you need in this format.

Enjoy!

 Go to http://www.htmlgoodies.com/book/seamless.html *for a couple examples of seamless frames in action.*

Changing Multiple Frame Cells

 You can see multiple frames in action by going to http://www.htmlgoodies.com/ 2atonce.html. *Go see it. It's fun to watch it happen.*

What we're doing here is allowing your user to change the content in more than one frame window with one click. You already know how to use TARGET commands to get this effect in one frame window. Now we'll set it up so that one click changes many windows. Figure 6.20 shows what you start with.

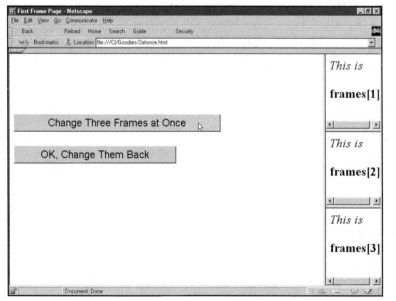

Figure 6.20
Before clicking the Change Three Frames at Once button.

And now for my first trick: The pointer in Figure 6.21 is poised on the Change Three Frames at Once button (insert drum roll sound effect). When I click one I get the results shown in Figure 6.21.

Figure 6.21

The results after clicking the Change Three Frames at Once button.

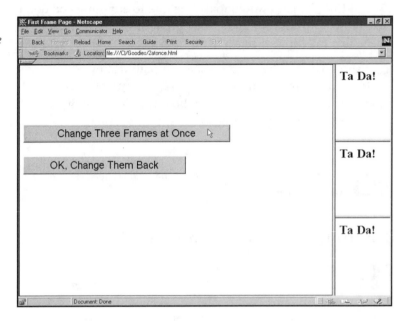

(Insert cymbal crash sound effect.) I clicked the OK, Change Them Back button and restored the original frames shown in Figure 6.20.

Good trick, huh? Unlike the true magicians, I will reveal my trick to you. I am using some simple JavaScript commands to change the three frames to the right. (By the way, if JavaScript is new to you, keep reading. I'll get you through this tutorial, and then you can read more about JavaScript in Chapter 11, "Java Applets and JavaScript.")

We need to start with the code I created to make these four little frame cells:

```
<FRAMESET cols="85%,15%">
  <FRAME SRC="zippy1.html" NAME="A">
  <FRAMESET rows="33%,33%,33%">
      <FRAME SRC="zippy2.html" NAME="B">
      <FRAME SRC="zippy3.html" NAME="C">
      <FRAME SRC="zippy4.html" NAME="D">
  </FRAMESET>
</FRAMESET>
```

Please note that the pages that appear in the three smaller windows are named zippy2, zippy3, and zippy4. But in Figure 6.20, I labeled them frames[1], frames[2], and frames[3]. There is a reason for that—keep reading.

Look at the code. See how there are four frame cells? I have given them the names "A" through "D", in case I want to target any of my HREF link outputs. What you may not already know is that the frames had names before I named them. The browser already has "ordered" them for you.

Frame Order

When displayed, frames are given number names in the order they appear in the code.

The numbers, however, do not start with 1. They start with 0. Look to the right side of Figures 6.20 and 6.21. See how they are named frames[1], frames[2], and frames[3]? That's how the browser sees them. Where's frames[0]? That's the large frame on the left. Here's how the frames break down using the preceding code:

```
<FRAMESET cols="85%,15%">
<FRAME SRC="zippy1.html" NAME="A"> This is frames[0]
<FRAMESET rows="33%,33%,33%">
<FRAME SRC="zippy2.html" NAME="B"> This is frames[1]
<FRAME SRC="zippy3.html" NAME="C"> This is frames[2]
<FRAME SRC="zippy4.html" NAME="D"> This is frames[3]
</FRAMESET>
</FRAMESET>
```

See how the frame windows are numbered starting with 0? Please also note that the word used is *frames* with an *s*. There are more than one. Forgetting the *s* will mess up the whole deal. Now that you know that, go on to use it to your advantage by changing multiple cells.

FAQs from the HTML Goodies Web Site

Q. Your tutorial on changing multiple frames at once is interesting, but why go to all that trouble when you can just load a new frame template page and get the same effect?

A. Mine's faster. It also requires only the new pages to load. Your method will work just fine, but it takes longer and taxes the server more than it should. That said, yours makes it easier to bookmark specific pages in the frame windows.

Here's the command I used to change the three cells:

```
<FORM>
<INPUT TYPE="button" Value="Change Three Frames at Once"
onClick="parent.frames[1].location='zippy5.html';
parent.frames[2].location='zippy6.html';
parent.frames[3].location='zippy7.html';">
</FORM>
```

Here's a breakdown of the code:

- `<FORM>` tells the browser a form type is going here.
- `INPUT TYPE="button"` is does what its name implies.
- `VALUE=` denotes what will be written on the button itself.
- `onClick=` denotes that what follows should happen when the button is clicked. Please keep the capitalization on the letter *C*.
- `parent.frames[1].location='zippy5.html';` is the JavaScript command that does the trick for you.
- `"parent"` is the main page, the frame page.
- `"frames[1]"` is the frame that will be affected.
- `"location='###'"` denotes what fills the frame when clicked. In this case it's pages called `zippy5`, `zippy6`, and `zippy7`.

  Please make note of the semicolon (;) at the end of each frame command line. Without it, you will get errors like crazy.
- `</FORM>` ends the entire deal.

You can add as many or as few of the location commands as you want. If you have 20 frames, you can change them all with one click. Just make sure to add a new `parent.frames[#].location='###';` for each one. However, you only need one `onClick` command.

Let me also caution you that the quotation marks surrounding the location page are single. There are double quotation marks surrounding the run of `parent.frames[#].location='###';` commands. Make sure you get the quote marks right, or errors galore.

Well, there you go. As many frames as you can write—that's how many you can change with the click of a button. Good luck with this, but remember that when you are reloading multiple frames, you are loading multiple pages. The process may be very slow. If you use this function, do your best to offer low-byte pages for the shortest loading time.

Enjoy!

 Go to `http://www.htmlgoodies.com/book/coupleframes.html` *and you'll see another example. You'll also see how to lose the button and do it simply through a blue-letter hypertext link.*

Frames Border Color

Well, I guess the HTML Goodies Web readers really want to know how to do this. The number of letters lately has been huge; I guess colored frames are the "in" thing as of late.

Used correctly, adding color to frame window borders can look great. Better yet? They're super simple.

See the green frame in Figure 6.20? I made it by adding the command BORDERCOLOR="###" to the main <FRAMESET> command. I set the color to lime green. It looks awful, but makes the point.

You can get multiple colors across different frame windows, but you can only do it if you are using multiple <FRAMESET> commands. For instance, if you have your main <FRAMESET> breaking the page into two areas, you can change that border color by following the method outlined earlier.

You can use another color if you then add a second FRAMESET command to break one of the columns into smaller sections.

Enjoy!

FAQs from the HTML Goodies Web Site

Q. Can I set only some frame window walls to color and leave the others without?

A. Yes—if you use multiple <FRAMESET> commands. That way you can set some of the frame borders to a specific color and the rest to "#c0c0c0", their default color. You'll be setting their color, but the computer will think you've done nothing.

Chapter 7

Adding Link Buttons and Forms

Link Buttons

You know that the World Wide Web is held together through a series of hypertext links, or, as a student of mine called it, "A web of blue words." Actually, that's not a bad way of putting it.

Now it's possible for you to use hex codes to change the color of the links and visited links (see Chapter 1, "Playing with Text," for more on that). You can also make an image clickable by placing it in the hypertext anchor command (see Chapter 3, "Adding Images and Backgrounds"). You can also make an imagemap (see Chapter 4, "Creating Imagemaps").

In this chapter I show you an easy way to make your own link button, with your own wording—a nice, classy departure from all the blue words.

Figure 7.1 shows a typical link button.

If you click that thing it will jump you to a new page. Plus, the button moves when you click it! Movement! Cool!

I really think these buttons look professional, and they're not all that tough to make. Contrary to what some of you new to HTML might think, the button shown in the figure is not an image (like a .gif or a .jpeg). It is made through FORM commands.

Figure 7.1
A clickable button.

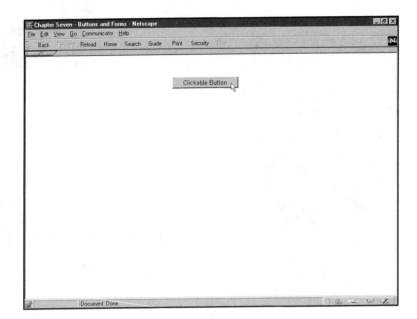

How to Make a Link Button

Here are the commands I used to place the button in Figure 7.1:

```
<FORM METHOD="link" ACTION="http://www.htmlgoodies.com/page1.htm">
<INPUT TYPE="submit" VALUE="Clickable Button">
</FORM>
```

The first command, FORM, has three parts. Here's what each means:

- FORM tells the computer a form item is going here.
- METHOD tells the computer how to handle the FORM command. In this case, you are making a link.
- ACTION denotes what connection you want to make. I made a connection to something called page1.htm at http://www.htmlgoodies.com.

Note

When using these buttons, make links using the entire URL. For example, http://www.etc.etc.etc.

The second command, INPUT, places the button. It has two parts:

- INPUT TYPE tells what type of input will occur (duh!).

- `submit` indicates just what it implies. In this case you want to "submit" something. You see, the `FORM` command is looking for a link—you are "submitting" a link. Get it?
- `VALUE` is the wording that appears on the button.

And finally, end the whole deal with this:

```
</FORM>
```

What About That "?" Mark????

Don't look for the question mark on the page shown in Figure 7.1—it isn't there. The question mark shows up when you use one of these link buttons on your page. Let's say you create a link button that goes to my site, HTML Goodies (`http://www.htmlgoodies.com`).

After you click your button to go to the site, the address in the browser's location bar will read as such:

```
http://www.htmlgoodies.com?
```

Just make sure you place a slash after the end of the URL you are jumping to:

```
<FORM METHOD="link" ACTION="http://www.htmlgoodies.com/">
<INPUT TYPE="submit" VALUE="Clickable Button">
</FORM>
```

See the slash after the end of the address? That eliminates the computer adding that silly question mark, which makes the link bad.

There is one other concern when dealing with these form buttons and their question mark additions. You can only move forward, linking to a page. If you use a link button to go to a page and then try to use another link button to go back, it can cause trouble with the question mark. You'll get an error that says the page `"?"` doesn't exist.

You would think there's a way to rid yourself of the question mark, but not so. I've experimented endlessly and I've asked four different Webmasters who had no idea how to get rid of it. I take great comfort in that.

Enjoy!

Lining Up Link Buttons

You need to separate the link buttons in order to get them to line up and point at different places. You have to make it so the other buttons don't know that other buttons are on the same page. Sounds covert, huh? It's a rather simple idea, but it does get a bit involved; you separate the buttons using table commands. You can read all about tables in Chapter 5, "All About Tables."

Some of the newer browsers (version 4 and later) allow you to separate the buttons with a simple <P> command. However, keep in mind that not everyone on the WWW is using the highest browser. You will do a little more work if you follow the table format I am about to describe, but you will be more certain the buttons will work on all browser levels.

Using tables also allows you greater control over page layout.

Figure 7.2 shows several link buttons all lined up in a neat row. They all work and they all go to different pages.

Figure 7.2
Clickable buttons all lined up.

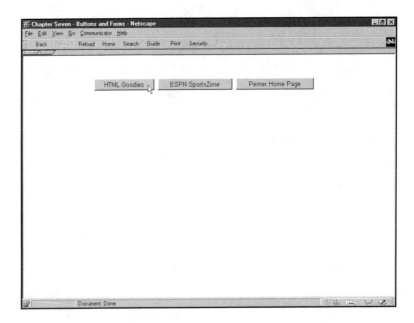

Here's the code that lines up the buttons:

```
<TABLE BORDER="0">
<TR>
<TD><FORM METHOD="LINK" ACTION="http://www.htmlgoodies.com/">
<INPUT TYPE="submit" VALUE="HTML Goodies">
</FORM></TD>
<TD><FORM METHOD="LINK" ACTION="http://espnet.sportszone.com/">
<INPUT TYPE="submit" VALUE="ESPN SportsZone">
</FORM></TD>
<TD><FORM METHOD="LINK" ACTION="http://www.perrier.com/">
<INPUT TYPE="submit" VALUE="Perrier Home Page">
</FORM></TD>
</TR>
</TABLE>
```

Here's a play-by-play:

- TABLE BORDER="0" tells the browser a table format will go here. The BORDER="0" part just tells the browser to place no defining lines around the cells you create.
- TD stands for table data. It denotes the information that will go in the individual table cell. In this case, the data will be a form button.
- TR stands for table row. It denotes the beginning of a new row of table cells.
- <FORM> through </FORM> is the form button format explained in the form button.
- </Table> wraps up the whole deal.

If you want to line up your link buttons vertically, as is done in Figure 7.3, you only have to make a couple of additions to the code already discussed.

Figure 7.3
Stacked, clickable buttons.

Here's the code that aligns the buttons vertically:

```
<TABLE BORDER="0">
<TR>
<TD ALIGN="center"><FORM METHOD="LINK" ACTION="http://www.htmlgoodies.com/">
<INPUT TYPE="submit" VALUE="HTML Goodies">
</FORM></TD>
</TR>
<TR>
<TD ALIGN="center"><FORM METHOD="LINK" ACTION="http://espnet.sportszone.com/">
<INPUT TYPE="submit" VALUE="ESPN SportsZone">
```

```
</FORM></TD>
</TR>
<TR>
<TD ALIGN="center"><FORM METHOD="LINK" ACTION="http://www.perrier.com/">
<INPUT TYPE="submit" VALUE="Perrier Home Page">
</FORM></TD>
</TR>
</TABLE>
```

Notice that I just added a couple of `<TR>` and `ALIGN="center"` commands. The `ALIGN="center"` command is my preference, you don't need it in order for them to be up and down. If you leave it out, the buttons will be left-aligned.

You can align the buttons in just about any order. How they line up is not the table cells' real use, although it helps a good deal. Their real use is to separate the buttons, so they work apart from each other. Just enter the button's commands as table data.

Again, later browser versions allow for easier separation, but I suggest following this format. This ensures that the buttons work across different browser versions; in addition, the tables allow you a lot more control over page layout.

May you have many buttons.

Enjoy!

Simple Forms

Forms are a good idea. A form does basically what email does—it sends information. Forms also look professional when you allow Net surfers to enter information right to your page, rather than using a `mailto:` command.

Please be advised that at the moment, only MS Explorer browser version 4.0 supports the `mailto:` command in terms of forms. The form commands will work in Internet Explorer. You get the elements to appear on the page, but Internet Explorer does not recognize all the form commands as one item, a guestbook for instance, the way Netscape Navigator does.

The First Step to Building a Form

The first thing you must tell the computer is that you are starting a form and what you want done with the form data. The command is as follows:

```
<FORM METHOD="POST" ACTION="mailto:your email address">
```

The command did three things:

1. It told the computer a `FORM` was starting.

2. It stated that the METHOD of dealing with the form data is to POST it.

3. The data should be posted to your email address through the ACTION="mailto:*your email address*" command.

Remember that you need to put your email address immediately after the mailto:, without a space. This is where the results of the form will be sent.

That's nice and simple. Now that the computer knows a form has begun, it's looking for any one of a number of form styles to deal with. I will go over five here: TEXT, TEXT AREA, RADIO BUTTON, CHECKBOX, and POP-UP BOX. These are, by far, the most used on the WWW.

The Text Box Form

This is a basic, long box that allows for one line of text (see Figure 7.4). When placed on a page, your reader will be able to type in information such as her name or email address.

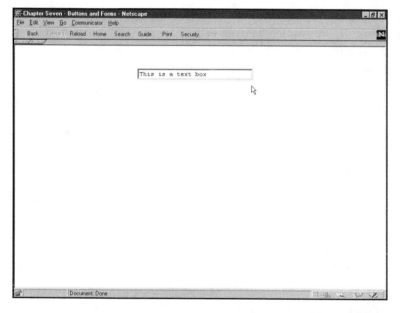

Figure 7.4
A text box.

You may have to click the box to activate it, but it works. If this is your first time making forms, you might think that the box is a .gif or a .jpeg. Not so. The box is placed on the page via HTML, not as an image. This is the command that places it on the page:

```
<FORM METHOD="POST" ACTION="mailto:your email address">
<INPUT TYPE="text" NAME="name" SIZE="30">
</FORM>
```

You already know what the <FORM> and </FORM> commands do. There are three parts to the text box command:

- INPUT TYPE tells the computer that a form item is going to be placed here. Remember when you placed the command to alert the computer that form items will be placed on this page? Well, here's your first form item. This form type is text.

- NAME= is where you define the name you assign to the box. Remember that this is a form that will be sent to you through the mail. When you receive the mail, it won't be just like the page. Only the text will arrive, so you have to denote what each piece of text will be. When the mail arrives from this text box, it will say NAME=*(whatever is written in the box)*.

  That way you know this information was written in the box marked *name*. Also remember that you don't have to call the box *name*—call it whatever you want. It will come to you with that name. If you're using the box to get the reader's name, call it name. If you're using the box to get the reader's email address, call it email.

  You can extend what text you use in the NAME="###" section by separating words by an underscore (_). For example, if you wanted to write something more specific than "*name*" in the preceding example, you could use:

  ```
  NAME="name_of_person_writing_from_my_web_page"
  ```

  It will work just fine; just make sure you use an underscore between each word. Underscore, good! Spaces, bad.

- SIZE denotes how many characters long this box will be. Make it 60 or 100 if you'd like. I've found that 30 is usually a good size for people entering text. You should understand that you can also "force" an answer this way. Let's say you are asking for a zip code: You could reinforce that by only making the text box seven spaces wide. If you are interested in a state but only want the two-letter code, only offer two spaces. It won't always work, but it does help.

The Text Area Box Form

This is a larger box, like the one before, that allows your reader to enter text. The difference between the text box (earlier) and the text area (this example) is that the text box only allows for one line. The text area, however, is much larger and will allow for as many words as you want. Take a gander at Figure 7.5.

Neat, huh? Go ahead and write in it; it'll work. You may have to click the box to activate it. Here's the command that made it appear:

```
<FORM METHOD="POST" ACTION="mailto:your email address">
<TEXTAREA NAME="comment" ROWS=6 COLS=40>
</TEXTAREA></FORM>
```

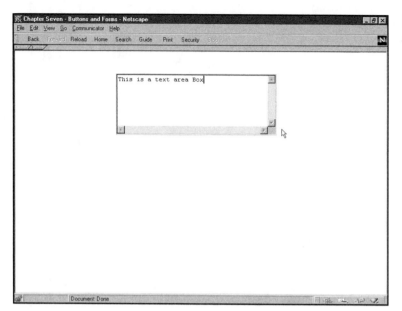

Figure 7.5
A text area box.

Please note that <TEXTAREA> requires a </TEXTAREA> flag, whereas the <TEXT BOX> flag does not. Here are its parts and what they mean:

- TEXTAREA yells to the FORM command that here will sit another form item. This one will be a text area box.

- NAME is the same as before. The reader information in this box arrives in your email box denoted by the name you use. In this case, what is written in this box will arrive in your email box with the word comment. Again, this can be as involved as you like, just separate the words with underscores.

- ROWS tells the computer how many rows of text it will accept.

- COLS tells the computer how many characters will be in each row. This text box will accept 6 rows of text, 40 characters each. Go ahead and make the box bigger or smaller. You're in charge here.

The Radio Button Form

This is a neat little deal that places a circle on the page. That circle is active and a reader can use the mouse to click it. When the radio button is chosen, it darkens. Figure 7.6 shows three radio buttons.

I have three of them there to prove a point, and it's not that I prefer hamburgers! The point is that radio buttons are a one-choice deal only. Only one button can be selected when you use radio buttons. When another is selected, the first one becomes unselected. Go ahead. Try it.

Figure 7.6
Three radio buttons.

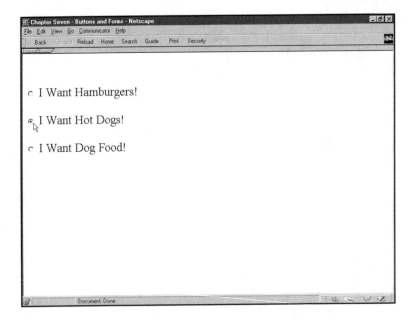

Why are they called radio buttons? They act as the radio buttons used in older car radios. When you pushed one, the dial moved. When you pushed another, the first button popped out and the dial moved to your new choice. You're probably too young to remember. It was back when only AM was a big selling radio, back before dirt. Here's the command for placing a radio buttons on your page:

```
<FORM METHOD="POST" ACTION="mailto:your email address">
<INPUT TYPE="radio" NAME="I_want_to_eat" VALUE="hamburgers"> I Want Hamburgers!<p>
<INPUT TYPE="radio" NAME=" I_want_to_eat " VALUE="hot_dogs"> I Want Hot Dogs!<P>
<INPUT TYPE="radio" NAME=" I_want_to_eat " VALUE="dog_food"> I Want Dog Food!
</FORM>
```

The radio button form command is long, but it's not that difficult to understand. Here are its four parts and what they mean:

- TYPE tells the computer what type of form item it will be. In this case, it's a radio button.
- NAME indicates the category the button is in on your form page. The example asks people to choose one of three foods. All the foods fall under the NAME of "I_want_to_eat". That's the radio buttons' group heading.
- VALUE is the name assigned to the button. Notice the choice of hamburgers has a value of "hamburgers", and so on.

Why on earth would I want to label all those buttons with different names?

Remember that this is going to be sent to you through email. You have to be able to read what the person chose. Say you had a guestbook with a section of radio buttons asking which page the user is signing in from. Your NAME in the command might be "signing_in_from". Each of the radio buttons is assigned the VALUE of each of your pages. Say a person chooses the radio button assigned to your home page. That button's VALUE might be "home_page."

Thus, when the form arrives to you, the email would read signing_in_from_home_page.

If the hamburger button in the food example is chosen, the text that arrives in your email box would read I_want_to_eat hamburgers.

Pretty darn slick, huh?

The Check Box Form

The check box is pretty much a clone of the radio button except for two features (see Figure 7.7):

- The item it places on the page is square and is marked with an X when chosen.
- You can check as many as you'd like.

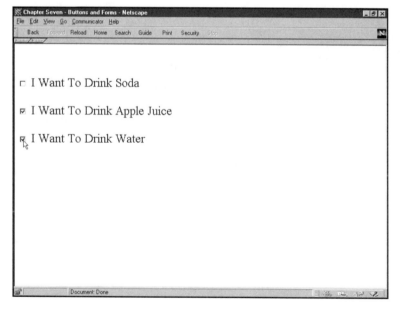

Figure 7.7
A few check boxes.

You'll note that you can chose one, several, or all of the check boxes. I've chosen two in the this example. This check box is basically a fancy radio button. Here's what placed the check boxes on the page:

```
<FORM METHOD="POST" ACTION="mailto:your email address">
<INPUT TYPE="checkbox" NAME="I_want_to_drink" VALUE="soda">
I Want To Drink Soda!<p>
<INPUT TYPE="checkbox" NAME="I_want_to_drink" VALUE="apple_juice">
I Want To Drink Apple Juice!<P>
<INPUT TYPE="checkbox" NAME="I_want_to_drink" VALUE="water">
I Want To Drink Water!
</FORM>
```

Each of the items mean the same as they did for the radio button form, so there's no need to go over them again. Please note, however, the TYPE is now checkbox instead of radio.

Remember that when the text from a check box arrives at your email box, the output from every box the user checks shows up. It can fill up your email pretty quickly. With radio buttons, only one item under each NAME heading arrives. With check boxes, every item can be checked; thus, every item can arrive.

I like radio buttons much more than check boxes. The reason is that the radio button forces a choice. Check boxes invite people to check everything every time. That can waste your time reading through it all. I like to make a one-choice deal. It's easier on me and if people want to leave more information or ask questions, there's always the TEXT AREA box for that purpose.

The Drop-Down Box Form

I love these drop-down boxes, but I don't use them too often. I like to have all the items people can choose out in the open. The drop-down box, unless clicked, only shows one item. But this is your form and you can do anything you want. Figure 7.8 shows a drop-down box; you have to click it to see all the choices. This one is for people to choose their favorite color.

Here are the commands that placed the drop-down box on the page:

```
<FORM METHOD="POST" ACTION="mailto:your email address">
My favorite color is: <SELECT NAME="Favorite_Color" SIZE="1">
<OPTION SELECTED>Blue
<OPTION>Red
<OPTION>Yellow
<OPTION>Green
<OPTION>Black
<OPTION>Orange
<OPTION>Purple
</SELECT>
</FORM>
```

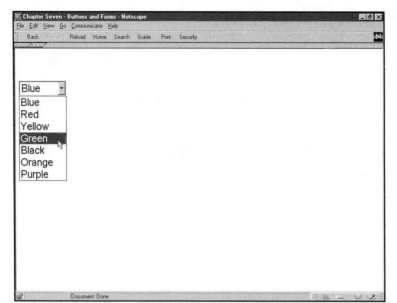

Figure 7.8
A drop-down box.

Although this looks a little bit more involved, it really isn't. It's the same thing again and again. Here are the parts and what they mean:

- SELECT tells the computer another form is going here. This time it's a selection, or drop-down form.

- NAME means the same thing it always means. This is the heading of the form item. It denotes how the results of the reader will arrive at your email box. In this case it will say Favorite_Color= and then the reader's choice.

- SIZE denotes the size of the box. Here, 1 means one line or item is shown. Try putting 2 there if you'd like to see what it does. I prefer 1; more than one item tends to defeat the purpose of the drop-down box.

- OPTION SELECTED denotes which option will appear in the box. Note in the figure that Blue is the first item in the list. Blue would be visible before you click the drop-down box. You may want to avoid using an item someone can choose in this position, but rather something that reads Click to Choose, or words to that effect, to provide the user more instruction.

- OPTION denotes another choice that will be visible when you click the item.

- </SELECT> finishes the entire deal.

Send and Reset Buttons for Your Forms

Now that you have placed all the form items you want on your page, you need a way to have the results sent to your email box (or wherever you said this would go in the original form statement). You should also give your Web visitors a way to quickly erase the information they've entered in your forms. To do these two things, you'll create Send and Reset buttons for your forms (see Figure 7.9).

Figure 7.9

Submit Query and Reset buttons.

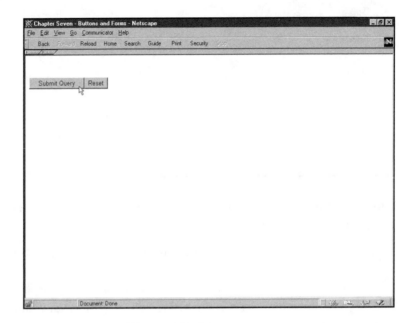

Here are the commands that put the buttons on the page:

```
<FORM METHOD="POST" ACTION="mailto:your email address">
<INPUT TYPE="submit"><INPUT TYPE="reset">
</FORM>
```

Easy, huh? Now when you click the buttons, the form will enact the ACTION you noted in the original FORM command. In this case it would have been mailed to my email box.

If you would like to put your own words on the Submit and Reset buttons, add VALUE="####" to the previous commands:

```
<INPUT TYPE="submit" VALUE="Click to Send It!">
&ltINPUT TYPE="reset" VALUE="Wait! Start over.">
```

Finally!

Make sure you end your form with this:

```
</FORM>
```

That's a beginning on forms, but you can do much more than what I have described here. There are forms with which you can connect to Common Gateway Interfaces (CGIs), databases, or other data-collection devises. All I wanted to do here is give you a very basic, very easy form for you to use on your Web pages. I believe I have; now off to help others. Thank you citizen.

Enjoy!

Creating a Guestbook

I get a great many emails asking me to put up a tutorial on making a guestbook. Here it is! I will go over three different types of guestbooks: Simple `mailto:` guestbooks, guestbooks that offer a page thanking the person for writing, and guestbooks that post what your visitors write to a separate page.

A Basic Guestbook

We'll start at the beginning. Figure 7.10 shows a simple guestbook.

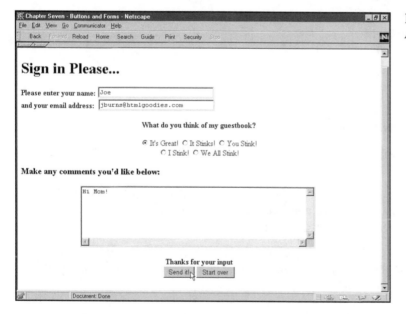

Figure 7.10
A simple guestbook.

This is the program that created the guestbook. Just copy it from here:

```
<H1> Sign in Please...</H1>
<FORM METHOD="POST" ACTION="mailto:user@writemehere.com">
```

```
<B>Please enter your name: </B><INPUT NAME="username" size="30"> <BR>
<B>and your email address: </B><INPUT Name="usermail" size="30">
<p>
<CENTER>
<B>what do you think of my guestbook?</B>
<P>
<INPUT TYPE="radio" NAME=I_think_that VALUE="It's_Great">It's Great!
<INPUT TYPE="radio" NAME=I_think_that VALUE="It_stinks">It Stinks!
<INPUT TYPE="radio" NAME=I_think_that VALUE="You_stink">You Stink!
<BR>
<INPUT TYPE="radio" NAME=I_think_that VALUE="I_stink">I Stink!
<INPUT TYPE="radio" NAME=I_think_that VALUE="We_all_stink">We All Stink!
<P>
</CENTER>
<H3>Make any comments you'd like below:</H3>
<CENTER>
<TEXTAREA NAME="comment" ROWS=6 COLS=60></TEXTAREA>
<P>
<B>Thanks for your input</B>
<BR>
<INPUT TYPE=submit VALUE="Send it!">
<INPUT TYPE=reset VALUE="Start over">
</CENTER>
</FORM>
```

Simple `Mailto`: *Guestbooks*

What you have in the preceding code is a very simple guestbook set up using two text boxes, five radio buttons, and a text area.

If all you want is a simple guestbook that sends mail to you, boom—you're done. Just cut and paste the guestbook to a page, place your email address where it says `user@writemehere.com` and put it up for the world to use.

This approach only works with Netscape-style browsers and Explorer 4.0. Earlier Explorer browsers do not recognize this as a form working with a `mailto:` command. It simply puts up the email box as if it was a regular `mailto:` HREF command.

- There is no confirmation of sent mail.
- The text arrives as one long line, like so: `Hello+I'm/+very=glad/=to=meet+you. +/ I+like+/your+%guestbook.$`. You can read it, but it's tough.
- The mail arrives as an attachment labeled a `.dat` file.

The .dat file suffix stands for data. It has to be opened in a text editor or after changing the suffix to .txt. You may be able to alter this in your email program. There is often a configuration you can alter that puts attachment right into the email body. Look through your configuration settings for that.

Augmenting Your Guestbook Output

Here are a couple of commands you might want to play around with. The first helps you read the email that arrives in your box. Add enctype="text/plain" to your FORM command. It will look like this:

```
<FORM METHOD="post" ACTION="mailto:your email address" enctype="text/plain">
```

In most cases, that delineates the mail and sets it to plain text. The output of the guestbook should then look something like this:

```
NAME = Joe Burns
EMAIL = jburns@htmlgoodies.com
COMMENT = Hi Mom!
```

Wouldn't it be great if you could set up your guestbook so that the subject line were filled out automatically? That way you would immediately know where the mail came from. If you had multiple guestbooks, you could keep better track of where people were writing you from. Well, here's how you do it:

```
<FORM METHOD="post" ACTION="mailto:jburns@htmlgoodies.com?subject=
This appears in your email's subject line" enctype="text/plain">
```

I used my personal email address for this example; you would put your email address in place of mine. After the email address, I just added a question mark, the word subject, the equal sign, and the text I wanted to appear in the subject line of the email.

It's not necessary to have underscores in the text for the subject line. Also notice the patter of quotation marks. There is no quotation mark before the subject line text. Just follow the pattern given here.

FAQs from the HTML Goodies Web Site

Q. Can I make it so that the guestbook sends mail to two different addresses?

A. You mean like a CC? Yes, in some cases. Many later browsers allow you to post as many email addresses as you'd like, as long as you separate them by commas (with no spaces).

Guestbooks with Virtual Pages

This is a guestbook that allows the viewer to fill in information. When the viewer sends the form data, another page pops up, thanking the viewer for the input. The viewer must then select Back to return to the main page.

 My current guestbook is this kind. You can see it in action, online at http:// www.htmlgoodies.com/feedback.html.

Sending the user to a virtual page is done by attaching a guestbook form's email output to a CGI. A CGI is a small program, usually written in Perl, Java, or C++ computer languages, that does little tricks.

It gets a little involved, but fear not. I have full instructions, just not right here.

For instructions on how to attach your guestbook to a CGI, see Chapter 12, "Common Gateway Interface (CGI)." It is a tutorial that gives you the HTML document, the CGI, and instructions on how to get them both up and running on your server.

Image Submit Buttons

Here's an example of what I'm talking about: Figure 7.11 shows a simple form. However, instead of a link button starting it off, the user clicks an image.

Figure 7.11
A guestbook with an image submit button.

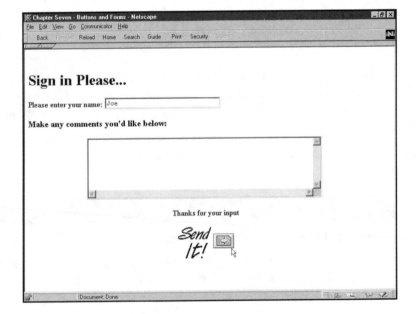

There's no need to show you how the form is made. I go over that in the forms and the guestbook tutorials. What I am concerned with here is the input button. Here's the format I used to make the button:

```
<INPUT TYPE="image" SRC="hgbutt.gif" HEIGHT="24" WIDTH="129"
 BORDER=0 ALT="picture button">
```

Notice it's the same format at the normal link button, except instead of the type being SUBMIT, it's now IMAGE. The SRC has to be added to call for the image; the HEIGHT, WIDTH, BORDER, and ALT commands define the image for the browser and lose the blue border that comes with an active image link.

I hope you can use this in your own pages.

Enjoy!

So You Want a Searchable Database, Huh?

I am asked this question time and time again: "How do I set up a searchable database?" There are actually a few different ways. Some are harder than others.

Here's a quick look at the three main methods.

Search Someone Else's Database

Ever been at a page and the author invites you to search Yahoo! or Webcrawler right from his or her own page? You think this person must pretty high up the ladder to be able to pull off this kind of deal. Not really—anyone can do it. Figure 7.12 shows an example of a page on my site that allows you to search three different search engine databases.

Actually, I lied (and I may lie later). Even if you were to use the items and search Yahoo!, my site didn't actually perform the searches. The search was done by Yahoo!. I just allowed you to initiate the search from my home page. When you get your results, you would no longer be in Kansas Goodies anymore—you would have been transported to the Yahoo! site. If this seems a bit confusing, hang in there. All I am doing is allowing you to search Yahoo! from my page.

Let's look at the code I used to create the Yahoo! search:

```
<FORM ACTION="http://search.yahoo.com/bin/search">
<INPUT SIZE=30 name=p>
<INPUT TYPE=submit value="Search">
</FORM>
```

It's a simple set of FORM commands, set up much like you would to create a link button or a simple mailto: guestbook. However, in this case you are using the form to send the information contained within the text box to a search engine. That's what you call the actual program that searches the Yahoo! database, a *search engine*. In the previous example you are sending the info to Yahoo!'s CGI bin to be worked on by something called *search*.

Figure 7.12
Various search engines.

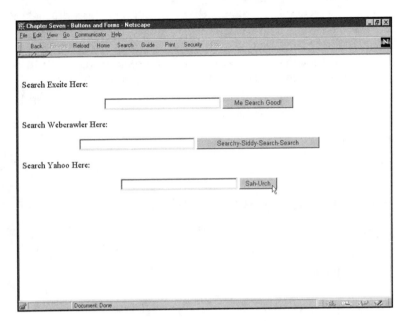

Here are the Webcrawler and Excite lines:

```
<FORM NAME="wcsearchform" ACTION="http://webcrawler.com/cgi-bin/WebQuery"
 METHOD="GET">
<FORM NAME="search" ACTION="http://www.excite.com/search.gw" METHOD="get">
```

Notice they also sent the text box's output to a search engine. One goes to something called WebQuery and the other goes to search.gw. Once the data is sent to the search engine, the site's database is rummaged through and you get your results.

Note again, however, that you do not use my site to search—you only send the information from my site. Once that's done, I'm totally out of the picture and you're at the search engine's site.

Once more thing: Notice the METHOD and name="p" in the Yahoo! search? Those are little items that each search engine uses to denote how to manipulate the data it receives and what to name the output sent through the text box. Each search engine works differently and you must make sure to use the search engine's format, exactly, on your page.

Where do you get the format for all this? Directly from the search engine itself. It's not that tough. Go to the search engine site and look at the source code. Just grab the part that goes from <FORM> through </FORM>. You may need to knock out some stuff in the middle, like extra text or table commands, but it's all right there. Put it on your page.

One thing, though: You may notice when you get the code that the ACTION section does not include the search engine's entire address. That's because the full address wasn't needed when the code was on the original site.

Because the domain is added as the default, you know that you don't need to put the full address on links to pages within your own site. Now the code you took from their site is on your site and it needs the full address.

For instance, let's say you took some code from a search engine at http://www.joe.com. The code you take from the site may read like this:

```
ACTION="/search/findit/"
```

Notice the slash before the first directory? That tells the computer to add the domain before the slash as a default. Now that the code is on your site, you need to add the full address right into the code. The code should be altered to look like this:

```
ACTION="http://www.joe.com/search/findit/"
```

Remember, the code now requires the full address because it is going from your site to perform the search. Without it, the code looks for something on your site called /search/ findit/ to perform the search. The server doesn't find it and you get errors.

But I Want to Search My Site!

This is a tough call. I have gone through the process and can tell you that it is rough and outside the scope of this book. The process occurs in two steps:

- You need to create a database and place it on your site.

  This database has to be in a format the server understands. Excel often works, as does Lotus.

- You need to write a CGI to do the searching.

  Maybe you are one of the people who have access to someone who will write one of these for a small amount of money.

There is another solution, but it isn't cheap. You can use the Excite search engine. It is a self-contained package that your Webmaster may already have. Mine did: $275.

The search engine was wonderfully easy. It installed quickly and made an entire directory searchable. All I did was point it in the right direction. It compiled the data and was up and running in a matter of minutes. After a month, I had to take it down. So many people were using it that the search engine was taking up 3 out of every 5 cycles of the computer's brain.

In layman's terms, it was about to crash the whole system by overworking it. I still have it and I still use it to search, but I don't make it available to others. It slowed the site tremendously.

There's not a whole lot more I can tell you. You know how to search other databases from your site, and have a couple of ideas about how to set up Excite and other, CGI-driven searches. You may want to contact your site administrator to look into those paths.

But I Want to Search My Site! (Take Two)

 If the Excite database is unavailable to you or you'd rather not spend the money, here's another suggestion: Use a JavaScript-based search engine. I have one you can have for free on the HTML Goodies site. Point your browsers to http://www.htmlgoodies.com/db.html.

You can search my site using the JavaScript database. Afterwards, select the link on the page that sends you to a tutorial on how to alter the database for use on your own site.

The process is simple. The JavaScript doesn't search your site, but instead searches itself. You enter all of your page names, their addresses, and keywords that denote each page into the JavaScript itself. Then when someone puts in a keyword, the JavaScript searches what you have put into it and returns the results. It's a self-contained process that works very well.

Go see my JavaScript database in action. If you like it, it's yours. Just follow the instructions online for altering the Script to search your own pages.

But I Want to Search My Site! (Take Three)

Okay, there's one more way to go about searching your own site. I was given this tip by the technical editor of this book, Bill Bruns. (Thanks Bill, great tip!)

Here's what you do: First submit all of your pages to a search engine that allows you to use a hidden value. I'll explain what that means in a moment. I don't know that this works with all search engines, but I know HotBot (http://www.hotbot.com) and AltaVista (http://www.altavista.com) allow it. What you'll do then is create the same basic search format I talked about earlier, which allows people to use search engines from your site. This differs in that you are going to add to your code a hidden field that denotes your domain.

Let's say I do this with my HTML Goodies site. The domain is htmlgoodies.com. I would submit all of my pages to HotBot; then I would create the code that allows people to search HotBot from my site. The search, however, would be altered in the code because I would have added a hidden field. That hidden field tells HotBot to search only for files that are on the domain htmlgoodies.com.

By limiting the search to that domain, I am in a sense setting up a search of my site only. Very clever.

Here's the code I would use to set up a search of HTML Goodies on HotBot:

```
<FORM action="http://www.hotbot.com/" method="GET">
        <INPUT type="hidden" name="SPID" value="2904">
        <INPUT type="hidden" name="_v" value="2">
        <INPUT type="hidden" name="domain"
value="www.htmlgoodies.com htmlgoodies.com">
        <INPUT type="hidden" name="SM" value="phrase">
        <INPUT type="hidden" name="RD" value="DM">
        <INPUT type="hidden" name="OPs" value="R">
<B>Search </B>our site with <a href="http://www.hotbot.com/">Hotbot</a>:
        <INPUT type="text" size="15" maxlength="25" name="MT">
        <INPUT type="submit" value="Search">
</FORM>
```

Most of the code was taken right from the site. The extra code that creates the hidden field was entered to limit the site to my pages only.

Remember that you are sent to HotBot (or whatever search engine you're using) when you use this method. The Excite and JavaScript method allow you to remain at your site for the search.

You need to play around a bit to get the correct format, but you'll find it. It's usually pretty clear from the remainder of the code.

Somehow, some way, you'll get a search on your page.

Enjoy!

Chapter 8

Cascading Style Sheets and Layers

Basic Style Sheet Format and Commands

Wouldn't it be nice if you could say "This is how I want you to handle my text" to all browsers that enter your page? You could make all <H3> commands Arial font. You could make all paragraph commands indent a half inch. You could specify a distance between your lines! You could ask for the world on a string! You wouldn't get it, but you could ask. It's the other stuff I'm talking about.

 This tutorial is online at http://www.htmlgoodies.com/ie_style.html.

Explorer 3 and 4 and Netscape 4.0 (and those to come) offer you more control through the use of what are called *style sheets*. It's actually a novel concept. Instead of writing font size, weight, margin commands, and so on and so forth, again and again, you write them once and the whole page feeds off that one master list—that one style sheet.

In fact, the 4.0 version of HTML expects that you will depend on these style sheets for a great deal of your writing. That's not to say you have to—the more traditional method of tagging every item will still work just fine—but if you read my synopses on HTML 4.0, you'll see that a few commands are going to the trash heap in favor of using style sheets for the effect. It's not a bad idea, but don't think that the methods you already know will be out of date any time soon. Read this over and if you think this is a better method, great. If not, feel free to tag everything individually. That will work just fine.

FAQs from the HTML Goodies Web Site

Q. **I went through your style sheets tutorial and put some on the page. It worked in Internet Explorer, but Navigator gave me some problems. It didn't do some of the commands and didn't understand others. Some it produced just fine. What's with that?**

A. You probably had problems because the style sheet commands used were not standard code. Microsoft's version of style sheets was the one adopted by the W3C (they're the people that decide what will and will not be standard HTML code). Netscape implemented the standard code into their browser Navigator so all standard codes should run just fine. You must have run into code not in the W3C standard, thus not understood by the Netscape Navigator.

So are these things called style sheets, cascading style sheets, or CSS? Choose any one—they all mean the same thing. I'll tell you what I really find funny: I had the original style sheets (sometimes called Explorer style sheets when referenced on other pages) up for six months when Netscape 4.0 came out. All of a sudden I was overrun with letters asking me when I was going to put up a tutorial on cascading style sheets and CSS, even though they mean the same thing. Yet this pup had been sitting and waiting all the time. The name had just changed a bit so it was thought of as a new thing.

The term *cascading style sheets* is used because more than one style sheet can affect the same page. For instance, assume you are using a style sheet on the actual document—called an *inline*—and a style sheet that is being referenced by multiple pages—called a *span*. Both can have an effect on the items in the page. If both the inline and the span style sheet attempt to affect the same item, an <H1> command for instance, the closest to the <H1> command wins. In this case it's the inline.

In case you're wondering, if two inline style sheets attempt to affect the same <H1> command, the one listed second in the actual HTML document wins. It's closest to the command going from the top of the document.

There are two ways to implement a style sheet:

1. You can put a separate style sheet on each page.
2. You can create one style sheet and link all your pages to it.

 Point your browser to http://www.htmlgoodies.com/book/stylesheet.html *to see a page with a rather large style sheet. Make sure to look at the source code.*

One Style Sheet—One Page

This is the way I see style sheets being used most often: You simply include the style sheet commands directly in the HTML document. If you look at the source code of some popular pages like CNN.com or ESPN's Sportszone, you'll see this type of style sheet being used.

I also use this method on the HTML Goodies site. The style sheet commands are placed between the `<HEAD>` and `</HEAD>` flags, and it looks like this:

```
<HEAD>
<STYLE="text/css">
<!--
BODY {background: #FFFFFF}
A:link {color: #80FF00}
A:visited {color: #FF00FF}
H1 {font-size: 24pt; font-family: arial}
H2 {font-size: 18pt; font-family: braggadocio}
H3 {font size:14pt; font-family: desdemona}
-->
</STYLE>
</HEAD>
```

In all fairness, I should mention that when used like this, it technically isn't a style sheet, it's an inline style *block*. But another term just pushes something useful out of your brain, so if I continue to call it a sheet, it's habit more than anything.

Follow these rules to place a style sheet (block) on your page:

- It must be within the `<HEAD>` and `</HEAD>` commands.
- The text must be surrounded by `<STYLE TEXT="text/css">` and `</STYLE>`.
- Remember that CSS from earlier? It stands for cascading style sheets? The style sheet is text, so if you type it on the page, it will show up and we can't have that. In addition to the style commands, surround the text with `<!--` and `-->`. Those happy little commands make the text invisible. Like Wonder Woman's jet. Man, I loved that show. I think it was called *Superfriends*.

Hey! Make with the Style Sheet Already, Bub!

This gets a little confusing, but there is a method to this madness. Now that you know the big picture, let's look at the format for individual style commands:

```
TAG {definition; definition; definition}
```

Here's a sample line from a style sheet:

```
H2 {font-size: 16pt; font-style: italic; font-family: arial}
```

225

Here are a few things I want to point out about the individual style command:

- Notice the thing surrounding the definition is a curly brace ({), not a parenthesis or a square bracket.
- Notice the spaces! You don't have to leave them, but it helps when you read your style sheets later. Just don't forget the semicolons.
- Notice each definition is separated by a semicolon, but the definition contains a colon! Confusing, I know, but that's the way it goes in Internetland.

You're not limited, either. If you can somehow find a way to use 30 style sheet commands to affect the same <H2> flag, bully for you! Just remember to separate them all by semicolon.

What HTML Tags Can I Define?

As far as I can tell, you can define any HTML tag.

Now, some definitions will be silly with some tags. I mean, a font definition with an <HR> tag seems a bit goofy, don't you think? I see the style sheets using these flags the most:

- <H1> through <H6>
- <P>
- <BODY>
- A:link (denotes the unvisited link)
- A:visited (denotes the visited link)
- <DIV> (denotes a division of the page)

Twenty-Eight Style Sheet Command Definitions

Here are 28 very common style sheet commands. You can put together a myriad of looks with these. However, this list is less than half of those available. At the end, I'll give a couple of links to full command lists—but I'll bet these become your work-horses. Most of the other commands are overly specific.

The FONT/TEXT definitions:

1. font-family   Denotes typeface.

   H2 {font-family: arial}

2. font-style   Denotes the style of the text. Use normal, italic, small caps, or oblique for commands.

   H3 {font-style: small caps}

3. font-size   Denotes the size of the text. Specify in points (pt), inches (in), centimeters (cm), pixels (px), or percentage (%).

   H4 {font-size: 20pt}

4. `font-weight`   Denotes text presence. Specify in extra-light, light, demi-light, medium, bold, demi-bold, or extra-bold.

   `A:link {font-weight: demi-light}`

5. `font-variant`   Denotes a variant from the norm. Specify `normal` or `small-caps`.

   `H2: {font-variant: small-caps}`

6. `text-align`   Justifies the alignment of text. Specify as `left`, `center`, or `right`.

   `H1 {text-align: center}`

7. `text-decoration`   Lets you decorate the text. Specify as `italic`, `blink`, `underline`, `line-through`, `overline`, or `none`.

   `A:visited {text-decoration: blink}`

8. `text-indent`   Denotes margins. Most often used with the `<P>` flag. Make sure you use `</P>` also! Specify in inches (`in`), centimeters (`cm`), or pixels (`px`).

   `P {text-indent: 1in}`

9. `word-spacing`   Denotes the amount of spaces between words. Specify in points (`pt`), inches (`in`), centimeters (`cm`), pixels (`px`), or percentage (`%`).

   `P {word-spacing: 10px}`

10. `letter-spacing`   Denotes space between letters. Specify in points (`pt`), inches (`in`), centimeters (`cm`), pixels (`px`), or percentage (`%`).

   `P {letter-spacing: 2pt}`

11. `text-transform`   Denotes a transformation of the text. Specify `capitalize`, `uppercase`, or `lowercase`.

   `B {text-transform: uppercase}`

12. `color`   Denotes color of text. See Appendix B for a few color codes. If you use the six digit hex codes, make sure you place a pound sign (#) in front.

   `H3 {color: #FFFFFF}`

The `MARGIN/BACKGROUND` commands (when used with the `<BODY>` flag, these commands affect the entire page!):

1. `margin-left`   See margin-top.

2. `margin-right`   See margin-top.

3. `margin-top`   Denotes space around the page. Specify in points (`pt`), inches (`in`), centimeters (`cm`), or pixels (`px`).

```
BODY {margin-left: 2in}

P {margin-right: 12cm}

BODY {margin-top: 45px}
```

4. `margin`   Denotes all three margin commands in one command. The pattern follows top, right, and then left.

   `P {margin: 3in 4cm 12px}` (note no commas or semi-colons)

5. `line-height`   Denotes space between lines of text. Specify in points (`pt`), inches (`in`), centimeters (`cm`), pixels (`px`), or percentage (`%`).

   `TEXT {line-height: 10px}`

6. `background-color`   Denotes page's background color. Specify the color in hex or word codes, or use `transparent`.

   `BODY {background-color: #ffffff}`

7. `background-image`   Denotes the background image for pages. Specify the image you want through that image's URL.

   `BODY {background-image: http://www.page.com/dog.jpg}`

8. `background-repeat`   Denotes how the image will tile. Specify `repeat-x`, `repeat-y`, or `no-repeat`.

   `BODY {background-repeat: repeat-y}`

9. `background-attachment`   Denotes how the image will react to a scroll. Specify `scroll` or `fixed`.

   `BODY{background-attachment: fixed}`

The positioning/division definitions:

These commands come into play when you begin working with text and image positioning. Note that these examples are given using a specific item.

1. `position`   Denotes the placement of an image or a division of the page. Specify either `absolute` for specific placement or `relative` for placement relative to other images.

   `<IMG STYLE="position:absolute" SRC="joe.jpg">`

2. `left`   Denotes amount of space allowed from the left of the browser screen when positioning an item. Specify in points (`pt`), inches (`in`), centimeters (`cm`), pixels (`px`), or percentage (`%`).

   `<IMG STYLE="position:absolute; LEFT: 20px;" SRC="joe.jpg">`

3. `top`   Denotes amount of space allowed from the top of the browser screen when positioning an item. Specify in points (`pt`), inches (`in`), centimeters (`cm`), or percentage (`%`).

```
<IMG STYLE="position:absolute; LEFT: 20px; TOP: 200pt"
  SRC="joe.jpg">
```

4. width Denotes width of image or page division. Specify in points (pt), inches (in), centimeters (cm), pixels (px), or percentage (%).

```
<IMG STYLE="position:absolute; WIDTH: 80px; LEFT: 20px;
  TOP: 200pt" SRC="joe.jpg">
```

5. height Denotes height of image or page division. Specify in points (pt), inches (in), centimeters (cm), pixels (px), or percentage (%).

```
<IMG STYLE="position:absolute; HEIGHT: 55px WIDTH:80px;
  LEFT: 20px; TOP: 200pt" SRC="joe.jpg">
```

6. overflow If the item is too large for the specified height and width, this tells the page what to do with the overflow. Specify visible, hidden, or scroll.

```
<IMG STYLE="position:absolute; overflow: hidden;
  WIDTH: 80px; LEFT: 20px; TOP: 200pt" SRC="joe.jpg">
```

7. z-index Denotes an item's position in the layering structure. The lower the number, the lower the layer. An image marker with 20 goes over the top of an image marked with 10. Specify by number.

```
<IMG STYLE="position:absolute; Z-INDEX: 10; overflow: hidden;
  WIDTH: 80px; LEFT: 20px; TOP: 200pt" SRC="joe.jpg">
```

What It All Looks Like

Here again is the style sheet from the online version of this tutorial:

```
<STYLE TYPE-"type/css">
<!-- BODY {background: #FFFFFF}
A:link {color: #80FF00}
A:visited {color: #FF00FF}
H1 {font-size: 24pt; font-family: arial}
H2 {font-size: 18pt; font-family: braggadocio}
H3 {font size:14pt; font-family: desdemona} -->
</STYLE>
```

Now remember, this is all you have to do. There are no commands to put in the text itself, no extra items to place. This style sheet in enacted automatically when one of the listed items appears; you just sit back and watch the show. Unless you want the same command handled differently in two different parts of the page.

What if I Want the Same Tag Handled Different Ways?

What you do is assign different "classes" of tags. Real simple. Look here:

```
H3.first {font-size: 20pt; color: #FF00FF}
H3.scnd {font size: 18pt; color #DD00FF}
```

See what I did? I labeled the <H3> flags separately by adding a period and then a suffix. I used first for the first type and scnd for the second type. You can use whatever you want; I like these determinants. When you place them on your page, you do this in the text:

```
<H3 CLASS="first">This will be affected as outlined in"H3.first"</H3>
<H3 CLASS="scnd">This will be affected as outlined in "H3.scnd"</H3>
```

One Style Sheet—Many Pages

First, create a style sheet following the format given earlier. This is the only thing on the page. Do not make this an HTML document, just the style sheet commands! You will make the file so that if I wanted, I could just copy and paste what you have right into my own <HEAD> flags. Which is just about what you will be asking the computer to do. The style sheet will be a simple text file with a .CSS suffix.

Let's say you name your style sheet fred. Its name would become fred.css. The suffix is required for browsers to recognize it as a style sheet rather than a simple mesh of letters. Place this command on your page to call for the style sheet:

```
<LINK REL=stylesheet HREF="http://www.yourserver.com/fred.css"
 TYPE="text/css">
```

Here's what's happening:

- LINK tells the browser something must be linked to the page.
- REL=stylesheet tells the browser that this linked thing is relative to this page as a style sheet.
- HREF="*www.yourserver.com/fred.css*" denotes where the browser will find the style sheet.
- TYPE="text/css" tells the browser that what it is reading as text will act as a cascading style sheet. If the document isn't text with a .CSS suffix, no dice.

Every page that contains this command is affected by the one style sheet you created and placed in your directory. One sheet, many pages.

FAQs from the HTML Goodies Web Site

Q. I have followed your style sheet tutorial but I'm not getting the effect.

A. The most common reasons include misspelling or miscoding the commands themselves. Check that carefully. If you're positive they are correct, it might be that your browser does not support the commands you are calling for. I'm sorry to say that not all style sheets commands are universal. If you're sure your version does support that specific style sheet command, it might be that the browser has "turned off" the use of style sheets. In Internet Explorer, look under Options or Internet Options, depending on your browser version. In Netscape Navigator, look under Preferences. There you find a box that allows you to "turn on" style sheet capabilities. If it's already clicked to allow style sheets, it has to be your coding.

Can I Use These Style Elements on Individual Items?

Yes you can. They simply sit inside the flag you are working with. Just make sure to denote them using the STYLE command inside the command. Since they sit inside another command as just a defining command, they don't require a </STYLE> flag. In that position, they affect only what you say they will, rather than the entire page. Like so:

```
<FONT STYLE="font-weight: extra light; font-family: courier">
affected text</FONT>
```

Follow this format and you can define a style for just about any HTML flag. There's also a method of setting up classes of items that works pretty much the same way. But that's another chapter.

See these sites for a full list of CSS commands:

- C-Net's Table of Style Sheet Commands: http://www.cnet.com/Content/Builder/Authoring/CSS/table.html

- The World Wide Web Consortium's Style Site: http://www.w3.org/Style/

 Point your browser to http://www.htmlgoodies.com/book/stylesheet.html *to see a page with a rather large style sheet. Make sure to look at the source code.*

Positioning Things Precisely on Your Web Page

Wouldn't it be great if you could make a point of placing every item on your page exactly where you want it? Even better, make that placement exactly the same on every browser your page is viewed in? It looks like the answer is a series of cascading style sheet commands that allow you to denote—to the pixel—where you want an item to be pinned up.

You should know that style sheets are not universal at the time of this writing. Netscape Navigator version 4.0 and Explorer 3- and 4-level browsers understand the style commands, but not always exactly the same way. It's still a bit buggy at the moment. In fact, it's quite buggy. Netscape Navigator understands the "standard" style sheet code, but not all of the code available through Internet Explorer is standard. You need to make sure those viewing your page are using one of the listed browsers for this to work. I stress the word *need*. If the browser doesn't get these positioning commands, the page will look either like crud or just straight text.

FAQs from the HTML Goodies Web Site

Q. Since style sheets are not universal yet, how do I make it so that people see the pages the way I want them to look on any browser?

A. For one, don't make overly intricate pages, but that's not always possible. The next best step is to not make the style sheet effects vital to the page. Those effects that are vital should be done the traditional way—by placing the tags individually. You could also set up a JavaScript browser choice that first recognizes the type of browser the user is working with and in turn send them to a page made just for that browser. There's one in Chapter 11, "Java Applets and JavaScript."

 I have a few positioning examples for you at http://www.htmlgoodies.com/book/ position.html.

Positioning an Image

You may notice soon that I am doing this by including all of the style sheet commands inside the items that I am positioning. You might wonder that if these are style sheets, why not put these in a text.CSS file or in the HEAD commands inside a <STYLE> flag? You can do that, but in order to teach this, it is easier to include the commands with the item that I am positioning. In addition, I like doing it this way. To each his own...

You are going to state to the browser that it should position the upper-left corner of an image in a specific plot point on the page. The image in Figure 8.1 is positioned exactly 25 pixels from the top of the page and 170 pixels from the left.

Here's the code I used to place the image at that specific plot point:

```
<IMG STYLE="position:absolute; TOP:35px; LEFT:170px; WIDTH:50px;
   HEIGHT:50px" SRC="circle.gif">
```

Here's how it works:

- IMG denotes that this will be an image.
- STYLE= proclaims that what will follow are style commands.
- position:absolute; states that the image will go exactly where indicated. If text or another picture is already there, tough—this goes right over top of it. That is one of the drawbacks to this positioning stuff.

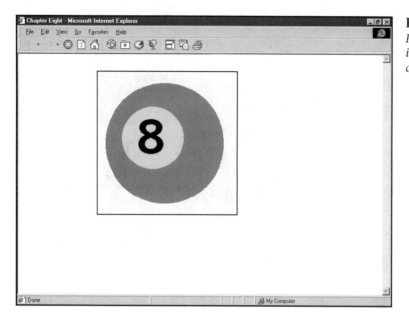

Figure 8.1
Precisely positioning an image with the <STYLE> command.

- ⬤ `TOP:35px; LEFT:170px;` are the plot points for the image: 35 pixels down from the top and 170 pixels in from the left.
- ⬤ `WIDTH:50px; HEIGHT:50px` is the height and width of the image itself.

Notice the semicolon between each section.

Now, when the style sheet commands proclaim that the position is absolute, they're not kidding. Here's the same example with some text on the page. Notice the image didn't care that there was text around (see Figure 8.2). It was put into position and that's that. Keep that in mind when positioning items.

FAQs from the HTML Goodies Web Site

Q. Can I set the position with percentages? That way I could say 20% from the left and the screen size wouldn't be such a problem.

A. I have never seen it done with percentages. My quick experiment with them failed. I would say that pixels are your friends for now.

Positioning Text

You can position text in the same way you positioned an image. Figure 8.3 shows an example where a block of text is positioned 80 pixels from the top of the window and 400 pixels from the left of the browser window.

Figure 8.2
A positioned image sitting on top of text.

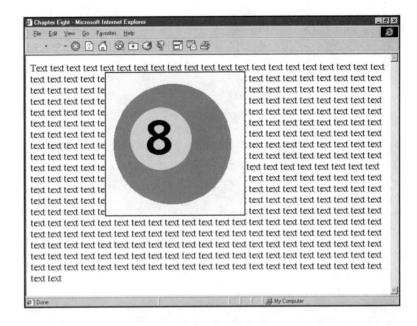

Figure 8.3
Here is some positioned text.

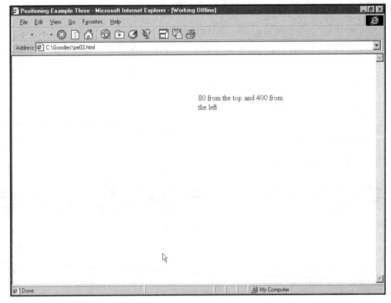

Here's the command I used to position the text:

```
<DIV STYLE="position: absolute; TOP:80px; LEFT:400px; WIDTH:200px;
  HEIGHT:25px">80 from the top and 400 from the left</DIV>
```

Here's what's happening in the code:

- DIV denotes that this is a "division" of the page. A section, if you will.
- STYLE= denotes that some style commands will be put to work.
- position: absolute; denotes that this division will be placed exactly where you want it placed.
- TOP:80px; LEFT:400px; is the positioning of the division.
- WIDTH:200px; HEIGHT:25px denotes the height and width of the division.
- /DIV ends the division section.

The text in Figure 8.3 wrapped to the next line because I made the width of the division too small for the text in it. Figure 8.4 shows the same example with the division width set to 300px.

Figure 8.4
Text does not wrap with the DIV *width set higher.*

FAQs from the HTML Goodies Web Site

Q. It looks like I could use this to place an image and then place text. If I do it correctly, it appears I could put text across the picture, sort of like a label.

A. Yup. That's true, but I would suggest doing it through layering commands, or through a table cell so that you can ensure that the text is laid on top.

You can add color to the text by adding the following command to the mix. Now the division you set up is filled in with the chosen color (see Figure 8.5).

```
background-color: yellow
```

Figure 8.5
Background color added.

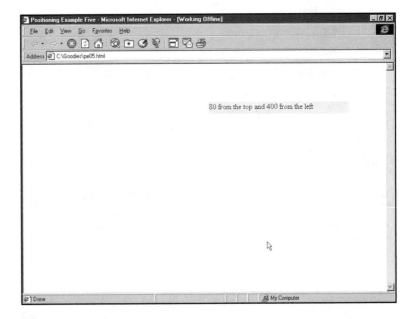

This works with either word or hex color codes. However, if you use a hex color code, make sure to place a pound sign (#) in front of the six characters, like so: background-color: #FFFFFF. It is required in this style sheet format, unlike basic HTML code.

FAQs from the HTML Goodies Web Site

Q. How do I set the positioning so I am sure it fits all browser screens from lowest to highest resolution?

A. You really can't make an exact science out of this, but the best answer I have is not to avoid using these commands on just one item. The purpose is more to create the full layout of the page by sectioning it off through divisions. Using it on one item creates problems.

Can I Set Other Styles?

Sure! You can set just about any style command that works on text. Just make sure that you give the division enough space to house the text if you set the font size higher. Figure 8.6

shows an example where I've used as many text-based style commands as I could find before it got boring. The code looked like this:

```
<DIV style="position: absolute; font-family: arial; font-style: italic;
 font-variant:small-caps; font-weight:bold; text-decoration:underline;
 letter-spacing: 2px; top: 80px; width: 400px; left: 400px;
 height: 25px; background-color: yellow">
 80 from the top and 400 from the left</DIV>
```

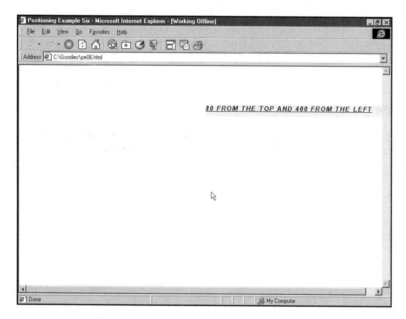

Figure 8.6
Multiple style sheet commands in positioning.

Using Classes and IDs

There are a great couple of ways to quickly use CSS commands. When I speak to people about CSS, the main thing I hear about is the time the sheets save them. They've set up a series of formats for certain commands and the sheet takes care of the styles without any extra work.

The reason I like these two commands in particular is that they're quick, even for those who do not regularly use style sheets. They're easy to understand and save on the fingers by cutting down on the typing. I swear my finger used to be longer.

I had a student call these commands "style sheets lite." That's a good way of thinking about it. People who understand HTML can understand the class and ID format much easier than learning how to create a full style sheet block. I offer this tutorial if for no other reason than the ease of learning.

It should be said that style sheets are not universal as of the writing of this book. I know I've said this before, but here we go again. Your viewer needs to be using Netscape 4.*x* or any version of Explorer. Even then, the commands are very buggy. You do not need to be overly concerned that a browser that doesn't read style sheets will be baffled by this. Earlier browsers are great at ignoring commands they do not understand. The text just appears as normal. You could also make a point of using a JavaScript meant to "see" the user's browser and send them to a page that is suited to their system. I have one in the JavaScript section of this book—use classes and IDs, but don't rely heavily on them.

First off, you need to have a general understanding of style sheet commands. Don't be put off at this point. They are very easy to grasp. At the end of this tutorial, you'll have no trouble implementing them on your page.

This is a style sheet model, so you need to do two things to get started: Set up the style section within the <HEAD> flags and then set up the classes.

FAQs from the HTML Goodies Web Site

Q. Do my inline style sheet commands have to go in the <HEAD> flags?

A. Technically, no. Just make sure they are above the actual item that is calling for them, so that the commands are already in the browser's memory before you call on the effect. That's why I suggest putting them in between the <HEAD> commands; that way they load first and are out of the way without jumbling up your page.

Setting Up the STYLE Section

To get started, you need to insert the following code between your HTML document's <HEAD> flags:

```
<STYLE type="text/css">
<!-- Classes and ID's will go in here... -->
</STYLE>
```

Setting Up the Classes

Now the fun part. Let's set up a class. For the sake of argument, let's say I want to set up a class of text that is Arial font, 20pt size, bold, and orange. You could do it this way:

```
<FONT FACE="arial" COLOR="orange" SIZE="+2"><B>text in here</B></FONT>
```

That's a good bit of text, plus I'd have to type it every time I wanted that class of text to come up. If I'm doing a Netscape table where I wanted every cell to have that type of text, I'd have to write it every time for every cell. Yeah, I could copy and paste it again and again, but I'd rather write it out once, assign a class to it, and refer to that class when I want it.

Here's the class structure that equals the text:

```
.pumpkin { font-family: arial; font-size: 20; font-style: bold;
color: orange }
```

The class is identified through a period and then a code name. I chose pumpkin for this example, mainly because I am setting the text to orange.

What follows are the style sheet commands, separated by semicolons and encased within those fancy braces. See that in the class statement? Place that class statement inside the <STYLE> flags from earlier. It should look like this between your <HEAD> flags:

```
<STYLE type="text/css">
<!-- .pumpkin { font-family: arial; font-size: 20;
font-style: bold; color: orange }-->
</STYLE>
```

Putting the Classes to Work

Okay, you're ready to go. The class is in place and you can call on it anytime you want within the same document. Obviously, if you follow the steps to use an external style sheet, you can use this across pages, but this tutorial is set up to work within the same page.

You can call for this as part of any command that is used to alter text. Figure 8.7 shows a few examples.

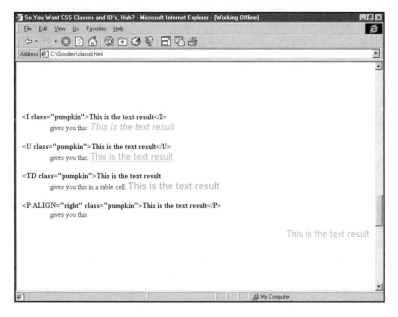

Figure 8.7
Showing classes.

Can I Have More Than One Class?

Sure. You can have as many as you'd like, as long as you keep using different code words to denote the many classes. Just keep lining them up, one after the other in the style sheet section up in the <HEAD> flags.

What About Those IDs?

The ID command works exactly the same way as the class command. It exists to allow you to incorporate these style sheet models into JavaScript or DHTML. I wouldn't get too worried just yet; that's still a bit into your HTML future. Unless you are attempting to use these with JavaScript, stick with the class command. You can use the ID command, but it won't do anything different or better than the class command. In case you want to give it a whirl, here's how to use it.

In the style section of your <HEAD> flag, denote the ID by a pound sign (#) and a code word. Like so:

```
#pumpkin { font-family: arial; font-size: 20; font-style: bold; color: orange }
```

From that point on, it's the same format as the class commands (see Figure 8.8). Like so:

```
<P ID="pumpkin">This is the text result</P>
```

Figure 8.8
Orange text!

The ID and the class formats can be used on the same page. I'm using both on this page, with the same code word. I think these are great. You could put together your entire style sheet system using only these class models. Here's to good pages.

Enjoy!

 I have a few more examples of classes and IDs at `http://www.htmlgoodies.com/book/` `classid.html.` *Make sure you look at the source code to see the style sheet commands.*

CSS and Forms

Please note that these commands only work with Microsoft's Explorer browser version 4.0. If you haven't already, you may want to read through my tutorial on cascading style sheets and forms before you attack this one; it will help a great deal. That said, let's get started. Dig the fancy guestbook shown in Figure 8.9 (notice the ToolTip, the thing that looks like a pop-up text box where the mouse cursor is).

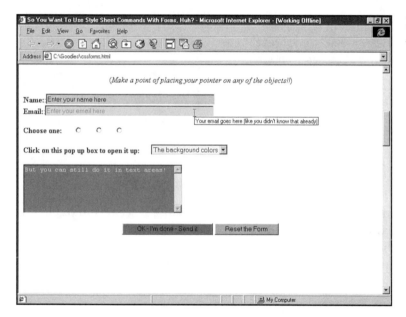

Figure 8.9
A multicolored form.

Here's the code I used to create the form:

```
<FORM method="post" ACTION="####@######.###">
<b>Name:</b>:
<INPUT TITLE="Your name goes here" TYPE="text" SIZE="50"
 STYLE="background:00BFFF" VALUE="Enter your name here">
<BR>
<b>Email:</b>:
```

```
<INPUT TITLE="Your email goes here (like you didn't know that already)"
 TYPE="text" SIZE="50" STYLE="color:ff0000" STYLE="background:00ff00"
 VALUE="Enter your email here">
<p>
<b>Choose one:</b>
<INPUT TITLE="You can't change the color of checkboxes or radio buttons,
but you can add this text" TYPE="radio" STYLE="background:00BFFF">
<INPUT title="ditto" TYPE="radio" STYLE="background:00BFFF">
<INPUT title="ditto, ditto" TYPE="radio" STYLE="background:00BFFF">
<P>
<b>Click on this pop up box to open it up:</b>
<SELECT SIZE="1" STYLE="background:ffff00">
<OPTION SELECTED>The background colors
<OPTION>even work with
<OPTION>pop-up boxes.
<OPTION>Cool, Huh?
</SELECT>
<P>
<TEXTAREA TITLE="another yellow box" ROWS="6" COLS="40"
 STYLE="color:00ff00" STYLE="background:ff0000">
But you can still do it in text areas!</TEXTAREA>
<P>
<INPUT TITLE="Send it off to me" TYPE="button" STYLE="background:871eb0"
 VALUE="OK - I'm done - Send it">
<INPUT TITLE="No Wait!  Stop!" TYPE="button" STYLE="background:87b4b0"
 VALUE="Reset the Form">
</FORM>
```

Eeeeew! That's gross!

Agreed. You are seeing this in shades of black and white. If you'd like to see this in full living color go to the HTML Goodies site (`http://www.htmlgoodies.com/cssforms.html`). Wear sunglasses; it's quite bright, but it does the trick for this tutorial. Without looking directly into the awful colors, direct your attention there one more time. There are four new things you can add to your MSIE guestbook forms:

- Background color
- Separate text color
- ToolTip (pop-up text box) on mouse-over
- Colored buttons

Each of these is created via style sheet commands added right into the form element.

242

FAQs from the HTML Goodies Web Site

Q. If I use these commands and a person running Netscape uses the forms, will it still work?

A. Yes. The browser just ignores the commands and produces a normal-looking guestbook form.

Now let's take a look at each of the four new things we've added, shall we?

Adding a Background Color

The background color is added to all of the items through the background STYLE command. Here's a basic text box with the command added to it:

```
<INPUT TYPE="text" SIZE="50" STYLE="background:#00BFFF">
```

That STYLE="background:#00BFFF" is the command that does the trick. Simply add that to any of the form elements, except radio buttons and check boxes, and you get the color denoted by the hex code. For a whole lot of hex codes, see the Goodies color chart in Appendix B, "Useful Charts."

The reason you can't get color in the radio buttons or checkboxes is quite scientific and difficult to understand: They don't have backgrounds to color in. So far, so good? Stunning. Let's move along...

Adding a Separate Text Color

Notice again that there is text in the preceding boxes. That's fairly easy to do, as is changing the color of said text. Let's use the previous example, but add some green text. It looks like this:

```
<INPUT TYPE="text" SIZE="50" STYLE="background:#00BFFF"
STYLE="color:#00ff00" VALUE="This text appears in the box">
```

See the two new commands? I added them right after the background commands. They look like this:

```
STYLE="color:###ff00" VALUE="This text appears in the box"
```

The VALUE= command denotes the text and STYLE="color:###" denotes the color of the text. Use it for any form item that accepts text, and you're good to go. Is that stuck on a brain cell? Going forward...

Q. Can I use word color codes in style sheets?

A. Maybe by the time you're reading this. Try one and see; I wasn't able to when I wrote this tutorial.

Adding a ToolTip on Mouse-Over

I think this is the coolest thing in this tutorial: A little text box pops up if you place your pointer on top of almost any of the items. That box is called a ToolTip. It works the same way the ALT command does with images.

The little yellow box you see is created via a TITLE command. Here's the code that produced the text box in the preceding image. See how the pointer is sitting on it and it's producing a yellow ALT-type box?

```
<INPUT TITLE="Your email goes here (like you didn't know that already)
" TYPE="text" SIZE="50" STYLE="color:#ff0000" STYLE="background:#00ff00"
VALUE="Enter your email here">
```

That's not so tough, huh? It's a simple trade. You add the TITLE="###" deal and the computer gives you the box. Supply and demand.

Q. Why can't I get a yellow box to pop up on the Select drop-down box?

A. Because the code won't allow it. I assume that's because the box itself requires being clicked to work—but that's a guess.

Adding Colored Buttons

There was a time when my email was full of requests for colored form buttons. There was no such thing at the time, so I created one through images and onClick JavaScripts. It's really involved and might not be worth the trouble. This, however, is so super simple I can't believe it. Plus, I've already shown you how to do it. Here's the code for the Send button from before:

```
<INPUT TITLE="Send it off to me" TYPE="button"
STYLE="background:#ff00ff" VALUE="OK - I'm done - Send it">
```

There you go. It's a simple submit button with many of the commands from earlier in this chapter stuck in for good measure.

FAQs from the HTML Goodies Web Site

Q. Is there a way to change the framing around these images to a different color?

A. I don't understand why people want to create items with so much color it would be blinding. Luckily, no. There isn't.

That's That!

Now, please. I made the color scheme to prove a point. This is not a contest. Do not attempt to create a form with the worst grouping of hues. I cannot be held responsible if you do. They're your eyes.

Enjoy!

Using Layer Commands

You can almost guess from the title of this section what these commands do. If you have already read the cascading style sheet tutorials in this chapter, you know it is possible to position an image on a page down to the pixel. You should also know that if there happens to be text where you position the image, tough. The image lays over the text. You have, in effect, created two layers, one over the other.

In this tutorial you learn how to use what might be considered a mistake in position of images to your advantage. You can place items on top of each other via the layer commands. You can place text over an image, place an image in the corner of another image, or lay three images over top of a background image. I've found these layer commands quite helpful. I'll bet you do, too. So let's get started.

Let us imagine I have these three images, as shown in Figure 8.10.

All three images are wonderful by themselves, but I would really like to lay one on top of another, sort of build an "X" with the first two layers and put the smiley face over both of them; something like Figure 8.11.

Neat, huh? Let me state right up front that I am able to make such an "X" because I made the images that lay on top transparent, so you could see through the top images. If the top image, the smiley face, weren't transparent, it would simply cover the bottom two images. See the information on transparent images in Chapter 3, "Adding Images and Backgrounds," if you don't already know how this is done.

What you see in Figure 8.11 are three images, all the same size. I did that on purpose. They are all 250×250 pixels. I then denoted that each image be placed in the same space. I then denoted that each image is a layer section in and of itself. Here's the code that makes the layered image:

Figure 8.10
Three separate images.

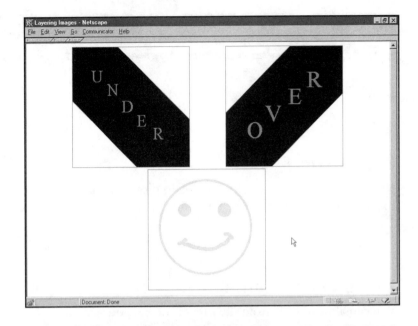

Figure 8.11
Same three images layered on one another.

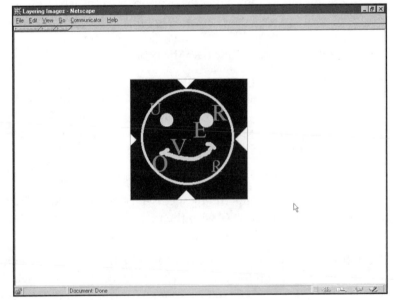

```
<LAYER NAME="under" LEFT=250 TOP=100>
<IMG SRC=x1.gif>
</LAYER>
<LAYER NAME="over" LEFT=250 TOP=100>
<IMG SRC=x2.gif>
```

```
</LAYER>
<LAYER NAME="overagain" LEFT=250 TOP=100>
<IMG SRC=x3.gif>
</LAYER>
```

Here's what's happening in the code:

- LAYER denotes to the browser that this is a layer. Please note that the first layer you place is the bottom layer. They continue to go over top as you add layers.

- NAME names the layer, obviously. This won't come into much play in this tutorial, but is important in later layer get-togethers.

- LEFT and TOP denote the image's placement *on the browser window*. Allow me to state that again...*on the browser window!*

- LEFT is from the left of the screen to the upper-left corner of the image. TOP is from the top of the screen to the upper-left corner of the image. The numbers are pixels. There is a lot of playing with numbers to get the image exactly where you want it. Think of the browser screen width as around 600 pixels and the height as around 500 pixels.

- IMG SRC acts just like any old image command. You can add HEIGHT and WIDTH if you'd like.

- </LAYER> ends each layer.

As shown, you'll need to do one of these LAYER commands for each layer you want.

FAQs from the HTML Goodies Web Site

Q. Is layering the same as absolute positioning?

A. Very close. The difference is that in layering, the items can be given a pecking order. This one goes on top of this one, on top of this one, on top of this one. Positioning sets it so the last one listed goes on top. These layers allow you have an image move horizontally through multiple images. You can then denote which goes on top and which goes underneath the horizontal image.

Q. Can I use the layer commands to set up an imagemap like your fake image?

A. Yes, you'll just need to surround the image command with the hypertext commands to activate the image.

 I have a few examples of layering that incorporate JavaScript at http://www.htmlgoodies. com/book/layering.html; *it will knock your socks off. So don't wear your shoes while looking.*

Layering in General

The process of creating a layered image is not difficult. However, there are a few items that might trip you up. I learned most of this from a lot of trial and error so here are a few items you should know before you waste time messing around.

Layered images do not react to ALIGN or CENTER commands. They do not care if there is text in the way, they place things right where you say to place them without any regard for what's around.

See the three-layered image in Figure 8.11? All three images are placed 250 pixels from the left of the screen and 100 from the top. That's why they layer. I have them all in the same place. The thing is that the layered image will be at 250 in and 100 down no matter what. You must write the rest of your page accordingly, leaving a big enough text space so that the image has a place to sit. If not, it will layer directly over what is sitting in its space. Which itself might be a neat effect...

If you want it to sit in the open like mine, you need to leave a big space right where you want it to sit. I do it by adding these:

```
<P>   <P>.
```

Each one of those adds two open lines. You need the   to add a space on a line. You see, just putting in a lot of <P> commands won't do it. There has to be something on a line for the next <P> command to work. You can't use any character because you need the blank line; use a space. That space is created by . And no, just putting a space by hitting the Spacebar won't do it.

The layers do not have to be in the exact same space. I have them that way more for demonstration purposes than anything. If you have two oddly shaped images and you only want part of one overlapping the other, it will work. The best method I have found for placing through layering? Creating a deck of cards fanning out in a hand. Clever. You'll have to play with the LEFT and TOP pixel number a bit, but you'll find the correct placement.

Don't go crazy layering things because it currently only works with Netscape 4.0 or later. If you have a chance to see a layered page in a browser window that doesn't support the commands, do it. You'll see how bad it looks when the commands aren't supported. All the images show up, they just aren't where you want them to be. Bummer.

Enjoy!

Part 4

Beyond HTML

Chapter 9

Behind the Scenes on Your Web Site

HEAD Commands

Try this for fun: Without telling them what you are doing, ask a few of your friends what the <HEAD> commands on an HTML document are for. I'll bet you get widely differing answers. I received a letter from a person who really chewed me out for not involving the HEAD commands in the HTML Goodies primers. I asked why this struck such a chord with her and she answered that the commands have to be in the document for it work correctly. "No they don't," I replied. "Yes they do," she replied back. "No they don't," I wrote back. "Do too," she replied. The conversation went downhill from there.

Actually we're both right. Here's a very basic HTML document format. You've seen this example 100 times I'm sure:

```
<HTML>
<HEAD>
<TITLE></TITLE>
</HEAD>
<BODY>
Displays in browser window
</BODY>
</HTML>
```

When I was learning to use HTML, I saw that same example over and over again. I thought the HEAD commands made things pop up in the blue bar at the top. You see, the <TITLE> commands were all I ever saw inside. Because I was left to my wits to learn this language, I figured I didn't need those commands. I wrote without them for a good long time. None of the pages ever seemed incorrect or flawed, so I never felt I needed them.

It wasn't until I started playing with JavaScript and META commands that I even cared what they did. This is all true. When I teach HTML in a classroom, I do not incorporate the HEAD commands until after the students learn to manipulate text with bold, italic, and other types of commands, and that's usually well into the semester.

I'm sure that statement is right now driving someone out of his skull. Again, I say what would you tell students who are just being introduced to the language what those commands do? Header commands are a great part of HTML. I know that now. I still think they are to be taught separately as something to incorporate rather than be required.

I don't know why I told you that...I guess I just love sharing with you people. So let's get started.

What the <HEAD> Commands Actually Do

The HEAD commands do three things:

1. They contain information regarding the document. This data does not appear in the browser window when the page is loaded. The data is mainly used for helping search engines with page descriptions, browsers with base domains, and other data not generally regarded as display content.

2. They separate the page into two distinct sections. Ever go into a page that won't load, but somehow the title is up there? It's inside the HEAD commands.

3. They are loaded first and the stuff included between them is run first by the browser.

FAQs from the HTML Goodies Web Site

Q. A friend told me she uses the HEAD command because it helps the page load faster. Any truth to that?

A. If she means that she incorporates in the HEAD commands items the page will need later so that the page doesn't load each event separately, yes. There's a ring of truth to what she says.

Q. I am using an HTML helper program that puts the HEAD commands in for me every time I write a page. Since I don't put anything other than the <TITLE> commands in there, should I take the HEAD commands out?

A. Nah. The effort isn't worth the benefit. The HEAD commands are only 10 extra characters; they're not slowing the page. Let 'em go. You may update the pages later and need them.

Information Regarding the Document

The following commands are used to describe information contained within the HTML document.

TITLE *Commands*

This is the command that appears most often between the HEAD commands. It places text within the color bar at the very top of the browser.

I must say I liked it before the newer-version browsers placed their names after the TITLE text. That didn't use to be the case. It was just text you wrote. In addition, if you wrote a lot of TITLE commands, they were all compiled, one after the other. You could have animation in the blue bar at the top—it was great. The newer browsers don't go for more than one TITLE command these days.

Man, I'm starting to sound like Dana Carvey's Grumpy Old Man. We had lotsa TITLE commands. And that's the way I likes it!

At this point in time we begin constructing the fully functioning HEAD command extraordinaire:

```
<HEAD>
<TITLE>Big Fat Head Commands</TITLE>
</HEAD>
```

META *Commands*

I have a full tutorial on META commands and what they do. You should check it out for gobs of META commands information. Here, I quickly outline some of the more popular ones:

- `<META NAME="keywords" CONTENT="key,word,key,word">` This offers key words to the search engines that use them in their searches.

- `<META NAME="description" CONTENT="Great page! Come see!">` This offers a description of the page for search engines that use them.

- `<META NAME="generator" CONTENT="Notepad">` This tells search engines what program was used to create the document.

- `<META NAME="author" CONTENT="Some Body">` This tells search engines who wrote the document.

- `<META NAME="copyright" CONTENT="Copyright © 1997 Me">` This tells search engines...blah, blah, blah.

- `<META NAME="expires" CONTENT="15 September 2000">` This automatically expires the document in the search engine's database.

Our super duper HEAD command section grows to this when you add those commands:

```
<HEAD>
<TITLE>Big Fat Head Commands</TITLE>
<META NAME="keywords" CONTENT="key,word,key,word">
<META NAME="description" CONTENT="Great page! Come see!">
<META NAME="generator" CONTENT="Notepad">
<META NAME="author" CONTENT="Some Body">
<META NAME="copyright" CONTENT="Copyright © 1997 Me">
<META NAME="expires" CONTENT="15 September 2000">
</HEAD>
```

The BASE HREF *Command*

The BASE HREF command is one of those commands some tell me has to be used, while others can't see a reason for it. You decide for yourself. Here's the format:

```
<BASE HREF="HTTP://www.htmlgoodies.com/>
```

The command acts as a reference for the remainder of the page. When you use BASE HREF, whatever you place between its quotation marks is added in front of any links you write. For example, I wrote this link:

```
<A HREF="page.html">
```

Since my document employs the BASE HREF command, the link now becomes http://www.htmlgoodies.com/page.html.

"So what?" you say. "It already does that on my machine." That's true. And it will continue to do that as long as the document remains on the site that possesses the correct BASE HREF. What if someone downloads the page and runs it off of her hard drive? The link would be dead without the BASE HREF command. With it, the domain is added and the link works from anywhere.

I have yet to adopt the BASE HREF command because of the setup of my pages; I include page jumps a lot. If I use a BASE HREF, the page jump only works on the server. If the document is on the hard drive, it won't jump because the BASE HREF command won't stop adding the domain to it. However, when the page is posted to the Net it tends to reload the page with the entire domain attached, rather than jumping to the page section I want. It's way too much of a hassle.

Let's continue making our super duper HEAD command section:

```
<HEAD>
<TITLE>Big Fat Head Commands</TITLE>
<META NAME="keywords" CONTENT="key,word,key,word">
```

```
<META NAME="description" CONTENT="Great page! Come see!">
<META NAME="generator" CONTENT="Notepad">
<META NAME="author" CONTENT="Some Body">
<META NAME="copyright" CONTENT="Copyright © 1997 Me">
<META NAME="expires" CONTENT="15 September 2000">
<BASE HREF="HTTP://www.htmlgoodies.com/>
</HEAD>
```

FAQs from the HTML Goodies Web Site

Q. Can I put any HTML code, like an image, into the HEAD commands?

A. Yeah. It runs first and appears first on the page. Try it.

Parts Two and Three

Earlier I said that the HEAD commands break the page into two distinct sections and also are loaded and run first. That comes into play when you have a script of some sort. Let's take JavaScript, for example.

If you place your JavaScripts in the HEAD commands, they are run first. The JavaScript usually has two parts: a script and something that calls for that script to place an object on the page.

Separating the script from the element that calls for it speeds the use. The script is already running by the time the call is made for its services.

As for separating the document into two parts, it is often possible that two entities won't run together—again, use two JavaScripts for an example. Placing one inside the HEAD commands and the other inside the BODY commands tends to separate them enough to calm the fight. They often then both run.

What about style sheet commands? If you are running any on your page, you need to denote to the browsers where to find the CSS files or what each class means.

Adding a JavaScript and some style sheet commands to our super duper HEAD command section, we get the finished product:

```
<HEAD>
<TITLE>Big Fat Head Commands</TITLE>
<META NAME="keywords" CONTENT="key,word,key,word">
<META NAME="description" CONTENT="Great page! Come see!">
<META NAME="generator" CONTENT="Notepad">
<META NAME="author" CONTENT="Some Body">
<META NAME="copyright" CONTENT="Copyright © 1997 Me">
<META NAME="expires" CONTENT="15 September 2000">
```

```
<BASE HREF="HTTP://www.htmlgoodies.com/>
<SCRIPT LANGUAGE="JavaScript">
</SCRIPT>
<STYLE="text/css">
</STYLE>
</HEAD>
```

Well, there it is. The ultimate HTML document HEAD section. Of course, all of that is not needed, but it can't hurt to add it. You'll be helping search engines and some of your site users. I've altered the program I sometimes use to write HTML to include the six META commands already. I'm not so sure about the BASE HREF command, though...

Enjoy!

 I have an HTML document that uses multiple commands between the HEAD commands at http://www.htmlgoodies.com/book/headcommands.html. *Make sure you look at the source code.*

Declaring Your Version of HTML

If you've made your way through the HTML Goodies site, you probably have looked at the source of some of my documents. I know some of you are looking because every now and again, I get a letter asking what that strange, cryptic command at the top stands for. If you don't know what I'm talking about, this is the command:

```
<!DOCTYPE HTML PUBLIC "-//W3C//DTD HTML 4.0//EN">
```

FAQs from the HTML Goodies Web Site

Q. Do I put the declaration between the HEAD commands?

A. No; it goes on the page first thing—even before the HTML command.

That's a strange looking thing, huh? It's called an "HTML Declaration." Basically it's declaring what version of HTML the browser is to use when reading this document. It also tells the viewer, if they care to look. It's long, but rather easy to understand. Here's what it means:

- ○ !DOCTYPE HTML PUBLIC proclaims this is an HTML document type that can be read by public browsers.

- ○ -//W3C represents the HTML organization that proclaims what HTML flags are to be considered standard. You can visit the World Wide Web Consortium's (hence, WWW3C) page at http://www.w3.org and read about HTML until your brain is full.

- ⦿ //DTD HTML 4.0 stands for Document Type Description Hypertext Mark-Up Language (version) 4.0.

- ⦿ //EN means the document will be written in English.

FAQs from the HTML Goodies Web Site

Q. Must I use an HTML declaration? What if I don't?

A. It's up to you. I've been told by those in my school's Computer Science department that if you fail to use a declaration, the default HTML version, usually the highest version out, is enacted. At the moment, that's 3.2. Yes, 4.0 is out, but isn't its use isn't widespread enough to make it a default (as of the writing of this book).

My assumption is that once you read this, you will right away ask if you need to hurry and go put the command on your pages. I can tell you that I use it on every page now. I started putting it on when I first learned about it. Some of my very early pages do not have the command and I'm in no real hurry to get it on them, mainly because the pages use very early (and very basic) commands that do not belong to a higher version of HTML. Besides, I've been told the default is the highest HTML version. I would not be doing myself any good by altering the page.

I would suggest using the declarations if you are trying to write in HTML 4.0 specifically or in the new language that's coming up the pike—XML (extensible mark-up language). I have tutorials on both with sample declarations in the book; see Appendix A and Chapter 15, respectively.

I'll tell you the two rules of thumb that one of the HTML big-heads told me: Use the declaration if you're using META commands or plan to use HTML validators.

 Here's an example of a page using an HTML declaration intended to allow the page to run HTML 4.0: http://www.htmlgoodies.com/book/declair.html.

So You Want an FTP Directory, Huh?

A while ago, I started getting letters asking me how to make an FTP directory. Apparently, people have a series of items they want to offer as downloads. An FTP site can be a great add-on for your main Web site, but there are a few things you have to do differently.

FTP is a totally different *protocol*, or set of instructions, than HTTP (Hypertext Transfer Protocol). This means that an FTP directory has to be set up as a totally different section of the hard drive. You must have your Webmaster or ISP set up an FTP area for you; you can't do it yourself because the FTP and HTTP protocols are totally different and cannot be mixed. There cannot be an ftp://www.htmlgoodies.com and a http://www.htmlgoodies.com existing side by side in the same place. The FTP needs to be a totally separate directory, with its own totally separate Internet protocol number.

You can set up an FTP site just by using HTML, but it's not the best thing to do. I played until I got close to what I wanted; take a look at Figure 9.1.

Figure 9.1

An FTP style listing on an HTTP server.

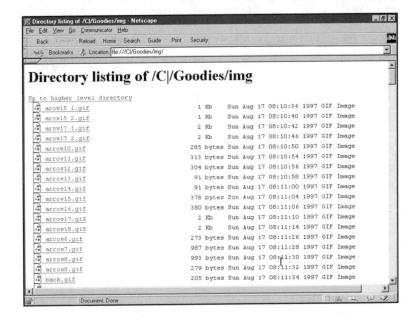

Please understand that I by no means set up a true FTP directory. I am simply giving the impression. All the rules of HTML still apply. This is more visual than it is functional. Downloads do not just happen as they do in a true FTP setting, but I'll give you some hints to get people downloading from you directly from your site.

The thing about an FTP directory is the availability of downloading. If you clicked any of the images displayed, you would notice they just appeared like any other hypertext link. Try this: Netscape people hold down the Shift key while you click an image name; MSIE people, click the right mouse button on the image link; Macintosh people can click and hold, then choose to download. Go ahead try it.

FAQs from the HTML Goodies Web Site

Q. How do I go about getting a real FTP directory? Your idea is good, but I want the real thing.

A. You'll probably have to pay for it. An FTP directory takes up a lot of server time, especially if you are offering large image or movie files. A site's FTP directories usually are on their own server so they don't interfere with the regular Web pages. In addition, they follow a different protocol. That's why when you go to a real FTP directory, the address begins with `ftp://` rather than `http://`. The best first step is to talk to your Web server people and ask them.

Those Shift-Key and Mouse-Click Tricks

In case you're wondering, the Shift key or specific mouse clicking shortcuts work with any link to an image or file. If you do what your browser requires while clicking any hypertext link, you'll initiate a download of whatever is at the other end of the HREF link.

Better still, the Save As that is initiated automatically saves as All Files (or the correct file format), making sure you don't corrupt whatever you are grabbing. Neat, huh?

Using Zip Files

Have you ever clicked something and had the browser ask you what you wanted to do with the file? One of the options was to save the file to disk. That's a *download*. You received that message because the browser, or the server more likely, wasn't configured to display or run that type of program. Therefore, it asked you what to do with it—you downloaded it.

Zip files are compressed versions of your regular files. Browsers don't display them, and even if the browser is configured to understand what the zip file is, the Save As window pops up. It can then be downloaded. Instead of offering the normal version of the file, offer a zipped version. It eliminates all that fancy clicking stuff.

So now all you need is a program that will zip and unzip files for you. My favorite is WinZip, available at `http://www.winzip.com`. This program both creates and opens zipped files. The program is *shareware*, so you'll get it free to test out for about a month and then, if you pay a few bucks, it's yours for good.

I've paid for a good many of my shareware programs. It gets rid of the nagging "pay me" window and usually sets the program up to do more than it did before. Plus, it's only fair. You wouldn't want someone using your stuff without compensating you.

Why the FTP Style Directory Displays

When you posted your HTML pages to your WWW server, you were told to make the home page a specific name. Usually it was `index.html`. Why? Because that is the default file the computer looks for when someone tries to come into the directory. Remember what it said at the top of my images listing: "`Index of /images`".

Keep in mind that this is not a true FTP directory; it is a listing of what is in the directory. It just gives the impression of being an FTP directory.

So why did it display the index as a list of files rather than as the page index.html? Because there wasn't an index.html for it to display. I left it out on purpose to get that effect.

Now, don't be concerned if your WWW server wasn't a different name other than index.html for the main page. I've had servers ask for default.html, www.html, and HomePage.html. You can set it to any name you want. Whatever the name of the default index page is on your server, leave it out on purpose and you'll get a listing like I did earlier.

Making the FTP Directory

You need to create a directory in order to have an FTP directory. If you have a program that creates directories for you, great. Use it. Those of you who do not have it need to make the directory by hand. Follow these steps:

1. Telnet into your server. Enter your login and password.

2. Get to the directory where you place all your WWW files. You should be able to get to it (if you aren't already there) by typing cd *[directory name]* and pressing Return. Do not use the brackets ([ ]).

3. Once there, enter mkdir *[name]*. Replace *[name]* with what you want to call the directory. Do not use the brackets.

4. If you don't get errors, you did it. Now type chmod 777 *[name]*. If this is the case, you're done and now have a directory ready to accept files and to allow people in.

5. Log out. Put your FTP files in your new directory and forget the index.html on purpose.

6. If you do not have Telnet capabilities, ask your server people how you go about making subdirectories. If they tell you you're not allowed, you might want to look for another server.

There you go; nothing to it. Just remember to tell people to do the Shift key or mouse-click stuff—or make it easier on your users by zipping the files for them.

Enjoy!

 Go to: http://www.htmlgoodies.com/book/download.html *to see an FTP directory in action, try the downloading tips above, and grab a zip file I have posted there. There's a surprise inside when you open it.*

Web Pages Without the .html Extension

After I put up Java Goodies I began getting letters asking how I post pages that do not require the .html extension. To some it may seem simple enough, but to those new to the HTML game, it isn't. So here's the trick.

This tutorial is online at http://www.htmlgoodies.com/directory/. *Please note there is no* .html *extension on* directory—*just the slash afterward.*

My assumption is that you have a WWW site right now, correct? That means that you have a general idea that you need to place files from your computer to a server so the whole world can see them.

When you upload, you are uploading to a directory. That directory is a little section of the server's hard drive set aside and given a name. Let's say your home page address is as follows:

```
http://www.fred.com/~wwwuser
```

The name of the directory that you upload or FTP all your files to is named wwwuser. See that? What you may not know is that the directory has a certain set of rules that it follows. The main rule is that it allows any and everybody to look at its contents. It's a WWW directory and people can access it, right? Another rule is that you are given personal access, with the use of a login and password, to place and remove files.

The rule you may not be aware of—and the one that will be of the utmost importance to this tutorial—is that the directory has been told to look for a specific filename when someone logs on. Notice the address again. It doesn't call for any specific page. It could, of course, just by adding a slash and then the page name, like so:

```
http://www.fred.com/~wwwuser/joe.html
```

But that's not what happened. The directory's name is all that was listed. Again, look at the online example. Here's the URL:

```
http://www.htmlgoodies.com/directory/
```

None of these addresses calls for a certain page, but one comes up. That's because of the third rule I spoke of earlier. I hope you were paying attention...and spit out that gum.

The Index Page

When you got your WWW site, you were told to give the home page a certain name. The vast majority of the time that name is index.html. Why? Because the directory that holds your WWW files has been told when someone tries to get access to the directory, by default, display the index.html page. Get it?

Don't get flustered if your default page isn't index.html. I have been on many different servers. One wanted www.html, the other wanted HomePage.html (note the capitalization), and a third wanted default.html. My Webmaster wizards here at HTML Goodies tell me that you can configure a server to search for booger.html if you really wanted. But that would lead to a sticky situation. Rim-shot. (Thank you folks, good night! Try the Veal.)

How to Do It

It took me a while to get to this didn't it? I tend to ramble. How do you do it? The rule of thumb here is to remember that any *subdirectory* (a directory inside a directory) retains all the properties of the parent directory. Any directory inside a bigger directory will do what the big directory does just because. That's my best "Gen-X" speak.

If you make a directory inside of wwwuser, then that directory will also display its own index.html. If you make a smaller directory inside that directory, then it will display its own index.html. Get it?

FAQs from the HTML Goodies Web Site

Q. I am following your tutorial on losing the .html. The problem is that now I have two different index.html pages. I have already erased my original by saving the new one right over it. How do I solve this?

A. I have done that at least 10 times. The best way to keep it straight is to create the same directory structure on your computer's hard drive as is on your server. If your WWW address uploads to a directory called wwwuser, create a directory on your hard drive named the same. Then create the subdirectories so that your computer reflects the server. Now you'll lessen your problems. My hard drive is set up as an exact duplicate of HTML Goodies. Of course, always make backups. You don't know this, but HTML Goodies is fully posted on three servers. You only get to see one. If that one crashes, the next one can be used immediately.

Creating a Directory

I have received so many letters telling me that I go the long way in making a directory. True, there are software programs out there that will do all of this with the click of a button, but in case you don't have such an animal, try this. If you do have a program that will do all of this on-the-fly, go nuts. You may save yourself a few hours by first calling to ask your server people how they want you to create subdirectories, or if they want you to create them at all.

I know this listed just a minute ago, but so you can avoid flipping back and forth, here's the process again:

1. Telnet in to your site.
2. Get to your directory. Usually when you Telnet into your site, you are either in, or are one directory above, your WWW directory (where you keep all your files).
3. Try typing cd *[name of your www directory]* at the prompt.
4. If that doesn't work, type cd .. (two periods) and then try Step three again. If you don't get any errors, you're there.

5. If you like, you can type `ls` at the prompt; that gives you a listing of all your files.

6. To create the directory, type `mkdir [directory name]`.

7. Do another `ls` command; you should see that directory sitting there.

8. Some servers need for that directory to be "turned on" before anyone can use it. Just to be safe, type `chmod [directory name] a+rx` now. If the server won't take that command, try substituting `a+rx` with `777`.

9. Log out. You're done.

Now you have a second directory sitting inside your `wwwuser` directory. That directory responds to its own `index.html`. Let's say you named the directory *skippy*. Now you can tell people to go to the following URL and they'll get the main page with no html. Now, how easy it that?

```
http://www.fred.com/~wwwuser/skippy
```

 There's an example of losing the `.html` *across many pages.* Go to `http://www.htmlgoodies.com/book/.`

Chapter 10

Adding Sound and Video

Sound on the Net

Sounds on the Net are a great thing. If you have a computer equipped with a sound card and a few shareware programs, you can hear as much as you care to download. Van Halen is my favorite music group. I was able to download the sound files of two new songs before their Greatest Hits album came out. I still bought the CD, of course. The sounds are neat, but are not quite yet the quality of my Sony home sound system. I can rattle pictures off the walls with that pup.

This is not to say that only music can be played over the Net. Any sound—from a dog barking to full orchestras—can be turned into a computer file and played over the Web. This chapter covers two ways of offering sounds over the Internet: helper applications and embedding the sounds.

FAQs from the HTML Goodies Web Site

Q. Before I ask about putting a sound on my page, I have to ask...is it legal to do that?

A. If you wrote and performed the song, yes. If you didn't, we get into a gray area. Permission conquers all in discussions of copyright. If you have permission to play the music, then you're good to go. BMI and ASCAP (the two big music licensing firms) are now selling site licenses; your server may have one. If so, all you need to do is report to

continues

them you're playing the song. In turn, they report it back to the firm. Past that, just grabbing a portion of your favorite group's music and playing it is treading on thin ice. They might care, they might not. Even if you don't play the entire song, they might still get upset. Be prepared to take the sound down if you are asked to.

 When I posted the first version of this tutorial, it was the most popular one on the HTML Goodies site. It's still visited often. Go to http://www.htmlgoodies.com/embed.html *to see it yourself.*

Helper Applications

When the World Wide Web got started, back when Mosaic was the browser and this new thing called Netscape Navigator 1.0 had just come out, sounds were available. They were played with the use of a helper application.

Helper applications are programs that were called upon by the Netscape Navigator browser, but were not part of the Navigator itself. (You can still do it all this way, don't get me wrong. Plug-ins, covered later, are making helper applications a bit of an endangered species.) You're using helper applications right now. Every browser has a different way of displaying the helper applications it's currently using. In some versions of Navigator, for instance, just click the **Options** menu. Choose **Preferences** and then choose **Helper Applications**—there they are. Roll down the list and you'll see a lot of extra applications and Ask User statements. In order to play a sound file (.wav, .au, or .aiff), you need to attach an application that the browser can use to play the sound.

I used (and still do) a program called WHAM. It's great and it plays all types of sound files.

Here's how helper applications work:

- The browser goes and gets the sound file, downloading the entire thing into a temporary directory.
- The helper application is launched once the file is complete. Some helper applications, like RealPlayer, actually launch and begin playing the file before it is completely downloaded.
- The operating system (Windows 3.*x*, Windows 95, MacOS, and the like) loads the sound file into the application.
- The application plays the sound.

I always thought it was a pretty good system. Yeah, it took a bit of time, especially using a 14.4 or 28.8 modem, but it always worked.

Figure 10.1 shows a helper application playing a sound file on the HTML Goodies site. The helper application is one you'll find on most computers running Windows: the Media Player. All I did was go into the Helper Applications mentioned earlier and assigned it to play certain types of sound files.

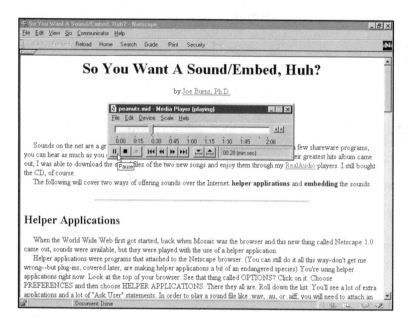

Figure 10.1
Helper application playing a sound file.

Putting Sound on the Page

Follow this format if you have a sound you'd like to offer. This will make your Web visitors use a helper application

```
<A HREF="http://www.yoursite.com/filename.wav">Click Here</A>
```

Of course, there are sound formats other than .wav. Keep reading for information on a few more you can use.

Notice that the preceding code is nothing more than a simple link format pointed right at the sound file. All you need to do is offer the sound file. Place it in the same directory as the page that calls for it; the browsers take it from there. You just sit back and watch it happen. Just be sure to FTP-transfer the sound file to your site as binary or raw data; any other way can corrupt it. You can read more about FTP transfers in Primer 7.

Embedding Sound on a Page

This is a relatively new way of doing things. Embedding a sound means that you include the sound commands in your HTML document and use a plug-in to run it.

Plug-ins are programs that help your browser perform at a higher level. They are called *plug-ins* because they must have the browser open to work. Helper applications are independent of the browser. Plug-ins are not.

A sound plug-in does basically the same thing the helper application does, but the sound plug-in works inside the browser window rather than starting up as a whole other program. Instead of WHAM popping up and the browser being pushed to the back as the sound runs, a sound plug-in works inside the browser. That allows you to play with the page while the sound is running.

Figure 10.2 shows a plug-in playing a sound on the HTML Goodies site.

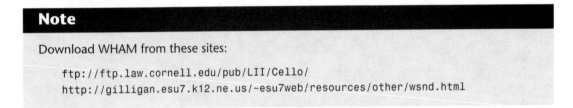

Note

Download WHAM from these sites:

```
ftp://ftp.law.cornell.edu/pub/LII/Cello/
http://gilligan.esu7.k12.ne.us/~esu7web/resources/other/wsnd.html
```

Figure 10.2
Plug-in application playing a sound file.

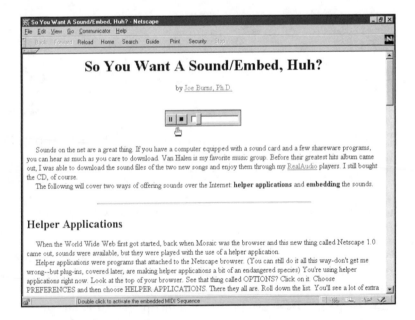

Notice the hand on the player that pops up? It is pointing with two fingers. I set up this embed so that the user has to click to start it, but there are ways to make it start all by itself.

If you head to the Netscape home page or to Yahoo! and enter plug-ins, you'll be able to scan a ton of little programs that cover everything from sound to video to 3D VRML. They all have specific requirements for browser types and platforms. Be sure to read the instructions before downloading. Not all four plug-ins that I installed dealt with sounds, but they have all worked right away.

If you're using a later version of Netscape Navigator, you might have run into something odd: a page that requires a plug-in and a pop up in your browser window asking if you'd like to get the appropriate plug-in. If you answer yes, it takes you to the Netscape plug-in page and you then download what you need.

FAQs from the HTML Goodies Web Site

Q. The tutorial about embedding sound is fine, but how do I make my sounds?

A. You must have a computer that can create sound files first. If your computer came with a sound card, you most likely can. Look for a utility called Sound Recorder (or something similar). Open it. It usually looks a lot like the controls on a cassette machine (see Figure 10.3). If you have a sound card, you most likely have a microphone and CD player too. That recording device simply starts recording what is coming through the speakers when you hit the red button. Once you have the piece you want, save it as one of three formats: .wav (a PC format), .au (a Sun format), or .mid (the MIDI format). Although there are other formats, these are the most popular in the Net.

Figure 10.3
Sound recorder tool panel (Windows 95).

What is MIDI?

It's an acronym that stands for Musical Instrument Digital Interface. That's a program that acts as a go-between for an instrument and something that creates the sound. Sort of like running a guitar through a computer and out a speaker.

MIDI files work over the Net like a little program that runs the sound card. The MIDI file is not simply read like a .wav or an .au file. The MIDI file sort of "plays" the sound card. It tells the sound card what note to produce and for what duration. Put enough of them together and it sounds like music.

The Format for an EMBED *Command*

I'm going to show how to embed a sound file on your Web page. In this example I'll use a MIDI file. In fact, if you have the ability to play MIDI files, and have already visited this tutorial online, you probably clicked and have listened to a MIDI of the Peanuts theme. I like it. This is the code you need:

```
<EMBED SRC="sound.mid" AUTOSTART=FALSE LOOP=
WIDTH=145 HEIGHT=55 ALIGN="CENTER">
</EMBED>
```

I should probably make it clear that EMBED is not an HTML standard command. At the time of this writing, it only works with the Netscape Navigator browser. If you use an EMBED command on your page, you should follow it immediately with this command:

```
<BGSOUND="###">
```

That basic command allows those running Internet Explorer to hear the sound you've embedded on your page. If you add one, add the other. Be good to all your viewers. Here's how EMBED works:

- EMBED tells the browser an embedded sound is here—go get the plug-in. Embed commands are associated with plug-ins.

- HEIGHT/WIDTH deal with the embedded object's size on the page. That little control panel at the top of the page in Figure 10.2 was created with a size of 145×55. You can read more about HEIGHT and WIDTH commands in Chapter 3, "Adding Images and Backgrounds." The embedded object is offered almost as if it were an image; that way the browser understands what the embedded thing is.

- SRC stand for *source*. It tells the browser where to go in order to get the audio file.

- AUTOSTART deals with whether you want the sound to play by itself or by the viewer starting the file after the plug-in box pops up. TRUE starts the file straight away; FALSE prompts the viewer to play it.

- LOOP works basically the same way as AUTOSTART. TRUE loops the sound so it plays forever. Make the loop FALSE if you only want it played once.

- HIDDEN works to allow you to hide the controls. Use YES and NO. By the way: If you hide the control, it might be a good idea to AUTOSTART the sound.

Note

The browser does one of three things if there are no plug-ins available:

1. Nothing. Very early level browsers and Internet Explorer use this tactic.

2. Put up a dialog box asking you how you want to handle the file. Earlier versions of Navigator might do this.

3. Tell you a plug-in is needed and ask if you'd like to go get it. (W95 browsers do this.)

FAQs from the HTML Goodies Web Site

Q. How do I make it so that the EMBED plays multiple audio files, one right after the other?

A. You need to take the files you want play and edit them all together into one big file. I know of no other way.

Q. When I have an EMBED on my site, it plays great. When the person leaves the page, however, it stops. How do I keep it playing?

A. You must keep the window that contains the embed commands open. Either make all links on the page open new windows, or use the new window JavaScript to open a small window that contains the embed. (For more information on the new JavaScript window, see Chapter 11, "Java Applets and JavaScript.") That window keeps it playing, unless the person closes it.

Q. Isn't there a way to set the loudness of the EMBED?

A. Nope.

More About Embed

You can EMBED just about any type of sound file as long as the person using your page has the capability to read it. My plug-in plays just about any file except RealAudio. You can read more about RealAudio later in this book.

RealAudio still works as a helper application. What's great about RealAudio is that it plays the sound as it is being downloaded. The play is almost instantaneous. Great invention.

Download time with an EMBED is not sped up or slowed. The entire file must download before the plug-in plays it. What is different (and better) about this is that an EMBED starts the download process without anyone clicking blue words. You can also play with the page while the download is occurring, rather than just sitting and waiting, like you had to do with helper applications.

FAQs from the HTML Goodies Web Site

Q. What format would you suggest using to play sounds on the Net?

A. I suggest WAV first, MIDI second. Both are pretty popular. Of course, you can always offer an array of formats. Just find a shareware sound program that has the capability to save in multiple formats and then offer three or four—or offer any one you want. If someone wants the sounds bad enough, he can get the plug-in.

That's about it. Try embedding a few MIDI files and see what kind of response you get. I have one here and there; no one has complained yet.

Enjoy!

 You can listen to me speak via an embedded sound file. I have a soft, yet soothing voice. It's at http://www.htmlgoodies.com/book/voiceembed.html.

RealAudio: A Special Format

I have stayed away from RealAudio mainly because in the past it couldn't be performed straight off a WWW server. You needed a RealAudio server to run the format.

 You can, however, hear me speak in RealAudio! Point your browser to this tutorial on line at http://www.htmlgoodies.com/ra.html.

The process of RealAudio was explained to me by two different Internet server tech people. (These guys know words that don't exist in any language.) After they explained for a good 15 minutes, they stopped, noticed that my eyes had completely glazed over, and decided to give it to me in simple terms. Note that the process is much more involved than this, but here's the general idea:

You put a sound on your WWW page, say a .wav or a MIDI. You are using what is known as a helper application or a plug-in. Either way, you are calling on a piece of software other than the browser itself to play the sound. The problem with that is that it takes some time because the entire file has to download and then be loaded into the application before it can play. Depending on download speeds, Net congestion, file size, and your modem speed, this could take a long, long time.

Where RealAudio beats them all is that it plays the sounds almost instantaneously. It amazed me the first time I heard and saw it work. If you did what I did, you went to the RealAudio site, didn't bother to read any of the documentation, grabbed the RealAudio converter, and placed a few files on your server.

Mine didn't work either.

It didn't work because of downloading time and pace. For example, if you download an image file and sit there watching the numbers tick by in the status bar, you'll notice that the numbers are by no means consistent. You get a burst of data here and there, but there are also downtimes. You have to remember that you are not the only person being serviced by the system and that other people need the file too. That's the *downtime*—while others are being helped, or while the telephone line path to your house is very busy.

FAQs from the HTML Goodies Web Site

Q. I got RealAudio files to work by downloading them and then playing them off my hard drive.

A. Yup, that'll work. But it defeats the purpose of the files. You might as well have used .wav.

RealAudio works by creating a *buffer*, or specific connection, between your computer and a RealAudio server. Once the connection is established, the transfer of data is consistent and at a set pace, usually the pace of your modem. It's a process known as *streaming*. That way the file can be played as it is being downloaded. The pace is the key here. HTTP servers don't offer the pace the RealAudio server does.

"But there has to be a way to play these things off of my site," you say.

"There is now!" I reply.

FAQs from the HTML Goodies Web Site

Q. I want a RealAudio server. How much do they cost?

A. The last time I checked into buying one (I really did this) the costs were up around 10 grand to get it running. That's before even attempting to find a server that would allow me to place the machine and hook up to the Internet. You see, RealAudio servers are *bandwidth* (the width of the pipe coming out of the Internet server) monsters. They use a ton of it. It can shut the place down. You need a very large investment in not only space, but in number of connections.

RealAudio from Your Site

In order to run RealAudio sound files from your HTTP server, you're going to need a few things. Luckily they're all free for the downloading. You'll need the following:

1. The RealAudio player version 3.0 or later
2. The RealAudio sound encoder
3. A RealAudio meta file

These items and more are available at the RealAudio web site `http://www.realaudio.com` and their site `www.realstore.com`. I'll show you how to make one of those meta deals yourself.

First things first. If you're going to do this, your server must have two MIME type settings:

- `audio/x-pn-realaudio` Files with an .ra or .ram file extension.
- `audio/x-pn-realaudio-plugin` Files with an .rpm file extension.

These settings are nothing that you can do yourself. You need to contact your system administrator and ask for the settings to be made. Most servers already have these settings, but it's best to check.

Those settings tell the HTTP server to load the RealAudio server when it sees a file with the .ra or .ram extension.

FAQs from the HTML Goodies Web Site

Q. You tell us all the time to contact our system people. I don't know who they are. I am on Geocities (or Anglefire, or the like) and they tell me they can't allow me to do these things.

A. Well, those are free home page sites. What you are getting is free, so the system people can claim far more control over what you can and cannot do. Allowing someone to do a lot of this stuff can mess up a server. If you are very serious about doing the things in this book, you need to perhaps buy space on a server that allows more freedom. I like Geocities, but they are smart not to let everyone place CGIs, set MIME files, or create directories. It can cause many problems.

Creating the RealAudio Sound File

You will use the RealAudio encoder to do this. If you haven't installed it on your computer yet, do it. It's rather simple to use. The hardest part is getting the .wav file to convert to RealAudio. That's the catch of this tutorial. You have to be able to make a sound file. Most newer computers have a mic or a sound recorder program on them. Use it to make a file and then open that file in the RealAudio encoder and encode it. You should now have a file with the same name as the original but with an .ra extension. It stands for RealAudio.

Creating the RealAudio Meta File

Now it gets a little tricky. If this were a simple .wav or MIDI file, you could just transfer it to your server and make an HREF link to it to get it to play. Not so here. You need a buffer between the page and the RealAudio sound file. That buffer is the meta file. Here's what you do:

1. Create a simple text file with a text editor. The file should only have the path to the RealAudio file on your server.

   For example, your file is called joe.ra. You place it on your server named http://www.server.com/~fred. Your meta file contains only this line of text:

   ```
   http://www.server.com/~fred/joe.ra
   ```

   Don't use any HTML commands. Don't use any quotation marks. Don't put anything else in the file other than the path to your RealAudio file. Just that.

2. Now save the small text document with the extension .ram. If you want to name the meta file *joe*, save it as `joe.ram`. Get it? Now you have your meta file ready to go.

3. Transfer the sound and the meta file to your server. Make sure the sound file goes as binary or you'll mess it up. You can read more about FTP transfers in Primer 7.

RealAudio in the HTML Document

Now it's time to call for the RealAudio file in a document. It would make sense to make a link straight to the sound file. Not so. In this case you make a link to the meta file. Note that the meta file only has the path to the RealAudio file inside it.

- The HTML document calls on the meta file.
- The call on the meta file denotes to the server that a RealAudio file will be used here.
- The RealAudio file begins a download.
- The file starts playing after enough has downloaded to be read and understood.

...and off it goes.

So What's the Downside?

There are a few downsides to servingRealAudio on your Web site:

- The viewer must have the RealAudio player 3.0 or later. The players are a free download from the RealAudio site, so you're pretty safe.
- The meta file text will display if the MIME settings are incorrect.
- The Net may be congested; the download will be so sporadic that it won't work.

But it's better than nothing.

FAQs from the HTML Goodies Web Site

Q. I went to the RealAudio site and they now have RealVideo and an encoder, too. Will the video work like the audio in your tutorial?

A. People have told me it will. I have never tried it, but videos are usually so huge that I suspect Net congestion will get you. Go ahead and try it.

 I have an example of a RealAudio file running off a Web server. You can find the example at `http://www.htmlgoodies.com/book/realaudio.html`.

Video on the Net

A video? On your home page? Yes. Videos have been on the Internet for a while now, and if you don't mind spending a healthy chunk of change for the required hardware and software, they're pretty simple to create.

 This tutorial can be found online at `http://www.htmlgoodies.com/video.html`.

There are many different video formats that will play on one type of computer or another, depending on the software the user has installed. There are, however, three formats that are used almost exclusively over the Internet.

I am not including the streaming videos like RealVideo, Vivo, or NetShow. Remember that streaming means that the video is played in what's known as *real time*—it is played as it is being downloaded. I'm talking simple video formats.

- AVI—This stands for audio/video interleaved. It's a video format created by Microsoft that allows for video and audio to be saved together. This is the premier video format on the PC because it allows for many different compression schemes and reproduces a good picture. It also requires a lot of space. The extension for a file in this format is .avi.

- Quicktime—This is Apple computer's Macintosh-based format for playing movies. Apple has made the format quite popular on the Internet by creating players that allow the format to be run on an IBM. The Quicktime format is also popular because of its compression scheme. Files in Quicktime are usually less than half the size of their AVI equivalent, but do lose quality. The extension for a file in this format is .mov.

- MPEG—This is a video format created by the Motion Picture Experts Group; thus the name. The format runs on both Macintosh and IBM platforms and is valued for its compression rate. A large file can be transferred to MPEG and lose little quality while dropping the bit rate a great deal. The extension for a file in the format is .mpg.

I own PCs, so I capture in AVI format. Once I have the video in AVI, I use two separate pieces of software to change the video from AVI into one of the other two formats. AVI can be turned into MPEG straight away. The encoding process takes around two minutes for every one second of AVI video. Quicktime is a different story. The entire AVI file must be re-saved with a different compression rate, known as *Intel Indeo*. The AVI can then be run through a Quicktime converter. That process is very fast.

Figure 10.4 shows three file formats with the same four-second video of me saying "Hi Mom. Look, I'm on the Internet." Then I wave. It's pure movie magic.

Let's note the differences in file size between formats. Forget that. Note the file size, period. There's no doubt about it people—these things take up a lot of space. How are they produced? First, let's look at how a real video is put together. It will help later.

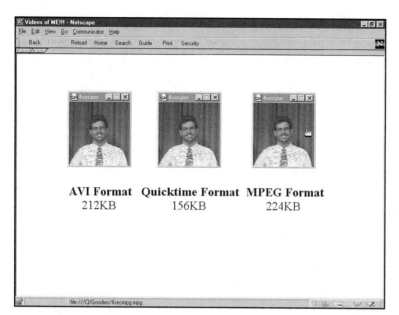

Figure 10.4
Three video formats and their sizes.

Film and Video

I have no doubt that all of you have seen a piece of film. A film is put together through one little picture replacing the one before it. As the film strip passes over the light, each frame (the frame is the little picture) is displayed. The frames roll past fast enough that your eyeballs perceive some sort of motion. The pictures on a film strip do not carry motion; your eye just perceives the quick passing of static frames as motion. It's a neat little trick that will help us later.

In case you're wondering, 24 frames pass over a film projector's light every second.

Video

Ah, video. A big fat cassette tape that carries pictures and sound. And it's not a whole lot more than that.

It would seem that if film used 24 frames per second, that video would just follow through and do the same. Not so. You see, video is used mostly on television; television uses a 30 frame per second speed, so video does too.

What about those slower video speeds like SLP and LP? They do run the tape more slowly, but still produce the 30 frames a second. By running the tape more slowly, the VCR is asking more and more information to be saved in a smaller and smaller space. This makes for a less pleasing picture. The slower speeds are a trade-off between picture quality and amount of data on a VCR tape. This little ditty of information will also be helpful later.

Video is easy to serve up on your Web site. Think of video the same way you do an audio file. You can use the same link and embed format you would in order to run the audio. Just remember that when you embed a video, it will show up in the browser window as a gray square until it fully loads. Make room for it. The real trick is in making the videos.

Digital Video

The three video files in Figure 10.4 are all digital video. Each is a different format, but they basically do the same thing. They play back a "video" in digitized form. Just as a scanner makes a digital photocopy of a picture, a video card makes a duplicate of a video movie.

It will make a digital copy of a video rather than a film because film is not in the correct frame rate format; 24 doesn't go into 30 cleanly. (In case you're wondering, the mathematical method used to put film on video tape is 1.5 video frames to one film frame. Add it up. It equals out.) In addition, video is already movement in a mechanical format. Video is captured motion played back through electronic *transducing* (change of one form of energy into another) of metal particles into color and motion.

Huh? Every time one of the 30 frames rolls past, the information saved on the VCR tape is read by a video reader or *head*. That head is electrified and the magnetic particles on the tape disrupt the electrical field the head is producing. That disruption is displayed to you as a picture. That's as un-technical as I could explain it and not resort to hand puppets.

Since the magnetic field is already there, why can't you just send that disrupted signal to a computer rather than another VCR or TV? You can. That's how those three pups in Figure 10.4 were produced.

FAQs from the HTML Goodies Web Site

Q. You've mentioned compression in a few different tutorials. What is that?

A. In layman's terms, *compression* is the capability to make an image or a video smaller by combining multiple pixels into one. Imagine an image with four dots all a slightly different shade of brown. By using compression, you can make it so that the four are combined into one—all the same color brown. That takes fewer bytes. You could store the image as only one pixel, but display all four pixels when the image is shown. Video is the same. If you can borrow from the frame before without loading a brand new frame each time (or combine pixels), then you are using fewer bytes and compressing the file size.

The Trick Is Compression

It's my opinion that the future of TV and video is all in the compression rate. What if you could purchase a TV show to watch whenever you wanted? Say you want to watch the evening news right now. It may not be on right now. But what if you could put your credit card into a computer and order the show over the Internet? Would you? I would. I'd even pay a little more to get a copy without commercials. Video on demand—if it can ever be perfected, it will put a serious dent in video stores and movie houses.

At today's compression rates, a half-hour show would take up more than 75MB. That's where the future is: compressing a show so it downloads in a minute. It's coming; I can feel it in my bad knee.

FAQs from the HTML Goodies Web Site

Q. I'm working with a piece of video. You're right—these things are huge. Any suggestion on how to make my video smaller in terms of bytes?

A. I have a couple: Go with Quicktime format. It usually produces the smallest amount of bytes. Use compression to create the video; I usually set mine at 50%, capture 15 frames a second rather than 30, go in black and white if I can, make the screen smaller, and lose the sound. Those will help.

Getting the Hardware

The equipment you need to capture video is quite simple: something that plays the video, like a VCR, and a video capture card that slides into your computer. In addition, you need a fairly strong computer with memory...lots and lots of memory. A big hard drive doesn't hurt either. You hook the VCR's out ports to the video capture card's in ports, install some software, and you're pretty much good to go. I'm sure the software will come with the card. Barring any unforeseen problems, you should be able to grab video with the best of them.

Cost is a factor, I'm sure. As with anything else, the better you buy, the more you will pay. The more options you want, the more you pay. My video card is Video Magic, made by Hauppaugue; it has the capability to capture a full 30 frames a second in two different formats using a few different types of compression rations. I paid $600 for the card and the software to be able to capture and then edit video on my desktop.

 Head to http://www.htmlgoodies.com/book/videos.html *to play a couple of videos. You also get a full explanation of the exact equipment I use to capture, create, and edit my own digital video. It's the exact setup I use to teach to my university classes.*

Video Player Software

If you have attempted to play the three videos via the online version of this tutorial and couldn't, it's not because I don't like you—it's because you don't have the correct video player. You should have them; they're free. Some may have even come with your computer.

Try to grab a plug-in version of your player. It works much better than the older, helper application model. If there isn't one available, don't worry about it. Just get one that plays the video on my site, so that you can see my smiling face. That's what's really important.

Net Notes

Most computers are already configured to play AVI and Quicktime formats. Some also have MPEG capabilities. If you are having trouble, try these sites for movie-playing helper applications:

> AVI format: `http://www.scdm.com/` and `http://www.udel.edu/ps/sw/aviplay2.htm`

> Quicktime format: `http://quicktime.apple.com/`

> MPEG format: `http://www.geom.umn.edu/docs/mpeg_play/mpeg_play.html`

> MPEG format for UNIX: `http://www.mpegtv.com/`

These sites offer multiple-format movie-playing applications:

> MacZilla, Movie Player for Macintosh: `http://maczilla.com/`

> CineWeb: `http://www.digigami.com/cineweb/`

Chapter 11

Java Applets and JavaScript

What's the Difference Between Java and JavaScript?

So what is the difference between Java and JavaScript? Java is an object-oriented programming (OOP) language created by James Gosling of Sun Microsystems. JavaScript was created by the fine people at Netscape and is also an OOP language. Many of their programming structures are similar, but JavaScript contains a much smaller and simpler set of commands, which make it easier for the average weekend warrior to understand. JavaScript is also much easier to work with because you embed JavaScript directly into your HTML documents.

Java is a much larger and more complicated language that creates standalone applications. A Java *applet* (so called because it is a little application) is a fully contained program. With Java you have to create separate files, compile them, and go through all kinds of other black magic to make your work usable.

Java applets run independent of the HTML document that is calling for them. Sure, they appear on the page, but the HTML document did little more than call for the application and place it. If the programmer allows it, oftentimes parameters can be set by the HTML document. The delivery of the applet is done through a download. The HTML document calls for the application, downloads to the user's cache, and waits to run. JavaScript is wholly reliant on the browser to understand it and make it come to life.

What's the benefit of using one over the other? There are several. If you can understand Java, it is amazingly versatile. Because of the size and structure of the language, it can be used to create anything from small Web page events, to entire databases, to full browsers. Java is the program I use to track my advertising banners.

In my opinion, JavaScript's main benefit is that is can be understood by the common man. It is much easier and robust than Java and allows for fast creation of Web page events. Many JavaScript commands are what are known as *event handlers*. They can be embedded into existing HTML commands. JavaScript is a little more forgiving than Java; it allows more freedom in the creation of objects. Java is very rigid and requires all items to be denoted and spelled out. JavaScript allows you to call on items that already exist, like the status bar or the browser itself, and play with just that part. JavaScript is geared toward Web pages. Java is geared toward where it is needed most at the time.

Both create great Web page events. Both can offer interaction between your user and your Web page. But they are not created equally.

Which to use where? Use whichever fits your needs. That sounds like a cop out, but remember that the applets and JavaScript are most often offered on the Net as fully functioning items. You simply grab them and use them on your page (provided you are given permission). There are many sites out there that do nothing more than hand out applets or JavaScript. I have a list of them in Appendix C, "Valuable Links." HTML Goodies has a sister site called Java Goodies (`http://www.htmlgoodies.com/javagoodies`) that hands out JavaScripts. We have over 500 at the time of this writing.

The following tutorials teach you to implement these items on your pages. They do not teach you to write the languages, but rather instruct you on placing functioning applets and JavaScript scripts on your Web pages. It is a good introduction to the formats. Once you know how to get these pups on your pages, you'll understand more about their structures and can then more easily attempt to learn the language and create functioning JavaScripts or applets yourself.

FAQs from the HTML Goodies Web Site

Q. Where do I learn to write Java or JavaScript?

A. That's a very hard question to answer. I did a lot of searching of the Internet and found some help, but not much. What I did find started at an advanced level. My suggestion is to purchase a book on the subject of Java or JavaScript programming and set aside a weekend. Remember, this is a language. It's just the same as if you were going to purchase a book on learning to speak Chinese. See if a local college is offering a class on the programming language. If so, that's the way to go. If not, read through a few books, pick one, and give yourself time. Lots of time. I can write JavaScript pretty fluently, but it took me a good six months to get to this point.

Enjoy!

Java

This section deals with installing existing Java applets on your Web site. You must have a 32-bit platform computer system in order to run any applet correctly. That means you require Windows 95/98, OS/2, or a newer Macintosh operating system (Mac OS). Yes, Macintosh is a 32-bit OS, but earlier versions do not run Java applets.

This also requires a browser that has Java capabilities. This means a Netscape Navigator, Internet Explorer, or equivalent 32-bit browser. If the browser you have on your system was made for Windows 95/98 or Macintosh, it is ready to go. My apologies, but this does not work on Windows 3.*x* for workgroups, even with the 32-bit extension software installed.

I have been told that plug-ins for Windows 3.*x* are being devised so that you can view applets on that platform, but as of this writing I wasn't able to find one. They may be available now. I would start my search for a plug-in at the Netscape home page (`http://home.netscape.com`).

There are a great number of people who have mastered the Java language and have created numerous applets for you to use on Web pages. Really. I have long list of sites in Appendix C whose entire reason for being around is to hand out functioning Java applets. Cool, huh?

I see applets handed out basically one of two ways. Either the applet sits on the creator's server and you attach to it or the applet is given right to you and you place it on your own server. We'll go over attaching to an applet on another server here and how to place the applet on your own server in the advanced applets tutorial coming up next in this book.

 This tutorial can be found online at `http://www.htmlgoodies.com/bookchat.html`.

The applet we work with here is a very cool one. It sets up a chat room. You can use it to do real-time chats with other people all over the Web. Plus, is won't make your server people angry because all the work is done somewhere else. It doesn't get any better than this.

Well, it does, but we're not there yet. Before we get into sliding this chat room into your site, let's find out just what we're dealing with here.

How Does Your Browser Know It's a Java Applet?

If you've read over my primers or have been working with the World Wide Web for a while, then you know the Internet works by giving everything a filename and a suffix. In computer terms it's called *association*. The name `image.gif` is an example. `image` is the name of the item and `.gif` is its form. A page on the Web is done the same way. The title of the this tutorial's online version is `bookapplet.html`. The name of the page is `bookapplet` and the type of page is `.html`.

By doing this, the computer can tell all these different file types apart. It associates an application with the item's format. Images are displayed using an image viewer, .html pages are displayed using the browser, and so on. Once the computer sees the item's format by its suffix, it knows what application to open in order to use the item.

These applets work the same way, yet they run on their own, inside the browser window, without opening another program. The computer sees the applet as a name and then a suffix. In terms of an applet, the suffix is .class. Remember that applets are models made up of many little parts—a class of parts. Just as species are broken up into classes, so are applet parts. An applet is a class of like parts. Thus, you name the applet you are using in this fashion: applet.class. Still with me?

You're saying "Wait, my PC won't let me put five letters after the dot." I'll bet you are using Windows 3.*x*. That won't work here.

I said earlier that there are numerous sites that hand out applets through the grace of the authors' hearts. Those are great sites and I'll show you how to use some of those applets. Once you learn this, you'll be able to go to any site running a Java applet and—just by looking at the page's source code—see the text required to make the applet run and maybe even grab the applet itself.

I'm asking you nicely to not do that. There are enough free applets out there that you do not need to take without permission.

If you do find an applet you like and it's not being offered for download, ask the author if you can use it. Most people on the Net are quite accommodating. If the author says no, respect that.

You see, it's really tough to use an applet and take the author's name off. Usually the copyright and author's name are in the compiled code. You might not know yet that applets are not text—they are compiled machine language. You can't get into it and that makes it super simple to show who actually wrote it and that you're using it without permission.

That's copyright infringement and that's not good.

The Chat Room Applet

Here we go! People believe this Java stuff must be hard because it requires all these little stipulations. Actually, Java is pretty easy to implement once the applet is compiled. It's just reeeeeeeaaaaal testy. It likes everything to be just so. If it isn't, tough—no Java for you!

What you need:

- An applet (no kidding)
- A series of lines in your HTML document that call for the applet

Here's the process we'll follow: The chat room applet is being offered to you through the fine people at ChatPlanet, the largest Java Chat site on the Internet (http://

`www.chatplanet.com`). They know I am mentioning it in this book and have given me full permission to do so.

What you do is go to the ChatPlanet site and choose the link that reads `Get Chat For Your Site`. There you are asked a bunch of questions, including your name and your age, plus a few other not-so-delving queries, including what the title of the page on which you intend to use the applet and what the topic of chat will be.

You are given the ability to choose five different interfaces (graphical looks) for your chat room.

Submit all of this, and bingo! You receive some code to place on your page; that code runs the applet right from the ChatPlanet server. The entire process took me less than two minutes, but I type fast.

Once all is right with ChatPlanet, you receive your code and the applet is up and running. You get something that looks like Figure 11.1.

Figure 11.1
ChatPlanet chat room interface.

I should say here that if you really like the applet, there is a way you can download and run it right from your own server. You need to read the advanced Java applets section later in this chapter to understand how to do that.

The Code I Got

After I submit all the information ChatPlanet wants, I receive this in my email box about an hour later:

```
<APPLET CODEBASE="http://c29453.channels.chatplanet.com/
chatplanet-codebase" CODE="eweb.chat.ChatApplet.class"
 WIDTH="640" HEIGHT="400">
<PARAM NAME="access" VALUE="public">
<PARAM NAME="channel" VALUE="HTML Goodies">
<PARAM NAME="host" VALUE="c29453.channels.chatplanet.com">
<PARAM NAME="port" VALUE="5030">
<PARAM NAME="style" VALUE="">
</APPLET>
<BR>
<FONTSIZE = 8><a href ="http://www.chatplanet.com">
Chat provided by ChatPlanet: The Internet's Largest Java Chat Network
</a></FONTSIZE>
```

It might look a little goofy to you if this is the first time you've seen an applet's code, but it helps the applet run correctly.

I should say here that this code does not work if you simply transcribe it to your page directly from here. This code was created just for me. You have to go and have code created for yourself.

Let's look at the main APPLET command first:

```
<APPLET CODEBASE="http://c29453.channels.chatplanet.com/
chatplanet-codebase" CODE="eweb.chat.ChatApplet.class"
 WIDTH="640" HEIGHT="400">
```

Here's what's happening:

- APPLET tells the browser that it will now have to contend with an applet.
- CODEBASE denotes the name of a directory on the server where all the applets are held. You see, an applet is created just for you when you sign up with ChatPlanet. It's placed in a directory after it's created. In this case the direct URL to the directory is http:// c29453.channels.chatplanet.com/chatplanet-codebase.
- CODE tells the browser which file inside the directory to use. I keep this straight by thinking of CODE as an equal to SRC in an image command. In this case I am using an applet called eweb.chat.ChatApplet.class. Note the class after the period.
- WIDTH and HEIGHT define parameters in which the applet can work. You have to have this; applets work inside their one little window. The height and width settings define the window. Some applets allow you to change the height and width. This one does not. Go with the sizes you are sent.

Now let's look at the applet's parameters.

All the `<PARAM>` commands come immediately under the main APPLET command. These are commands that set parameters allowed by the applet. Keep in mind that every applet is unique; it is up to the author whether to allow you to alter parameters. Just because a parameter setting works in one applet is no guarantee it will work in another. Here are five parameter settings:

```
<PARAM NAME="access" VALUE="public">

<PARAM NAME="channel" VALUE="HTML Goodies">

<PARAM NAME="host" VALUE="c29453.channels.chatplanet.com">

<PARAM NAME="port" VALUE="5030">

<PARAM NAME="style" VALUE="">
```

Each setting has three commands:

- PARAM denotes that this is a parameter.
- NAME denotes the name of the parameter
- VALUE is the parameter setting.

If you read through the parameter settings you'll note that this applet is open to the public. It's to be used on HTML Goodies; the host is `c29453.channels.chatplanet.com`. People attach through port 5030 and no `style` value is set.

Can you change these parameters? No; they're pretty well set. That doesn't mean you can't change any parameters. When you install your own applet, you can change parameters to your heart's content.

Finally, the end applet command, `</APPLET>`, ends the entire deal.

When you call for the page in your browser, the applet should download into the browser, run, and post the chat room on your page for all to use.

FAQs from the HTML Goodies Web Site

Q. Can I align applets?

A. Yes. Just add the `ALIGN="###"` command inside the main APPLET command. However, when I want to center the applet, I surround the entire code with `<CENTER>` and `</CENTER>`. It's habit, I guess.

It is possible you'll get a big gray box where the applet should be. That could mean you have altered the code, which you shouldn't be doing anyway, or that the applet server is down.

These things happen. Give the people in charge a little time and they'll get it up and running again soon. Believe me, they know it's not working. I've been in a server house when someone kicked the plug out by mistake. It is total mayhem.

Is That It?!

Yup. That's it. The applet should run just fine. I've gotten this pup to work three different times on three different servers. The applet downloads and then runs like the little program that it is.

Where Do I Get Other Applets?

 There are a myriad of places. As I said earlier, I've listed a few in Appendix C. Enjoy! Want to use my chat room? Go to `http://www.htmlgoodies.com/chat.html`.

Advanced Java Applets

The previous applet section was fairly basic. The purpose was to familiarize you with a lot of the commands you'll be seeing here. This section is advanced because you are now going to install an applet right onto your own Web server. This means you need to install the applet, create the HTML document that runs it, and set the parameters so that it does what you want it to do.

It's not as complicated as I'm making it sound. Again, however, applets like everything to be just so or they simply refuse to work.

The Dancing Text Applet

Figure 11.2 gives you a look at what you're going to install. It's a little tough to grasp what this little gem does in the book, so I'll try to explain a little bit more. The text inside the black box is multicolored. Every letter is a different shade. The text is rolling up and down like waves.

 All the parts you need to create this applet are available at `http://www.htmlgoodies.com/book/dancingtext.html`.

The applet was written by Sohail Nasim. He was nice enough to make the applet available to a download site called Gamelan (`http://www.gamelan.com`). Pronounce that *gah-meh-lan*. The Gamelan people were then nice enough to allow me to use the applet in the HTML Goodies book.

Figure 11.2
Dancing text applet.

It's eye-catching and a great example for your first applet installation. Here's what you need:

- ○ The applet. Its name is SNSineText.class and I'll give you a link in a moment so you can download it straight away from the HTML Goodies Web site.

- ○ The code that calls for the applet.

Let's take them in order...

The Applet

First let me quickly explain what this thing is again. An applet starts as a text document written in the Java programming language. Once the author has finished the work, she runs the text document through another program called a *compiler*. That compiler changes the text into what's known as *machine language*. Now the applet is a fully enclosed function program.

Compilation is not new. Most any program you receive on disk or CD-ROM is compiled into this, or another type of machine language. Ever wonder why you can't look at your Windows 95/98 code? Because it's in machine language, that's why.

Now that the applet is an application unto itself, you need to be a little more careful with how you handle it. Remember that it is no longer text, so it cannot be treated as such. When you FTP the applet either from my site to your hard drive or from your hard drive to your server, you must make sure the applet is sent as binary or raw text.

The easiest way to keep it all straight is to think of an applet as an image. It isn't, of course, but if you apply all the FTP concerns to it that you do an image, you'll have little problem.

If you'd like to read more about FTP concerns, I have a piece on just that after Primer 7.

 Let's go get the applet. If you point your browser to http://www.htmlgoodies.com/ SNSineText.class *(note the capitalization pattern), you'll have it. There is also a link from the online version of this tutorial.*

When you arrive, you may think I've tricked you because all that is on the screen are some squiggly lines in the upper-right corner. Stop! That's it! Now you can download it by choosing Save As from the File menu and saving it directly to your hard drive. Just make sure that when you save it you do so as All Files.

I have found that Windows 95/98 often wants to put the extension .exe on the end of the name. Don't let it. Erase the .exe and save it just as SNSineText.class. Do not change the name. Save it just as I show it.

FAQs from the HTML Goodies Web Site

Q. When I download an applet, can I change the name?

A. I wouldn't. Some you can and some you can't, and there's no real way to tell which is which. I would go with the name the author chose.

The Applet Code

All right, you're halfway there. Now for the code that calls for the applet:

```
<APPLET CODE="SNSineText.class" WIDTH=592 HEIGHT=80>
<PARAM name = text       value = "Welcome To My Page  Enjoy it!">
<PARAM name = TextColor value = "rycwopg rB cy rcwr ycwrBc op">
<PARAM name = BackColor value = "b">
<PARAM name = FontName  value = "TimesRoman">
<PARAM name = FontStyle value = "Bold">
<PARAM name = FontSize  value = "30">
<PARAM name = Amplitude value = "20">
<PARAM name = GapSize   value = "5">
<PARAM name = Offset    value = "15">
</APPLET>
```

You can transcribe it from here or go to the online version of this tutorial and copy and paste it from there. Either way, look at the main APPLET command:

```
<APPLET CODE="SNSineText.class" WIDTH=592 HEIGHT=80>
```

You can pretty much pick out what each part means:

- APPLET alerts the browser that an applet will go here.
- CODE tells the browser the name of the applet.
- WIDTH and HEIGHT set the window in which the applet will run. By the way, the applet allows you to change the WIDTH and HEIGHT commands to fit the text you will put in the box.

If you just finished reading the applet tutorial before this, you might be asking where the CODEBASE command is. You don't need it. Remember that CODEBASE denotes the name of the directory where the applets sit. Since the applet and the HTML document that is calling for it sit inside the same directory, there's no need to look anywhere else. The CODE command alone does it.

The Parameter Commands

Here's where this little gem shines. You have the ability, thanks to the author, to change this to your heart's content. Here are the parameters and what they do:

```
<PARAM name = text      value = "Welcome To My Page  Enjoy it!">
```

This sets the text that will appear on the applet. Remember that you need to resize the box in the HEIGHT and WIDTH commands if you change the text. That way there isn't a lot of extra space around the items.

```
<PARAM name = TextColor value = "rycwopg rB cy rcwr ycwrBc op">
```

No, this isn't written in Klingon. The line allows you to denote a separate color for each different letter. Notice there's an equal number of codes as there are letters? *Welcome* has a code of rycwopg. I have a letter code for color for every letter in the word *Welcome*. See how I have a letter color code for each letter and a space where the spaces fall in the text that appears on the applet? That's how you set the colors.

Why is it done this way? Because the author wants it done this way. There's no better reason for it.

Here's the color chart:

Black = b	Magenta = m
Blue = B	Orange = o
Cyan = c	Pink = p
Dark Gray = d	Red = r
Gray = G	White = w
Green = g	Yellow = y
Light Gray = l	

You need to set all the letters to the same color if you want as entire word to be the same color.

By the way, you must have a color code for each letter. If you don't, you'll get an error and the applet will not run.

```
<PARAM name = BackColor value = "b">
```

This sets the background color. Notice I have it set to black. I did that to show the shape of the applet. If I were using this on the page, I'd set the background to the same color as the background of the page. The letters would then appear to be floating. Of course, this effect dies if you use a background image or the user has his own colors set. I'd still do it, though.

```
<PARAM name = FontName  value = "TimesRoman">
```

This sets the text font. You have your choice of TimesRoman, San Serif, or Helvetica.

```
<PARAM name = FontStyle value = "Bold">
```

This one's pretty self-explanatory also. You can set the text to Plain, Bold, or Italic. If you want a combination of two or all three, separate them with plus signs (+); bold+italic is an example.

```
<PARAM name = FontSize  value = "30">
```

If you use a large font, make sure you make the HEIGHT and WIDTH larger to accommodate it.

```
<PARAM name = Amplitude value = "20">
```

This is the height of the wave.

```
<PARAM name = GapSize   value = "5">
```

This is the amount of space between the letters.

```
<PARAM name = Offset    value = "15">
```

This is how far from the left edge the letters begin.

Finally, the </APPLET> commands ends the entire deal.

FAQs from the HTML Goodies Web Site

Q. Do I have to fill in every <PARAM> when I put an applet on my page? Sometimes I don't know what they are asking for.

A. Yeah, lots of times the author uses some cryptic message to denote something simple. Often an author creates a default so that if a parameter is not denoted, one is put in by the applet. I suggest you simply try running the applet without the parameter set; just leave empty quotation marks. If you get an error, you'll know you need to put in something. You might have to ask around or play the guessing game.

Q. Can I run more than one applet on a page?

A. As long as you install each applet correctly, you can install as many as you'd like.

Now Put Them On Your Server

Once you have all the parameters where you'd like them, try it. The applet runs right off your hard drive. If it doesn't, you may have corrupted it in the download from my site.

If it works, FTP the applet and the HTML document to your server. Make darn sure the applet goes as either binary or raw data. If you send it as text, you will corrupt it and the whole process comes to a stop.

FAQs from the HTML Goodies Web Site

Q. I keep getting the "Java class error" and "applet not found" errors.

A. First check to make sure the applet made it to your site in the upload. That is very seldom the reason, but it's good to check anyway. The most common reason for those types of errors is that you have corrupted the applet in one or more of the transfers. Let's work backward. The applet worked on the site you got it from, right? Did it work on your hard drive? If so, the upload to your server is the problem. If not, you corrupted it when getting it from the site yourself. Remember: Always treat these applets as if they were an image. You may need to ensure this because relying on an FTP program is not wise. They often see applets as text and upload them in ASCII format. That kills it. Force the FTP program's hand to send the applet as binary.

If you've sent everything correctly, open your browser and watch the fun.

Applets are not hard to install, they just need you to pay attention to what you're doing.

Hopefully you have gotten this one to work. If so, you can get just about any applet to work; they all work the same way. You get the applet (or applets—many effects are accomplished using three, four, or more!); get the code; set the parameters to your liking; upload the applet as binary; upload the HTML document as text. You should be good to go.

As I said before, I grabbed this applet from Gamelan, but there are many other sites that are just as helpful. You'll find a long list of them in Appendix C. Have fun—these things are a blast.

JavaScript

JavaScript is a programming language, and I love it! I really enjoy writing and posting JavaScript to my own Web pages. You can make a myriad of events that spice up what otherwise would be pretty static pages. As you delve deeper, you'll begin to understand why the WWW—and I—have taken so strongly to JavaScript. JavaScript basics are discussed in this tutorial and you receive a JavaScript that posts this text:

```
You arrived at the page on [the date] at exactly [current time].
```

This appears where it usually reads Document Done. It's a neat little script that lets your user know you're thinking about them.

This is an important disclaimer, however: I wrote this JavaScript. Because I wrote it, I get to put a copyright on it. When I send you to go get the code, or when you read the code shown here in a second, you'll see where I put it. I entered it right into the code.

This is very common in the world of we who write JavaScript. There are people all over the Net who write JavaScripts and then hand them out for free. I'm one of them. We don't ask for money, but we do ask that you keep our copyright statements intact.

Follow this tutorial straight away and you'll see what I mean.

Let's Get Started

 First you need the script to place on your HTML page. I have it printed here. You can transcribe it from here, or better yet, you can get it online at http://www.htmlgoodies.com/ jstext.html. *I will refer to the script often, so take a quick look at it. If you go for it online, you may want to download the page into your own computer. While you're online, see the script in action at* http://www.htmlgoodies.com/javabook.html *so you know the look you're going for. Now go!*

Welcome back. That was fast. Here it is:

```
<SCRIPT LANGAUGE="javascript">
<!-- Hide from browsers that do not understand JavaScript
//This script Copyright 1998 by Joe Burns, Ph.D.
//Keep this and the line above intact if you use this script.
//Thanks - Joe
    function dateinbar()
      {
      var date = new Date();
      var m = date.getMonth() + 1;
      var d = date.getDate();
      var y = date.getYear();
      var h = date.getHours();
```

```
            var mn = date.getMinutes();
            var sc = date.getSeconds();
            var t = m + '/' + d + '/' + y + ' at
            exactly ' + h + ':' + mn + ':' + sc + ' ';
            defaultStatus = "You arrived at the page on " + t + ".";
            }
// end hiding -->
</SCRIPT>
<BODY BGCOLOR="#ffff00" onLoad="dateinbar()">
```

The JavaScript looks like chicken scratch, doesn't it? Yeah, it did to me too when I got started. Now let's get it up and running:

1. Open the text editor you use to write your HTML documents. Mark the page with <HTML>, <HEAD>, and <TITLE> commands like you would to start any other document. This JavaScript must be put into an HTML document to run. It is not a small application (as is a Java applet).

   Keep in mind that not all JavaScripts work this way. In fact, many are self contained and you just plop them on the page where they run. That wouldn't make much of a tutorial. This is a somewhat involved, but also a very common style of JavaScript.

   When you are editing pages that contain JavaScript, you need to use an editor that does not have any margins. NotePad and Macintosh's SimpleText are great for this. I don't mean margins set to their widest point—I mean no margins, period. Using margins might corrupt the shape of the JavaScript, causing longer lines to break into two smaller lines. That halts the process completely.

2. Now copy and paste the entire jstext.html file you just looked at—the whole thing. Copy it from the browser screen. Don't download the page and take it from there. I wrote the script so it would display on the browser screen rather than running as the script that it is. Just copy it directly from the screen. Of course, you can also transcribe it from here, too.

   Place the script immediately following the <TITLE> commands, but still inside the </HEAD> you just wrote in the text editor. Please make a point of copying it exactly. Remember, not only must the script retain the same lettering, but it must retain the same shape.

FAQs from the HTML Goodies Web Site

Q. I did exactly what you said and my JavaScript keeps giving me errors.

A. The most common reason for getting errors on a JavaScript from my site is that you are attempting to edit it in an editor that has margins (and are hence corrupting it by changing the shape of the script). If in the script a line is very long, do not break it into two lines. Using margins will do that, so edit without margins and don't try altering the format of the script. You'll only cause problems...and errors.

3. Look again at the script. I have allowed you permission to use it as long as you leave in my name. That's already done for you if you copy the whole deal.

4. Now look toward the bottom of the JavaScript. The very last line reads like this:

```
<BODY BGCOLOR="#ffff00" onLoad="dateinbar()">
```

This is not actually part of the JavaScript. It's going to act as the BODY command for the HTML document you're writing the script into. If you want to use BGCOLOR, LINK, VLINK, ALINK, or BACKGROUND commands in this document, put them in the BODY command just like you would in any other BODY command. Get them in the front part of the command before the onLoad command starts.

You'll note that the second half of the BODY command has an onLoad= command and then some attributes immediately after. That command is JavaScript and it tells the browser that when the page is loaded (the command is onLoad, get it?), start the JavaScript section in the HEAD commands titled dateinbar().

You'll find that dateinbar() function in the script you pasted between the HEAD commands.

Let me explain the process of this tutorial. It will help you understand why you need all these little parts and what they all do.

First the browser loads the page. That means the JavaScript you pasted into the HEAD command is placed into your computer's brain. But it doesn't go to work. It just sits there waiting to be called upon.

Next, the BODY command loads and the onLoad="dateinbar" command is seen by the browser. That onLoad command triggers the browser to start running the JavaScript.

The JavaScript itself reads part of your browser. It gathers the day, the month, the year, the hour, the minute, and the second. Once it has all the parts, it puts them all together in a nice sentence and displays it in the browser status bar for all the world to see.

Is That It?

Yes! Think of this JavaScript as just another piece of the puzzle. There are rules to implementing JavaScript just as there are rules to altering text with HTML. You should be able to save and run it as long as you have followed the instructions, placed the script within the HEAD commands and after the TITLE commands, and made sure to add the onLoad command to your BODY commands.

JavaScript is a lot less scary than you'd think. Most people run into trouble in the script itself.

FAQs from the HTML Goodies Web Site

Q. My JavaScripts work in Netscape but not in Explorer.

A. Netscape reads JavaScript and Explorer reads something called VBScript (Visual Basic Script). The two are very close, but there are some differences—especially when JavaScript 1.1 came out. Simple JavaScripts often run on Explorer, but any script containing JavaScript 1.1 commands will work in Netscape and not in Explorer.

JavaScript Requirements

Here are a few items to keep in mind when posting a JavaScript to one of your HTML documents:

- You need a higher-level browser—This should go without saying, but if your browser can't read JavaScript, you'll get nothing on the page. Netscape Navigator 2.02 and Explorer 2 are the lowest you can get away with.

- Denote image height and width throughout your HTML page—JavaScripts are a little picky in that they like for everything on the page to be denoted. This includes adding the height and width of each image.

- Hide the script from less-powerful browsers—JavaScript is text. If the browser viewing your page does not have Java capabilities, the text is displayed. You can hide the text from earlier-version browsers by adding <!-- at the beginning of the script and //--> at the end of your script. This does not affect the script's performance.

  If you look at the script I just gave you, you'll see where I used those commands. I also added some text; that's allowed. The text is not for the JavaScript, but to allow me to keep things straight.

- Keep the shape—JavaScripts like to retain their shape. You should make a point of editing your JavaScript/HTML documents in a text editor that does not have margins. Suggestions for editing JavaScript/HTML documents include Notepad (PCs), Simple Text (Macintoshes), or turning off the word wrap in your current HTML editor.

JavaScript Troubleshooting

Here are some suggestions of what to do if you can't get a script to work properly on your Web site:

- The script doesn't work—The quick answer is that it does. All scripts in this book and on the HTML Goodies and Java Goodies site have worked for me before I handed them off to you. You can be sure that the script does work; there is just a problem elsewhere.

- Nothing happens—Nothing? Then you might not have a browser late enough to run JavaScript. It may also be that you don't have the entire script. There are many scripts that have two parts, one on the HEAD commands and one on the BODY command. It won't display if you do not have the command in the BODY that calls for the script. For instance, nothing would happen in the status bar if you forgot the onLoad command. If the script is functional and you have installed every part, you should either get the script's effect or an error code.

- I get an error code—You saw that coming, didn't you? Make note of the line the error code is coming from. That is the line from the *top of the page*, not from the top of the JavaScript. Count your <HTML> as line one. Remember to count the blanks lines, too.

- Fix the error code—Remember, form is key here. Most times, error codes can be fixed by making sure the script is in the exact form it was in when you took it from me. Make sure the line hasn't been chopped off early or jumped to the next line before it should have been. This solves most error codes. I know the code worked when you grabbed it from me; the error occurred somewhere in the transfer.

- It works on my computer, but not when posted—You have corrupted it in the FTP transfer. Change the form you sent it in. If you sent it ASCII, try binary and vice versa.

Careful now. If you get into these JavaScripts, you'll get hooked. I did. In fact, I created an entire site around them: Java Goodies at http://www.htmlgoodies.com/javagoodies. Enjoy!

 Just to show you that JavaScript is very versatile, I have posted another JavaScript that acts much the same as the one in this tutorial, except the text scrolls along the status bar. Woohoo! See http://www.htmlgoodies.com/book/scrolljs.html *for all the parts.*

Advanced JavaScript Commands

In the original JavaScript tutorial, the one just before this one, you implemented what one might call a "well-formed" JavaScript. The script was a huge scary thing that sat up in the HTML document's HEAD commands. The script started with the traditional <SCRIPT LANGUAGE="javascript"> and ended with </SCRIPT>. It was then triggered to begin running by an onLoad command stuck in <BODY>. That format is very common and you'll see it a great deal as you write your own Web pages.

One of the great things about JavaScript is that it can be as complicated as the tutorial you just got through or as simple as the many examples in this tutorial.

Here we're going to go over a certain class of JavaScript commands called *event handlers*, which are commands that work directly with existing HTML commands. They work so closely, in fact, that they work by being embedded right into the HTML command itself.

They're called event handlers because they create events. They do things when your users do things. That's a terrible description, but I'm on a tight schedule here. Read on...

 To see these scripts in action, point your browser to `http://www.htmlgoodies.com/` `adv_js.html`.

We're going to go over a few different JavaScript event-handler commands here. I'll list them up front. I want you to keep an eye on their capitalization patterns—you must keep that pattern every time you use the command. If you don't, the commands won't work.

- `onMouseOver`   This creates the event when the mouse is passed over active text or an image.
- `onMouseOut`   This creates the event when the mouse is taken off an active text image.
- `onClick`   This creates an event when active text or images are clicked.
- `alert`   This brings up a dialog box that contains text and an OK button.

The `onMouseOver` *Event Handler*

I'm going to show you the format for using this command in a hypertext link first, explain what the parts mean, and then show you what it does. Here's the code:

```
<A HREF="http://www.htmlgoodies.com" onMouseOver="window.status=
'Click here to go to HTML Goodies'; return true">HTML Goodies</A>
```

Please keep in mind that that full line of code should all go onto one line. (It can't be shown here that way because of margin constraints.)

Now let's break it down. You should notice right off that the format is a hypertext link with some text stuck in right after the `htmlgoodies.com` URL. That's how these event handlers work; they are embedded right into an HTML command. You don't need the traditional `<SCRIPT>` and `</SRCIPT>` commands. The code just runs inside the HTML when your user passes his or her mouse over.

This line of JavaScript code does the work:

```
onMouseOver="window.status='Click here to go to HTML Goodies';
  return true"
```

Let's break it down:

- ● onMouseOver is the event handler. It denotes that something will happen when the mouse passes over the active text.

- ● window.status is JavaScript code for the browser window status bar. That's the bar at the bottom of the screen where it reads Document Done after a page has loaded.

  The words that follow in single quotation marks are the words that appear in the status bar when the mouse passes over the active text. Please also notice the semicolon.

- ● return true is also JavaScript that checks to see if there is a status bar. If it finds one it reports back that the text can be placed. I know it seems strange, but you have to play by JavaScript rules to get this effect.

- ● Finally, please take a long slow look at the pattern of equal signs and single and double quotation marks. It can get confusing, but it has to be just so to get the effect.

Now, after all that mind-numbing detail, you get the results shown in Figure 11.3.

Figure 11.3
The onMouseOver *effect.*

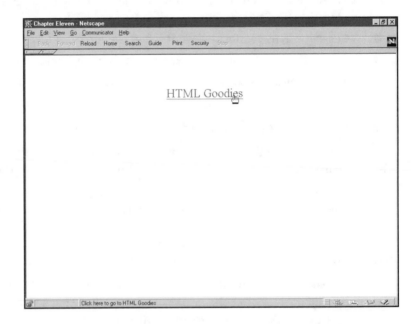

Look at the bottom line on the browser in Figure 11.3. The text Click here to go to HTML Goodies popped up in the status bar when the mouse passed over.

Let's go a little further, keeping the exact same format but adding another event handler. Oh yes, these little puppies can be used in combination. What you're going to do is add the onMouseOut event handler so that when your users pass their mouse over the link, they get words in the status bar. When the mouse moves off the link, they get different words.

It gets very long and a little confusing. It also has to all go on one line. Here it is:

```
<A HREF="http://www.htmlgoodies.com" onMouseOver="window.status=
'Click here to go to HTML Goodies'; return true" onMouseOut=
"window.status='I said click!'; return true">HTML Goodies</A>
```

You get two messages every time your mouse moves on or off of the text.

onMouseOver *and Background Colors*

onMouseOver is good for more than just posting text. This code allows your users to pass their mouse over text and change the actual background color of the page:

```
<A HREF="" onMouseOver="document.bgColor='black'">Black</a>
<A HREF="" onMouseOver="document.bgColor='green'">Green</a>
<A HREF="" onMouseOver="document.bgColor='yellow'">Yellow</a>
<A HREF="" onMouseOver="document.bgColor='red'">Red</a>
<A HREF="" onMouseOver="document.bgColor='brown'">Brown</a>
<A HREF="" onMouseOver="document.bgColor='white'">White</a>
```

Once again, notice the hypertext link format—except this time the onMouseOver is not pointed toward the window.status, but document.bgColor (note the capitalization pattern).

bgColor is JavaScript for the HTML document's background color. The background changes every time your user passes her mouse over a new color.

Figure 11.4 gives you a general idea of what it looks like in the browser.

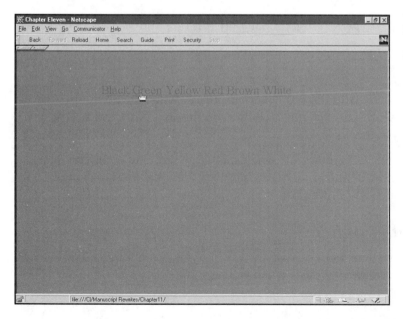

Figure 11.4
The onMouseOver *background color changer.*

You can set this up with any hex or word color code. There is a long list of them in Appendix B, "Useful Charts."

You can make as many or as few choices as you want by adding or subtracting A HREF commands. What will not work are TEXT, LINK, or VLINK commands. They are a bit more stable.

Just for kicks, I'll give you one more little piece of code using the onMouseOver event handler. This is a fun little piece that can keep your users guessing. Look at this:

```
<A HREF="http://www.htmlgoodies.com" onMouseOver="parent.location=
'dude.html'";>HTML Goodies</A>
```

It all should look familiar by now. The only new item is the parent.location command. That is JavaScript for a new page.

This script basically loads the dude.html page (or whatever page you denote) when the mouse passes over.

It's a hypertext link that doesn't need to be clicked. Use it in good health.

The Alert *Event Handler*

I'm going to show you the alert event handler using the onMouseOver, since you're already familiar with it. Here's the basic format:

```
<A HREF="http://www.htmlgoodies.com" onMouseOver="alert
('Hello out there!')";>HTML Goodies</A>
```

Notice again that it's a simple hypertext link format, only this time the onMouseOver is going to enact this line of code:

```
"alert('Hello out there!')";
```

That code brings up an alert box with the text Hello out there! when the user passes the mouse over the link. The user has to click the OK button on the alert box to make it go away. Figure 11.5 shows what this looks like.

Just change the text inside the parentheses and single quotation marks to configure this for your own use. Whatever you write shows up on the alert box. Yes, you can type long sentences. The text just wraps right on the box.

The onClick *Event Handler*

You may be well ahead of me here, but I'll say it anyway. OnClick works exactly like onMouseOver, except onClick creates the effect when you click the active text or image.

Figure 11.5
onMouseOver *calling on an* alert *event handler.*

Here's the background color change code from before using onClick commands:

```
<A HREF=""onClick="document.bgColor='black'">Black</a>
<A HREF=""onClick="document.bgColor='green'">Green</a>
<A HREF=""onClick="document.bgColor='yellow'">Yellow</a>
<A HREF=""onClick="document.bgColor='red'">Red</a>
<A HREF=""onClick="document.bgColor='brown'">Brown</a>
<A HREF=""onClick="document.bgColor='white'">White</a>
```

This creates the same effect, only now the user must click to get the background color to change. Here's the alert event handler example using onClick:

```
<A HREF="http://www.htmlgoodies.com" onClick="alert
('Hello out there!')";>HTML Goodies</A>
```

Same effect, but you have to click it first.

Now, you may be thinking that onClick is just another version of onMouseOver and can only be used in hypertext links. Not so. Where onClick really shines is when you use it with form buttons. If you need to read about form buttons you'll find them in Chapter 7, "Adding Link Buttons and Forms." Let's get into a few examples, shall we?

Back and Forward Buttons

Why make your users click on the Back and Forward buttons way at the top of the browser screen when you can plop them right on the page? Take a gander at Figure 11.6.

Figure 11.6
Back and Forward buttons.

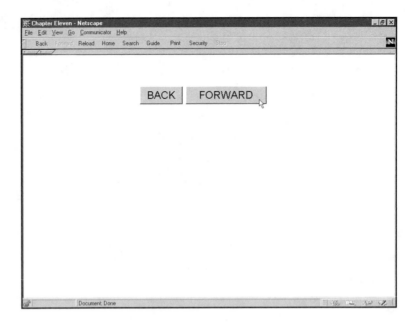

Here's the code that placed them:

```
<FORM>
<INPUT TYPE="button" VALUE="BACK" onClick="history.go(-1)">
<INPUT TYPE="button" VALUE="FORWARD" onCLick="history.go(1)">
</FORM>
```

Here's what's happening:

- <FORM> starts the button.
- INPUT TYPE="button" is pretty self-explanatory.
- VALUE="###" denotes what will be written on the button.
- onClick= denotes that the event will activate when clicked.
- "history.go" is JavaScript that denotes movement through your history file. That's the file that keeps a record of everywhere you've been during that particular surfing jaunt; (1) sends it forward one step, (-1) sends you backward one step.

  If you'd like you can raise or lower those numbers. Setting it to (-4) takes your user back four pages if he has that many pages in his history file. If not, the button will not function.
- </FORM> ends the button.

You should also know that you can separate these two, employing only one button. Just make sure you keep the beginning and end FORM commands in place.

Links Within Pages

People ask me all the time how to get link buttons to do jumps within pages. The quick answer is that you can't. The link button places a ? on the end of its links—that messes it up. Through the magic of an onClick event handler, however, you can create a button like the one shown in Figure 11.7.

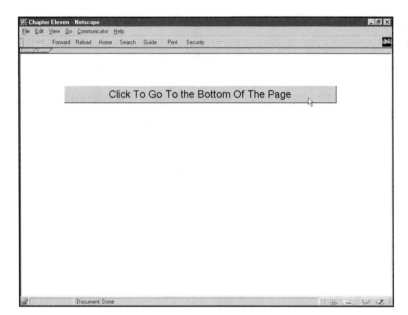

Figure 11.7
Internal link script.

Here's what made it. Copy the code and place it on your page where you want the button to appear.

```
<FORM>
    <INPUT TYPE="button" VALUE="Click To Go To the Bottom Of The Page"
    onClick="parent.location='#code'">
</FORM>
```

Please note that the full INPUT TYPE line of text should all be on the same line.

Here's what's happening. The button is created the same as earlier, except for these things:

● onClick="parent.location='#code'" You saw parent.location earlier. You know that means to load a page into the browser window.

● '#code' denotes the point where this script will jump to. You're not offering a new page, so the script must look to the current page. On that page there is a place called #code. If you haven't already, read all about page jumps in Chapter 2, "Making Links." It will help you understand this a little better.

This code denotes the point where on the page the button will jump:

```
<A NAME="code">
```

It's the same format as the page jump link. You need to choose a new "code" for every point you denote on the page.

Making an Email Button

If you could click the button in Figure 11.8, you'd send me a piece of mail. It works. Go ahead, click. I said click! Click! Oh, wait. This is a book. Right.

Figure 11.8
An email button script.

Here's how to make the email button:

```
<FORM>
<INPUT TYPE="button" VALUE="Click Here to Write to Me"
onClick="parent.location='mailto:jburns@htmlgoodies.com'">
</FORM>
```

Please note that the full INPUT TYPE line of text should all be on the same line.

The button works the same way as the link button, but this time it is enacting a simple mailto: (like you would use to create an email hypertext link). See Primer 4 if you don't know what I mean.

If you use this button, be sure to change out your email address where mine sits now. Remember, no space between `mailto:` and the address.

FAQs from the HTML Goodies Web Site

Q. Can I set the button up to write to more than one person?

A. On later browsers you can add as many email addresses as you want as long as you separate each with a comma and no spaces.

Well, that's a quick look at some JavaScript event handlers. They are great items because they're quick, they sit inside the HTML, and they do great tricks.

By the way, in case you're wondering, the `onLoad` command you used in the first JavaScript tutorial is also an event handler and works just like the others did; it just enacts the event when the page loads. If you'd like an alert box to pop up when the page loads, change the `onMouseOver` to `onLoad`.

If you haven't take it from the tutorial, these event handlers are quite interchangeable. Try swapping out one for another. You'll find great new events just from playing around. Just be very careful to keep the double and single quotation mark patterns the same or you'll get errors.

Enjoy!

 I have a few more intricate JavaScripts that employ `onClick` and `onMouseover` commands at `http://www.htmlgoodies.com/book/morejs.html`.

Opening New Windows

I can always tell when there is a new command that is in vogue. I start getting all kinds of email asking how to do it. Well, this is the new thing. I don't know why, but everyone wants to know how to create these little windows that pop up. All the Geocities.com pages have them. Other pages use them as control panels operating the main window.

Figure 11.9 shows an example of what you'll be creating through this tutorial.

If you decide to go with this kind of pop-up window, use it sparingly. I think they become an annoyance after a while; you start yelling at the screen every time another one pops up. I do, at least. It really scares the cat.

If you insist on doing one, let's do it right! We'll start at the beginning.

Figure 11.9
A new Window script.

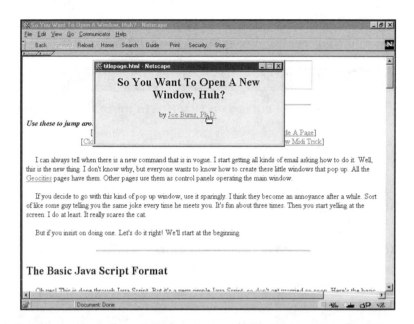

Q. What's the command that makes it so that someone cannot close the extra windows I make pop up?

A. There isn't such a thing. You always run the risk of users closing windows as soon as they pop up.

The Basic JavaScript Format

Oh, yes! This is done through JavaScript. But it's a very simple JavaScript, so don't get worried so soon. Here's the basic format:

```
<SCRIPT LANGUAGE="javascript">
<!--
window.open ('page.html')
-->
</SCRIPT>
```

Heck, you're already familiar with most of this stuff. Since this is a script, you need the opening `<SCRIPT LANGUAGE="javascript">` statement, and the `</SCRIPT>` statement at the end. The `<!--` and the `-->` are used to hide the text from older version browsers (under 2.0) and text-only browsers that don't read JavaScript. You see, if you didn't have those in there, the text would display.

But it's the stuff in the middle that makes the magic.

`window.open ('page.html')` does just what it says—it opens a window (a new browser screen, actually) and fills it with the page within the parentheses and single quotation marks. The HTML document in the example that fills the window is called `page.html`.

That little script opens a new browser window and you get the effect. Wouldn't it be great if we actually had the ability to configure the window any way we wanted? You bet. Here's how.

Configuring the Window

Now you get to the commands I used to get the little window effect. You can place this JavaScript anywhere on the page. Toward the top or in between the HEAD commands ensures that it runs sooner in the process than if you put it at the end. It's a pretty robust script that doesn't need a special placement. This is exactly what I have:

```
<SCRIPT LANGUAGE="javascript">
<!--
window.open ('titlepage.html', 'newwindow', config='HEIGHT=100,
WIDTH=400, toolbar=no, menubar=no, scrollbars=no,
resizable=no, location=no, directories=no, status=no')
-->
</SCRIPT>
```

Please make a point of getting everything from `window.open` to `status=no')` on one line.

Here's what's happening:

- `<SCRIPT LANGUAGE="javascript">` starts the JavaScript.
- `window.open` is the JavaScript command that opens a new browser window.
- `'titlepage.html'` is the name of the page that will fill the window.
- `'newwindow'` is the name of the window. This you need. We are going to use commands intended to alter the window that the script is opening. The item has to have a name so that the JavaScript knows what item it is dealing with. I went with `newwindow`, but it could have just as easily been zork, or woohaa, or raspberry.
- `config=` denotes that what follows configures the window. (This command really isn't required, but it's a good idea to use just to keep things straight.)
- `HEIGHT=100` denotes the height of the window in pixels.
- `WIDTH=400` denotes the width of the window in pixels.
- `toolbar=no` denotes if there will be a toolbar on the newly opened window. Set this to yes if you want one, to no if you don't.

The *toolbar* is the line of buttons at the top of the browser window that contains the Back, Forward, Stop, Reload, and so on.

- menubar=no denotes whether there will be a menu bar. Set this to yes if you want one, to no if you don't. The *menu bar* is the line of items labeled File, Edit, View, Go, and so on.

- scrollbars=no denotes whether there will be scrollbars. Ditto with the yes or no deal. I wouldn't make a new window that would need scrollbars, anyway. I think it kills the effect.

- resizable=no denotes whether the user can change the size of the window by dragging.

- location=no denotes whether there will be a location bar on the newly opened window. Use yes or no again. The *location bar* is the space at the top of the browser window where the page URL is displayed.

- directories=no denotes whether there will be a *directories bar* on the new window. Use yes or no. This is the bar at the top of the browser window that has the bookmarks and such.

- status=no denotes whether there will be a status bar. Use yes or no. The *status bar* is the area at the very bottom of the browser screen that says Document Done.

- </SCRIPT> ends the whole deal.

FAQs from the HTML Goodies Web Site

Q. I want two windows to pop up.

A. Then create two JavaScript commands that open a new window, and list one right after the other. You'll get two windows.

Page Inside a Page

The example I gave relies on two pages: The first is the main HTML document that carries the JavaScript. The second is the HTML document that is displayed inside the new window.

Here I get a little fancier with the JavaScript code. I show you how to set it up so that the new window is included inside the main HTML document completely. One page, two windows.

```
<SCRIPT LANGUAGE="JavaScript">
function openindex()
    {
OpenWindow=window.open("", "newwin", "height=250,width=250,toolbar=no,
scrollbars="+scroll+",menubar=no");
OpenWindow.document.write("<TITLE>Title Goes Here</TITLE>")
```

```
OpenWindow.document.write("<BODY BGCOLOR=pink>")
OpenWindow.document.write("<h1>Hello!</h1>")
OpenWindow.document.write("This text will appear in the window!")
OpenWindow.document.write("</BODY>")
OpenWindow.document.write("</HTML>")

OpenWindow.document.close()
self.name="main"
        }
</SCRIPT>
```

This is a very basic script written by Andree Growney and myself. This JavaScript creates a "function" that opens a new window. Look at the top line of the script after the <SCRIPT LANGUAGE="javascript"> line.

The function starts with the line: function openindex(). What that does in JavaScript speak is create a function called openindex. Then whatever is inside the curly braces following that statement is what the function is supposed to do. With me so far? In the case of this function, a new window is opened. The next lines of the script are quite similar to what we've seen so far:

```
OpenWindow=window.open("", "newwin", "height=250,width=250,toolbar=no,
scrollbars="+scroll+",menubar=no");
```

The line calls for the creation of a new window. As you can see, no external page is called for. There are just the empty quotation marks. This forces the JavaScript to look at itself for the information.

The name of the new window is newwin, and the statements following define what the window will look like.

Now we get to the meat of this little ditty. Each of the lines that start with this:

```
OpenWindow.document.write()
```

These lines denote a new line of text that is written onto the window that is being opened. Now look down the code—note that the text inside the quotation marks of each new line is HTML code. Thus, the text written to this window is going to be read as HTML code. I only have a few lines here, but you can add as many as you'd like. Just be sure to preface each line with the OpenWindow.document.write command. Follow the format closely; one missing quote or parenthesis can kill the entire script.

Be sure to end the script that same way I have: OpenWindow.document.close().

Calling for the Function

No, you're not done yet. When you create a function such as this, something must be used to "trigger" the function to work. Usually, as is the case here, you use a command in the BODY portion of the main HTML document. Here's the deal:

- Configure the script and place it in the <HEAD> section of your main HTML document.
- To trigger the function, place onLoad="openindex()" in the <BODY> command of the main HTML document. That tells the browser to initiate the openindex function when the page is loaded.

Closing the Window

This seems like the next logical step in the process. You made it open, now make it close. There are three ways of doing it:

- Every window carries what I call the "goodbye box" on the upper-right corner. It's the gray square that has a little X on it. Click that and away it goes.
- You could offer a button on the page that closes it when the user clicks the button.

I'm starting here because I don't think I need to go over the little goodbye box. Here's the code for the button:

```
<FORM>
<INPUT TYPE='BUTTON' VALUE='Close Window' onClick='self.close()'>
</FORM>
```

Either place that pup on the page that will go into the new window or place it in the code in the previous JavaScript format. You get a little button that closes the window when clicked.

A New Window MIDI Trick

I am asked at least once a day how to keep a MIDI playing in the background while a person surfs your site. It's a little rough because the page that has the MIDI embedded stops playing the file once you leave it. Here's a suggestion: Place the EMBED commands on the page that will fill the new window. That way people can surf all over the place on the main browser window and the MIDI will play away. The only real downfall is that the MIDI party stops cold if the person closes the little window.

I said it was a suggestion, not the end all.

Exciting, huh? Now you can make little windows pop up all over town. Again, I suggest that one new window might be a welcome help to your pages' users. However, a new window every other page would bring you to level of telemarketers in some people's minds. Use this only when they are really needed.

Enjoy!

 I have an example of a window opening and then closing by itself! Go to `http://www.htmlgoodies.com/book/openclose.html`.

Image Flip

This is one of the most asked-for items on the HTML Goodies site: an image flip. The image-flip script shown here works cross browser with no trouble. Plus, it's a snap to configure for your own use. Even better? It's an active image, so it can be clicked and take you to another page! Here's the effect: First, Figure 11.10 shows the mouse pointer on the image. Figure 11.11 shows the mouse cursor off the image.

 You can see the tutorial and get all the parts you need online at `http://www.htmlgoodies.com/imageflip.html`.

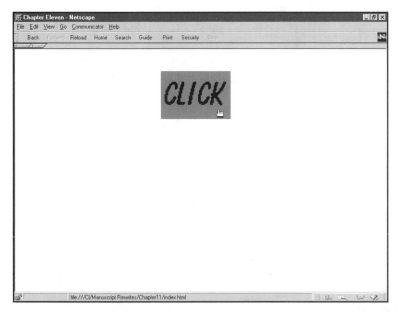

Figure 11.10
An image flip with mouse cursor on the image.

FAQs from the HTML Goodies Web Site

Q. How do I make it so that text highlights when my mouse pointer moves over it?

A. You could us an image flip to highlight one image and not the other. That would give the effect.

Figure 11.11

An image flip with mouse cursor off the image.

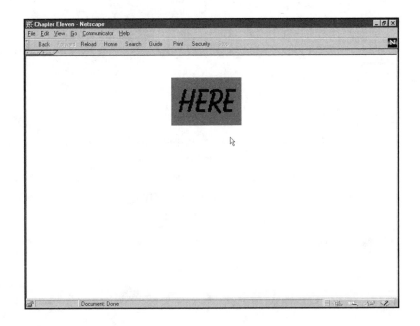

You need four things to make this work: two images, a JavaScript, and a command that calls for the images and the effect of the script. You can get them right from the online tutorial: `http://www.htmlgoodies.com/imageflip.html`.

The effect I put together is done with two images named goof3.gif and goof4.gif. Why goof? Because I'm your father, that's why! Actually, that's not the answer, but I've always wanted to say that.

There. Now that that's settled...

The Script

You should have been able to get the two images from the links. If you haven't already, do so. Now you need the script. It goes between the <HEAD> and </HEAD> commands on your page. You can transcribe it from here or get it from the online version of this tutorial.

```
<SCRIPT LANGUAGE="JavaScript">
<!-- hide from none JavaScript Browsers
Image1= new Image(75,50)
Image1.src = "goof3.gif"
Image2 = new Image(75,50)
Image2.src = "goof4.gif"
function SwapOut() {
document.imageflip.src = Image2.src; return true;
}
function SwapBack() {
```

```
document.imageflip.src = Image1.src; return true;
}
// - stop hiding -->
</SCRIPT>
```

Denote the Graphics

Now that you have placed that script into your document between the HEAD commands, you need to denote what graphics will be used. You do that in this section of the script:

```
Image1= new Image(75,50)
Image1.src = "goof3.gif"
Image2 = new Image(75,50)
Image2.src = "goof4.gif"
```

When you start editing, remember that the image that appears first (without any mouseover) is the one listed second. Remember, this is a flip. When this script is made functional, the second graphic will be the first to display, then the original image will come back again. With me?

Put in the names of your images in reverse order. Next, be sure to denote the images' width and height. The images I am using are 75 pixels wide by 50 pixels high. See that in the code? Put your height and width numbers in where I have (75,50). Width is listed first.

Before you ask, no, the images do not have to be the same size. But it does better the effect if they are.

Also keep in mind that these images need to load quickly. You see, the second image is not loaded when the mouse first goes over the area. When the mouse passes over, the script is activated and the second image is called for. There is a slight loading time span. With that in mind, go with small graphics.

Call for the Script

Now we set up the magic. Here's the command you place in the <BODY> section of your document where you want this image to appear:

```
<A HREF="index.html" onMouseOver="SwapOut()" onMouseOut="SwapBack()">
<IMG NAME="imageflip" SRC="goof4.gif" WIDTH="75" HEIGHT="50"
BORDER=0></A>
```

You know this format well. It's a simple HREF link command with some JavaScript event handlers. You can read about event handlers in the advanced JavaScript tutorial in this very chapter. Notice that the hypertext link is constructed so that the image is what is active. The height and width of the image are denoted and the image's border is set to 0.

The image that is being called for is the image you listed second in the script. Again, the script hasn't been called into play yet. The command is just displaying the image you tell it to—in this case, goof4.gif.

FAQs from the HTML Goodies Web Site

Q. Can I make an imagemap that works like an image flip, like in sections?

A. Sure! Make a fake imagemap and then make each image an image flip. It's involved, but what a great effect! (See the fake map tutorial in Chapter 4, "Creating Imagemaps.")

I have built a fully functioning fake imagemap out of image flips. See it work at http://www.htmlgoodies.com/book/fakeflipmap.html. Be sure to look at the source code!

Q. Can I get it so that more than one image flips at the same time?

A. Yes, but it's quite an involved JavaScript. I have some in the Images section of the Java Goodies site (http://www.htmlgoodies.com/Javagoodies.img.html). See if that's not what you're looking for.

Creating More Than One Image Flip on a Page

 Go to the HTML Goodies site at http://www.htmlgoodies.com/Javagoodies.img.html *and download the JavaScript there. As you can see, the script and the command that calls for it are pretty well married. If you haven't seen it so far, note that the script has two lines that read as follows:*

```
document.imageflip.src
```

If you look at the command that calls for the script, you'll see that a name is given to the image: IMAGEFLIP.

I'm sure there are other ways of doing this, but I add more image flips to the page by choosing a new word that will go in place of imageflip in the previous example. Let's say the new word is just *image*. I would then change out the word *imageflip* with the word *image* three times—once in the command and twice in the script. See that?

I would then change out the script with two new images and redo the entire process again—a new script for each image flip I wanted, each with a different name used so that the browser can keep them separate.

Again, there are probably other methods, but the script is so small that I can copy and paste faster that by creating new JavaScript lines.

And that's that. Now go start flippin'.

Enjoy!

Using External JavaScripts

People ask me all the time how they can set it up so that one page is inserted into a whole slew of HTML documents. Others want to only post a JavaScript once and have it appear in multiple HTML pages without copying and pasting on every page. Well, here's how you do it: Use an external JavaScript.

For the most part, I always tell you to place the JavaScript you want to run directly on the page it will affect. That rule holds true for more involved JavaScript, but what if you could place a single JavaScript file into your site and run it off of every page, similar to what happens in a cascading style sheets model?

For instance, say you want a current date on every page. You could either copy and paste a date JavaScript into every page or you could place it once as its own page and link all the other pages to it. One script, many date stamps. Here's how you can do it.

The Date Stamp

The JavaScript that posted the date in the online version of this tutorial does not appear on that HTML page. Feel free to go and look at the source code on the tutorial if you want, but it really doesn't. The script is written somewhere else. I know it's killing ya...you want to look at the source code. Don't do it! Don't give in to the pressure! Be your own person!

Or go look...I don't care.

In order to get that date on the page, I created what is known as a *JS* file, or a *JavaScript* file. The JavaScript file is nothing more than a JavaScript saved as a text file and given the extension `.js`.

Let's say you have a JavaScript like the one that placed the date shown just before. In fact, let's say you have exactly that script. Here's what it looked like when I started:

```
<SCRIPT LANGUAGE="JavaScript">
<!-- hide script from old browsers
test = new Date()
month = test.getMonth()
month = (month * 1) + 1
day = test.getDate()
year = test.getYear()
document.write(" ",month,"/",day,"/19",year," ")
// end hiding script from old browsers -->
</SCRIPT>
```

There you go. It's a very short, simple script. Even if you are not overly schooled in JavaScript, you can pretty much pick out how it works. It gets the day, the month, and the year from your computer and posts them all in a row with slashes between the numbers. Ta da! You have a date.

Creating the JS File

Take the script and write it, all by itself, into a text editor. It should be the only thing on the page. Now, knock off the beginning and end SCRIPT commands. These things:

```
<SCRIPT LANGUAGE="JavaScript">

</SCRIPT>
```

Get rid of them. Erase them. You'll pick them up again later. Now the page should look like this:

```
<!-- hide script from old browsers
test = new Date()
month = test.getMonth()
month = (month * 1) + 1
day = test.getDate()
year = test.getYear()
document.write(" ",month,"/",day,"/19",year," ")
// end hiding script from old browsers -->
```

Now do a Save As command and save the file as text only, just the same way you would an HTML file. Give it a name of eight letters or less and add the extension .js.

Let's say you want to name this file george. Do a Save As, making sure you are saving as text alone, and give the file the name george.js. Again, make sure you give the file a name of eight letters or less. I have found that more than eight letters messes up the process. Why? My guess is that it's a leftover DOS concern. But that's a guess. You're now done with that.

Moving along...

Calling for the JavaScript File

You have the JavaScript file saved; now you need to call for it in another document. Let's get back to the JavaScript that produced the date. I followed the same instructions I just gave you and created a file called datestmp.js.

I placed these commands to get its effect on my page:

```
<SCRIPT SRC="datestmp.js">
</SCRIPT>
```

See, I told you you'd pick up those two commands again—that's all you need. The JavaScript denoted by the .js extension appears anytime you place those commands on your page. Just remember to lose the beginning and ending SCRIPT commands in the JavaScript file or you'll get an error.

This is how I tell people to set it so that they can change one page and content in multiple pages change. You set up this same format of a JS file, except the JS file is made up of `document.write("")` statements. Remember them from the new window tutorial?

Whatever you write in the quotation marks shows up on the page as text. Use enough of them and you can enter full paragraphs. That way, you change the text in the JS file and the text on all the pages that use the file update. Simple.

FAQs from the HTML Goodies Web Site

Q. I want to use the external JavaScript using a script that is called for using an `onLoad` command. You only show it with a self-contained script. Can it be done?

A. You have to write the `onLoad` command on each page. That's not going to come along with the script because it has to be placed in the `BODY` command on the page.

A Few Things to Keep in Mind

I found a couple of concerns through my experience:

- The `.js` filename cannot be more than eight characters long.
- Remember that JavaScript sometimes gives Internet Explorer fits. Be sure to test your pages in IE before posting them. If the script causes trouble, use a browser detect script (coming up next) to move IE users away from the pages that employ these external scripts—or any script for that matter.
- This works best with self-contained JavaScripts. Scripts that have multiple parts throw a lot of errors. It's better to just paste the script onto the document in those cases.
- This does not work with multiple scripts in the same `.js` file. You will often find that an effect is created by two JavaScripts, one following right after the other. No dice here. In order to get the effect, you either need to have a `<SCRIPT>` command in the `.js` file or call for two JS files. Either kills the effect. It's best to just paste the scripts onto the page in cases like that.

Remember the `<!--` and `//-->`

That's the general idea. Now go and JavaScript your viewers to death. Just remember to surround your JavaScripts with these two commands: `<!--` and `//-->`.

I did that earlier, see? Those commands hide the text from viewers that cannot read JavaScript. It won't make the browser run the script, but it will stop JavaScript-impaired surfers from getting any error codes when they access your page.

Enjoy!

 See an online example of an external JavaScript at `http://www.htmlgoodies.com/book/` `externaljs.html`.

Browser Choice Script

 This effect is tough to show in book form, so I'll take a moment here to explain what happens. This script sits on a page that your user logs onto. The script looks at the user's browser and loads the page you specify, depending on what browser the user is running. You can see this tutorial online at `http://www.htmlgoodies.com/browserpage.html`.

This JavaScript is great for pages that have Internet Explorer– or Netscape Navigator–specific commands or Netscape–specific JavaScripts. You can create two different versions of each of your pages, one for Internet Explorer and one for Netscape Navigator, so that your user gets far fewer errors from your site. It's more work for you, and of course you don't have to double every page, but it's a great effect if you take the time.

"But," you ask, "if Internet Explorer has trouble with JavaScript, how can you use a JavaScript to get this effect?"

Internet Explorer has trouble with JavaScript 1.1 commands. This JavaScript is written using only 1.0 version commands. That can be read by Internet Explorer, so this script works just fine with both.

Why Would I Want This?

I do and I do for you, and this is the thanks I get.

The two browser powers that be, Netscape and Microsoft, are having a bit of a tiff. They are in a fun game of one-upmanship. Each is trying to created a bigger and better mouse trap to squash the other. In doing so, the browsers are moving further apart in terms of *events* (things it will do). That means that you get an error code, or a nasty message, or nothing if you are using one browser and the page you're visiting has stuff intended for the other browser. You can read a whole bunch of tips on how to get around some of these differences in Chapter 15, "Other Stuff You Should Really Know."

This little beauty of a JavaScript saves a lot of surfing headaches by solving the major problem of browser type right off the bat. If you wrote a page intended for Internet Explorer use alone—bingo—Internet Explorer users go to the page you set up for that browser. Netscape Navigator users go to another page you created for them.

This is a very simple script that assumes your users are running either Navigator or Explorer. I don't know that that's such a big assumption; the two browsers do own the majority of the market. However, the script is written is such a way that other browser types are supported and browsers that do not support JavaScript also get a page.

Let's Look at the Script

The script is rather small. You can transcribe it from here or go online and copy and paste it from `http://www.htmlgoodies.com/mybrowserchoice.html`. It looks like this:

```
<SCRIPT LANGUAGE="javascript">
<!-- begin hiding the script
//This little ditty written and copyright 1998 by Joe Burns Ph.D.
//Keep this in the script if you plan to use it.
if (navigator.appName == "Netscape")
{
parent.location="nspage.html"
}

else

{
parent.location="msiepage.html"
}
// end hiding the script -->
</script>

<NOSCRIPT>
**** Place a text version of the page here ****
</NOSCRIPT>
```

The script is very simple. The first section makes the statement, `If this browser is Netscape Navigator, then go to this page`. That's the part that reads as follows:

```
if (navigator.appName == "Netscape")
{
parent.location="nspage.html"
}
```

The second section is an `else` statement, which tells the computer what to do if the browser is not Netscape Navigator. It send the user to a page designed for Internet Explorer called `msiepage.html`.

Notice, then, the `<NOSCRIPT>` and `</NOSCRIPT>` commands. Those commands surround a *text*, or much simpler version, of the Netscape and Explorer pages. You can, of course, change the names of the pages. Just go into the script and where you see `nspage.html` and `msiepage.html` and put in your own page names. If you need to use the full path (`http://www.blah.blah.blah.com`), you can do that too.

The process goes this way: The user logs into the page that has the JavaScript. If the browser is Netscape Navigator, he is sent to a page called nspage.html. If the browser is Internet Explorer, he is sent to the msiepage.html. If the browser is neither or does not understand JavaScript, the user stays at that page and the simpler version between the <NOSCRIPT> command displays. It's a pretty simple system.

How Do I Do It?

You need at least three pages:

1. The page with the JavaScript and the simple version of the pages
2. A page intended for Netscape Navigator users
3. A page intended for Internet Explorer users

Once you have all three pages ready, FTP them all to your server. Remember that all hypertext links to this system need to go to the page containing the JavaScript, or no one will get the effect. See this JavaScript in action online at http://www.htmlgoodies.com/book/ choosebrowser.html.

Enjoy!

Shopping Cart

This is easily one of the most requested items at HTML Goodies. And with good reason. The shopping cart is becoming a large part of Internet commerce. Anyone with a number of items to sell would want to display their products in this across-page format.

This is a very involved tutorial. Seeing it online will help a great deal. Go to http:// www.htmlgoodies.com/shoppingcart.html.

As you go through this tutorial, you'll see why I have had to wait a while to get one of these carts to hand out. They are huge undertakings that require a great deal of talent and knowledge to write. When I went out looking for a cart to use in a tutorial, I ran across a lot of free but cheaply built items. The good ones were all a pay-for deal. Until this one showed up on my doorstep.

This shopping cart was written by Gordon Smith for his Scottish Gifts On-Line World Wide Web Page (http://www.mearns.org.uk/scotshop/). Gordon has a great online shop selling Scottish items direct. He uses a shopping cart program to run the site.

I'm a big fan of Gordon's site for a few reasons. One, I'm Scottish. The Burns' have their own tartan and everything. Second, he allowed me to use this shopping cart programming to help you. Finally, he sells great stuff.

I'm a fan of Gordon himself because he's a heck of a JavaScript programmer.

What's a Shopping Cart?

A *shopping cart* is a series of pages linked through some sort of programming (usually Perl or JavaScript) that allows data to be transferred along with the viewer as she moves from page to page. This is an example:

A woman enters a site. That site sells clothing. One page displays the dresses the site has for sale, another displays the shoes, and yet another displays the accessories. The woman clicks to purchase a dress. The purchase is then added to her shopping cart. She then moves to the shoes page and clicks to purchase a pair. That item too is added to her shopping cart. Finally, she moves to the accessories page and adds a scarf. After choosing the items she wanted to purchase, she clicks the order link and a page pops up, listing all of her purchases with a final price. That's the concept of a shopping cart.

It seems like a rather simple process on this side of the curtain, but behind the scenes it's quite a difficult task to get that purchase data to move along from page to page as the viewer shops around.

How Does This Shopping Cart Work?

I should state it right up front so that there is no mistake: This shopping cart uses cookies.

FAQs from the HTML Goodies Web Site

Q. I hate cookies. Is there any way to do a shopping cart without them?

A. Yes, but the results you dislike are still there. You see, you need to move information across pages to make a shopping cart work. Either a cookie does it or some other means holds onto the information. Any way you go about it, something must retain the items purchased as the user moves from page to page. Cookies are the quickest way to go.

If cookies are a new concept to you, please read the cookie tutorial in Chapter 15 for a lot of important information. I make that statement because many people believe cookies are the scourge of the Internet high seas. I see them the same way.

Plus, if you want this shopping cart effect, you need to store the information somewhere as the viewer moves from page to page. The user's cookie is the easiest way to do it without inventing some new method of writing to the user's hard drive or to a file online.

Cookies are in wide use today and as long as your user knows you are using them, I don't see the problem. Be honest.

Here's the great thing about this shopping cart: It is already fully self-contained and requires little assembly. In fact, the entire set of pages and programming were sent to me and I went in and cut away anything that wasn't specifically needed for the cart to work. I then entered a great deal of comment lines into the code. Every time you need to alter or enter a piece of information to make this script work for your needs, it is denoted right in the page's code.

What you get here is a bare-bones template that allows you to add your own images, text, and prices. As long as you do not alter the JavaScript programming, the cart should work straight away.

Let's See It

I'll let you go and play with the shopping cart program online so you can get a feel for it; then come back to the book and I'll tell you how to alter it. Figure 11.12 shows a picture of the shopping cart template. Actually, you can probably figure all this out just by looking at the source codes of each page, but I'll go through it all anyway. You can view the shopping cart in action at `http://www.htmlgoodies.com/shopcartindex.html`.

Figure 11.12
A shopping cart.

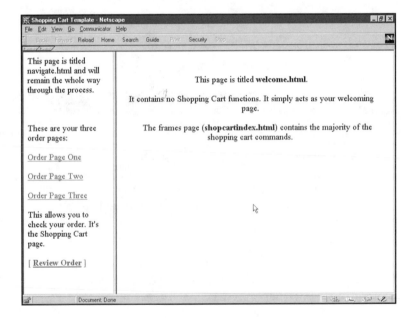

Here's what you'll be looking at: The shopping cart is in a frames format and it must stay that way or you get a warning and errors. There are three pages of items you can buy.

1. Page 1 has only one item on it, valued at $1.11.

2. Page 2 has three items on it, valued at $2.22, $3.33, and $4.44.

3. Page 3 also has three items on it, valued at $5.55, $6.66, and $7.77.

You add an item to the cart by clicking the button that reads Add This Item to My Total. Take a choice away by clicking the button that reads Subtract This Item from My Total. You can click to review your order at any time; you'll see the total of what you've chosen.

The Pages

You need a series of seven items to get this to work on your server. You can download them one at a time or grab them all in a little zip file from the online version of this tutorial. Please remember that you need all the pages in order for this to work. The effect does not display outside the frames format and you get a bunch of errors. In short, get them all and put them in the same directory. Here are the pages you need to grab:

- shopcartindex.html is the main frames page.
- navigate.html is the page that appears in the left frame.
- welcome.html is the page that appears in the right frame.
- pageone.html is the first page of items.
- pagetwo.html is the second page of items.
- pagethree.html is the third page of items.
- order.html is the page that appears when you ask to review your order.

You can go into these template pages and add text and images to your heart's delight. I won't be going into that here. What I am going to do here is explain how to alter the shopping cart functions so that you can set prices and get the information sent to you.

There are really only four pages you need to alter: the three pages with shopping cart items (pageone.html, pagetwo.html, and pagethree.html) and the order.html page.

Altering pageone.html

If you understand how to alter this one page, you can alter the other two shopping cart item pages. They all work the same.

Let me state again that these instructions are printed again right in the code of pageone.html. Here's the basic shopping cart item format pasted from pageone.html:

```
<INPUT TYPE=button NAME=addbox VALUE= "Add This Item To My Total"
onclick=Loc_additem('p1i1','1.11','Page_1_item_1','pageone.html')>
<INPUT TYPE=button NAME=subbox VALUE= "Subtract This Item From My Total"
onclick=Loc_subitem('p1i1','1.11','page_1_item_1','pageone.html')>
You Have Ordered This Many Of This Item:<INPUT TYPE=text NAME=p1i1
SIZE=2>
```

Here's what's happening:

- INPUT denotes a data input item.
- TYPE=button denotes that will be a button.
- NAME= denotes a name for this item so that it can be recognized across pages. This is the addbox.
- VALUE= denotes what will be written on the button.
- onclick=Loc_additem denotes that when this button is clicked, the item in the parentheses needs to be added.
- ('p1i1','1.11','Page_1_item_1','pageone.html') denotes the parameters of the item represented by this button.
- 'p1i1' is the item's identifier. p1i1 stand for page 1, item 1.
- '1.11' is the item's price. At the moment it's a dollar and eleven.
- 'Page_1_Item_1' is the page and item identifier that accompany this information when it moves to the order page.
- 'pageone.html' dittos. You see these items listed when you run the order form. The second button works the same way, except it subtracts the item.
- INPUT TYPE=text NAME=p1i1 SIZE=2 denotes the little box that keeps a running total of how many of this item were ordered. Note the NAME= command—it is p1i1, thus linking this box to the buttons.

Actually, ('p1i1','1.11','Page_1_item_1','pageone.html') is the only section you should really be concerned about. It denotes the item identifier and price. If you alter it, as you have to in order to change the price, you must change each item in two or three places. See that earlier? If you change the price, it must be changed twice. If you change the identifier, it has to be changed three times. With me so far?

There is no reason you couldn't have 20 or more items on each page. You just have to come up with new identifiers for each of the items so that the JavaScript shopping cart can distinguish one from another. The easiest way to do it is to simply copy and paste what is there earlier in this chapter and change out the little section within the parentheses.

FAQs from the HTML Goodies Web Site

Q. You say we can add items to the shopping cart program. Can we take them away? I only want two on each page.

A. Yes, just be sure to remove the entire block of code or you get errors.

Altering order.html

This page requires a great deal of information so it can send the results of the shopping cart to your email box. Slowly go through the page looking for sections written in all capital letters. I put them there, along with some comment statements pointing out some very important parts. (Note that all items that must be changed are not commented out. Look for CAPS.)

The biggest concern is that you make sure to change out the main FORM command that contains the mailto: section. This is set up to work just like a basic mailto: guestbook, so that must be changed out with your email address.

Using a CGI with the Order Form

The author of this shopping cart, Gordon Smith, has also included a CGI that works with this order form. The CGI is a Perl script and is named formmail.pl. The CGI is only available in the zip packet shown earlier. You'll also notice that a thanku.html page is included in the zip packet. That is the page that the CGI displays after someone has filled out and sent the form information to you.

Installing the CGI is a chore unto itself. I have three tutorials that walk you through the process of installing a very similar type of CGI in Chapter 12, "Common Gateway Interface (CGI)." If you follow the format I have laid out in my CGI tutorials, you will be able to get this one up and running. Again, the CGI is only available in the zip packet download. No, it is not required to make this work. The order form acts as its own simple mailto: form so the information will get to your email box.

A word of warning: This system is set up so that information is transmitted. That information is not secure. That means that if someone really wanted to, she could intercept it without your knowing it. Notice there is no slot for credit card numbers on the order form. There was originally, but they have been taken out because I do not want to be responsible for anything that happens with someone's card number. If you do add a slot for a user to enter a credit card number, you do so at your own risk—and at the user's.

Go with an email bill after the form arrives. That is a lot safer.

FAQs from the HTML Goodies Web Site

Q. You say not to ask for credit cards with the shopping cart program. Then what do I need to do to be able to accept cards over the Net?

A. The first place I would go is your local bank. You need an affiliation with a financial institution to accept cards. They will most likely be able to put you in touch with a company that sells the software (maybe Visa or MasterCard themselves). The software

continues

---

uses something called *encryption*. That means it encodes the numbers so they cannot be easily stolen. If you're using that method, go ahead and request cards. Having people send card numbers across regular email is just asking for trouble.

Q. How much does it cost to be able to accept credit cards over the Internet?

A. Prices vary but the pay structure is similar. There is always a setup fee and a monthly fee after that. It also costs a few cents every time someone swipes his card. 30 cents a swipe is what I've heard.

Thanks again to Gordon Smith of Scottish Gifts On-Line for his generosity. Please take a moment to look at his page if you haven't already (`http://www.mearns.org.uk/scotshop/`)—if not to look at his wares, to see this shopping cart in action with all the bells and whistles. I have this shopping cart online in its bare-bones form: `http://www.htmlgoodies.com/book/shopcart.html`.

Enjoy!

Chapter 12

Common Gateway Interface (CGI)

What You Need to Know About CGI

What is this thing I'm calling CGI? It's an acronym for Common Gateway Interface to start. When I first started hearing about CGIs myself, I thought it was a programming language. Not so. CGI is pretty much an all-encompassing term that refers to an application that acts upon data that is offered to it. A CGI can be written in a great many programming languages, but the most popular are Perl, C++, and lately, Java.

The three CGIs that are being offered to you in this chapter are all in written in Perl.

This chapter walks you through attaching to already-existing CGIs and adding three very popular CGIs—a hit counter, a guestbook CGI, and a bulletin board server—to your own site.

Please let me state up front that CGIs are very touchy things. It took me close to two weeks to get all of these CGIs running on my own site, but follow along, keep a close eye on what you're doing, and hopefully you can beat that pathetic time record.

Using a Hit Counter

This is without a doubt the number one item people ask me about. Everyone wants a counter. Why? I don't know. My guess is because someone else has one. I don't have a lot of room to talk. I have one. Heck, I have 20 on the Goodies site!

Actually, there are some valid reasons to have a counter. The best I can think of is to track your site's traffic. If you have a counter on every page, you can get a general idea of what people find most interesting on your site and start gearing your content more toward your audience's interests.

If you get into selling advertising on your site, a counter is quite helpful when the person paying for the banner ad wants to know how many people actually came to see it.

Having one is a pretty good thing...and it does look cool.

 This was one of the original HTML Goodies tutorials! It's online at `http://www.htmlgoodies.com/counter.html`.

If you have already attempted to surf the Net to find a nice, easy page telling you how to put up a counter, you have probably encountered something that uses words like *bitmap*, *standalone daemon*, *config file*, and *inetd*. Right? Not exactly an easy "how to."

Here's the reason the pages are so darn technical: Counters are technical. It's a fact of Internet life.

Here's the information you didn't want to read: I cannot give you a set command that plops a counter in place. What I can do is tell you how to go about finding the command that will plop the counter on your page. Stay with me here and I'll get you a little closer to having a counter.

Granted, counters look great. They do, however, have several drawbacks:

- They slow the completion of the page.
- If the counter CGI is down, the page transfer comes to a complete stop.
- Counters can be faulty and count incorrectly.
- The viewer might have his inline images turned off, thus never seeing your count.
- Honestly, how good does a counter that only reads 15 look?

FAQs from the HTML Goodies Web Site

Q. I want my counter to start at 50,000 so it looks like I have a lot of visitors. How do I do that?

A. It depends on the counter in general. Some allow you to do that, some don't. You need to check out your counter's properties with the owner to find out.

If I haven't talked you out of a counter, let's go on...

Formatting a Counter

A counter is an image. In most cases, it's a bitmap. Remember that word from before? Don't let it throw you. An image is an image is an image. It shows up on your page. This little image, however, comes from the CGI that you attach to. Here's the command I used to get a counter on my page:

```
<IMG SRC="http://www.htmlgoodies.com/cgi-bin/counter?width=5&link=
{http://www.htmlgoodies.com/} {counter.html}">
```

Looks pretty scary, huh? It isn't really. The command is doing four things:

- ◯ `IMG SRC=` is telling the computer that what is returned from the CGI is an image. Where you place the counter command on the page denotes where the image will fall.
- ◯ `"http://www.htmlgoodies.com/cgi-bin/counter?` is the path (the URL, if you will) to the counter CGI.
- ◯ `width=5` tells the CGI how large a counter to return.
- ◯ `{http://www.htmlgoodies.com/}{counter.html}"` is the path back to the page that should receive the counter.

I liked this, too. This is the very basic format almost all counters follow:

```
<IMG SRC="PATH TO THE COUNTER CGI/width=#&link=PATH TO THE PAGE">
```

Since there are many different ways to write counter CGIs, the actual format that works for you may differ slightly from this one, but not too much. The concept is that it's an image.

I have seen some counter formats that do not have the `WIDTH` command and others that do not enclose the path to the page in the braces, but this is the format for the most part.

I told you this gets technical.

Finding a CGI Counter on the Net

The format works for my server and my server alone. You might think (spoken with evil British accent) "Hah! The fool! He has given us the path to his counter CGI! I shall change the information in the command with my page's address so the counter will return a bitmap to me!!! Ha ha ha ha ha ha!" No dice.

You see, people who write these little counter CGIs know they are very popular. In turn—as is the case here—the CGI is written so that unless you are on the same server as the CGI, you get a nasty message in return. Here's what you get if you attach to the CGI noted here:

```
Counter Only Counts Our Pages OK, Joe. You're beginning to anger me! Can I get a
counter or not?
```

Sure you can; there are three ways. All three will work, but one is just better than another.

From Your Internet Service Provider (ISP)

Always an easy answer, huh Joe? Well, yes. It could very well be that the people in charge of your server have a little CGI waiting just for you. All you have to do is attach to it. Contact her and ask. Either that, or you can surf to other pages on your own server and see how they got their counters to work. My guess is that there's a counter CGI just waiting for you if you're on a server of any size or that allows imagemaps.

From the Public Domain

They have those things?! Yeah, you'll find a few on the Web. They are very over-taxed and can slow your page considerably, but they're out there. I have a few listed in the "Net Notes" section of this chapter.

These are nice sites that allow you to choose the type of counter you want and then allow you to fill out a form that hands you the IMG format to place on your page. Read it over carefully before attaching! There might be costs if your site gets more than a set number of hits in a day and they make no commitment that the counters will work every time. Some are done through a CGI as I explained earlier, others are done through Java, and others take a different tilt. Read the pages and make sure you understand and can handle how the counter is placed on your page.

A Counter CGI from a Private Site

Remember a little while back in this chapter where I have you talk in the sinister British voice and say that you'll just attach to my counter by just changing the command line from my page? Well, that's not too far from what you can do. But you should do this one thing:

Ask permission!

If you see a page that has a counter on it, look at the page's source. (You can see its source by opening **Source** under the **View** menu at the top of the page.) Look for the IMG command that put the counter on the page. The path to the counter CGI is going to be an URL. Take just the main URL (before all the directories) and log on. The main page will more than likely have a hypertext link that allows you to write to the Webmaster of that specific site or to the people who run the server itself.

Write and ask for permission to make an attachment to the counter.

Disclaimer: *I did not* tell you to go and attach to counters at will until you find one that works! Doing that can really tee off people who put a great deal of work into assisting their own server's patrons.

Although you might get a counter for a short while, if you perturb the people who run the server, you can be locked out just that quickly. Be nice—ask. I bet you get a nicer note than if you're found using a counter CGI without permission.

FAQs from the HTML Goodies Web Site

Q. How can I get a counter that only I can see?

A. You probably already have it. Ask for permission to read your access file log; that keeps a running count of how many times you have been accessed.

Q. I can't get access to my log files. Now how do I get a counter only I can see?

A. Set a counter on the page and then set the counter's height and width to 0 so it disappears. Create an entirely new page with the exact counter commands on it. Look at the new page—it tells you the count of the other page.

Well, that's about all I can tell you. I know it's not a direct answer, but it at least sends you in the right direction. First ask yourself if you really want this counter thing. If so, do the legwork! It will pay off. You'll get a nice counter sitting right where you want it.

Enjoy!

Net Notes

Here are a few links to public domain sites that offer you the ability to attach to their counter CGI:

> Page Count: `http://www.pagecount.com`
>
> Webtool's Counter: `http://www.webtools.org/counter/`
>
> WebCounter Analysis: `http://www.portset.co.uk/webcounter.htm`
>
> WebCounter Home Page: `http://www.digits.com/`

Just for fun:

> The Anti-Counter: `http://www.cs.wisc.edu/~jenner/anti-counter.html`
>
> The Fake Counter Home Page: `http://www.geocities.com/SiliconValley/Heights/5910/counter.html`

I have installed a counter from one of the public domain counter sites listed here; it's on `http://www.htmlgoodies.com/counters.html`.

Putting a Counter on Your Site

The preceding section discusses attaching to a counter CGI located somewhere outside your personal site. Now I get into how you can install a counter CGI on your own site.

Click Here *This tutorial is online at* http://www.htmlgoodies.com/countcgi.html. *The script for this section in both text and download form can also be found at this URL.*

Please note that this section uses UNIX commands. The majority of servers on the Net are UNIX. If yours runs a different system, contact your Web server's technician to ask what additional steps you need to take.

In seems like everyone wants a counter on his page. I can understand. I love the look of a counter proclaiming to all that my page is cool enough for a couple hundred thousand to roll through. The problem is that counters are not all that easy to come by if you don't own the CGI. I do own the CGI and now I'm going to give it to you. You'll get a counter if you follow this section straight away. The counter will look just like the one in Figure 12.1.

Figure 12.1
Hit counter style on the HTML Goodies site.

Counter —

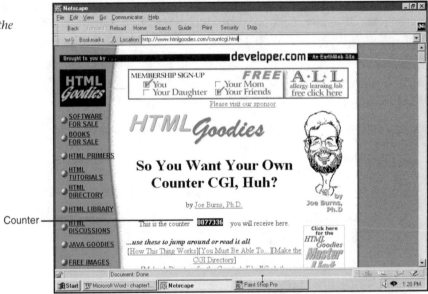

Be careful. There are many not-so-nice people out there who will attach to your counter without your knowing it. Later I tell you how to lock those people out of this counter. I should say that this section does get tricky. CGIs are tough sometimes.

How This Thing Works

This is a very simple counter CGI. It returns a bitmap image counter like the one shown in Figure 12.1. The process is this:

1. The page is requested by a server.
2. There is a code word on the page that is used when contacting the CGI.

3. The CGI checks in a counts directory for a file named after that code word.

4. If the file exists, the CGI adds one to the count in the file and returns the bitmap image of the count.

5. The CGI creates the file if it doesn't exist. The count starts at 1.

You need to create two things: the cgi-bin directory (if you don't already have one) and a directory where this CGI can keep record of all your counts.

In order to do this, you must be able to do a few things with your Internet account. You must be able to

- Gain access through Telnet or FTP (discussed in the next section)
- Create directories
- Change directory modification

If you don't know if you have these permissions, contact your server's technician or just start following along. You'll be told soon enough if something doesn't jibe with the server.

Here we go...

FAQs from the HTML Goodies Web Site

Q. I don't have access through Telnet. What do I do?

A. Contact your server people and ask if you have access at all. You must be able to create and configure directories and place CGIs. Ask if you can do all that. If you can't, you may want to look for another server that allows you those privileges.

Creating Directories with FTP

Creating a directory on an FTP site is as easy as creating a directory on your own hard drive. You'll need some FTP software, though. If you don't know how to FTP, read Primer 7 for details.

Creating Directories with Telnet

For those of you who don't know, Telnet is another way to attach to your Internet server. With Telnet you are attaching directly to the server *shell*. This is where you can enter commands that directly affect the UNIX settings.

You should have received a Telnet program when you signed up with your Internet service provider (ISP). If not, read the section on Telnet in Chapter 15, "Other Stuff You Should Really Know."

All Telnets work the same way. Open the program, choose to connect, and type in your WWW address without the `http://`.

You're good to go. Keep following along...

First, you need to Telnet into your server. Upon connecting, you are asked for your username and password. Put them in. Usually you get a few welcome greeting messages and then a prompt of some sort. I have worked with seven different servers and the prompt has been different on all seven. It should look something like this: `telnet%`.

Does that look familiar? If not, don't worry, you will see the blinking cursor, which is where you enter information.

Why is this done? When you send files to your server, you send the files to a directory in order for them to be seen by the entire Internet community. It has a name; you need to find that name. Most of the time it is something like *public-html*, *www*, or *default*.

For the sake of demonstration, let's say the directory's name is www. (That's the shortest name and thus easiest to write a couple hundred more times.) Depending on your system setup, you will either be in that directory when you Telnet in, or you will be in one above it. The smart money is that you are one above it. Type this at the prompt: `telnet% ls`.

Please note that I am using `telnet%` to represent the prompt. Your prompt may look different.

Press Return; you get a listing (that's what `ls` means) of everything in that directory. If you see the names of all your HTML documents that Internet viewers can access, you are already in the correct directory. Skip the next part.

If you see your Internet directory's name (I called it www earlier), you are one above the directory. This is probably where most of you are.

You need to get into your www directory. Do that by typing this at the prompt: `telnet% cd www` (or whatever your directory's name is).

`cd` stands for change directory; that's what you just did. Put in the `ls` command again and you should see all of your HTML documents.

Making the CGI Directories

This may already have been done for you. You should check that first. If when you typed one of the `ls` commands you saw a `cgi-bin`, you need not do this.

You need to create a special directory for your CGIs. No, they cannot sit where all the other files are located—it becomes clear why in a moment. I suggest you name the directory you are about to create `cgi-bin`, as that is what I am going to call it the rest of the way through this chapter. Please notice that is a hyphen between the `cgi` and the `bin`. You make the directory by typing this: `telnet% mkdir cgi-bin`.

If you get another prompt and no error messages, you did it. This is the first point at which you may be told you do not have the ability to place a CGI. If you do get an Access Denied type of error, you may not have been granted permission to create directories within your site. You can try contacting your service provider to ask for permission. If the answer is still no, you need to think about how badly you want to be able to do this. It may mean moving to a totally different server to gain access.

If you'd like to see your work, type this: `telnet% cd ..` (Those are two periods.)

And then type this: `telnet% ls`

You should see the new directory `cgi-bin`

Now you need to make a directory for the counter files. Follow the same steps as described earlier, but this time create a directory called `count`. This is where the CGI stores the count it is keeping of visitors to each of your pages. Again, do an `ls`. You should see the two new directories, `cgi-bin` and `count` sitting before you.

Log out by typing `logout` at the prompt.

Grabbing the CGI Script and Modifying It

The CGI I am giving you is the exact CGI I use on my system. You need to copy it and save it to your hard drive as `count.pl` or `count.cgi`, depending on what format your server wants. You need to find out from your server's technician which one is preferred.

You can view and download the CGI counter script in text form at `http://www.htmlgoodies.com/countcgi.txt`.

The script may not be ready to go as is. You need to check a few things first:

1. Look at the first line: `#!/usr/bin/perl`

   That is the path to the Perl program in your server. It must be correct for this to work. The CGI will not do most of the work, the Perl program on your server will. This little CGI just sort of "brings" the information to Perl for manipulation. Find out if this path is correct by asking your server's technician. If it isn't correct, change it. Just be sure to open and configure the CGI in Notepad, Simple Text, or another text editor that does not have margins. Altering this CGI's shape by allowing word-wrapping stops it from working.

2. Look at the third line down: `$counterdir="/directory/sub/sub/counts`

   That's the absolute path to the directory, which contains the counts for the CGI. You made it when you created the `count` directory.

Why is this eliminated? Absolute path is a tough concept to grasp at first. Let's say your home page has this URL:

`http://www.server.com/~joe`

That little squiggly line before `joe` is called a *tilde*. It's a neat little space-saving trick. It says to the computer, "There is one directory on this entire server called `joe`. Find it!" There might be five directories between the server name and `joe`, but you'd never know because of the tilde. The actual path to `joe` might be this:

```
http://www.server.com/names/men/tall/joe
```

This is the absolute path to `joe`. Get it?

Finding the Absolute Path

You have to log back into Telnet.

Follow the commands outlined earlier to get into the directory that contains your WWW files for all the world to see. Perform an `ls` command. You should see the `cgi-bin` and `count` directory sitting there.

1. Open the `count` directory by typing `cd count`.
2. When the prompt comes back up, type `pwd` and press Enter.
3. What is sitting before you is that directory's absolute path.
4. Copy it and enter it in the CGI.
5. Log out of Telnet.
6. FTP the CGI.

   Use whatever method you use for placing files on your server to now transfer the count CGI to the `cgi-bin` directory. Do not put the CGI in the `count` directory; it will not work there.

7. Transfer the file as ASCII. Yes, I said ASCII.

   We're getting close. Stay with me here. Log back on with Telnet and get to the directory where you keep your WWW files. You should see the `cgi-bin` and `count` directories using an `ls` command. Now "turn on" both directories. You are basically setting the file's modification instructions so that the server knows that this directory can be written to and read by other servers. Type this at the prompt:

   ```
   telnet% chmod a+rx cgi-bin
   ```

   If you get no error codes, success. If you did get an error code, try this instead:

   ```
   telnet% chmod 775 cgi-bin
   ```

   Sometimes that's allowed and the other isn't. If neither works, you don't have the correct permissions. Talk to your server technician to see if you can get them.

8. Now go ahead and "turn on" the `count` directory by following the same steps as detailed earlier—use `count` instead of `cgi-bin`.

9. That done, you need to "turn on" the counter CGI itself. Type the following at the prompt:

```
telnet% cd cgi-bin
```

You just opened the directory. Now type this:

```
telnet% chmod a+rx [cgi name]
```

10. Put in the name you gave to the CGI. Again, if a+rx doesn't work, try 775.

11. Log out. You're ready to count.

FAQs from the HTML Goodies Web Site

Q. My server people tell me that they don't want me using Perl. What else can I attach to in order to make your script run?

A. Nothing. This script is created to run Perl.

Q. Don't I need images 1 through 0 for this?

A. No. The CGI creates the images as bitmaps for you.

Getting the Counter on the HTML Page

Here's the command you need to place on your page to receive a count:

```
<IMG SRC="/cgi-bin/count.cgi?codeword">
```

Here's what's happening:

- IMG denotes that it's an image that will be returned.

- SRC is the source path. Notice it's pointing toward the cgi-bin you created and then to the CGI inside the directory. Make sure to put in the exact name you used for the CGI. It may differ from what's shown here.

- ?codeword is the way you denote each page that receives a count. The code word can be up to 40 characters. Make up a different one for each page.

That's the general idea. If you have all the paths correct, and the permissions turned on correctly, you should receive a count straight away.

You Shouldn't Do This, but I'll Tell You Anyway

If you want your count to start at a certain level—10,000 for instance—you can do so by adding this to the end of the previous command:

```
&count=####
```

Just replace #### with the number you want to start with. Keep in mind that this only works the first time you access the page. If the counter already has a count of 1, no dice.

The only legitimate reason for doing this is if you're already using a counter, switch to a new one, and want to carry over your current numbers. If you use this command for any other reason, you're probably cheating.

Keeping Others from Using Your Counter

You put this counter on your site to count your pages. If someone is nice enough to ask to use the counter CGI, it's up to you to decide whether to let them. There are some swarthy individuals out there who just muscle right on in. It's not tough to steal into this one; you just copy the command and—poof!—you're counting. This CGI is not advanced and doesn't have a lock-out function. You need to do that by hand.

First log onto the Telnet again. Get to your count directory (where all the counter's numbers are kept) and do an ls to see all the files inside. The files are named after the code words you used. If you see one you didn't put there, someone is stealing from you. Lock them out. Now I tell you how to do just that.

For the sake of demonstration, say there's a file there named fred. It's not your file, so some person is getting free counts from you without asking. Type these commands at the Telnet prompt:

- ○ telnet% touch fred.LOCK   Now press Enter.
- ○ telnet% rm fred   And press Enter.

The touch command creates the file you write. In this case, you created a file named after the bad file with the .LOCK suffix. You then removed (that's what rm indicates) the file fred. You switched fred for fred.LOCK. Now the file fred is locked at 0—it cannot be written to.

The thief might change his code word. Lock them out again. He'll soon get the message.

I do this once a week for the fun on of it. I kind of feel like Matlock.

FAQs from the HTML Goodies Web Site

Q. I cannot get this counter of yours to work! It's driving me nuts. What am I missing?

A. Make sure your paths are correct. Don't guess—check it carefully. That is what usually messes me up.

There's no doubt about it, this is a tough one. If you get it to work, you'll be very pleased with your own counter. It works very quickly and it runs right off your own server. It's a great upgrade to your site.

Enjoy!

Putting a Guestbook on Your Site

This section covers placing a guestbook CGI on your site (see Figure 12.2). It's a topic that HTML Goodies online readers requested for a long time. If you follow it, you are guided through the steps for placing a guestbook CGI on your server. The CGI will hopefully work the same as my guestbook CGI, mainly because it's the same one. You can see it work at
`http://www.htmlgoodies.com/feedback.`

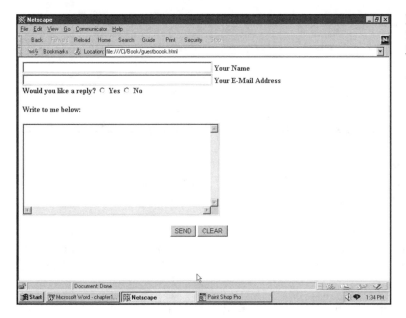

Figure 12.2
The guestbook from the HTML Goodies Web site.

When you use this CGI, it returns a page thanking the user for writing (see Figure 12.3).

I assume here that you have already read the preceding section on setting up a `cgi-bin` directory on your site. That is where you store the guestbook CGI you get in this section. Just think of that `cgi-bin` you made as the future home of all the CGIs you get through the rest of your Internet life.

Getting the Guestbook on the HTML Page

Sounds like a new movie, doesn't it? I have links to the script; its HTML buddy is at the end of this section.

You need to copy the script and its HTML buddy from the HTML Goodies online site as two files.

Figure 12.3

The guestbook Confirmation page from HTML Goodies.

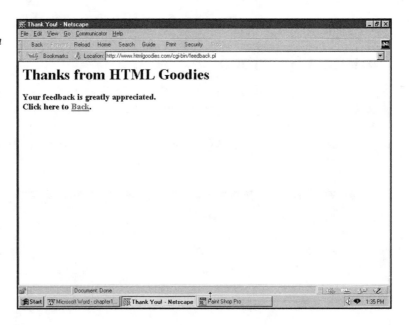

You can view and download the CGI guestbook script in text form at `http://www.htmlgoodies.com/gb_cgi.txt`. You can view and download the guestbook HTML document in text form at `http://www.htmlgoodies.com/gb.txt`.

Save the CGI script as `gb.cgi` (or with whatever suffix your server requires). (Some servers use `.pl`. Ask your server technician what suffix you should use.) You need to save the HTML document as `gb.html`. Save them both as `source` so that they keep their shape. It this getting loopy enough for you yet?

You need to make a few changes to the HTML document so that it knows where the CGI is located. Look at this line in the script:

```
<FORM method="post" Action="/cgi-bin/gb.cgi">
```

This attaches this form's output to the CGI. Change that line so that the output is directed at the `cgi-bin` you created in the preceding section. This is fairly easy. Take your full URL and add `cgi-bin`, a slash, and the name of the CGI file. For instance, your address is `http://www.server.com/~fred`.

The preceding `Action` statement would read as follows:

```
http://www.server.com/~fred/cgi-bin/gb.cgi
```

Get it?

You are now done altering the HTML document. Remember that these two documents were written for each other. They work together. You can change the text or add graphics to the HTML document, but you cannot change the FORM commands at all. If you attempt to add a third text box or another radio button, it won't work.

Modifying the CGI Script

You are concerned about two things here: the path to Perl and the path to Sendmail.

What happens is that the guestbook information is sent to the CGI. The CGI and the information are loaded into the Perl program, or *shell*. The data is manipulated and then returned to your mailbox.

How the mail gets to your mailbox is the Sendmail question. Look at the CGI script:

```
open(MESSAGE,"¦ /usr/lib/sendmail -t");
```

That is the path that the server uses to find a little program that sends the mail. It needs to be correct for your server.

These paths will be correct for the most part. Most servers are set up basically the same way, so you may not need to change anything. Then again, you may need to change them both. Talk to the tech people where your pages are located.

FAQs from the HTML Goodies Web Site

Q. How do I change it so that my return pages don't say what yours say?

A. The return page comes from the CGI, it is not another page. Look at the CGI's text in a text editor. Toward the end, you'll see the text thanking the person for writing. Alter that so that it says what you want.

Activating the Guestbook

You now need to use your FTP program. Attach to your site like you would any other time you were going to transfer files. Send the HTML document to where the other HTML documents are. Do not put the HTML document and the CGI in the same directory; they will not work that way. Remember making a path to the CGI? That's because you will place the CGI in the cgi-bin directory.

Depending on how your FTP is set up, you should see the cgi-bin directory in your window as you transfer the HTML document. Click the cgi-bin directory to open it and then send the CGI.

Send the CGI script as ASCII!

Yes, that's correct. Send it as ASCII text. Do not send it as binary. It is written to be sent as ASCII text. There. I said it three times so you know it's not a typo. Log out of the FTP program.

Now log onto your `cgi-bin` and "turn on" the guestbook CGI in the same manner you used to "turn on" the counter CGI earlier.

If all the paths are correct and you have turned on all the correct files, you should be able to open your browser, log on to the guestbook HTML document, and run the CGI.

FAQs from the HTML Goodies Web Site

Q. This thing just will not work!

A. Almost every time I get to the bottom of this guestbook CGI not working, it winds up being one of the paths. Check them carefully.

You might get a service error first time through. Read it. It will tell you what the problem is. The most common problems are that it cannot find Perl, it cannot find a file due to incorrect paths or filenames, or your server doesn't support post capabilities. The first two can be repaired. The third cannot without first contacting your server technician.

Good luck. Please understand that placing a CGI is very difficult and there are only about a million little things that can go wrong along the way. Take your time and make sure the paths and filenames are correct. It took me two weeks to get this working. See if you can beat my record.

Enjoy!

Net Notes

See this guestbook CGI in action: `http://www.htmlgoodies.com/feedback.html`.

BBS CGI

People have been writing to me through the online site for a while now asking how they can get a billboard server or a newsgroup-type effect. Others want to post the results of their email guestbook without all the hassle. The answer is my BBS CGI, which you can see at `http://www.htmlgoodies.com/gstbk.html`. If you decide to post a message using the CGI on my site, please keep your comments clean. They are posted to another page for all to see.

If you're following this chapter in order, you should have already been introduced to creating a `cgi-bin` directory, placing CGIs in the directory, and turning them on so they run as the CGIs they are meant to be. If not, start reading from the beginning—you'll do yourself a world of good.

Grab the CGI

 The CGI I give you here is the CGI I use on my server. The file is in text format. You need to save it to your hard drive from HTML Goodies online as bbs.pl *or* bbs.cgi, *depending on what format your server wants. You must find out from your server's technician which one is preferred. The script is available to you in text form at* http://www.htmlgoodies.com/ bbscgi.txt.

Altering the Script for Your Server

Creating this BBS page of emails is done almost totally in the CGI itself. Open this CGI in a text editor and configure it for your server and your site. Again, make sure you only edit the CGI in a text editor that does not have margins! Use Notepad on an IBM and Simple Text on a Macintosh. If you want to use any other text editor, turn off the word wrap; just moving margins to their widest setting is not enough—lose them totally. If you alter the shape of this CGI script through word wrapping it will not work.

Let's make some changes:

1. Look at the first line: #!/usr/bin/perl. That is the path to Perl on your server. Make sure the path is typed correctly.

2. Look at the third line: $guestbook="/directory/sub/sub/page.html";.

That it the absolute path of the page that this CGI creates to post the email messages. You need to offer the absolute path. A straight URL address won't do.

Look down to the fourth line of text. It should look like this:

```
$entriespage="http://www.server.com/~joe/bbs.html";
```

This should be your home page address, followed by a slash and the name of the page you want the emails posted to. See that?

"But why do I need to enter the same thing in two different formats?!" Because that's the way the CGI is set up. One posts the message, the other creates a link. They do different things, you see.

Now look at line seven:

```
$maintainer="user\@emailaddress.com";
```

That's where you put your email address. Please make a point of keeping the backslash before the @ sign. If you remove that backslash, the whole process stops.

If you want, you can also go into other parts of the script and alter what is posted to the browser window. Look at the script under where it reads:

```
sub thank_you{.
```

That's the text that pops up when someone sends a message. Change it to whatever you want. I suggest you keep a clean copy of this CGI before messing with it too much. Losing just one little character kills the whole deal real quick.

FTP the CGI

Use whatever method you use for placing files on your server to now transfer the BBS CGI to the cgi-bin directory. Do not put the CGI in just any directory. It will not work anywhere but in the cgi-bin.

Transfer the file as ASCII. Yes, I said ASCII.

Now go back in using Telnet and turn on the BBS CGI.

The HTML Document

 Remember when you saw my BBS work? You entered the data into a guestbook sort of file. You need to have that for this CGI to work. The HTML document is available in text form at http://www.htmlgoodies.com/bbsform.txt.

Now that you have the document, you can gussy it up to your heart's content, but you cannot change, alter, or add to the form items. This document was written for this specific CGI and vice-versa. Altering it will stop the process cold. Wham!

See this line:

```
<FORM ACTION="/cgi-bin/bbs.cgi" method=post>
```

That's the line that attaches this document to this CGI. If you followed the instructions to the letter, the path is already correct. However, if you changed any of the names or altered any of the paths, you need to make sure this is pointed at the right place to find the CGI.

Transfer the file into your regular www directory (where your home page sits).

The BBS.html Page

You're basically done. If everything is set correctly, you can log on to your new page, fill out the elements, and get a bbs.html page created for all the world to see.

The problem is that this page fills quickly. It quickly becomes huge—and it will also happen that some idiot will post an obscenity or some other numbskull comment thinking he or she is really cute. You'll want either to get rid of that or empty the page now and again. Here's how:

1. Log into Telnet. Use the preceding commands to get into your www pages directory. That's where this bbs.html page is sitting.

2. Type `rm bbs.html` and press Enter.

3. Type `touch bbs.html` and press Enter.

4. Type `chmod a+rx bbs.html` and press Enter. (Use 775 in place of a+rx if it doesn't work.)

You just removed the `bbs.html` page and replaced it with a page of the same name, but blank. You then "turned it on" again. Easy, easy.

FAQs from the HTML Goodies Web Site

Q. How can I make your BBS post the newest messages at the top of the page rather than the bottom?

A. You can't do that without changing around the entire CGI.

Q. How can I block out those people I don't want from coming in and posting? You know, people who are writing nasty things.

A. That something you need to work out with your server people. They can block that person completely. That's what I'd do, anyway.

Q. Can I limit the amount someone writes?

A. No. The CGI simply re-posts what is written. Another downfall of the process is that people can write HTML code to the page. If you install this, you need to keep a steady eye on it.

That's It!

Have fun. Now you can create BBS pages to your heart's content. Just remember that these pages fill very quickly and must be kept up. I just hope mine doesn't get too big that I have to take it down for sanity's and space's sake. Enjoy!

Chapter 13

Internet Explorer Tutorials and DHTML

Using Microsoft Internet Explorer-Specific Commands

Doesn't Microsoft's Internet Explorer Web browser do everything Netscape Navigator does? Just about, but Netscape and Microsoft are in a fight for browser supremacy. Each is doing its best to offer features that the other will not handle. Some feel that's good, others feel it is making the World Wide Web a hard place to write for. There will be conflict as long as some commands are supported by both browsers, and some aren't. There will be some errors and there will be some strange-looking mistakes.

"Internet Explorer, Joe?"

"Yeah."

"I've used it a great deal lately. I like it. It allows for a very smooth page scroll and the little rotating "e"/globe up on the right corner is pretty spiffy. I also like the fact that I can manipulate its interface (its visual form) a lot more than Navigator. I only show the Back and Stop buttons now. Plus, I really like the ability to very easily manipulate the Favorites section."

Its downfalls are that Navigator still seems to load faster, but Internet Explorer hasn't crashed yet. My Navigator still does that now and again. Go grab your own version of Internet Explorer at `http://www.microsoft.com/ie` and you be the judge.

FAQs from the HTML Goodies Web Site

Q. Since you're talking about browsers specifically, I would like to know how people who make browsers make any money. Internet Explorer and Netscape Navigator are free over the Net. You can buy them, but why would you when they're free? Where do Microsoft and Netscape make their money?

A. Advertising. Netscape's home page and Microsoft's Internet Explorer page are two of the most visited sites on the Net. Every time you log on, you see advertising banners. It's the same thing with Geocities, which gives away free home page space. There's always an ad banner popping up. You create a product and give it away so people will see the ad banners. HTML Goodies works the same way—it's free because I can sell enough advertising to keep it that way.

I attempt here to provide a quick reference to what features and commands Explorer supports that Netscape won't. Please note that a lot of these are add-on commands to many existing tutorials that I have already posted. When possible, I make reference to the main topic tutorial.

There are three major features Explorer supports that Navigator has some trouble with: scrolling marquees, active channels, and inline frames.

Each of these features is covered in this chapter.

Setting Static Backgrounds

This is a great effect. Add BGPROPERTIES="fixed" to your BODY command and the background images remain stationary while the text scrolls over them.

Specifying Page Margins

These go inside <BODY> and affect the entire page in that position:

- ○ LEFTMARGIN="###" denotes left margin in inches.
- ○ TOPMARGIN="###" means top margin in inches.

Loading a Background Sound

If you've read Chapter 10, "Adding Sound and Video," for how to embed sounds, you have a general idea of what these commands do. They offer, as suggested, a background sound for the page.

Follow this format:

```
<BGSOUND SRC="sound.wav" LOOP="###">
```

- BGSOUND means a sound will be placed here.
- SRC is the source of the sound. Sound can be in most any sound format, including MIDI; Explorer supports them all. Use this command in addition to the EMBED commands to make sure your sounds plays across platforms.
- LOOP designates the number of times the sound will play. Using infinite will play it forever and ever...until you go crazy.

Setting Table Properties

I get at least a letter a day asking how one changes the background color of a table or table cell. Well, here's how you do it with Explorer. All commands are placed within the <TABLE> command, except where noted.

- BORDERCOLOR="###" refers to the color of the border. See the chart in Appendix B, "Useful Charts," for a few color commands.
- BORDERCOLORLIGHT="###" offers a softer version of the color requested.
- BORDERCOLORDARK="###" ditto. This and the preceding two commands also work inside the TH and TD commands.
- FRAME="###" tells the browser to display certain outside borders on the 3D table cell frame. Use these attributes:

  ABOVE   Border on top only

  BELOW   Border on bottom only

  LHS   Left border

  RHS   Right border

  HSIDES   Top and bottom borders

  VSIDES   Left and right borders

  BOX   All sides get a border

  VOID   No sides get a border (so there!)

- RULES="###" same deal, but on the inside borders. Try these:

  ROWS   Shows borders between rows

  COLS   Shows borders across columns

  ALL   Gives them all borders

  NONE   No borders

FAQs from the HTML Goodies Web Site

Q. Why doesn't Internet Explorer support the simple mailto guestbook format?

A. It does with the release of Internet Explorer 4.0, but I don't know otherwise. They knew about using forms as a guestbook and a few versions still came out that didn't support it. I thought that was a big oversight and based on the mail from my users, others did too. All's well that ends well.

Hopefully you can use what I have here. Do yourself a favor: Go get Internet Explorer if you don't have it already. Most computers already come with it. It opens a whole new realm of HTML writing. Whether you make it your main browser or not is up to you. I still use Netscape Navigator for the majority of my HTML work. I usually use Internet Explorer to surf.

You can install both browsers on your hard drive at the same time. I've even had them both open at the same time—no problems. Happy exploring!

 See a few of these commands in action at `http://www.htmlgoodies.com/book/iecommands.html`.

Using IE Marquees

If you go to `http://www.htmlgoodies.com/marquee.html` with Netscape Navigator, you see the hilariously funny joke in text form at the top of the screen as shown in Figure 13.1. If you were using Microsoft Internet Explorer, that text would be scrolling, allowing you to read the joke again and again and again. As we all know, jokes get funnier the more you tell them.

Marquee? It looks like a scroll. It is a scroll, but <MARQUEE> is the flag that makes it happen. It's a throwback to the marquees that used to scroll, announcing a movie or show at a theater. That said, here's what posts the fancy scrolling text in Figure 13.1 to your Internet Explorer Web page:

```
<MARQUEE BGCOLOR="#80FF00" LOOP="infinite" >text text text</MARQUEE>
```

Here's what's happening:

- MARQUEE tells Internet Explorer that a scrolling marquee is going here.
- BGCOLOR tells the marquee what color to put behind the text. This color is in hex code, but you can also use word color codes. I have a whole list of them in Appendix B.
- LOOP="infinite" tells the marquee to roll that text forever. Put a number in place of infinite to tell it how many times it should roll.
- /MARQUEE ends the whole deal.

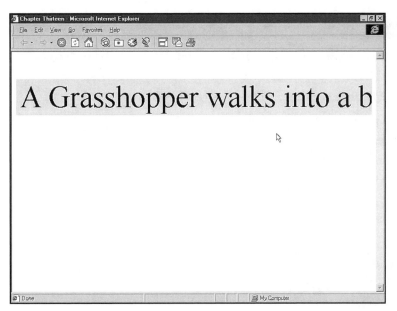

Figure 13.1
Scrolling marquee with Internet Explorer.

Can I do other things? You betcha. I only used a few of the available commands. Here are a couple more. You'll place them inside the first MARQUEE command, just like the BGCOLOR and LOOP command in the preceding code.

- HEIGHT="###" specifies the marquee's height. Do it in percentage of the screen height or pixels.
- WIDTH="###" denotes the marquee's width. Do it in percentage of the screen width or pixels.
- ALIGN="###" uses top, left, or middle in the marquee banner.
- DIRECTION="###" uses left or right. That's where the text comes from. right is default.
- BEHAVIOR="###" has scroll as default. slide has the text come in and stop; alternate makes the text come from both sides every other time.
- HSPACE="###" tells the marquee how much space to leave on each side of the text. Write this in pixels.
- SCROLLAMOUNT="###" tells the browser how much space between successive scrolls. Do this in pixels.
- SCROLLDELAY="###" is the number of milliseconds (thousands) between each scroll.
- VSPACE="###" denotes the top and bottom space before the text. Do this in pixels.

FAQs from the HTML Goodies Web Site

Q. What happens if you use these commands in a page displayed by Netscape Navigator?

A. The text between the marquee commands displays normally—no scroll.

Q. What's up with the marquee tutorial? I can get that on Netscape Navigator using a scrolling JavaScript.

A. Yeah, I know, but this scroll is done using simple MARQUEE commands and it is an Explorer-only deal. Microsoft is selling ease here, not anything new.

Just like a movie, huh?

Enjoy!

 I have this same marquee scrolling at `http://www.htmlgoodies.com/book/marquee.html`. *You get to see the entire joke. Make sure you look at the source code.*

Using IE Active Channels

Have you seen the icons shown in Figure 13.2 floating around lately?

Figure 13.2
Active channel icon—
Internet Explorer.

They're pretty popular little pups with the Internet in-crowd. In fact, requests to put to-gether a tutorial on the subject of active channels have been filling the Goodies mailbox. Here we go. This is a basic instructional look at what an active channel is and how you can get one on your site.

FAQs from the HTML Goodies Web Site

Q. Is there a way to use JavaScript to make it so that when someone logs onto your site they are automatically given an active channel?

A. I'm sure there is by using an onLoad command (see the Advanced JavaScript section of Chapter 11, "Java Applets and JavaScript") with a function that forces the browser to look at the active channel .CDF file. Despite this, don't use it. I would be pretty cheesed if you did that without my permission.

An active channel is another idea from the laboratories of Microsoft. As such, you require the use of the Microsoft Explorer browser, version 4.0 or later, in order to get in on all the actively channeled fun. I have no doubt that Netscape will include it very soon.

Think of it this way: the people who come to your site have the ability to set up a pathway in which you can *push* (give information to the viewer) information other than what is on the page. In activating this *pathway*, or channel, the user allows you a bit more leeway in bombarding them with information. You can push or *pull* (take information from a site)—depending on what side of the argument you prefer—just about anything: a monthly newsletter, new site info, or a listing of new tutorials.

FAQs from the HTML Goodies Web Site

Q. If I set it up so that I push a newsletter to people through my active channel, where does it end up? I mean, where is it on the computer?

A. I found the few that I signed up for in my browser's cache (Temporary Internet File folder in Windows). I see that part as a bit of a downfall. If the items you push aren't pushed to the desktop, they are kind of hard to find.

What's more, the user who clicked to create an active channel with you now has an additional bookmark to your site. In fact, that's how people started referring to these little gems in the first HTML Goodies emails. Users wanted to know how to create the fancy bookmark. If you haven't already clicked a page in order to set up a channel, use your Explorer 4.*x* browser, head to my tutorial, and click the Active Channel logo. You get a box that looks a lot like Figure 13.3.

For now, just choose to add the site to your channel bar as I have it earmarked in Figure 13.3. Go ahead, you can always delete it later.

Now you should have an active channel set up with my site. To see the fruits of your labor, look at the very top of your browser window. There should be a button there marked Channels. There's a little satellite receiver image near it. Go ahead and click that. The screen should split and you should see a little HTML Goodies logo next to the same satellite dish image. If there's no image, you may need to run your mouse over the text.

FAQs from the HTML Goodies Web Site

Q. I hate how the screen looks when I open the Active Channels menu. It's all pushed together.

A. That happens. Close the Channels menu and it will return to normal.

Figure 13.3

Internet Explorer Add Active Channel(TM) Content dialog box.

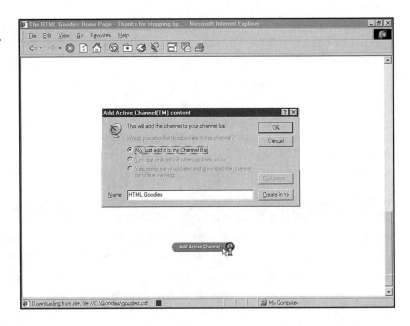

Creating an Active Channel Link on Your Page

Now that you have a channel that links you to my page, let me show you how to get one on your page so that others can begin channeling through you. Hopefully someone will begin channeling Elvis soon. (Uh, thank you very much.)

Here's the format:

```
<A HREF="http://www.htmlgoodies.com/goodies.cdf"><IMG SRC="add_chan.gif"></A>
```

Notice it's little more than a basic A HREF link command. The only real difference is that this link is headed toward a file with a .cdf extension. add_chan.gif is the image I am using as the link, but you don't need an image for it to work. You can put in straight text if you want. That little image is just how I usually see these things identified on other Web pages, so I'm using it here.

Using the Channel Definition Format (.cdf)

.cdf stands for Channel Definition Format. It's a text file that denotes what you have available on your site, and it's what sets up your active channel. Here's what my .cdf file, named goodies.cdf, looks like:

```
<?XML VERSION="1.0" ENCODING="UTF-8"?>
<CHANNEL HREF="http://www.htmlgoodies.com" BASE="http://www.
htmlgoodies.com">
<TITLE>HTML Goodies</TITLE>
```

```
<ABSTRACT>HTML/DHTML Tutorials and Java Script</ABSTRACT>
<LOGO HREF="http://www.htmlgoodies.com/goodieschannel.gif"
 STYLE="IMAGE"/>
</CHANNEL>
```

This .cdf, and all .cdf files for that matter, are simple text—just as any HTML document you've ever made. That text is then saved to a file and the file is given the extension .cdf. Again, think of it as creating an HTML file, except you use the .cdf extension instead of .html.

It may look like I have a basic HTML file here with a few mistakes. Not so. You see, the .cdf file is not written in HTML per se, but rather a cousin of HTML called XML (Extensible Mark-up Language). There's more on XML in Chapter 15, "Other Stuff You Should Really Know."

Now is when this thing starts to get a little goofy and people start to drop out saying "Ah, the heck with it."

Creating the .cdf File

Let's make a file the old fashion way—steal it from Joe.

Go ahead and copy the .cdf file from earlier and paste it into a text editor like Notepad, SimpleText, or WordPad—whatever you use to edit your HTML documents.

This .cdf is about as basic as you can get. It does one thing: It sets up a channel. There are many more events available, and I'll get to them, but we'll start with this.

You can see where to change out the text to suit your needs, but just so you know what your doing, here's the .cdf again, and what each part means:

```
<?XML VERSION="1.0" ENCODING="UTF-8"?>
```

This is the XML declaration statement. It tells the browser that the following document is in XML format version 1.0. The question marks at the beginning and end are a nice touch, don't you think? The encoding statement tells the browser what format is being used to build this .cdf file.

```
<CHANNEL HREF="http://www.htmlgoodies.com" BASE="http://www.
htmlgoodies.com">
```

This is the encompassing channel statement. Everything that sits within the `<CHANNEL>` and `</CHANNEL>` commands refers to the channel's traits. The HREF and BASE commands denote the base URL of each of the filenames that follows. These are the same because my channel is on the main page, which is also the base address. Make your BASE your site's main URL.

For example, if your site is `http://www.server.com/~bob/`, that's the base you put in this command. All other pages sit inside that base address. Get it?

```
<TITLE>HTML Goodies</TITLE>
```

This is the title that appears in the channel. (Remember when you clicked the channels icon at the top? That's where this pops up.)

```
<ABSTRACT>HTML/DHTML Tutorials and Java Script</ABSTRACT>
```

This acts as a small description of the site.

```
<LOGO HREF="http://www.htmlgoodies.com/goodieschannel.gif" STYLE="IMAGE"/>
```

This is the icon that appears in the channel list. The format is XML. Follow it; you must remember that this is not HTML. The image cannot be animated and cannot be any larger than 30×80. If it is, it just gets scrunched down to size and looks pretty bad.

This wraps up the channel section and this particular .cdf.

FAQs from the HTML Goodies Web Site

Q. What happens if I use an animated image for my channel?

A. Nothing, really. It doesn't animate and you get just the top level image. The entire thing still loads, so you're wasting bytes.

There are a slew of other commands that you can incorporate when you create your active channel. Here are a few to get you off the ground, with the most useful first.

```
<ITEM>
```

This is an item that you can push to the user, like an HTML file. It goes inside the CHANNEL commands. For example:

```
<CHANNEL>
<ITEM HREF="http://www.page.com/newsletter.html" PRECACHE="yes">
<CHANNEL>
```

What happens here is that an HTML page titled newsletter.html is pushed to the user. Notice the PRECACHE="yes" command. That addition to the ITEM command makes the browser go get the item and stick it in the cache. When you click the channel to read newsletter.html, it pops up straight away because it was precached.

```
<USAGE VALUE="###" />
```

This too goes inside the CHANNEL command. It tells how the browser is to use the thing within in the <ITEM> command. The available values include desktop component, channel, and screen saver. This is an example:

```
<CHANNEL>
<ITEM HREF="http://www.page.com/newsletter.html" PRECACHE="yes">
<USAGE VALUE="channel" />
<CHANNEL>
```

This HTML document appears in the channel.

<SCHEDULE>

This displays the schedule for the active channel content. If you are pushing information that has an end date, you can use the command to have the channel end on its own, rather than going in and changing out the information yourself. This is an example:

```
<CHANNEL>
<ITEM HREF="newsletter.html" PRECACHE="yes">
<SCHEDULE STARTDATE="1998.02.28" ENDDATE="1999.09.31">
<INTERVALTIME DAY="5" />
<EARLIESTTIME HOUR="5" />
<LATESTTIME HOUR="12" />
</SCHEDULE>
<CHANNEL>
```

- INTERVALTIME is the update frequency. You can use DAY, HOUR, or MIN.
- EARLIESTTIME is the earliest time during the schedule when an update can occur. You can use DAY, HOUR, or MIN to set parameters.
- LATESTTIME is the latest time during the interval that an update can occur. You can use DAY, HOUR, or MIN.

That's about all you need to put together your own active channel. All those fancy commands aside, the bulk of your work is done by the short .cdf format I showed earlier. Add an item to distribute, and you are pretty much good to go. The rest of the commands do a good deal of fine tuning, but are not needed to create a solid channel for your viewers.

Enjoy!

 Try heading to the HTML Goodies home page at http://www.htmlgoodies.com. *There you can see the exact active channel format in action.*

Using VBScript with IE

This section deals with VBScript and ActiveX discussions. You need to run Microsoft Explorer in order to use or see the script perform.

VBScript is a short way of stating Microsoft's Visual Basic Scripting. It is a strict *subset* (a little portion) of the Visual Basics for Applications (VBA) language (huh?). It's the Microsoft version of Java, sort of. It's also the leading scripting language used in ActiveX.

Around 1995 or 1996, someone said, "Let there be motion on WWW pages!" Someone else seconded the motion and everyone went off looking for a simple programming language to do it. The first one that really took was Java. It's an object-oriented programming language created by a guy named James Gosling at Sun Microsystems. You can read a great deal more about Java in Chapter 11.

ActiveX comes in through Bill Gates and the fine people at Microsoft. ActiveX is Microsoft's vision for interactive and movement-filled Web pages. I've used it a couple of times; it's actually pretty easy. One of the problems with Java is that you still need to write it out. ActiveX attempts to get rid of that. You can call up some activity, an *object*, with the click of a button. It's all pretty slick. There's one drawback though: It only works on Microsoft Internet Explorer (or Netscape with a plug-in). It will probably be that way for a few generations. Why? Because there is no real need to have it work everywhere, Java is supported by Internet Explorer and Netscape Navigator. Microsoft is pushing ease here, not something new and better.

FAQs from the HTML Goodies Web Site

Q. I have never heard of VBScript. Who uses it?

A. I see a good bit of it from users of Java Goodies, who send me items to post to the site. It's not in widespread use by any means, but some real Explorer enthusiasts still program it a bit. Microsoft's ActiveX technology uses it, but I wouldn't run right out and grab a manual on it just yet.

A VBScript Clock

Might you have the time? Yup—just see Figure 13.4. That's a VBScript. In order to join in the fun, you need Explorer or a version of Netscape that has an ActiveX plug-in. The links to get these items are at the end of this section in "Net Notes."

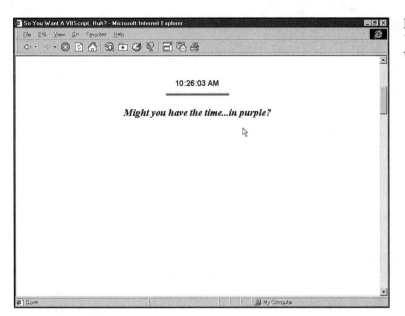

Figure 13.4
Web page clock produced with VBScript.

Let's take a look at the VBS script for the clock in Figure 13.4:

```
<SCRIPT LANGUAGE="VBScript">
<!--
Sub IeTimer1_Timer()
IeLabel1.Caption = time
end sub
-->
</SCRIPT>
<OBJECT ID="IeTimer1" WIDTH=39 HEIGHT=39
CLASSID="CLSID:59CCB4A0-727D-11CF-AC36-00AA00A47DD2">
<PARAM NAME="_ExtentX" VALUE="1005">
<PARAM NAME="_ExtentY" VALUE="1005">
<PARAM NAME="Interval" VALUE="1000">
</OBJECT>
<TABLE BORDER=2 BGCOLOR=PURPLE>
<OBJECT ID="IeLabel1" WIDTH=137 HEIGHT=39
CLASSID="CLSID:99B42120-6EC7-11CF-A6C7-00AA00A47DD2">
<PARAM NAME="_ExtentX" VALUE="3625">
<PARAM NAME="_ExtentY" VALUE="1005">
<PARAM NAME="Caption" VALUE="">
<PARAM NAME="Angle" VALUE="0">
<PARAM NAME="Alignment" VALUE="4">
<PARAM NAME="Mode" VALUE="1">
<PARAM NAME="FillStyle" VALUE="0">
<PARAM NAME="FillStyle" VALUE="0">
```

```
<PARAM NAME="ForeColor" VALUE="#000000">
<PARAM NAME="BackColor" VALUE="#C0C0C0">
<PARAM NAME="FontName" VALUE="Arial">
<PARAM NAME="FontSize" VALUE="12">
<PARAM NAME="FontItalic" VALUE="0">
<PARAM NAME="FontBold" VALUE="1">
<PARAM NAME="FontUnderline" VALUE="0">
<PARAM NAME="FontStrikeout" VALUE="0">
<PARAM NAME="TopPoints" VALUE="0">
<PARAM NAME="BotPoints" VALUE="0">
</OBJECT>
</TABLE>
```

Here's what's happening:

First look at the text. The actual script is quite small; it's only three lines long. Two OBJECTs follow. The <OBJECT> command starts off each one. To understand why, let's go back to 1991—that's when Microsoft began playing with this format they call OLE, Object Linking and Embedding. It was a way to create documents, spreadsheets mostly, that allows many different working parts to be stuck within the same domain. The parts all do different things, and they all work together. Each part was referred to as an OBJECT, each independent and each fully functioning.

Defining the First Object

Notice in the following code that each object has its own ID name and parameter settings. Just like Java, these little guys need to have their own defined space. classID denotes a specific thing that this object does. In this case, it sets up a timer. See the name: IeTimer1?

```
<OBJECT ID="IeTimer1" WIDTH=39 HEIGHT=39
 CLASSID="CLSID:59CCB4A0-727D-11CF-AC36-00AA00A47DD2">
```

You might have been asked to sign contracts when you tried to access this page. This is what's known as *digitally signed software.* You are asked if you accept terms laid out for you to see. If you do, click to accept. It's much like signing a contract to follow the rules. This VBScript is not fully recognized by Internet Explorer until some extra programs are installed. When you said OK to the download, the browser got the needed programming and installed it. It's a truly slick little system.

FAQs from the HTML Goodies Web Site

Q. I don't like how the objects were just "installed" for me. Isn't that sort of an invasion of privacy?

A. No—you allowed it. But I know what you mean. I am also used to downloading the entire item and then installing it myself. That way I can run a quick virus check and choose where I want it installed and such. You clicked Yes when asked, however. I wouldn't call it an invasion.

Defining the Second Object

This code has the clock face's actual look, thus the name IeLabel1. Note that this object is the one encased in TABLE. Here you can change background color, change text color, change font type, font name, and add a caption. Each of the parameters are fairly self-explanatory. Change them around and add new colors and text styles. The object responds.

```
<TABLE BORDER=2 BGCOLOR=PURPLE>
<OBJECT ID="IeLabel1" WIDTH=137 HEIGHT=39
 CLASSID="CLSID:99B42120-6EC7-11CF-A6C7-00AA00A47DD2">
```

Adding VBScript to Your Page

You can transcribe the entire VBScript from earlier or cut and paste it from the online version of this tutorial. You must be online when you run it because the VBScript calls Microsoft for the objects it needs. You are asked if you want them installed; click to indicate that you do. Next time you attempt to see this clock on your browser, you will already have the objects and it will run fine straight away.

When should you use VBScript? When you are positive that your viewers will be using Internet Explorer as their browser. If you're not sure, use JavaScript to post the time to your page. I have a script that will do just that in Chapter 11. Both script formats are supported by Internet Explorer to a point, but only JavaScript is fully supported by Netscape Navigator.

Keep in mind that if your page is complete without the VBScript, go ahead and use it. Netscape Navigator is wonderful at ignoring commands it doesn't understand. For example, if you use the clock, people using Internet Explorer get the time. People using Netscape Navigator get nothing. That's not bad if the clock is just an added extra. See what I mean?

Now, where to place this on your HTML document? The code you see should be placed at the point you want the clock to appear on the page. Think of the code as one element. You can center it using <CENTER> commands if you want.

I use both Netscape Navigator and Internet Explorer, and I like them both. To have a preference so strong that you refuse to use one or the other is beyond me. It's my opinion that if you're into HTML, learn it all.

Enjoy!

 See another VBScript in action at `http://www.htmlgoodies.com/book/vbs_example.html`.

Net Notes

Active X Plug-In for Netscape: `http://www.ncompasslabs.com`.

Using Inline Frames with IE

Inline frames appear within the page (see Figure 13.5). They resemble table cells, yet what appears in the frame is not text on the page, but rather a whole other page, like regular frames.

Figure 13.5
An inline frame in Internet Explorer.

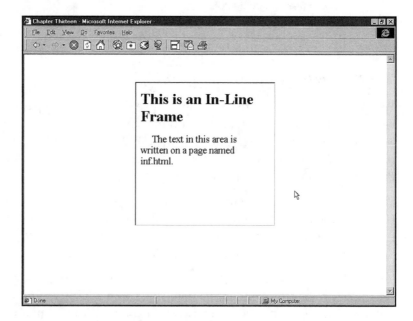

I know Figure 13.5 looks like a table cell, but it's really a frame with the text from another page displayed inside it. It's a page in a page. It's two, two, two pages in one. I'll stop now before I begin quoting Doublemint gum commercials. Here's how I did it:

FAQs from the HTML Goodies Web Site

Q. Can't I get the same look using table cells as I do with inline frames?

A. Yes, but you can't get that look of loading new pages into the frames unless you reload the entire page again and again.

Adding the IFRAME *Command*

The command for adding inline frames for IE browsers is as follows:

```
<IFRAME SRC="inf1.html"></IFRAME>
```

- IFRAME is the command that states an inline frame will go here.
- SRC denotes the source for the page, just like an image command.
- /IFRAME ends the entire command. You must have this for each IFRAME you post.

How's that for easy?

Adding Multiple Frames

If you can have one, you can probably have two. Dig Figure 13.6 and Figure 13.7.

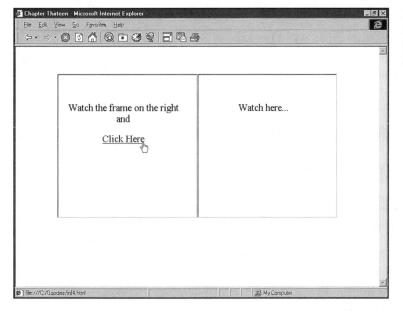

Figure 13.6
Multiple inline frames before clicking the Click Here link.

Figure 13.7

Results of clicking the Click Here link.

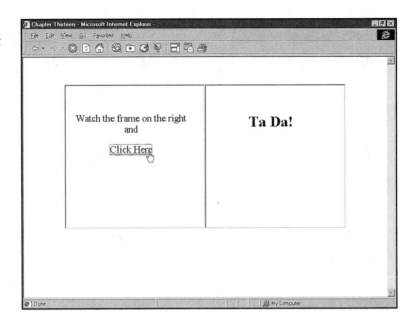

Here's the code that made the frames in Figures 13.6 and 13.7:

```
<IFRAME SRC="inf2.html" NAME="left"></IFRAME>
<IFRAME SRC="inf3.html" NAME="right"></IFRAME>
```

Now we get into the beauty of inline frames; you can have movement between them. First, let's look at the code.

I need you to see that I used an </IFRAME> each time I created a frame. Now notice that the format for creating the frames stayed the same. I added a new command:

```
NAME="--"
```

If you already understand the concept of frames and targeting the output of hypertext links within frames, you already know the drill here. If not, see the original frame tutorial's section on targeting; you'll find it in Chapter 6, "Using Frames."

That NAME command names the frame so that you can target where a hypertext link's page appears. The default is for the information to appear in the same frame as the hypertext link. What I did here, though, was name the frames—in this case, left and right.

Here's the format I used in the left frame to create the hypertext link:

```
<A HREF="inf4.html" TARGET="right">Click Here</a>
```

See? The right frame was named right; thus, the output of the click landed in the right frame. That's easy enough.

I Want a Button!

Calm yourself! You can have your button and click it too. Check out Figures 13.8 and 13.9.

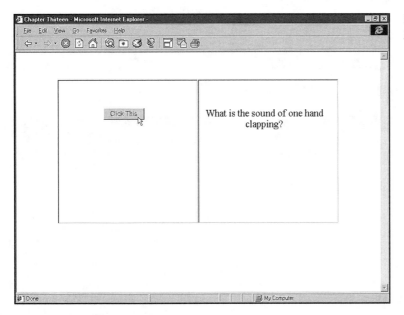

Figure 13.8
Before clicking the button.

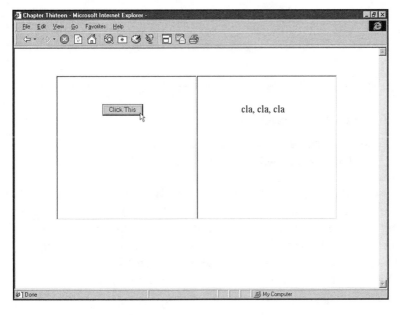

Figure 13.9
Results of clicking the button.

And here's the button's code:

```
<FORM ACTION="inf7.html" TARGET="right">
<INPUT TYPE="submit" VALUE="Click This">
</FORM>
```

Adding Invisible Frame Borders

Watch the browser screen shown in Figures 13.10 and 13.11.

Figure 13.10
Before clicking the invisible inline frame border link.

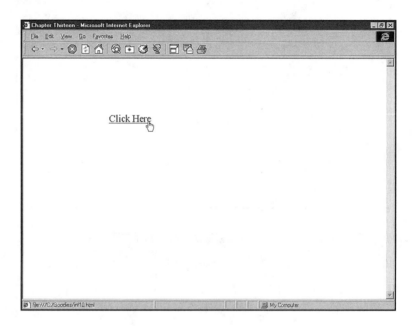

I think that's the neatest effect these frames offer. Here's the code I used to make the frames:

```
<IFRAME SRC="inf8.html" FRAMEBORDER="0" NAME="left"></IFRAME>
<IFRAME SRC="inf9.html" FRAMEBORDER="0" NAME="right"></IFRAME>
```

See the FRAMEBORDER="0" command I added? That's what does the trick. You have two settings to choose from: 1 and 0; 1 is the default. That gives you the slightly indented frame look I have; 0 loses the frame altogether. That's what I did in this case. Since I made the two source pages the same color as the main page—without the borders—it looks like the frame is simply part of the same page. I got the blank look on the right by creating a page that was the same color as the main page, but without text. I think it's a great effect.

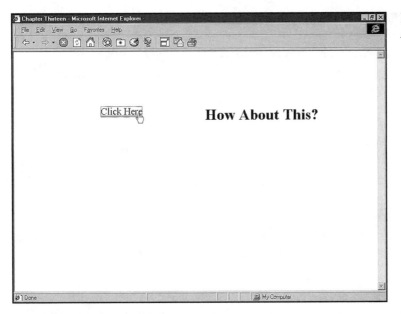

Figure 13.11
After clicking the link.

Altering Inline Frames

Here are a few more commands that you can use to alter the frames on your page. I've used them all just to make sure they work. Just stick the command, with whatever setting you want, into the <IFRAME> flag to see it work.

- HEIGHT="###"   This acts just like the HEIGHT command in terms of an image. It defines the frame's height in pixels or percentage.

- WIDTH="###"   Ditto this one in terms of frame width.

- MARGINWIDTH="###"   This sets the margin width in either pixels or percentage.

- MARGINHEIGHT="###"   Ditto, but on height.

- SCROLLING="###"   If the information inside the frame is too long to display, a scrollbar appears. You can stop it by adding this command set to no.

- ALIGN="###"   This works like the ALIGN command in terms of images. It denotes where text will appear when surrounding the frame.

- NORESIZE   Add this and the user will not be able to resize your frame.

These are great, but keep in mind that these are Internet Explorer–only deals. They do not display in Netscape Navigator browsers. Make a point of using these when you are sure a user is running Explorer or use a JavaScript in order to send users to certain pages depending on their type of browser. I have one in Chapter 11.

FAQs from the HTML Goodies Web Site

Q. What happens if I use inline frames in a Netscape Navigator browser?

A. Nothing—literally nothing. The commands are ignored and no frames show up.

Enjoy!

 Stop by `http://www.htmlgoodies.com/book/inlineframes.html` *to try out the examples in the tutorial.*

Using Dynamic HTML

What is Dynamic HTML? It's actually a little tough to get a handle on because it's beginning to mean different things to different people. The actual term stands for Dynamic Hypertext Mark-up Language.

The essence of the term stands for almost any coding that creates movement or interactivity by employing the standards of the 4.0-level Netscape Navigator and MSIE browsers. I've also heard DHTML discussed as being PowerPoint for the Web, but there was movement before with animation and interactivity with forms.

Yeah, see, that's the rub. For something to be considered DHTML it has to employ version 4.0 browsers. Again, there's an argument I've heard that DHTML is only viable if it occurs within the Explorer 4.0 browser.

On the other hand, some people have stated that DHTML includes Netscape's layering commands. Does it? It depends on whom you speak to.

FAQs from the HTML Goodies Web Site

Q. What do you think about DHTML?

A. This is actually the first new thing in a while that I'm really excited about. And what's better is these DHTML examples are starting to come out as fully functioning packages. You just drop the files in a directory and it works. I believe that in a year or so there will be so many applications of DHTML that you'll be able to find what you need. Plus, if I can run this game (the example used in this section) with a few simple steps, imagine what you can do if you really took the time. There are great applications here. This could be really big.

The best description I can offer is that DHTML is any combinations of style sheets, JavaScript, layering, positioning, and page division, at the 4.0 browser level, intended to create movement or user interactivity. (See the positioning tutorial in Chapter 8, "Cascading Style Sheets and Layers," for more on this.)

You'll find many examples of DHTML if you go to HTML Goodies online. I chose only two for the *HTML Goodies* book; the two included in this book are a good introduction to the formatting. The first example is a very large, very involved DHTML game. The second is about as simple as you can get without someone else doing it for you.

I wanted to show both ends of the scale in terms of DHTML. Once you go through these two sections, try the others online at HTML Goodies. You can quickly browse the examples at `http://www.htmlgoodies.com/layers.html`. *If you get these to work, you can get any DHTML packages to work. This tutorial can be found online at* `http://www.htmlgoodies.com/dhtml2.html`.

Is Dynamic HTML Really Being Used?

At the beginning of this year, I went to my handy dandy little Internet counting program to see how many people had stopped by my site. I rolled through the numbers until I got to the last block of statistics. Those are the percentages of browsers coming to the site. Netscape Navigator had ruled the roost for the entire run of HTML Goodies until that day: Microsoft Internet Explorer: 52%.

In December 1997, CNN Interactive (`http://www.cnn.com`) listed the top 10 most popular future Internet items. Microsoft's Dynamic HTML led the pack. To be really cool, you refer to it as DHTML. If you want to be really, really cool, you can no longer refer to the World Wide Web as W-W-W. You must now say Tri-W.

FAQs from the HTML Goodies Web Site

Q. What happens if I run a DHTML program and the user pops in with Netscape?

A. I have found nothing but problems. The images usually display but not in their assigned positions. Ditto any divisions you have set up. Oftentimes, a JavaScript error results because certain items aren't denoted or given correct properties. This truly is a one-browser deal.

Shortly after being posted, my original online DHTML tutorial quickly became one of the most popular pages on this site. Soon after, I received this letter:

Dr. Burns,

We are developing DHTML authoring software that utilizes inverse mechanic and artificial behavior. Our Web site has numerous examples of interactive DHTML with JavaScript. We would be pleased if you could have a look and send us your comments.

Thank you

Francoise White

So I went and looked. The SFAN Experimental Multimedia Page (`http://www.pompano.net/ ~sfan/`) is a great site that will only get better, I'm sure. Visually, it's stunning—images fly everywhere. In my most humble tone, I wrote back asking if I could use one of the site's examples as a DHTML tutorial. Here's what I got back:

Dr. Burns,

Yes you have our permission to use our site and our demos for your tutorials. We would reciprocate. Let us know. We will contact you when our beta version [of a program to help you create your own DHTML events] is available for downloading.

Sincerely,

Francoise White

That said, the following sections are what I have for you.

Using DHTML for an Interactive Game

This is a great, visually pleasing video game (see Figure 13.12). Here's the concept: You are flying an F-14 in space. (I know it's impossible, but go with me here.) There is a spaceship that wants to blow you up. You want to do the same to it. Your fighter jet is given missiles and cannon shots. The spaceship has lasers.

Avoid the lasers and shoot the spaceship. What's even better about this is that when you shoot the spaceship, it blows up!

- M fires the missiles. You get 5.
- C fires the cannons. You get 15.
- The mouse moves the fighter jet up and down.

FAQs from the HTML Goodies Web Site

Q. The DHTML game you offer is amazing. How can I learn to build something like that?

A. Get into programming. You need to have a solid understanding of JavaScript to begin with and a good knowledge of layers, page divisions, and style sheets next. I will probably never delve deep enough to learn to program this stuff myself because there are great people like Francoise White who will do it for me. Soon you'll be able to buy hundreds of DHTML applications on a CD-ROM. Mark my words. You can buy JavaScripts, applets, and animater GIFs now—DHTML won't be far behind.

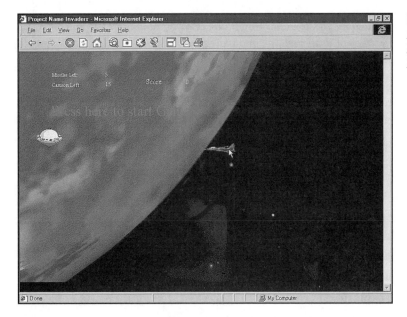

Figure 13.12
Interactive game using DHTML in Internet Explorer.

Putting the DHTML on Your Page

The news gets even better. This game is fully self-contained. Simply take all the parts and place them in the same directory. Run the `invaders.htm` file and you're good to go.

This is an example, so it would help for you to open and look at the codes. You'll see that two pages are actually at work here. There is the main page (`invaders.htm`) and an external JavaScript that work on the images. You can learn more about external JavaScripts in Chapter 11.

Each image is placed in a specific place through an absolute position style sheet command and then given a span in which it can move. The remainder of the scripts outline paths for that image. You'll note the randomness of the spaceship and the rather deliberate vertical movement of the F-14 jet.

In addition, there are commands that inform the computer to run a third image when two specific images intersect. For instance, if the `missile.gif` and `ufo.gif` images occupy the same space, a third image, `firea.gif`, runs at that spot. The effect gives the impression that a missile hit the spaceship and the spaceship blew up.

It's the same thing with the spaceship, the lasers, and the F-14. If they intersect, the game is over and you're dead. R.I.P.

It's very clever and very involved. Be thankful that it comes to you ready to go.

Setting Up the DHTML

 There are 10 items you need for this to work. Forget one and you're out of luck. You can either grab each one by itself or grab them all in a big zip file. The items are available from the online version of this tutorial at `http://www.htmlgoodies.com/dhtml2.html`.

Here are the text documents:

- `invaders.htm` This is the main page. It is still in .html format. Right-click to download. Macintosh users should hold the mouse down to perform a straight download. (30.9KB)
- `getpos.js` This is the external JavaScript. (29.9KB)

Images

- `cannon.gif` This is the cannon shot. (2.24KB)
- `earth.gif` This is the page background. (64.6KB)
- `f14.gif` This is the plane. (4KB)
- `firea.gif` This is the explosion. (27.6KB)
- `laser.gif` This is the UFO's laser shot. (.15KB)
- `missileh.gif` This is the missile shot. (.6KB)
- `ufo.gif` This is the bad guy. (4KB)

Sound

- `thrush.mid` This is the background music. (17KB)

Files

- `invaders.zip` This is everything in a big zip file. (116KB)

FAQs from the HTML Goodies Web Site

Q. I keep getting errors when I play.

A. You must not have downloaded the items or not placed them on your pages correctly. You have to follow the same rules using this stuff as you do using JavaScript. The text editors cannot have margins. If they do, you corrupt the scripts and you get errors. Use Notepad or SimpleText when you open the files to see the coding.

Thanks again to Francoise White at the SFAN Experimental Multimedia Page for allowing me to post this DHTML example. Good luck putting it one your site. It really is a clever piece.

Enjoy!

 Head to http://www.htmlgoodies.com/book/dhtml2.html *to play the game and get the parts you need to offer it from your site.*

Net Notes

Try these links for more DHTML fun:

Microsoft's DHTML Pages: http://www.microsoft.com/workshop/author/dhtml/

Macromedia's DHTML Zone: http://www.dhtmlzone.com/index.html

Inside Dynamic HTML: http://www.insideDHTML.com/dl/home.asp

Yahoo!'s HTML Formats: DHTML http://www.yahoo.com/Computers_and_Internet/ Information_and_Documentation/Data_Formats/HTML/Dynamic_HTML

Yahoo!'s DHTML Games: http://www.yahoo.com/Computers_and_Internet/ Information_and_Documentation/Data_Formats/HTML/Dynamic_HTML/Games

Using DHTML for Page Transitions

This is one of the latest and easiest DHTML items that allows you to create PowerPoint–type transitions when someone enters and exits your page. The effect is that one page is "wiped" over the last one. The only real downfall I have found so far is that the effect isn't rendered when the page is reloaded. You actually have to be coming or going for the first time.

Here's an idea of what I mean: I posted two pages, both containing the code. Then, using my Internet Explorer 4.0 browser, I jumped from one to the other. The transitions were set to random. Keep in mind that this image is a static picture. The circle continued outwards until the page had completely changed over (see Figure 13.13).

A good many tutorials come about because of email letters I get from readers who drop a command in my lap and yell, as much as one can yell in an email, "What the #$*% does this do?" That's where this topic came from, although Heath C. Ice had it pretty much figured out by the time he showed it to me. Thanks Heath, you're a gentleman.

Figure 13.13
Using DHTML for a page transition.

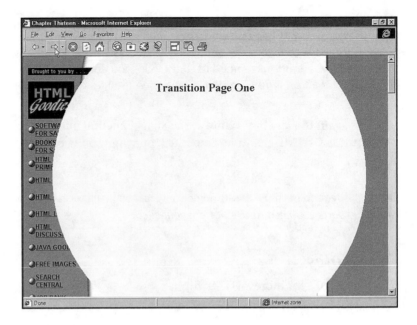

Setting Up the DHTML Transition

It kills me that this is so simple. Here's the code that creates the effects. They are META commands so they go between your document's <HEAD> commands, below the <TITLE> and </TITLE> commands. Here they are:

```
<META HTTP-EQUIV="Site-Enter" content="revealTrans
(Duration=1.0,Transition=23)">
<META HTTP-EQUIV="Site-Exit" content="revealTrans
(Duration=1.0,Transition=23)">
```

I'll only do the top command. You can take it from there to figure out the bottom one. I have not found any other levels of these commands other than the Site-Enter and Site-Exit attributes.

- META means that this command will tell about the page.

- HTTP-EQUIV stands for Hypertext Transfer Protocol Equivalent. That's a fancy way of saying, through HTTP, "Make an equal to this page." In simpler terms, do something to this page's display.

- "Site-Enter" means to do the transition when someone enters the page. I think this is why you cannot get the effect when simply reloading.

- revealTrans is DHTML script denoting that the page should be revealed.

- Duration=1.0 is the duration of the effect. It's set to one second right now.

- Transition=23 means to randomly choose from 22 other transitions.

What was that last one again? Why? It doesn't make perfect sense to you that 23 is the perfect number for a random transition? Me neither, actually. I base my statements on a totally unscientific process of entering the numbers 1 through 46 (2×23) into the transition statement and recording what happened.

You're right. I have no life. Here's what I found:

Specifying Transition Effects

You can try this for yourself. Just plug the numbers in and see. This is also pretty helpful knowledge if you want to set a specific transition.

The page will be revealed by the following:

1. Opening from the inside out
2. Scroll in from outer edges
3. Scroll out from center
4. Scroll up from bottom
5. Scroll down from top
6. Scroll left to right
7. Scroll right to left
8. Vertical blinds left to right
9. Horizontal blinds top to bottom
10. Combination of 8 and 9
11. Looks a lot like 8
12. Comes in pixels
13. Scrolls in from outer parts
14. Scrolls out from center
15. Closes from both top and bottom
16. Opens from center to top and bottom
17. Diagonal roll from right to left
18. Different angle diagonal roll right to left
19. Number 17; the other way
20. Number 18; the other way
21. Random horizontal lines
22. Random vertical lines
23. Completely random

Cycle appears to start again after this...

Enjoy!

FAQs from the HTML Goodies Web Site

Q. Do you see Netscape getting into DHTML soon?

A. Oh yeah. This is popular enough that it will happen. But that's not the concern. What's next is the concern. What will one browser do that's new and not supported by the other?

 See these transitions effects at `http://www.htmlgoodies.com/book/transitions.html`.

Chapter 14

Building Web Site Banners

I have been getting email from people asking how to create an advertising banner for their home page for a while now. This chapter walks you through the process. The purpose is to introduce you to the basic theory behind banner creation and enable you to comfortably create your own banner.

Software Tools Needed

You're going to need a lot more than a text editor and knowledge of HTML to build banners for your Web site—you're going to need some additional software. Before we begin, please go out and get the software described in this section.

Graphics Program

This chapter uses Paint Shop Pro. Those who are already in the graphic creation biz will now immediately go bonkers telling me that any number of programs are a better choice. Well, to each his own.

I use Paint Shop Pro because it has what we college professors call a *good learning curve*. That means that if you learn this graphics program, it is quite easy to get up and running on another. The menus are very basic and quite close to other great graphics programs like Photoshop or CorelDRAW, which I also own. The biggest problem moving from one program to another, I've found, is that the commands are in different menus. For instance, the crop function in Paint Shop Pro is under the Image menu, whereas in Photoshop it's under the Edit menu. That's a good example of the concerns you face going from this tutorial using Paint Shop Pro to using another graphics program. It's not a big jump.

That said, the best reason I can give for using Paint Shop Pro is that it's shareware. You can go and grab a copy and follow along. (No, there is no PSP yet for Apple, but use what image program you can get or already have. I taught at Bowling Green State University for three years using Macintoshes and the learning curve is equally as easy.)

Get your 30-day evaluation copy here:

- `http://www.jasc.com` (JASC Inc; these people make PSP.)
- `http://www.visitorinfo.com`
- `http://www.shareware.com`

Shareware.com lists a lot of download sites. When you arrive, you are asked for your system type (Windows 95, Macintosh, Windows 3.11). You can then search for the name of the product. Apple users can also use this site to look for graphic programs compatible with their system.

"I already have a graphics program," you say. You mean like MS Paint? Or maybe you got a more advanced program through all that great preloaded software. That's where I got CorelDRAW. If that's the one you want to use, great. The one downfall of MS Paint and the like is that they save images as bitmaps. That's a very vanilla format. I deal with GIF format in this tutorial. You will probably be able to follow along all the way up until the time we animate the images we create; then you need to find a program that converts the bitmap (denoted by a `.bmp` extension) into GIF format. Like Paint Shop Pro...

GIF Animator Program

The purpose of these advertising banners is to attract attention. It's nice that people see them, but you also want them to be clicked. An advertisement that isn't acted upon is not doing its job. In the four years I have run Goodies, I have seen maybe three static banners. The animation is what really makes a solid banner come alive—even if the animation is only two cells flipping back and forth. It just adds to the effect. So you're going to need an animator program.

There's an animation section in Chapter 3, "Adding Images and Backgrounds." If you've read it, you may already have the GIF Construction Set program. If not, grab it now.

Again, there are a lot of other animation programs. I learned on this one and I feel it's the best, plus that whole learning curve thing too. You can grab a copy from `http://www.mindworkshop.com/alchemy/gifcon.html`.

If you would like to browse elsewhere, the Animated GIF Artists Guild offers some great programs and instruction. See them at `http://www.agag.com/makeown.html`.

Banner Primer 1: Getting Started

This banner's main effect is a movie ticket that shows up in the middle of the banner. It tears in half as the two sides of the ticket pull away to the left and right ends of the banner. The text rolls by that and reads Admit One—To My Web Page—Click Here!. What you are seeing in Figure 14.1 is the very end, where the banner blinks Click Here. Please note that Figure 14.1 is a still picture. You need to see the banner online to get the full effect. You should see the banner in action at least once before you plunge into this series of primers. Point your browser to http://www.htmlgoodies.com/banner.gif *to see it.*

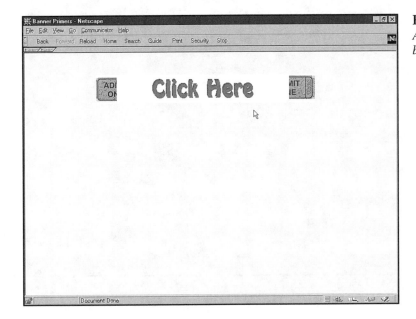

Figure 14.1
An animated Web site banner.

In the process of building this example, you perform six functions that are crucial to the creation of a good ad banner. Besides, I didn't expect that you would simply grab this one off the page and use it. But if you want to, go ahead.

Here's the plan from this point on:

- Banner Primer 2: Creating New Images
- Banner Primer 3: Learning to Crop
- Banner Primer 4: Importing Images—Copying and Pasting
- Banner Primer 5: Adding Text and Shadows
- Banner Primer 6: Animating the Images
- Banner Primer 7: Activating the Image and What to Do with It

The banner in Figure 14.2 was created using exactly the same steps I am going to cover here. I used Paint Shop Pro to create all of the images except the original ticket. I got that from the WebSpice Images provided for free on the HTML Goodies site. See http://www.htmlgoodies.com/images.html *to get them for yourself.*

The animated image in Figure 14.2 requires 13 different images to complete. The first group of images creates the tearing ticket animation.

Figure 14.2
Images needed for animated tearing-ticket GIF.

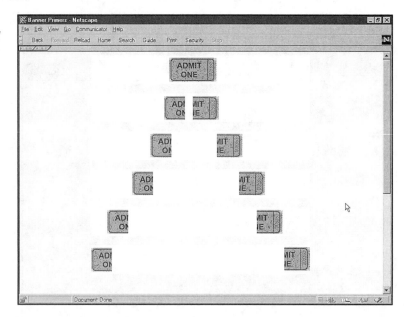

Figure 14.3 shows the second group of images used to create the text that will appear.

Don't bother to go to the HTML Goodies site and download any of them now. You'll create each one as you go along. The only image you really need from me is the ticket image, and you get that at the start of Banner Primer 3.

FAQs from the HTML Goodies Web Site

Q. Are we making the banner you did in the banner primers or do you want us to make one for ourselves?

A. Both, actually. Make the one I am showing first to get the hang of it and then make one for yourself.

First of all, grab the two programs noted earlier. Install them on your computer and make sure they work by opening and playing around with the buttons. If you don't get any errors, they work.

Figure 14.3
Images needed for text animation.

 *I have online links to download the software you need at* http://www.htmlgoodies.com/ book/pspgck.html.

Next, start thinking about what your banner is going to look like. I know you don't have the skills yet to create it, but so what? I'm not the president, but I still know what I'd do if I got into office. Sketch it out. Use arrows to show the motion you want. Create a sort of storyboard of your idea, but keep it simple. The more animation cells you have, the more bytes this takes and the slower it loads and runs. If your banner doesn't run, no one will see it anyway. Show your idea to a couple of people and see what they think. This little image is your site's welcome mat. It had better be nice—why would anyone visit otherwise? Get feedback on it. Creating a banner for your site should not be something you throw together in an hour or so. It should be given some thought. It is your representative in the real world.

Think about your site. What is good about it? Why should people come? Ask yourself what is so darn wonderful about your site that someone should take time out of their busy life and come see you. Whatever you land upon, that's what your banner should say, either in text or images.

Speaking of text, what will your banner say? The text needs to be very short. There are only 10 words on this banner (including those on the ticket). Plus, this banner rotates fully in just under six seconds. That's not a lot of time to read things over. So make your text big, exciting, and a very quick read.

And so we start.

Banner Primer 2: Creating New Images

At this point, you should have Paint Shop Pro (PSP) installed on your computer (or have the program you intend to use installed). If you are using PSP, you should have a screen that looks something like Figure 14.4.

Figure 14.4
JASC's Paint Shop Pro.

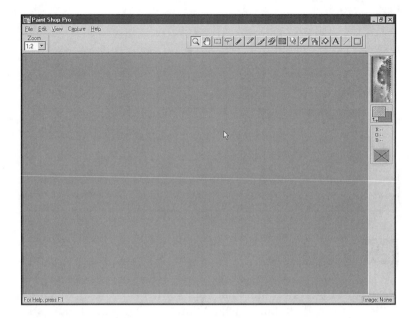

Creating a New Image

First off, you need to learn how to create a new image. Think of this more as a canvas; you create one image that is the correct size of our banner and then, using PSP, you add items to that palette.

The banner we are creating in this series of primers is the generally accepted size for an advertising banner. It is the size banner that sits on top of each HTML Goodies page. I don't know how this series of numbers was arrived at, but the banner size you want is 468 pixels wide by 60 pixels high.

A *pixel* is a little colored dot. You see, computer images are not like a photograph, where the color is consistent and smooth. Computer images are a lot more like the images you'd find in a newspaper. It's a lot of little dots up close, but when you move away and your eyes get the opportunity to blur the little dots together, it makes a pretty nice picture. Your television works the same way. Tonight, go right up to your TV, lick your thumb, and drag the spit across a small section of the TV screen. The liquid will offer enough of a "lens" that you can see the individual dots.

When I say the image is 468×60, that means there are 468 colored dots across, and 60 colored dots up. We are going to create an image made up of all white dots. It will look like just a big white rectangle.

There is a menu called **File** in the upper-left corner of PSP; click it and choose the **New** option.

Once that is done, you should get a dialog box that looks like Figure 14.5.

Figure 14.5
The New Image dialog box.

I doubt that the numbers in the width and height sections read 468 and 60 as the image does, so do that now. The fastest way is to click the number; it highlights in blue. Press your Backspace key. The number disappears and you can write in the number of pixels you want.

Notice the background color section. There are multiple colors to choose from, but we want to stay with white because this banner will be mostly white. Don't worry about the image type section. PSP takes care of that aspect.

Choose **OK**—ta da!—there's the new image. It should look like Figure 14.6.

Figure 14.6
Paint Shop Pro's new image.

Now let's save it right away.

Saving the Image

We want to save this image in GIF format. You choose GIF because you want to animate this image, and a few others, later. The animator requires that the images be in GIF. Click the **File** menu again and choose **Save As**; you get a familiar dialog box that looks like Figure 14.7.

First off, you need to choose where you want this image saved. Follow the same format you would to save any text file. Notice in the image that the section marked Save as Type is open. You open it by clicking the little arrow at the end of the line. Now you have a scrolling section where you can see all the different types of image formats you can use. We want to save in GIF—CompuServe format. Scroll up or down to that format and click when it is highlighted. You are now set to save in GIF format.

Figure 14.7
Paint Shop Pro's Save As dialog box.

In case you're wondering, the reason GIF format has the word CompuServe after it is because the format was created by CompuServe. Now look just above the Save as Type box at the File Name box. Here's where you give the image its name. To stay consistent with this chapter, call this image banner.gif.

FAQs from the HTML Goodies Web Site

Q. When I save the image, should I put the .gif at the end or will the computer do it for me?

A. Don't ever rely on a computer to do something for you. Be safe—put the .gif on the end.

Q. Why can't we save these images as JPG? Wouldn't that make the bytes smaller?

A. Because we're going to animate the images later and the animator program requires GIF format.

That's it! Success! You created and saved your first image. That wasn't so hard, was it?

You're creating and saving images like a pro. If you feel up to it, head to the next banner primer. Or take the night off and start again tomorrow. You do look a little tired.

 If you're having trouble making the template image, I have it for you to download at http://www.htmlgoodies.com/book/banner2.html.

Banner Primer 3: Learning to Crop

We are going to take the movie ticket image you should have downloaded from my site and cut it into two images. In technical terms, we will *crop* two sections. First you need the image. Once you have downloaded the image, open it in the PSP program by choosing

Open from the **File** menu and looking for the image in the dialog box. This is the same process you follow when you look for a text document in a word processor.

Cropping an Image

Click Here *Grab the ticket image at* http://www.htmlgoodies.com/book/banner3.html. *When you get it open, it should look something like Figure 14.8.*

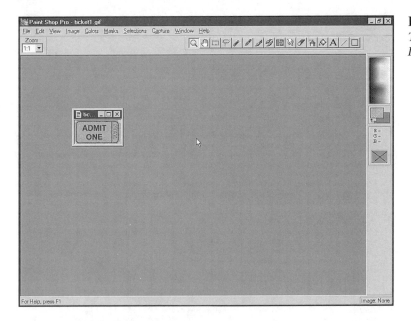

Figure 14.8
Ticket image in Paint Shop Pro.

Make sure you have saved the ticket image in the same directory in which you saved the image you made in Banner Primer 2. In fact, make sure you save all the images you make during these primers in the same directory.

Crop it!

Crop me? Crop you! (Sorry, easy joke.) This is so easy you won't believe it. We are going to turn the ticket image into two images.

Now let's put PSP in the crop mode. Look at the screen. There should be a little button that looks like a dotted rectangle. It looks like Figure 14.9 on the PSP screen, my pointer is on it.

Click it. Now you have placed PSP is the mode to crop out a section of the picture.

Once the crop button is clicked, place your mouse pointer over top of the ticket1.gif image. The pointer should change as shown in Figure 14.10.

Figure 14.9

The crop button on the Paint Shop Pro's toolbar.

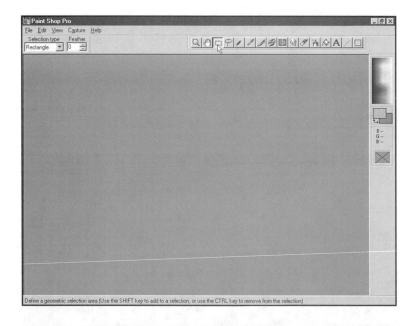

Figure 14.10

The Paint Shop Pro pointer in crop mode.

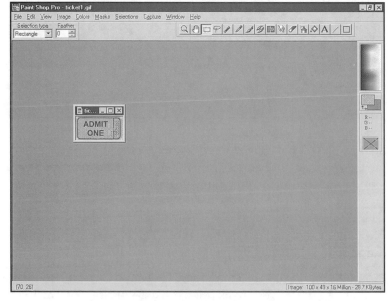

Do this: Put the cross in the upper-left corner of the image. Click and hold; then drag the mouse down and to the right. See the box forming? Try to cut the ticket perfectly in half. Once you have one half of the image set aside, let go of the mouse button. The box becomes a dotted line; it should look like Figure 14.11.

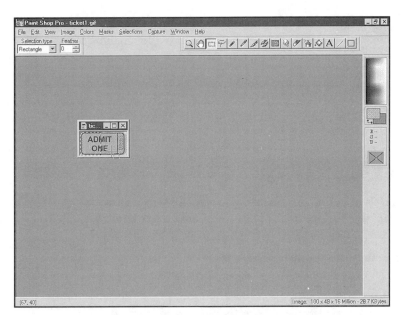

Figure 14.11
See the ticket image crop outline?

Got that? Good! Now let's perform the actual cropping. Look again at the top of the PSP window; there should be a menu called **Image**. Click it. **Crop** is a few commands down.

Once you choose **Crop**, your image should look like the one in Figure 14.12.

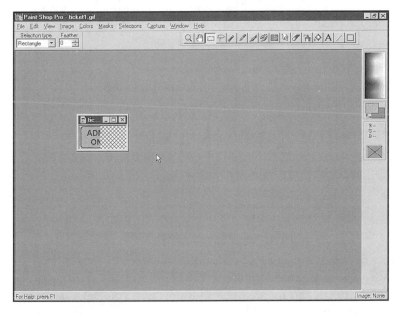

Figure 14.12
Cropped ticket image.

389

How about that? Now follow the same instructions from Banner Primer 2 and save that half image as `leftticket.gif`. After you've saved that new image, close it by clicking the gray X in the left corner of the image—not on the PSP program, but the X on the image.

Open the `ticket1.gif` image again and perform another crop, only this time crop the right side of the image and save it as `rightticket.gif`. Do your darndest to get the crop line in the same place as the last one. I did it by making the crop follow the left vertical line of the *m* in the word *Admit*.

FAQs from the HTML Goodies Web Site

Q. You say to cut the ticket in half by running down the vertical of the *m*. Shouldn't you tell people to look at how many pixels wide the image is and move their crop so that they cut it in perfectly in half by the pixels?

A. Yeah, but that's overdoing the purpose a bit. This ticket will split and fly away very quickly. A good eyeballing is sufficient.

Q. You could also do this by simply coloring one side of the ticket totally white and pasting it into the image. Since the image is white it would give the same effect.

A. That's true, but I was interested in showing cropping, too.

You now have the two ticket images you need to animate the ticket opening up.

Now you can crop with the best of them. I use this function constantly. It is a very basic of image creation. But there is also importing images. Thus we move on...

 I have the ticket image (and possibly the two halves images) at `http://www.htmlgoodies.com/book/banner3.html`. *You can download it from there.*

Banner Primer 4: Importing Images—Copying and Pasting

If you're following along at home, you should have four images in your banner folder by now: `banner.gif`, `ticket1.gif`, `leftticket.gif`, and `rightticket.gif`. Those four images are your building blocks. Now let's construct the sections.

This should be a fairly easy primer to follow because you have probably used this method a thousand times. What we intend to do is copy one image and paste it into another.

This is the same method as if you were writing a text document in a word processor. Let's say you want to move an entire paragraph from one section to another. You would high-light the text, choose to copy (or cut) it, and then paste it in the section you feel is a better fit. This is the same thing, except it's done with images.

Copy and Paste

Here we go. First off, you need to open PSP if you haven't already. Now open two images: ticket1.gif and banner.gif. Both of the images should now appear in the PSP window. They might be on top of each other. If that's the case, place your pointer on the blue bar at the top of one of the images, click, hold, and drag the image away from the other.

Notice this to begin with: Even though there are two images on the screen, they are not seen as equal by PSP. One of the images is in the *forefront*, meaning that is the image that is being acted upon at the moment. Look at the screen in Figure 14.13, which was taken from my own PSP while both images were open.

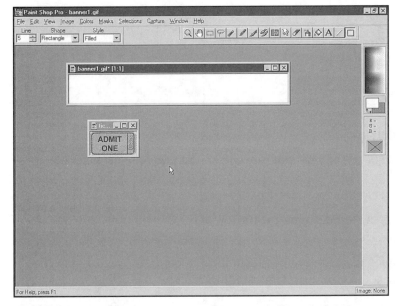

Figure 14.13

The banner image is in the forefront (the active window).

See how the banner.gif has a blue bar at the top (brighter here) and the ticket1.gif image has a gray bar at the top (darker here)? Look at your two images—one is one color and one is another. Your computer may be set to a different color scheme than mine. Usually one color is brighter than the other. The one with the brighter color bar at the top is the one that is in the forefront. That means that if you perform a copy, a cut, or a paste, that is the image that is acted upon. If you want the other image to be the one acted upon, click it. You'll see the colors flip. Do that: Click back and forth between the images to see them work that way.

Now you take those two images, banner.gif and ticket1.gif, and combine them to create a third image, which we call banner1.gif. It will look like Figure 14.14.

Figure 14.14
Ticket image pasted into banner.

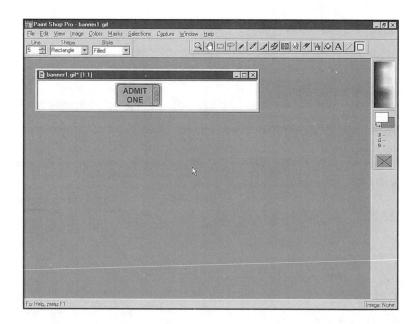

Performing the Copy

We will copy one image, the ticket, and paste it into the other image, the banner. Now we want the copy to act upon the ticket because that is the image we will copy. If it isn't already, click the ticket image to bring it to the forefront.

Once it is at the forefront, click the **Edit** menu at the top of the PSP window. You'll find **Copy** under that menu (see Figure 14.15).

The ticket image is now copied to a section of your computer's hard drive called the Clipboard. Think of it as having a Xerox of the image standing by.

FAQs from the HTML Goodies Web Site

Q. You might want to tell your readers that they can speed their copying and pasting by pressing CTRL+C to copy and CTRL+V to paste.

A. I do that, too. I find that older computer people like you and me who came up from DOS-based programs seem to do that more often. Thanks. I'll pass it along.

Performing the Paste

Now you need to bring the banner image to the forefront. Be careful about jumping to paste at this point. When you go back to the **Edit** menu, you'll notice that the **Paste** command has three options. Those options are shown in Figure 14.16.

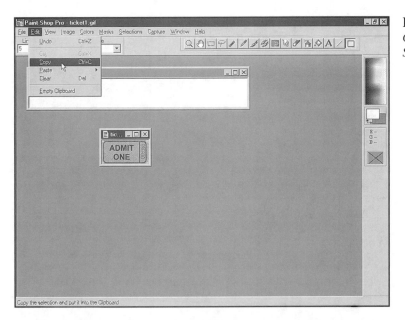

Figure 14.15
Copying an image in Paint Shop Pro.

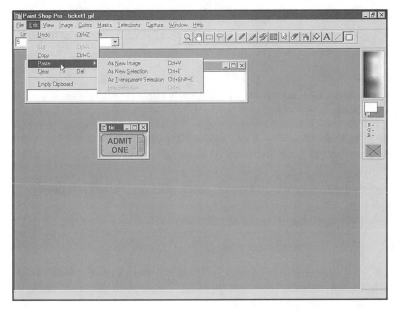

Figure 14.16
Paste *menu options in Paint Shop Pro.*

You are interested in pasting the copied image **As New Selection**. If you paste it **As New Image**, it pastes all by itself—and not into the other image. If you paste it as a transparent image, your effect is altered and you won't get what you're looking for. Go with the middle one. If the banner image is in the forefront, choose **As New Selection**.

You should now have something that looks like Figure 14.17.

Figure 14.17
Ticket image pasted into banner image.

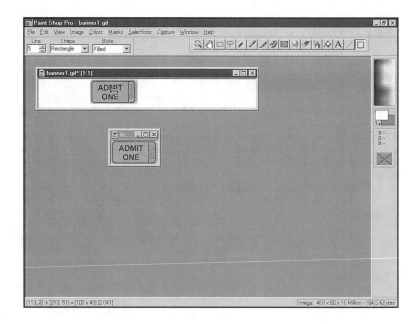

Go ahead and move your pointer around a bit. You'll see that the cross with arrows on the ends allows you to move the image wherever you want it. Try to get it right in the middle. Once you have it right where you want it, click but don't hold—just click it.

The image now locks into place and the same dotted line you saw in the crop function appears. Click again anywhere outside of the pasted image. Don't click inside or you'll get the arrows again. The dotted lines should disappear.

There's your new image. You now need to save it with the same commands you used to save the images you created. Make sure you choose **Save As**. You see, if you choose Save, you'll save right over banner.gif. You don't want to do that. You want to make a whole new image, so choose **Save As** and name it banner1.gif in the same directory you have been saving all your other images in.

Tearing the Ticket

Now you have the first banner with the full ticket right in the middle. The process now is to create the next five images where the banner splits and pulls to the outer walls of the image. That is done by creating five new banners that look like Figure 14.18.

You already have the tools to create the five images. You need to open four images in the PSP window for this: leftticket.gif, rightticket.gif, banner.gif, and banner1.gif. Once you have all of those images open, place banner1.gif just above banner.gif. The PSP screen should look like Figure 14.19.

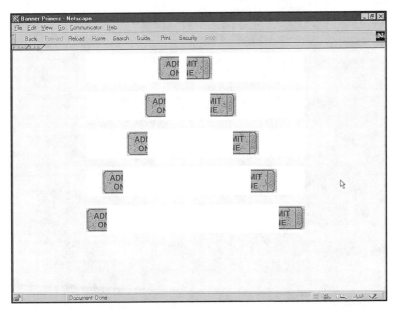

Figure 14.18
Tearing ticket sequence of images.

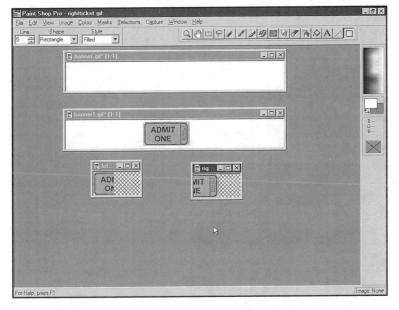

Figure 14.19
Four images opened in the Paint Shop Pro window.

I am having you do this because you use `banner1.gif` as a guide to create the next image. Notice how I have one lined up right under the other. Copy and paste `leftticket.gif` and `rightticket.gif` into `banner.gif` so that you get a little bit of a tear. It should look like Figure 14.20.

Figure 14.20
Pasting the left and right ticket halves.

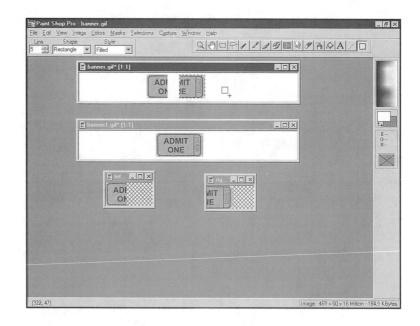

Save it as `banner2.gif`. Now leave `banner2.gif` open and reopen `banner.gif`. Place banner `.gif` below `banner 2.gif`. Now you can use `banner 2.gif` as a guide to make the next image, which is `banner3.gif`. The screen looks something like Figure 14.21 when you finish making `banner3.gif`.

Figure 14.21
Pasting the next sequence of left and right ticket halves.

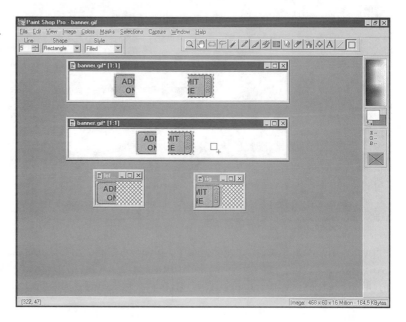

See how I am using one image as a guide to create the next image in the sequence? That's why I am asking you to create the images by looking at the image that comes before it. What you need to do now is create `banner4.gif`, `banner5.gif`, and `banner6.gif` so that they closely resemble the six images in Figure 14.18. They are all made by copying and pasting repeatedly, until the image is finished. Save the image by using the **Save As** command.

FAQs from the HTML Goodies Web Site

Q. I accidentally hit Save instead of Save As. I keep trying to choose undo, but it doesn't un-save.

A. And it won't. Saving something is altering it on the hard drive. You can't undo it. Next time save a backup of the item you're working on.

The `banner.gif` image is your canvas. It is the blank space that all other items will be placed upon. You use the image that came before it as a guide to creating the next image. Remember, these images are all going to be animated and need to be somewhat related to each other; otherwise the final animation will look way too jumpy to be enjoyed.

Make sure that `banner1.gif` through `banner6.gif` also end up in the same directory as the other images you have made. It's a little time consuming, but not as scary as you first thought, right?

 If you'd like to download the images created in Banner Primer 4, go to `http://` `www.htmlgoodies.com/book/banner4.html`.

Banner Primer 5: Adding Text and Shadows

Now the text. We are going to create four more images with text. They are shown in Figure 14.22.

We're concerned about three things when doing this: the text's color, font, and size. Let's take them in order.

Text Color

I know in the book these images are all shades of black and white, but if you've seen the images online, you see I went with shades of purple, mainly because the ticket is purple. If you feel another color is better on the eyes, knock yourself out. To get started, we need to play with the rainbow color block, known as the *color palette*, on the far right side of the PSP screen. My pointer is just below it in Figure 14.23.

Figure 14.22
Banner text images.

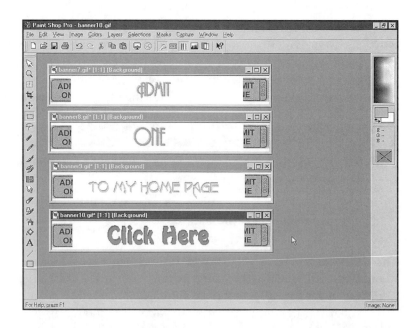

Figure 14.23
Viewing the color palette tool in Paint Shop Pro.

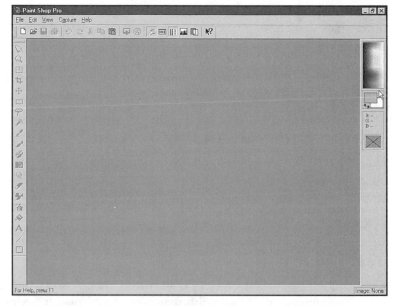

That's the designated area to pick colors. The rainbow item on top allows you to choose from a wide range of colors. At the moment, you can see the two colors that are chosen. One is a little lighter than the other. We don't want those two colors; we want shades of purple. You can do one of two things on your PSP, either run your mouse over the rainbow until you find the color you like or do what I do: Click twice on the box beneath the rainbow box that appears to be most forward. It's the one that is white. You should get a box that looks like Figure 14.24.

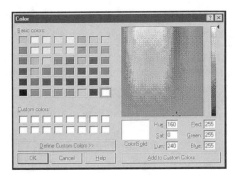

Figure 14.24
Paint Shop Pro's Color dialog box.

The colors in the small boxes are the most popular. I use them unless I need a really specific color. Choose a light shade by clicking the color; I don't care which. Choose **OK**. That shade should now appear in the little box to the right. Did it? Good.

Let's look at the color area again where you clicked to get the dialog box.

See the little arrow pointing to both of the small boxes below the rainbow box? Click it. Notice the two colors flip back to front? You just set background and foreground colors. We will use both.

Click the arrow so that the color you just chose is in the background. Now click the foreground box twice to again bring up the color palette. Now choose a dark shade of the color you just chose. Again, I went with shades of purple.

Make sure the dark box is forward. We are going to first lay down a dark shadow and then lay the lighter color over top. Basically we will paste the same text twice, one dark and one light. They will just be a bit offset from one another, giving the effect of a shadow. We have the text's color. Now we choose the text's font.

FAQs from the HTML Goodies Web Site

Q. How small can I go with text on a banner?

A. Not very. Remember that these words will be read on-the-fly. You may only get one shot at it. You might make supporting text smaller, but the main text should be big as life.

Text Font

To start this process, we need to once again display the image we intend to place this text upon. If you've been following along, you'll remember that we created `banner.gif` for the sole purpose of acting as a template so that we could paste other items onto it, namely the two halves of the ticket. Now we need a different template.

Notice that all the text appears between the two ticket halves when they are at their farthest point. The image we created that has that look now becomes our template. If you've been following my format, that is `banner6.gif`. Does that make sense?

Open `banner6.gif` in PSP and put PSP in text mode. Remember the cropping section of this primer series (when we clicked the button with the dotted square to place PSP into crop mode)? Same deal here. The button that places PSP in the text mode is near the crop button. My pointer is on it in Figure 14.25. Notice that a ToolTip box popped up, telling me that button deals with text.

Figure 14.25
The text button on Paint Shop Pro's toolbar.

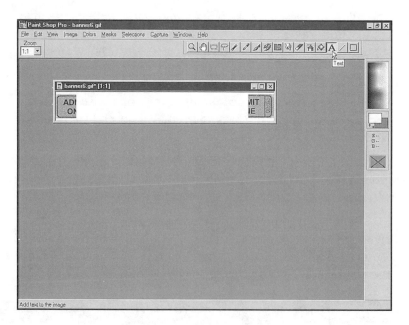

Now move your pointer over `banner6.gif`. It should look something like Figure 14.26.

That little A means that you are ready to place text on the image. Make sure your darker color is in the foreground. Let me repeat that: Make sure your darker color is in the foreground. Remember that we are laying down the darker shadowing first. Click the banner. You should get the dialog box shown in Figure 14.27.

Now the fun part: choosing the type of text. The upper left of the dialog box lists the available fonts. The example image uses Times New Roman font. That's not the font I used to create the first image that says Admit. I changed the font to something called Party. You don't have to use that font. In fact, you may not even have it available. The shareware version of PSP offers far fewer fonts than does the full version, which is what I have. If you dislike this font, or don't have it, look at some others. Click the highest font available in your own upper-left section. You'll see an example of the font in the gray window just below it. Now use your arrow keys to scroll down. You'll see fonts just whizzing by. Find one you like.

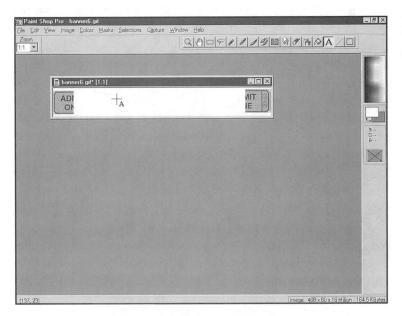

Figure 14.26
The text pointer is over a banner image.

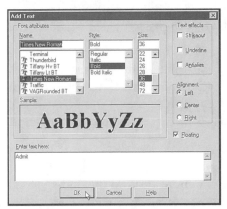

Figure 14.27
Paint Shop Pro's Add Text dialog box.

FAQs from the HTML Goodies Web Site

Q. Should we use the fonts you use on your primers?

A. You can use any font you'd like, but remember that these words have to be read and read fast. Make them large enough and choose a font clear enough that people can read them in one shot.

When you find the font you like best, type the text you want to appear on the image in the box marked Enter Text Here. In the case of this first image, we only want the word Admit. Click **OK**. You should now have something that looks a lot like Figure 14.28.

Figure 14.28
Selected text on the banner image.

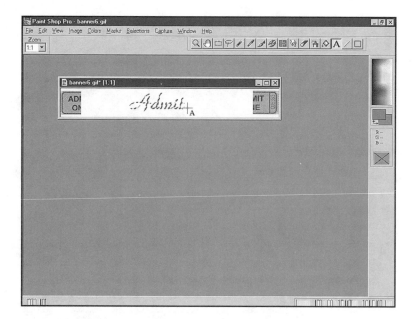

The text you put in should be there, surrounded by those familiar dotted lines and that same four-pointed arrow. Move it around. You can place the text wherever you want. Click the mouse to set it.

I hate it! That happens. I never get my text just right on the first try. To delete the text you just posted, go under the **Edit** menu and click **Undo**. That brings back the dotted lines. Go right back under the same **Edit** menu and choose **Clear** as it shows to the left. The text should be gone. Click the banner again to get the text dialog box and try another font.

Text Size

You can just about guess at this. There are two more areas on the Add Text dialog box (refer to Figure 14.27). One is marked Style and the other is marked Size. Both affect the look and size of the text. I have found that the Example box is helpful, but rarely my final authority on how large or small text will be. I always have to mess around trying nine or so looks before I arrive at the size and style I like most. Just keep posting text and erasing until you love it.

Adding Shadow

Here's the fun part of this. If you have followed the instructions, you should have laid down dark text somewhere on banner6.gif. That is the shadow text. Now go back over the color palette and click the arrow between the two color boxes. This flips it so that the lighter color now resides in the foreground box.

Make sure PSP is still in text mode and click the image again. The settings you used to lay down the dark text should still be there. Choose **OK**. Now you should have a light color version of the same text. Click the mouse, hold it, and lay the lighter text across the darker text (slightly offset). It should look something like Figure 14.29.

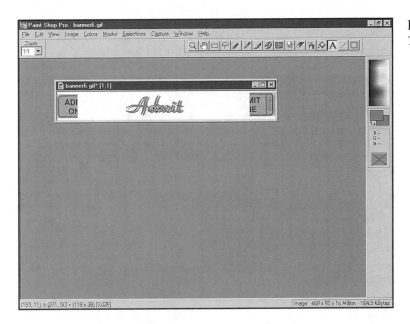

Figure 14.29
Text shadow overlay.

See the shadowing occurring? How much you set the light text off denotes how much shadow you get. Once you have the shadow where you want it, click, put PSP into the crop mode, and click the image once to set the text in place.

FAQs from the HTML Goodies Web Site

Q. Why don't you use the shadowing tool on the image program rather than double pasting?

A. Habit. This is the way I do it so this the way I teach it. I also think it's easier because I can play with the two levels rather than resetting and looking again and again.

There's an outstanding book called *Paint Shop Pro Web Techniques* by T. Michael Clark (New Riders Publishing) for any readers who want to delve deeper.

Now save the image using a **Save As** command. Remember: You just pasted two layers of text onto `banner6.gif`. If you simply choose Save you'll destroy `banner6.gif`. You need to save this as `banner7.gif`.

You only need three more banners. They are each created the same way as the banner we just finished. You use `banner6.gif` as a template for each, so you need to keep opening `banner6.gif` each time you want to create a new one. Just be sure to do a Save As each time you save a new image. The last three and a little about each follow.

Figure 14.30 shows `banner8.gif`. It uses the same colors as `banner6.gif`, but I flipped it so that the dark color is in the forefront. I also changed the font to Prom.

Figure 14.30
Text Image for
`Banner8.gif.`

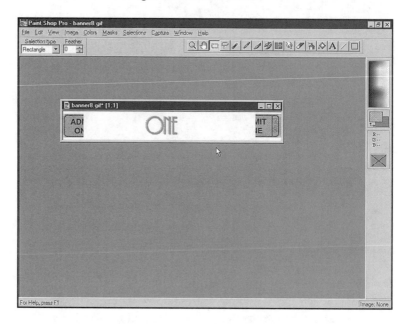

Figure 14.31 is `banner9.gif`. It uses the same colors, but the font is Isadora.

Figure 14.32 is `banner10.gif`. I have changed the colors for impact and made the text a little bigger. The font is Hobbit.

You're probably wondering what you thought was so hard about creating images. After you create the last three images, we will make them all one. See you then.

I have the text banner I created for this chapter for downloading at `http://www.htmlgoodies.com/book/banner5.html`.

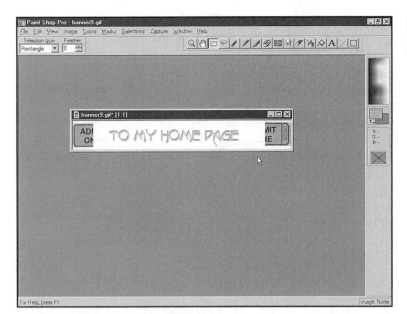

Figure 14.31
Text image for `banner9.gif`.

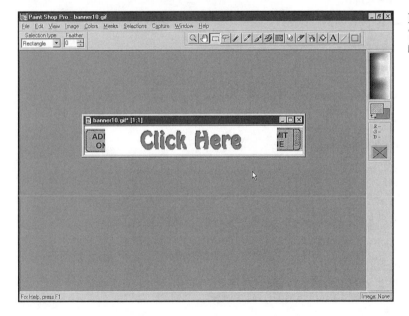

Figure 14.32
Text image for `banner10.gif`.

Banner Primer 6: Animating the Images

Click Here *This tutorial can be found online at* `http://www.htmlgoodies.com/banner_6.html`.

I should state right up front that if you haven't yet read the original Goodies animation tutorial in Chapter 3, "Adding Images and Backgrounds," then you may want to do that.

405

I am going to assume you have read it as you start this tutorial. This primer is for the creation of a banner. Since I have already written a piece on creating animation in general, I won't be going over it again here.

Create an Animation List

We have all the bricks and mortar. Now let's build the house. It is my opinion that when you are using a long series of images, it is best to write out what images will be used in the order they will be used. Remember in the first banner primer I said for you to draw out your ideas? This is where you try to make your vision come true.

 You may want to jump online again and look over the finished product again. The URL is http://www.htmlgoodies.com/banner.gif.

You should be quite familiar with the images that make up the animation. Here they are in the order they will be used:

> banner1.gif (full ticket)
>
> banner2.gif (torn ticket)
>
> banner3.gif (torn ticket)
>
> banner4.gif (torn ticket)
>
> banner5.gif (torn ticket)
>
> banner6.gif (most torn ticket)
>
> banner7.gif (Admit)
>
> banner8.gif (One)
>
> banner6.gif (most torn ticket)
>
> banner9.gif (To My Home Page)
>
> banner10.gif (Click Here)
>
> banner6.gif (most torn ticket)
>
> banner10.gif (Click Here)

Add Time Sequence

Next take that list and denote how long you want it to be between each animation cell. The GIF Animator Set works in tenths of a second, but since we don't have the cells actually denoted in the animation program, I do it through a simple method of S, M, and L, meaning short, medium, and long spans of time. I consider short around a quarter second, medium around a half a second, and long a full second or better. The time is how long it will be before moving to the next animation cell.

Here's what this banner looks like with times:

banner1.gif (full ticket)

(M)

banner2.gif (torn ticket)

(S)

banner3.gif (torn ticket)

(S)

banner4.gif (torn ticket)

(S)

banner5.gif (torn ticket)

(S)

banner6.gif (most torn ticket)

(M)

banner7.gif (Admit)

(L)

banner8.gif (One)

(L)

banner6.gif (most torn ticket)

(S)

banner9.gif (To My Home Page)

(L)

banner10.gif (Click Here)

(L)

banner6.gif (most torn ticket)

(S)

banner10.gif (Click Here)

Notice that the time is longer when there is text on the screen. I have found that a good second is required. Remember that you know what this says. The person who is seeing it for the first time does not. They have to read it. Give them time. Don't hustle through this.

FAQs from the HTML Goodies Web Site

Q. Why do you have banner 10, then 6, then 10 again?

A. Going from one to the other and then back again creates a sort of blink. Watch the animation roll through again online at `http://www.htmlgoodies.com/banner.gif`.

Q. I thought an animation was supposed to be equal, with the same amount of time between each image.

A. No. You want certain parts to go faster than others so you get a good show and so it doesn't become boring.

Create an Animated GIF

I have found that nothing wastes more time than trying to set times as you place each image in the GIF Construction Set. My suggestion is to get them all in the animator without setting any times. Just remember to have a control before each image and the LOOP command at the beginning. Yes, you want the banner to loop. Those that just go through the animation once do not attract as much attention. You may also want to set the final control to a longer time. That gives the impression that the banner is pausing before starting again. Nice effect.

Again, don't worry about setting control times yet, just get it all in there. We'll set times after this step.

Now that we have the skeleton, we can start to enter actual times. I wrote out all the images with an S, M, or L between each image; that resembles what is showing in the GIF Construction Set. All you need do is click each control and enter 20 for the short changes, 50 for the medium changes, and 100 for the long changes. Run it by pressing the **View** button.

Watch it run a few times, then go in and jimmy the times that look too long or too short. Believe me, doing an animation following this method saves you a bunch of time. Trying to enter the times while entering the control items to the GIF Construction Set very seldom works out right. I say go with the big picture first and whittle away after you have it.

Once you have it set to your liking, save it as `banner.gif`. Yes, I know that is the name of your original template, but we don't need it anymore and `banner.gif` is a really good name for a banner.

Now you have this thing. Now what? That's what Banner Primer 7 is all about.

Banner Primer 7: Activating the Image—Show Time

At this point it's likely that you haven't created your own banner. My guess is that you have done a re-creation of what I did for this series of primers. Maybe you simply took this design and changed a few words around. If that's the case, start again. In all honesty, this is not a stunning banner. It says nothing about the page you are to visit. It doesn't have a whole lot of information on it, and it's kind of dull. It is, however, a great example for teaching you the basics of banner creation.

Let me again state what I did in Banner Primer 1. Take some time; think about what makes your site great; think about what colors would be most eye catching without blinding the viewer. Try to come up with something that would make someone stop and watch your banner instead of scrolling down the page they came to visit.

To tell the truth, your banner is a bit of an intrusion. Think of your banner like a television or radio commercial. You're sitting there watching your favorite show when all of a sudden the show stops and you're expected to watch five or six 30-second commercials for any number of things.

I teach advertising. I know. People see commercials in a poor light...until they see a really good one. Then they wait for it to come on. One of the main attractions during the Super Bowl are the commercials. I actually used to wait to see who would win Bud Bowl.

So don't just copy what I've done here. Take a day or two—or three—and think about your site. Make the banner that people will stop and watch. Don't just hand them the same old, same old.

Getting Your Banner Out There

The purpose of the banner is to act as an advertisement for your site. It is to sit on pages other than your own. This banner is to bring people from other sites to your site. I think we can all agree on that. The question is, how do you get the banner on someone else's site? Here are a few methods.

Paying for Page Space

"Ugh!" you scream, "Money?! No way!!" Don't be so quick. Yes, I know that sites that pull in millions of people a month ask for big money—but there are tons of sites out there that are just like you, trying to build an audience. They would like to make a couple of bucks in the process.

The key to the entire process is finding your target audience. Let's say you have a page about watercolor painting. You want to get your banner on sites that have similar topics, sites that sell supplies, have artists displaying their work, display pages about oil painting, and so on. The topics do not have to be exactly the same, but close enough that someone who would visit that page might like to investigate your site as part of their surfing.

FAQs from the HTML Goodies Web Site

Q. **You say to find a target audience for your banner. Isn't the point to reach the largest audience so you have a better chance of hitting people who might want to come to your site? Just because someone likes art doesn't mean they'll come, and just because someone doesn't surf arts sites doesn't mean they won't come.**

A. You are attempting to make the exception the rule. Any advertiser will tell you that a mass audience is a shot in the dark. A targeted audience is far better hunting.

Now the part about price. I constantly receive requests from people asking me to advertise HTML Goodies on their site. And the prices are very low. I once got on a page with top center placement for a year for $30. Thirty bucks!! Unbelievable.

I have it a little easier finding advertisers because I own a site that pulls in millions per month. Many sites come to me regarding advertising.

You might have to seek out the sites yourself. Do it. Look around. Even if a site isn't displaying advertising at that moment, it doesn't mean they don't want any. Ask the Webmaster if she is willing to accept your banner for a small sum. Work out a deal. You may get your own $30 yearly rate, then again you may not. See what you can get.

Above all, remember that the pages you place your banner on must hit people that might have an interest in coming to your page. If not, it's wasted money and ad space.

By the way, Goodies has advertising representation and I am not supposed to buy my own advertising anymore as part of my contract.

Trading Banner Space

What a brilliant idea! Go surfing for sites that are most like yours and write to the owners of those sites suggesting that you start trading banners. You put their banner on three of your best pages and they do the same for your banners. Great! And it's free! If you get together with five or six sites, you can create a solid amount of cross-traffic. It's a great way to build your own visitors, maybe to the point where a real money-paying advertiser wants to get a banner on your site. Go figure. (Again, I am represented by a company to sell advertising. I cannot accept any banner trades.)

Joining a Banner Exchange Network

These things are really popular. What happens is that when you join you submit your own banner and in return you are given a bit of code to place on your page. That code is attached to the computers of the people who exchange banners. It keeps track of how many times your site displays banners. Some exchanges display your banner once for every 10 or so times you display a banner, while others just do a straight random display of banners. Either way, there's really not a guaranteed number of displays, and you must be running their banners to get yours displayed. Plus, you often do not have a say in what pages your banners display on; you may be missing the target audience completely. You may also get on pages that you wouldn't want to be on. Then again, it is free. Just be sure to read over the parameters of how large your banner can be and how may bytes it can contain. It's their banner exchange; they set the rules and you have to follow them.

I was a member of a couple banner-swap programs for a short time and have since left. I wasn't happy with the number of displays and clicks (people clicking the banner to come to my page) I was getting. You may have more luck. Some people swear by these things. The number of banner exchange sites has grown since I used them and many are quite targeted. Heck, there's one just for people with pages devoted to needlepoint.

The one I hear about most is Link Exchange, but look at a bunch before you decide to place your banner. You can find banner exchange networks everywhere by going to search engines and searching for the topics you think would make for good target audiences.

Offering Your Banner for Free

This sounds a little goofy but it has been fantastic for HTML Goodies. People who come to Goodies often ask if they can post the banner on their page as a link to the site. When they ask, I give them one. I can't tell you how many banners I have out there just from people posting them out of the kindness of their hearts. If you're one of those people, I can't thank you enough for doing that. I truly appreciate it. You have been quite helpful in building this site into what it is today. Word of mouth and links on other pages built the site. I didn't pay for the traffic; it came because other posted links and banners saying it was worth seeing. If you're not, go to the HTML Goodies home page and look toward the bottom of the page. There's a link so you can get one for your page.

Placing Your Banner on a Page

This is a good point of debate. The most popular placement is the top center, but I don't know that that's always the best place. You see, these things take time to load, especially if they are animations.

If the banner does not load quickly and the page has set aside all images with HEIGHT and WIDTH commands, all the page's text comes in and there's a hole where your banner should be. Users will simply start scrolling downward without ever seeing the image. It will come in and if you're using a program to count the number of times the banner displays, a count will be made. But did the user really see the banner?

I offer these suggestions to get your banner seen as often as possible:

- Go as small on the bytes as possible. The lower the bytes, the faster the load.

- Make the first image in the animation an eye grabber. It might make them stay for the rest.

- Try a placement lower on the page. See the CNN home page for a lesson in this. I always wait to see the top story. By the time I read the headline and start scrolling, the smaller advertisements halfway down the page are up and ready for my viewing. Yes, there are banners across the top, but I wonder if the banners down the pages aren't the better buys. It's a great method of placement, but you have to have a page design that stops people for a moment and then gets them to scroll.

- Try to get on more than one page on a site. If you are only on the home page and someone misses your banner, you're done. If you are on three or four pages, your banner is cached from its having been loaded on the home page. Now you pop right up when the user goes to the next page with your banner on it.

- Be sure to use the ALT attribute. If you don't know about the ALT command in images, read about it in Chapter 3. This command allows for the little yellow box, called a ToolTip, which pops up when you roll your mouse over an image. In addition to the rollover, the ALT command places text in the boxes set aside by the HEIGHT and WIDTH commands. Even if your image doesn't pop up, there will at least be some text there to catch some attention.

  Be sure to use the HEIGHT and WIDTH attributes so that there is a box for the ALT text to pop up in.

- Run your banner off the server that is displaying the page. This isn't always possible, but do it when you can. It gives you fewer possible problems and speeds the display.

FAQs from the HTML Goodies Web Site

Q. You say to go low on the bytes but then have us create an animated banner that can get huge. Which is it?

A. Both. Yes, a static banner might be smaller on the bytes, but many studies have shown that it won't catch the eye half as much as an animation.

Q. How about the bottom of the page? You didn't mention that.

A. Well, the bottom of the page might be a good placement if the page isn't very long. I say that because I go into ESPN's SportsZone just about every day to see how the Cleveland Indians are doing, and I don't think I have ever seen the very bottom of the page. I would shoot for the middle if I couldn't get the top.

Keeping Track of Visitors

How do you do it? Good question. If you have your banners on five different sites, how do you know which sites are being good to you and which are not? The method is so simple and so good, I shook my head in amazement that I hadn't thought of it earlier.

Let's say you are advertising on three sites: A, B, and C. What you do is have four home pages that are exactly the same. The first page is the original home page. This is the page you see if you came to the site through a Yahoo! search or by being given the address.

The next three home pages should be labeled in accordance with the three pages you are advertising on. The advertising banners you are running on site A should all be pointed to a home page called indexa.html. All the advertising on site B should be pointed at a home page called indexb.html, and site C should have all its advertising banners pointed to indexc.html. Put a counter on each page. Now you can keep a fairly straight record of which advertising is doing best for your site. You can also see if the advertising is working at all. If the original index page is bringing in the most traffic, you know the sites running your advertising ain't working.

You need to rely on the site you are buying advertising space on to provide you with simple information such as number of displays versus number of clicks. HTML Goodies has two separate programs running to keep track of that data. Smaller sites might not be as well equipped.

FAQs from the HTML Goodies Web Site

Q. What do you consider a good showing by an advertising banner?

A. I would like to see a 10%–15% increase if I am a low-visited site (2,000 or so people a month) and around a 5%–7% increase if I have more people coming through (10,000 or so a month).

Activating Your Banner

Okay, you have a site that offered a price you can afford (or wants to trade with you). The site asks for the code to run your banner on their site. What do you send them?

I first suggest you set it up so that you can run your banner off their site. There are a ton of things that can go wrong if your banner is being run on their pages from your server. There are still things that can go wrong if you are running your banner on their pages from their server—just not as many things.

Don't get fancy with the code. Don't try to run an applet or fancy image flip deals. Simple is easiest. Here's the basic code. I feel this is sufficient:

```
<A HREF="www.yoursite.com/yourpage.html">
<IMG SRC="banner.gif" BORDER="0" WIDTH="468" HEIGHT="60"
 ALT="Come to my page!">
</A>
```

A lot of people like the onMouseover look, where text pops up in the status bar. I think it's a bit much and might cause problems, but here it is before you ask:

```
<A HREF="www.yoursite.com/yourpage.html"
 onMouseOver="window.status='TEXT IN STATUS BAR'; return true">
<IMG SRC="banner.gif" BORDER="0" WIDTH="468" HEIGHT="60"
ALT="Come to my page!"></A>
```

You now have the basics of banner creation and use. Is there more? Oh, yeah. Will Paint Shop Pro do more than I showed you? Oh, yeah. But that's for you to find out on your own. You have the basics. Now go and make your site a banner.

 Want to put the HTML Goodies banner on your site (blatant plug)? Go to http://www.htmlgoodies.com/book/somebanners.html.

Chapter 15

Other Stuff You Should Really Know

Copyright Questions and Answers

A series of questions that have been asked of me at one time or another through email follow. People are concerned about what they can and cannot do in terms of copyright. I knew some of the answers and others I did not. After contacting a copyright expert at a local university, I was able to put together the answers to some of these common questions.

Please note that copyright law and copyright applications change. What is true in some cases may not be true in others. Here are a series of guidelines with, to the best of my knowledge, correct answers.

What Is a Copyright, Anyway?

Copyright is a form of intellectual property law. Copyright law protects an author or creator from his or her stuff being pirated and used without permission.

Keep in mind that it does not protect the idea, system, or method of the information. For instance, I have a copyright on HTML Goodies. That copyright covers my writings. It does not cover the idea of teaching HTML on the Net, the fact that I used English to do it, or that hypertext is employed. There are obviously other places on the Net trying to teach you how this stuff is done.

The Internet Is Public Domain, so Isn't Everything Fair Game?

No. The copyright laws that apply to written material, photographs, and a myriad of other items apply on the Internet too. You cannot just take and use whatever you feel like.

This topic has already been addressed by the Clinton administration's Information Infrastructure Task Force (IITF). The task force is attempting to shape existing copyright laws to apply more fully to the digital age. However, until laws that deal specifically with the Internet are on the books, existing copyright laws are the yardstick for existing pages.

So, Is Making a Link to Another Copyrighted Page Against the Law?

For the most part, no. You are only making a link to the page rather than displaying the information. That doesn't create a violation per se. However, since owners of copyright also own the rights to what can be done with their items, they do have the ability to deny you permission to create a link. Please understand that denying someone a link happens in very rare cases, but it has happened.

In fact, it has happened to me. I was sent a letter one day from a fan of the site. He told me that he had placed one of my banners on his home page and offered me a login and password to see it. I thought the need for a password was strange so I went to the site. There was my banner sitting above tons of hard core pornography. "Gaaaah!" I screamed. I then contacted the author and called upon my copyright law right and told him to take down my banner.

How Do I Get My Stuff Copyrighted?

It technically already is. The law states that a copyright can be placed on an item as soon as it is placed into tangible form (a Web page, for instance). There have been many cases where an implied copyright has stood up in court.

But don't test those waters. Put up a copyright insignia and text.

What Do I Put on the Page?

You should include the circle C (©) and the word *copyright*, plus the year and the name of the author. Like so:

```
This page © Copyright 1997, Dr. Joe Burns, Ph.D.
```

You may think you only need the circle C or the word *copyright* alone, but remember that the circle C is created in HTML through this command: ©. That does not show as a circle C when the source code is printed. Put them both to be safe.

Make a point of placing it on at least the main page. That's what I did. I made a blanket statement that everything inside htmlgoodies.com was written by me, except where noted.

Whether you put the copyright on every page, or just the top page, make a point of putting it in the text so that it shows when the page is displayed. You should also put it in the HTML code. Like so:

```
<!-- This page copyright 1998 by Dr. Joe Burns Ph.D. -->
```

Wait, Don't I Have to Send a Form to the Government?

That is voluntary. The Copyright Office catalogs your site if you want it to. It costs 20 bucks plus some shipping. No, this is not required in order to be able to bring a civil suit against someone else for copyright infringement. You can still claim money for damages and lost profit. However, you can only attempt to get punitive damages (punishment money) if you are registered with the Copyright Office.

How Do I Register with the Copyright Office?

You need to fill out the application form TX. There are other forms, but this is the one a Web site uses. The form is available from the Copyright Office home page at `http://lcweb.loc.gov/copyright`.

Fill it out, print a copy of your Web site, and send it in with a $20 check to this address:

> Register of Copyrights
> Copyright Office, Library of Congress
> Washington D.C., 20559-6000

You should receive confirmation in five to six months. Please note that the Copyright Office does not want two separate sheets of paper for the TX form. If you get the form from its site, it prints as two sheets. You need to photocopy them so they make one sheet, front and back.

Can I Just Send in a Disk?

No. A compact disc, yes. A floppy disk, no.

Do I Have to Register All My Pages Separately?

You mean like $20 a page? No. I registered HTML Goodies in one fell swoop. Updates go later. I looked upon it as chapters in a book.

How Long Does My Copyright Last?

Until you've been dead 50 years. Don't sweat it.

I'm Just a Kid. Can I Get a Copyright?

Yes. Minors are allowed copyright protection. Follow the same procedure I just described.

The Internet Is Global. What About Someone in Another Country Using My Stuff?

That depends on the country's policies. Some countries recognize a U.S. copyright and help with violators. Some don't. I haven't a list of what countries do and don't; I have yet to find one.

What If I Copyright Something and Someone Else Copyrights the Same Thing?

You mean in pure coincidence, right? If it comes to a lawsuit, it is up to you and the other person to decide who did it first. That's why you register with the Copyright Office. You then have a solid alibi for when you copyrighted the item. Not registering the item makes it harder to prove the date of copyright. It can be done, however. Some people mail their items to themselves so that there is a date stamped on the item. Other take their items to a notary public.

If you are not talking coincidence, and you mean that the person has simply stolen your idea, I hope you're quite sure you can prove the date you copyrighted your stuff. If you can't, I doubt the court is simply going to take your word for it. HTML Goodies is fully registered with the government Copyright Office. I don't want any misunderstandings.

I Call My Site "Dog Breath." Can I Copyright That?

No. Titles, names, and logos are not protected under copyright. You need to get into trademarks for that. Even then, you cannot trademark a word—just the design of the logo and the fact that the words represent your company. If you could copyright a word, I'd copyright the word *the*. I'd be rich.

This One Site Has a Great Image, but It's Copyrighted. Can I Use It?

Not without written permission. Period. I can't be more clear on that.

Can I Use Anything from a Site?

According to the Fair Use Doctrine (Section 110 [5] of the Copyright Act of 1976), it is allowable to use "limited portions" of a copyrighted item for works such as commentary, news reporting, academic reports, and the like. But you still have to give credit; you cannot claim the work as yours. You must cite where it came from.

The tricky part is that there is no set number of words that equal "limited portions." It's a tough call. My suggestion is to be fair to the person with the copyright. Don't post the whole site and give credit on only one page. I would fight someone posting a healthy portion of Goodies and only citing once. I also believe that on the Net the cite should include a hypertext link. (That's not law, I just believe that.)

I'll Just Post Everything and Cite to My Heart's Content

Wrong. There are limitations on Fair Use (17 USCS Sect. 107). Several factor are taken into account: whether you are attempting to make a profit, the nature of the work, the size of the portion you use, and the effect on the market place.

For example, say you re-post a large section of the HTML Goodies site and write some of your own stuff around it. You then register it with search engines calling people to come. Even though you cite me all day long, I would still have a hairy. You are putting a dent in my visitors and trying to use my work to bring people to you. Even if you quote a small amount of my work to gain visitors, I would still get upset. You are using my words to bring people to your site.

Now, before you ask, I am talking about direct quotes and the use of my language ("tutorials," "primers," and the like). If you read the tutorials and use the information to create your own page, great! That's the purpose. Here, I'm talking about a direct theft of my site. Feel free to use my ideas to death. Just don't use my exact words to attempt to get more people to your site.

What if I Take the Person's Page and Change It a Little. Can I Copyright It?

No. The changes must be "substantial and creative." In effect, there may be very, very few remnants of the original work. You might as well write it from scratch before trying to steal and alter. Editorial changes will just not cut it in a court of law.

The one possible exception to this rule is if you are creating a satire of a site. That is protected under the First Amendment. However, the satire must be obviously a satire. Subtle hints may get you in trouble. Make it blatant.

What Can I Do if Someone Uses My Copyrighted Stuff Without Getting Permission?

You can file a civil lawsuit in federal court to get an order stopping the person from using your material. A copyright attorney can get you started in the process. The U.S. Attorney can get involved if the person has used your work and is attempting to make a profit with it.

What Do You Do when Someone Posts Part of HTML Goodies Without Permission?

Usually I write a calm email letter asking the person to stop and take the pages down. If he has registered the pages with search engines, I ask him to place a redirect on the page so that hits come to the right place.

If that doesn't work, I contact the server's Webmaster and tell her to shut down the user's site—the entire site—or civil action will be brought against the server people for allowing copyrighted material to be pirated on their site. The next step would actually be to file a suit.

Has This Ever Happened?

A few times. I've only had to go to the server people once. When I did, the site was offline in a matter of hours. I've never filed a lawsuit.

Would You?

Yes. In fact, there is an obligation to file suit. If you are not willing to defend your copyright, it can be rescinded by the courts.

What if I Use Something I Didn't Know Was Copyrighted?

Take it down when you are asked to take it down. No one wants a lawsuit—they cost money. Usually you are asked to stop first. Just apologize and stop.

What if I Am Using Something That Is Copyrighted and I Know It?

You know you're breaking the law. The same answer applies from the previous question— take it down!—but don't be upset if you get served. You knew you were doing wrong to begin with.

I'm Just a Kid. I Don't Have Anything to Take. Go Ahead! Sue Me! You Can't Do Anything to Me!

You're right in one aspect. Because you are young and don't own a great deal, there is very little someone could take from you. What can be done is a conviction of a federal crime. Have you ever gone in to fill out a job application? Remember that line that asked if you had ever been convicted of a federal crime? You'll be checking Yes for the remainder of your life. Just try to get a job even related to computers with a conviction for copyright infringement.

What if I Don't Take the Image, but Make a Link?

You know, a link to the real site so that the image shows up on my page, but is coming from the actual copyrighted site? No go. You are still displaying it and you are breaking the law.

I Want Music or Video from My Favorite Group on My Site

You might be able to get that. ASCAP and BMI are the two big music licensing firms. They sell what are known as *blanket fee licenses* to servers. That fee allows the server to reproduce any song under BMI or ASCAP representation. If your server has paid the fee, go for it.

Without that fee being paid, you are breaking the law by playing the song.

But I'll only Play a Portion, Like in the "Fair Use" Deal

You're walking a thin line there. The purpose is entertainment in this case and might be a problem.

I'll Play My Version of the Song on My Keyboard and Post That

That's being done a lot and I didn't find much on it. Just remember that a song is more than just the performance and the recording. The melody is also under copyright. Your playing the song might still get you into trouble.

I'll Play a Recording of an Old Beethoven Piece

"He's been dead for over 50 years! The song's out of copyright and in the public domain," you say. Not always so. Authors can claim copyright on the sheet music, arrangement, and even performance of the song. You may not be upsetting Beethoven, you may be upsetting the person who arranged it.

Same deal with old pictures and paintings. Just because the artist has been dead and gone since the age of no indoor plumbing doesn't mean that a museum or a collector doesn't own the rights.

What Is in Public Domain?

As far as I could find, there is no government list or any other kind of list for that matter. You have to be careful about playing and posting.

What if I Scan Something That's Copyrighted?

That's not yours. That would mean you are trying to copyright the method. That's not allowed.

How Can I Be Sure Nothing on My Site Is Copyrighted?

Make it all yourself or ask permission at all costs. There are some sites out there that check for you, but I think doing it all yourself is much safer and more gratifying.

If you want to post something that is not yours, get permission from the owner. If the owner says no, too bad. If the owner says yes, get it in writing and hold onto it. You may also want to build good relations with people by giving them credit on the page in addition to asking permission.

Do You Do That?

Completely. Every time something appears on HTML Goodies or Java Goodies that was not written by me, I make a point of giving credit. If someone sends me a letter and I think it's postable, I ask if I can. Some people don't want any other names on their sites other than their own. I don't buy that. I cannot possibly know everything. When others help, I am happy and put a link. It is an equal relationship. The only thing I frown upon is someone else writing a tutorial. I like to do that.

I only accept JavaScripts from their authors. Now, it's rather easy to fool me and a couple have. They took someone else's work and put their name to it. I was then contacted by the real author and told to take it down. I did.

Another time, an author had placed his copyright on the HTML page but had not placed it in the code. By posting the code without the copyright, I was breaking the law. It was brought to my attention rather sternly. I apologized for what was truly an innocent mistake and took the page down.

Those are the only two times I ran into trouble. I try to be very careful.

Final Thoughts

The Internet is not wide open. The laws still apply there. Just because you can take it does not mean you should. Give credit as you would want credit given to you. That image may be really cool. Re-posting my site and claiming it as your own may impress your friends and a couple of visitors. Playing your favorite band's music may show you're a great fan.

...but none of it is worth a law suit.

Net Notes

Here are a few great links with much more detailed information:

U.S. Copyright Office: `http://lcweb.loc.gov/copyright/`.

The Copyright Web site: `http://www.benedict.com`. This is a great, great site.

Copyright Clearance Center, Inc.: `http://www.copyright.com`. This site allows automated rights clearance on the WWW.

The ILT Guide to Copyright: `http://www.ilt.columbia.edu/projects/copyright/index.html`.

Copyright and Fair Use—Stanford University: `http://fairuse.stanford.edu/`.

Thomson & Thomson: `http://www.thomson-thomson.com`. These guys offers services to determine whether your trademark or copyright can be adopted and protected.

For more, search copyright on Yahoo!: `http://search.yahoo.com/bin/search?p=copyright`.

What Are Cookies?

A cookie, huh? Either you are a real Web-head or you have stopped by to get the ingredients for that Neiman Marcus cookie that has been being shuffled around the Net. If you're actually looking for a food item, you're out of luck. (Okay, maybe I explain the cookie story at the very end of the tutorial.) This is a tutorial dealing with electronic cookies.

Cookies, Joe?

Yeah. *Cookies* are a small computer-generated text file (no larger than 4K) that you receive when you stop at certain sites. Unless you make a point of setting your browser's preferences to not accept cookies, write-protected your `cookie.txt` file, or have installed a JavaScript to do the same, you probably have a cookie sitting it your browser's directory right now. The use of cookies is quite widespread.

I have heard a few reasons the little file servers and browsers are called cookies. Each is probably less creditable than the last, but here are a few for entertainment purposes:

> In UNIX, files of this type had a name something like k00k.z. Thus the strange pronunciation as *cookie* (uh-huh...).

> The guy who got really, really, really rich by creating Netscape digs these particular chunky cookies—thus the name (hmmm...).

> Because distributing cookies is like leaving crumbs all over (uh....).

> Just because (which is probably the most likely).

But Wait!

Ben Buckner offers what sounds as if it could be a true story:

> About the term's origin: It's a very old bit of programmer slang (usually) for a piece of data stored to communicate between two processes, typically separated in time, and often as some kind of flag. The fuller form is "magic cookie." I know I've heard it used as far back as the late '80s anyway. The real defining point of the magic cookie is that some part of the data is unique to the process(es) so that the receiver can ensure that it's getting the message from the expected source. In the HTTP cookie, the server domain name serves that purpose, though in this case the client actually performs the verification to prevent server-based hanky-panky. I've heard that the term "magic cookie" was originally coined in reference to one of those old adventure games (perhaps "Adventure" itself) in which you had to give some character a magic cookie to get something from it (analogous to cookie verification), but that's just a vague memory.

Eh...I'll buy it.

What Do Cookies Do?

They themselves do nothing. Please do not be concerned that a virus or an evil program of some sort has been placed on your computer. The cookie is a text file. It is not executable. That means it can't run like a program.

The cookie was placed on your machine because you gave the server placing the cookie access to that section of your computer. Don't be alarmed. You have to give permission. Without it, you couldn't display any WWW files or pictures. (I am talking a SLIP or a PPP connection to the Internet here; AOL is a different story. You are not connected directly to the Internet on AOL.) And no, the server does not have access to other sections of your computer. Contrary to what some believe, HTTP servers cannot go into your computer and reconfigure unless you allow it. Again, don't be alarmed. Chances are very, very slim you allowed it by mistake.

But, as I said up earlier, you do have the ability, by going into your browser's preferences, to disallow the placement of cookie files. How does your computer know to allow all the regular image and text files, but no cookie files? The file's named `cookie`. Easy enough.

Getting Back to Cookies...

Remember that a cookie is used almost as a tag on your computer. You know, like they tag bears on those Saturday morning wildlife shows that play right before the football games. That "tag" holds information that the server that gave it to you would like to know. Such as the following:

- How many times your computer has stopped in—The server may post to a page a message welcoming you back for the nth time.

- What your computer did while you were in the site—Let's say you go into a shopping site. You order six things from four different pages. The cookie records the purchase and the price. At the end, you click a button and your total is displayed. In addition, the server knows you have purchased before when you return and may then send you directly to items you are interested in or offer a special as a return customer. You'll often hear this type of cookie usage referred to as a *shopping cart*.

- Keep track of a special name and password—No, I do not mean that the cookie has the ability to grab your actual server-side name and password. Let's say you join a sports page, and that you need to pay a bit of money in order to get very fast stats results on the games. This is common. After you paid the money, you are given a code word and password to log on with. After you log on the first time, those two bits of information are posted to the cookie. In the future you can then go back into the special site without having to fill out the logon form again and again. Plus, your favorite team's name may be added so that you are taken straight to the section you want without clicking.

Please remember that the cookie denotes your computer, not you. The server that uses cookies has no idea who you actually are unless you tell them by offering your name or email address.

Do You Hand Out Cookies on Goodies, Joe?

The HTML Goodies site is kept free thanks to advertiser support. There's a small ad banner at the top of each page. I use a rather expensive program to keep track of them. That program ensures that you get a new banner when you log onto a new page. In order for that to happen, I assign every page a code word. The online version of this page has a code word attached to it; the code word is oreo. In order to get a new banner on each page for you, that little program needs to keep track of the code words. It does so by placing the current page's code word in your cookie file. You get a new banner if you go to the next page and the code word doesn't match.

Do I use cookies? Yes. Do I use your cookie file? Yes. I am gathering nothing from you. I am only using your cookie file to keep track of code words, which are erased after you leave.

You see, I don't sell anything to the people who stop by. Everything on my site is free for the taking. Yes, I could place full cookies and use them for simple return visits data, but none of my advertisers have ever cared to know that.

The best reason is that I just don't need to do it. You see, every time you request files from my server (or any server), the path to your computer is recorded. It has to be. Without knowing where to send the files you request, you'd never get them. You do the same thing if you have a Web site.

Before someone explains to me that there are anonymous surfing sites out there, please remember that although the site that offers the information may not get the actual path to your computer, the anonymous surfing server does. It has to or you would never get the file. You're never going to do this totally anonymously.

All the paths to all the computers my server provides files to are held in a file. Usually the file is called logs. Mine is. You have one of these yourself; you just may not have access to it. I use a little program called Surfreport to take the contents of the log files and jumble them into a useable form. You can get the program yourself at http://www.surfreport.com. When I bought it the program cost $500.

This is what I get without using any cookies and just looking at my log files:

- Total completed requests: 170 240 (88 879)
- Average completed requests per day: 11 869 (12 697)
- Total failed requests: 1 425 (752)
- Total redirected requests: 3 007 (1 593)
- Number of distinct files requested: 89 (86)
- Number of distinct hosts served: 24 258 (13 456)
- Number of new hosts served in last seven days: 12 227
- Corrupt log file lines: 172

- Unwanted log file entries: 2
- Total data transferred: 1 016Mbs (537 710kb)
- Average data transferred per day: 72 515 kbs (76 816kb)

And so on and so forth.

Domain Report

```
Printing all domains, sorted by amount of traffic.

        #reqs: %bytes: domain

        ——   ———   ———

        38409: 21.74%: .com (Commercial, mainly USA)

        35007: 20.82%: [unresolved numerical addresses]

        31507: 18.54%: .net (Network)

        30149: 18.06%: .edu (USA Educational)

        5941:  3.58%: .ca (Canada)

        3301:  1.99%: .uk (United Kingdom)

        2636:  1.51%: .au (Australia)

        2509:  1.41%: .fr (France)

        2221:  1.38%: .se (Sweden)

        1808:  1.01%: .nl (Netherlands)

        1594:  0.86%: .us (United States)

        1191:  0.74%: .no (Norway)

        1153:  0.65%: .gov (USA Government)

        1069:  0.65%: .jp (Japan)
```

And so on and so forth.

This is information general enough that I can give advertisers good information about the amount of traffic that comes through my site and from where they came. I don't know a darn thing about any one computer or person specifically, just the total population.

In case you're wondering, as of July 1998, the HTML Goodies site is bringing in between 50,000 and 65,000 different surfers per day. Those surfers look at an average of between 90,000 and 100,000 different pages. The home page itself is viewed over 9,000 times a day. Do some quick math and you see that the Goodies site offers over 3 million page views per month by close to a 1 million people.

Midweek is the heaviest usage time. The lowest surf time is weekend days, and the most popular time for surfing Goodies is lunch time and early evening before 8 p.m.

I Want to See a Cookie

You can look at your own if you haven't altered your browser to stop receiving them. My guess is that if you've done any kind of surfing into any major sites like ESPN, Yahoo!, or WebCrawler, you've received a cookie.

Where Would I Find My Cookie?

Travel into the guts of your computer to find it. It will be somewhere in your browser's directory; look at the entire directory first. In later models it is sitting at the top level—and yes, it will be named cookie. In earlier browser models, you'll find it in your cache. You could also do a search on your hard drive for *cookie*. If you can't find it, no problem. Here's what mine looks like. I just cut and pasted it from my brand new Pentium 200MMX! 64Mb of EDO RAM! Woohoo!

```
# Netscape HTTP Cookie File
# http://www.netscape.com/newsref/std/cookie_spec.html
# This is a generated file!  Do not edit.
.sportszone.com      TRUE /FALSE      876509359
.netscape.com  TRUE /FALSE      946684799
NETSCAPE_ID    1000e010,138f8fd5
www.webcrawler.com  FALSE      /      FALSE      852076799
webcrawlerad    46162
```

What It All Means

You can pretty much see who has given me a cookie. I have one from Netscape and one from ESPN's SportsZone and others. The long numbers are actually dates, or time until expiration of the cookie in milliseconds. Those numbers were most likely placed by a JavaScript cookie script.

Are Cookies Bad?

I guess that depends on whom you speak to.

To be fair, the use of cookies does infringe on privacy. The server does know if someone stopped by before and knows what that person did while they were there.

If you haven't taken this tone from me yet, I don't believe cookies are all that awful. I also don't mind someone using them on me. A computer wizard with far more knowledge than me might prove me wrong, but I don't think we can expect to move around public phone lines and personal servers totally anonymously.

Let's look at some of the actual concerns people have written to me about cookies. I'll comment on each one.

- The people know I'm in their site—Yes, and K-Mart knows you're in their store. However, you're not being video-taped in a WWW server. You are in a lot of K-Marts.

- The server knows what I'm doing when I'm there—You bet. Where else other than your home can you have complete domain over all that is inside, taking whatever you want, while remaining totally anonymous?

- They know who I am—To a point. Your login or email login may be gathered because it's listed in the browser's general information, but it's not gathered by the cookie. The cookie can't do that. An applet can, and then it can be written to the cookie. This is a bit unnerving, I agree. But as I said before, it's hard to go around this web of computers totally anonymously.

- They'll spam me—If they do, a line has been crossed and the person who is using the unauthorized email addresses should be prosecuted.

- They'll get my picture—Not unless you offer it.

- They'll get my home address—Ditto.

- They'll get my SS number—Ditto ditto.

You really shouldn't be giving your SSN, name, phone number, or whatever else to anyone who doesn't need it. In this world of telemarketers and nasty people, giving your address to something as simple as a grocery story shopper's card can get you piled under with junk mail. I always try to sign up for items with my name only. If they refuse, I make a decision on whether the item is required for me to live a long and healthy life. Usually it isn't.

I agree to a point that surfing is invasive to your privacy, but it might be a trade-off you are willing to make in order to have this web of computers.

I've been informed that a fairly successful method of surfing anonymously is to enter false information into your browser, like an incorrect email address and a fake name—but stop and think. Phone bills, power bills, cable bills—each of those also gathers information about you. Plus, they probably asked for your SSN. Should we also be anonymous to them? It's a good debate if nothing else. It's up to you whether the cookies are good or bad.

On another note: Just for fun, I enjoy asking people if they would ever give a credit card number over the Internet even though great steps have been taken to ensure encryption of the numbers. Most people have a rather violent reaction against doing it.

They then hand their card to the waiter who walks into another room with it.

Is That It?

Well, yeah. I can't cover much more than what I've already told you. To go further, you need to get in touch with your own server people. They'll be able to place the CGIs or show you what is already being done log-wise for you.

What About That Neiman Marcus Cookie Story?!

Oh, that. This is what popular culturalists term an *urban legend*. It probably isn't true, but it gets told so often that people think it's true. Plus, it's always told as if it happened to someone's older brother's former friend's roommate, so it has to be true! One of my favorites is the story that the Mikey kid, who liked Life cereal so much, died in the early 80s by eating Pop-Rocks and chugging a Coke. It's not true, but the story goes around.

I also like the one where a woman, always distantly related, gets on an elevator with a very large, gruff-looking man who's holding tightly the leash of his huge growling dog. The woman is quite nervous. The large man yells, "Sit!" And she does.

Onto the cookie story. It seems that someone's brother's former roommate's friend took his daughter (wife, friend) to Neiman Marcus for lunch (dinner, breakfast). My version of the story had the daughter purchasing a scarf and a wool hat. Details make for a more compelling tale!

The people ordered and ate and were served three small cookies at the end of the meal. They liked the cookies so much the gentleman asked if he could purchase the recipe. The waiter said yes and told the price as 250. The man agreed. When his credit card statement arrived, he noted that it was $250 rather than $2.50. Apparently he'll sign anything at the restaurant.

Inflamed with cookie passion he said he would let the world know the recipe if they didn't take the charge off the card. They refused and he set to spamming this story all over the Net through BBS servers and email.

The recipe I received was actually pretty good. It called for finely ground coffee and oatmeal. In reality, it could be true but probably isn't. It is another reason to make cookies, and it's my opinion that we could all use a few more reasons to make cookies.

Enjoy!

Using META Commands with Search Engines

META what? Unless you are loopy into this HTML stuff like I am, you probably haven't heard about META commands until now. I would guess the reason is that the commands don't put anything on your page. There's no visual associated with them, but they can be quite helpful to the search engines that look over your page and tell others about it.

Search Engine...What's That?

A *search engine* is a program that takes key words from you, searches a database of Web pages, and gives you a list of pages that might be helpful. Yahoo! is a search engine, as is Excite.

When you submit your page to a search engine, or *register* the page as Web-heads like to say, you are asking the people who keep the page to place your page's text into a huge database.

You enter *key words* when you use the search engine. Let's say you are interested in fishing; you might enter "rod reel salmon. "The database is searched and returns any pages that contain those words.

When you register a page, some search engines ask you to enter a few key words. What you are allowed to offer is limited. Wouldn't it be nice if you could send the search engine a page that has all the key words written out in the HTML text? This way you could make the search engine's job a lot easier and get your page brought onscreen a lot more often. That means more people click your link and more people visit your site.

What You Can Do with META *Commands*

There are a few different things (in terms of search engines) that I know of:

- Offer key words to the search engine.
- Offer the name of the computer software, herein known as the *generator*, you used to make the page—it helps.
- Offer a description for use when your page is displayed. Some search engines do not show descriptions, so this won't work on all engines.
- Offer the author's name.
- Offer a copyright statement.
- Offer an expiration date so the search engine's database stops bringing your page up after a certain amount of time.

Let's remember that you are playing against a search engine here. You play by its rules, not the other way around. These items do not work on all search engines, but are successful on most.

I'll say this again later in the tutorial, but I'll do it here anyway: All META commands go between the HEAD commands, immediately following the TITLE commands. Just list one right after the other.

Offering Key Words

Follow this format:

```
<HEAD>
<TITLE>Page title</TITLE>
<META NAME="keywords" CONTENT="bring,my,Browns,back,Baltimore">
</HEAD>
```

Sorry, Ravens fans. I like who I like and I can't change for anyone. I grew up in Cleveland. No jokes!

See what I did? I offered key words, all separated by a comma. No space. Some servers don't like an added space and may not bring up the page because of the space being seen as part of the word. Offer words in the format shown here.

Some servers bring up one page over others because the key word appears more than once in the page. Why not offer 10 or 12 of each of the key words you are using? That tells the search engine that the key word appears many times inside the document. Something like "Browns,Browns,Browns,Browns,Browns,Browns,Browns."

You get the idea.

Just don't overdo it. Some search engines see excessive multiples of keywords as spamming and will not post your page specifically because of that.

Offering Your Page Generator

I don't get this one, but I always put it in anyway. It's another thing the search engine can use to isolate your page; it's simply the program you used to make your page. This is what mine always looks like:

```
<HEAD>
<TITLE>Page title</TITLE>

<META NAME="Generator" CONTENT="NotePad">
</HEAD>
```

Use it in good health.

Offering a Description of Your Page

If you use search engines to any great extent, you no doubt have seen those that return the title of the page and then something like the first 25 words. Most of the time, the text makes no sense. Wouldn't it be great if you could tell the search engine what description to place on the search-results page? Yes, it would! (It's a sign the mind is starting to go when you keep answering your own questions.)

Here's the format:

```
<HEAD>
<TITLE>Page title</TITLE>
<META NAME="description" CONTENT="Come to my page please!">
</HEAD>
```

Pretty self-explanatory.

Author, Copyright, and Expire

These follow the basic format as given earlier.

`<META NAME="author" CONTENT="Joe Schmoe">` tells search engines who wrote the document.

`<META NAME="copyright" CONTENT="Copyright © 1997 Me">` tells search engines the copyright.

`<META NAME="expires" CONTENT="15 September 2000">` automatically expires the document in the search engine's database.

Where Do I Place These on My Page?

Between the HEAD commands, just after the TITLE commands.

Make sure your page's title come first because that is the first item many search engines use. WebCrawler does that. Also, don't put something in the title that is different from the rest of the page when you submit a page to a search engine. It may be clever, but it's messing up the search for your information. Change it on your server, but be sure to submit a copy that is done correctly.

What if I've Already Submitted the Pages?

What to do now depends on the search engine people. Many will only take a submission once. Some might take updates, but they are last on their list of priorities. Go to the search engine you submitted to and read their policies and take it from there.

Good question. I should write a full tutorial on just that. In fact, I did. It's next. Enjoy!

How Do I Register My Pages with Search Engines?

Why this tutorial? Didn't you sort of cover this in a few other places?

Yes. I cover registering pages a bit in the META commands tutorial and in the database tutorial, but I'm still getting email letters asking how this is done, so I thought I'd put something together. It's a fairly simple process.

Registering Pages—What's That?

My guess is that you've used a search engine if you've used the World Wide Web to any extent. You go to the site, put in some key words, and the server searches a database and returns pages that contain your words.

"Wouldn't it be nice If I could put my pages on the search engine?" you ask. "You can," I answer happily. To *register* your page is to place it in the database of the search engine. That's what I talk about here.

There's a long list of search engines located in Appendix C, "Valuable Links," in case you want to register with more than one engine. I register my pages with 25.

How It's Done

There are really only two ways to register your pages. You can either head to each search engine separately and register your page, or go to a registration site or a registration program that allows you to register your page with many different search engines a once.

Registering at Each Page

I've registered my pages at a few different search engines. Here's a general idea of what you're going to find:

- ● Hierarchy sites—These are sites that build pages of lists. Yahoo! (http://www.yahoo.com) is a site like this. As such, Yahoo! wants you to help a bit. You'll log on there, look for the category (or page) you feel you should be on, and than click the Submit icon at the top of the page. Magic occurs—you are asked to enter your URL address, a few other fine points, and that's that. Yes, you can apply your same page to more than one category page. There is usually no letter telling that you've been accepted.

- ● Webs—These are databases that do not have a certain hierarchy about them. It is just one huge group of pages. WebCrawler (http://www.webcrawler.com) is one of these. These are fairly simple to register with. There is usually an icon that says something like Submit URL on the main page. Click it and answer the same question you'll answer anywhere else.

Sometimes you won't even have to answer any questions.

What Are These Questions?

Usually they want things like this:

- ● Your name—Good luck with this. Please use your real name. It feels silly returning an email to someone named Snoogums Face.
- ● Your email address—Give it to them straight.

433

- Keywords—Much, much more can be found on these in the META commands tutorial just before this one. Quickly, these are words some (stress *some*) search engines use to locate your page. Choose broad topic words. Also use the roots of words. Use "dog" instead of "doggie." If you use "dog," "doggie" will be found. It's a root. Using "doggie" eliminates "dog" because "dog" is smaller than "doggie." That may have been the dumbest example on this site.

- Description—Tell us all about your site in 15 words or less. Again, see the META tutorial for loads on this.

- Wanna pay?—Some search engines offer higher-level searches, certain placement, or more input text if you pay a bit. That's up to you.

- Passwords—Some ask you for passwords so that you can go back in and edit your entry later.

Please keep in mind that each search engine is different. Some ask for information, some don't. Some allow you to re-submit or edit, some don't. Some ask you to put a link to their search engine in return, some don't. I could do this for days.

Again, you probably won't get any letters telling you your site was cataloged. Sometimes you get a little return letter thanking you for registering. What you need to do is wait a couple of weeks and go back and search for your site. If it doesn't show up, try again in another week. If you still don't get an answer, re-submit.

Registering at Many Pages from One Page

This is how your old buddy Joe does it every time. I go to a site named Submit-It! (http://www.submit-it.com). There are other sites that do this, but this is the only one I've ever used. I have a list of Web sites that will do multiple registrations in Appendix C. Many are pay-for deals, as is Submit-It!.

You'll also run into sites that offer to sell you a program that helps you submit. You may also get letters from companies that submit and check for you. The downfall of these methods is that they cost a little money. I know people who have paid for both. Some were pleased, some were not. I've never paid to submit a site to a search engine.

That's about it. Go and register a page just for the heck of it. Let one of the engines walk you through the process. You'll find that the number of visitors to your site goes up a bit, if not a lot. Mine did. See you on the Net...

Enjoy!

Getting Them All the Same: Cross-Platform Tips for HTML Artists

Ever since the advent of the browser wars, I have been inundated with questions about why one Web page looks so different on Internet Explorer and Netscape Navigator (and now Opera and others). This question never seemed to go away: How do I get my pages to look and work the same in all browsers?!

Here's the short answer: You can't. The browser creators have seen to it. Internet Explorer and Netscape Navigator are very different animals. They have different margin settings, different browser screen sizes, and different methods for rendering tables, just to name a few fun problems to come.

Why are they so different? It's an attempt to create a browser that has something the others don't in an effort to get you to use that browser. I believe it comes down to marketing, pure and simple. Create the different, and hopefully batter, mousetrap and users will surf a path to your door.

Some might state that the easiest way to go about getting pages to look the same across browser platforms is to use a browser choice JavaScript. I have one for you in Chapter 11, "Java Applets and JavaScript."

I don't buy it. The real solution is to create a Web page that looks good across all browsers.

Here, in no particular order, I go over 21 basic tips that help make your pages presentable, no matter what browser you choose.

Tip One: Put Multiple Browsers on Your Computer

If you have the hard drive space, install a version on Netscape Navigator (NN), Internet Explorer (IE), and Opera (O) on your computer. I have all three on mine and they don't interfere with each other. That way you can open your HTML document in multiple browsers to see what they look like before posting them to the Web.

Tip Two: Write for the Browser That Is Pickiest About Coding

That is Netscape Navigator. If your page looks good in Navigator, it will probably look good elsewhere. This is especially true in terms of tables. IE allows you to get away without ending every <TD> and <TR> command. NN does not. Everyone must be closed, otherwise the table doesn't render properly. If NN requires a certain coding, that's the coding scheme you go with.

Tip Three: Allow the Browser to Decide When Long Pieces of Text Wrap

If you have paragraphs, do not break the lines yourself—just write the text and allow the browsers to wrap it. If you break the text yourself, you may run into trouble when people have smaller screen settings. You'll get that lovely one long line, one short line look all the way down the page.

Tip Four: Force Text Issues

Do not assume that if you use one <FONT COLOR> command that every table cell's text will be altered—they won't. NN sees to that. Make sure that every table's cell data is defined with HTML flags.

Simple rule: When in doubt, add the flags. Make a point forcing every text alteration you want.

Tip Five: You May Want to Stay Clear of Style Sheets for a While

According to the brochures, both NN and IE support style sheet commands. If you've ever tried writing with them, you'll know that isn't always true. The scoop is that the World Wide Web Consortium adopted Microsoft's template of creating pages using style sheets— that made it standard in the industry. Netscape then adopted the standard for its browser. That should have done it, right? Wrong. As you have probably noticed, there are many non-standard commands out there that do not work cross-browser. Case in point, the <BLINK> command works in NN but not in IE.

Furthermore, style sheet commands are fairly new. Believe it or not, there are still people out there browsing with version 2.0 (and earlier) browsers. I'm not kidding, there are. Even if you do use standard style sheet coding, they are left out in the code.

Everything that standard style sheet commands can do can be done with HTML flags. Either create your page so that it doesn't matter if the style sheet commands don't render or use the HTML flags.

Tip Six: Be Kind to Those Who Are Surfing Without Images; Use ALT Commands

Many people surf without wanting to see images—really. I do it now and again. All browsers that support graphics also allow you to shut off the inline images. That means just the text displays. I still know people who surf with LYNX and CELLO, which are text-only browsers; you can find links for them in Appendix C.

ALT commands place text with an image. Read all about ALT commands in the HEIGHT, WIDTH, and ALT command tutorial in Chapter 3, "Adding Images and Backgrounds." If the browser displays the image, you can get a ToolTip box to pop up using an ALT command. For those who are not using images, the ALT commands make their surfing life so much easier by telling them where the images are.

When you use ALT commands, set the image text aside by at least surrounding it with square brackets, and maybe adding the word IMAGE in all caps, like so:

```
<IMG SRC="image.gif" ALT="[IMAGE: A dog running across the lawn]">
```

You should also know that using ALT commands helps surfers who are blind. There are now computers that read text aloud. ALT commands allow the user to know where and what the image is.

Tip Seven: If You Use Imagemaps, also Offer Hypertext Links

Offer hypertext links to everything that is linked in the imagemap for all the reasons outlined earlier. Use an ALT command to denote that it is an imagemap.

Tip Eight: Do Not Use Frames Unless You Have a Very Good Reason

Frames are supported by a most browsers, but that's not the concern—speed, download time, monitor screen settings, and text wrapping are. Remember, you are trying to let all people see your pages. Not everyone has your 56K dial-up or your Ethernet-driven G3 chip. Many are still attached to AOL with 14.4 modems. Be kind. Unless frames are required, go with single pages.

Tip Nine: JavaScript—I Love It, but Don't Get Crazy with It

JavaScript is another item that is supported by most, but not all, browsers. If you use JavaScript, make sure it is not a pivotal part of the page. Your page should run just fine without it. I find you can use event handlers without messing anyone up. See the advanced JavaScript tutorial in Chapter 11 for more on these.

If you do have a JavaScript marvel you want to share with the people, put it on its own page and offer a link to it. Make sure the link tells the user what is coming. If it's cool enough, people will click.

Tip Ten: Only Use Applets if It Is Necessary—And It Probably Isn't

Applets require a 32-bit operating platform to run; that's a Macintosh or Windows 95/98. If your user doesn't have that, she gets a gray box where the applet should be. Follow the same rules as outlined with JavaScript. Use an applet only if it is truly needed, and even then put it on its own page and allow people to click to it.

Tip Eleven: Always Use both the EMBED and BGSOUND Commands

Neither is supported by all browsers. If you are going to put background sound on a Web page, use both commands. That way both NN and IE users will be able to hear it.

Tip Twelve: Force Your Page's Layout and Design

The best way to accomplish this is to always place your page's elements inside table cells; it lays the page out beautifully. You can then always make the table cell's borders invisible by adding BORDER="0" to the main TABLE command. Read all about tables in Chapter 5, "All About Tables."

Tip Thirteen: Force Your Page's Width

Remember that computer monitors can have many different settings. This plays havoc with Web pages. Use the TABLE method to force your page to stay within certain parameters. I do this by placing every page inside one large table cell set to a specific width. Here's the code:

```
<HTML>
<HEAD>
<TITLE></TITLE>
</HEAD>
<BODY>
<CENTER>
<TABLE WIDTH="80%" BORDER="0">
<TD>
****Content of page goes here****
</TD>
</TABLE>
</CENTER>
</BODY>
</HTML>
```

I choose 80% as my width. That leaves a nice 10% border on either side of the page because I centered the table cell. It also sets the text perfectly inside each window setting; nothing rolls off the side. Smaller screen settings might smoosh the text a bit, but that's a trade-off I am willing to make. You'll never get perfection every time.

By the way, the same thing can be done using FRAME commands. You make one frame a certain pixel width and set everything else to 0; put the HTML document into the larger frame and a page with the same color background into the other. Here's what the code might look like:

```
<FRAMESET COLS="640,*"  MARGINWIDTH="0" MARGIN HEIGHT="0"
FRAMEBORDER="0' BORDER="0' FRAMESPACING="0">
<FRAME SRC="page.html">
<FRAME SRC="page2.html">
</FRAMESET>
```

If you want it centered, you can always change the code to COLS="*,640,*. It will work, but again, you are incorporating multiple pages.

Go with the table commands version I showed you earlier.

Tip Fourteen: If Possible, Use Percentages When Forcing Widths

I think this is the way to go as screen settings vary; if you set a width to 850 pixels, those with 800-width screens get a horizontal scrollbar—and no one wants that.

Remember that this isn't always possible. For example, you must be using pixels when denoting an image's height and width.

Tip Fifteen: Use GIF Format for Icons, JPEG Format for Larger Pictures

This is the way I have found it works best. GIF helps the smaller items keep their detail and JPEG helps the larger items load faster by being a compressed format.

Tip Sixteen: Try to Avoid META Refresh Tags

You can read about META refresh tags in Chapter 2, "Making Links." These are the tags that create what I call "dynamic pages," by jumping to a new page after a set amount of time. I love the look, but a text-only browser cannot support the command.

If you decide to use META refresh commands, make sure you have also posted a hypertext link so that people who do not get the effect can then click to go on.

Tip Seventeen: Always Double-Align Text and Images

Never assume that using an ALIGN="###" command will do the trick. Even if your table cells include an ALIGN="center" command, still surround the text with <CENTER> and </CENTER>.

The same goes for ALIGN="left" and right. Use <P ALIGN="left"> and </P> too.

Tip Eighteen: DHTML Is only Supported by IE 4.0 and Later

Only those IE 4.0 users can see it. Make a link to the page using DHTML so that the user can choose to go. Don't simply assume they are using the correct browser.

Tip Nineteen: When Denoting Colors, Try to Use the 216 "Safe" Colors

Appendix B, "Useful Charts," has the 216 non-dithering color chart, which includes the 216 colors that most operating systems support fully. You might notice they are all hex command color codes made up from the values 00, 33, 66, 99, CC, and FF. You can use any one of the colors and be pretty darn sure the end user's browser will support it.

Tip Twenty: If You Need to Pick a Screen Resolution to Design for, Choose 640×480

Yes, that's small, but pages conform better to larger environments than they do smaller.

The easiest way to do this is to set your own monitor resolution to 640×480. You can always change it back when you're done. It's your computer.

Tip Twenty One: Write Simply

Yes, I know that animations, JavaScript, applets, and background are really cool. I like them just as much as you do. But go easy on the flash. Content should be your main concern. Text and static images make a very good page if the user is interested in what you've written.

Look, you've seen MTV. If you're my age, it's VH1. If you're my wife, it's CMT. You know that no matter how great a video is, if the song it's set to stinks, forget it. You may look once, maybe twice, but after that the flash is not worth that poor content you have to listen to. See the analogy here?

If you want your pages to render well across browser versions and screen settings, you'll have to reign in your want to go for the latest thing. I love DHTML, it's great—but not everyone can see it.

Stay with the basics. Many people do not dive on the next browser version the day it comes out. Their version 3.0 browser works just fine. Heck, their version 1.0 version browser works just fine. I still have Netscape Navigator version 1.0. I really do. It's great to surf with. Just text and images, nice and fast.

Some may not like that reasoning because it means you cannot fill your pages with bells and whistles and the latest scripts that make images jump around. Don't assume the user has computer or browser to run the fancy formats. Always let the user see your simpler cross-browser page. Allow them to choose whether they have the correct equipment and to see the latest thing.

So think about your users, not those you will impress. You may not be as flashy, but I'll bet you get more hits.

How Do I Get My Own Domain? How the World Wide Web Works

I often get letters asking me how to go about getting a domain. Most of the time I simply answer the letters by stating that you pay for it. It's not a good joke, but you have to love the classics.

In this tutorial I do my best to explain how to go about getting your own section of the World Wide Web, and hopefully explain a little how the whole Internet works along the way.

A Domain

So, what's a domain? A *domain* is a larger site on the Net. cnn.com is a domain, as is yahoo.com. My domain happens to be htmlgoodies.com. In order to get a domain you need to do a little more than name your site and hope people show up. You need to let the entire Internet community know you're out there. You need to get your own set of IP numbers.

Stay with me, here.

IP Number?

Yeah. *IP* stands for Internet Protocol. This protocol is used for moving files around this web of computers we call the Internet. You need to have an IP address that does not change in order for your site to be recognized as a drop-off point for a packet of information.

I Already Have an IP

You are assigned an IP each time you attach if you use an Internet service provider (ISP). This does not apply to AOL or CompuServe users because they are not attached to the Internet as such, but are only allowed to surf through the use of AOL's browser.

You see, you do get an IP when you attach to your ISP, but that is a floating number, is only good for the one session, and is used mostly to assist in a packet downloads.

I'm Lost!

I figured you might be at this point. Let me continue by first explaining how the World Wide Web works. It makes this all much less confusing. Please note that it does get far more complicated than this, but this is the general idea, and a pretty good explanation if I do say so myself. I've read it already.

What's Happening?!

You're sitting in your easy chair surfing the Web. You enter the address `http://` `www.htmlgoodies.com`, click the Enter button, and you start receiving files that display on your screen. Pretty cool, huh? I think so.

First let's look at the universal resource locator (URL): `http://www.htmlgoodies.com`.

By the way, URL is just a fancy computer-speak way of saying address. I use the term at cocktail parties to impress my parent's friends. Outside of that, I say *address*.

- `http` stands for Hypertext Transfer Protocol. This is the *protocol*, or set of instructions the browser is to use to handle what's coming up. What's coming is hypertext, thus the need for hypertext transfer protocol. That makes sense.

- `://` is some left over UNIX commands that I wish the powers that be had gotten rid of a long time ago, but didn't. Think of `://` as "everything that follows should be handled this way." Put the two together and you can see that the beginning is saying that the following address is to be handled using Hypertext Transfer Protocol. Still with me?

- `www.htmlgoodies.com` is the actual address. In Internet lingo it's the URL.

The URL

`htmlgoodies.com` is my domain's URL. Now, if you have read into anything dealing with computers, you know that computers do not read text; computers read numbers. Period. If you type the letter Z, the computer displays a Z, but records it in its own memory a seven-digit series of 1s and 0s. This is called the ASCII code.

For now, just take my word that computers do everything with numbers. Text is simply displayed so you, the smart human, can understand what is going on.

So you, the smart human, enter `www.htmlgoodies.com`. The thing is, the dumb computer didn't look for `www.htmlgoodies.com`. It looked for a site named 204.170.191.236.

204.170.191.236?!

How did you say that so fast? Yes! 204.170.191.236. That's my set IP address. Anytime a computer on the Net looks around it sees other computers as numbers. It makes the attachment via finding the correct number, not the correct text. The text has been placed there to make it a whole lot easier on you. It wouldn't be much fun if someone asked you for your home page address and you had to recite `"pi.pi.pi.pi"` on down the line to the fiftieth decimal place. It's easier to just say you're at `bob.com`, although not much easier.

How Does It Do That?

This is where the magic is—all the stuff you don't see that goes on behind the curtains: Somewhere between you and the site you want to find is something called a *DNS*. That stands for a domain name server. It has a really, really long list of domain names and the numbers that correspond. Usually, the ISP that you have your page on has its own DNS server. If not, they are attached to one nearby.

The DNS reads the text you put in, changing that text into the corresponding IP number, and then sends the request off and into cyberspace. If that seems like one more step than is required, it is. But isn't it worth it to be able to type in words rather than remember some long strain of numbers? I knew you would agree. All of you except that guy in Topeka, Kansas. He doesn't agree with anything I say.

Have you ever put in an address and received a message that the server you requested didn't have a DNS entry? Well, now you know what that means. The DNS server can't find a number that lines up with the text you entered.

Where Do These Numbers Come From?

The InterNIC Registration Service is the government agency that hands out IP numbers, at least for IP numbers in the USA. Yes Virginia, there is an Internet, Inc. These people are in charge of handing out the IP numbers. The cost was $100 for two years. It's now been lowered to $70—not a bad price. Plus you don't have to tip. You send them the request and you get back a number if the name you want isn't taken or offensive. In addition, that number is made known to all the world's DNS servers. Oh, it's quite a system.

I actually didn't fill out the forms myself. The company that set up my virtual domain did it for me. *Virtual?* Easy now. I'm not done explaining the IP numbers yet.

Who Gets What Number?

We have the fine people at the Department of Defense, the DOD, to thank for this Internet setup. They came up with the concept somewhere in the late 1950s. Back then, this system was to simply interlock a few hundred computers so information could be safely passed around even in the event of an attack. It was never thought that people would be using this marvel to download naked pictures of Terri Hatcher. Heck, she wasn't even born yet.

Class A

The IP numbers are in four sections called *octets*. If you encounter a site that has its first octet as 126 or lower, it is one of the first sites to ask for the use of an IP address. It is also very big. The problem is that there can only be 126 of these very big servers. IBM has one of these type addresses, as does the National Science Foundation and a few huge commercial servers. These sites can be found by DNS simply with the use of the first octet of its IP number. Any site with this type of IP number is known as a *class A server*.

Class B

Class B servers are found using the first two octets. They are servers that have an IP number from 127 through 254 in the first position. What is in the second position depends on what number was assigned to them by InterNIC. In case you're wondering, this allows for 64,514 different addresses.

Class C

Class C servers use the first three octets to denote who they are to DNSs. You can do the math, but the available number of these servers is over a million.

Class D

I'm a class D server. In fact, I'm not a server at all. More to come.

The IP addresses work to do two things. They find a host on the Internet and they choose a certain section once they get to the host. Imagine an IP number of 122.9.4.4.

It may be a real number, I don't know. I made it up for demonstration purposes. It's obvious that number is assigned to a big, huge server because its first octet is less that 126. Notice then that the next three octets are only one number each. That's because the IP address is being used to find other servers inside 122.

If 122 is IBM, maybe 122.9.4.4 is IBM's main business server, and 122.4.3.3 is their employee Web page server. Many larger universities have 10 or 12 different servers on campus. In fact, they could have up to 254, each receiving a different number at the end of the IP. The university is given an IP of class B and different assignment IPs under that. The technical name for these sub-servers is *subnets*. Once an IP is assigned, any sites under the umbrella of that IP are denoted by the first octets and the numbers that follow. In addition, subnets do not have to carry the server's domain name. It is possible for a server called joe.com to assign a subnet IP number to a domain called fred.com. As long as the number stays static, the DNSs will find it; they'll just find it as a subnet of the server it is on. This is that virtual server I spoke of earlier.

Starting to see how this all works?

I don't mean to imply here that only servers are assigned IP numbers. Any computer attached to the Internet has an IP assigned. The IPs assigned to servers are set; they are the same no matter what. If you attach with your home computer, you too have an IP assigned to your computer, but it is not a set IP. Rather, it is one assigned to you for the duration of your attachment.

How Do I Find Out What a Domain's IP Number Is?

You can do that using ping. Head to the Windows 95 DOS prompt after you are attached to your server. Use the Telnet command prompt in Macintosh and Windows 3.*x*. At the prompt, type in **ping** and then the address of the server you want the number for. Press Enter. A request is sent and an IP address is returned.

There are also many shareware ping programs available on the Internet. You can go to `http://www.shareware.com` to look through a few.

Getting Your Own Domain

Now we finally get to the real reason you came here. How do you get your own IP address and start you own domain, `www.yournamehere.com`! There are two basic ways:

- Buy a connection to the Internet, a DNS, dedicated ISDN lines, modem ports, hire a technician, and set up three or four very expensive Internet servers. $$$$!
- Get a virtual domain.

I opted for the latter. The first choice is good if you want to start your own server, sell space on the server, and make a true business of it all. I just wanted to write tutorials and answer email. I have a virtual domain.

Virtual Domain

I went to a gentleman here in central Pennsylvania and asked if I could have a domain on his big huge expensive server. He said "Yup." What he did was set aside a subnet of his server and called it `www.htmlgoodies.com`. He then applied for an IP address for that section of the server.

The IP number of the server I am on is 204.170.191.1. It is a class C server using the first three full octets as the DNS; my IP number again is 204.170.191.236. The numbers are the same, except that the fourth octet is extended from 1 to 236. When you put in `www.htmlgoodies.com` and press Enter, you are actually going to a domain called `Sunlink.net` in Sunbury, Pennsylvania. ISPs are usually not so much one server but a cluster of servers. You're going more to a domain than to a specific server. Once you get there, you are immediately routed to a certain section of one of the servers on the domain denoted as 236, or `www.htmlgoodies.com`. Ta da!

Don't I Have an IP Number Already?

Most people on the Web have an address something like `www.server.com/~fredflintstone` or `www.server.com/bedrock/~barneyrubble`. What you have is a section of the server just like I do, but your section does not have its own IP number.

When someone comes to see your site, they type in `www.server.com` first. That is the address. That carries the IP number. You are found after the IP address is used to find the server. Your portion of the server is denoted through a tilde (pronounced *till-duh*) or through the use of `/subdirectory/after/subdirectory`. After the server is found, the stuff written after the server address is then used to send the user to your site.

By the way, a tilde (~) is a UNIX shortcut that means, "there is only one directory in this entire server titled fredflintstone, find it!"

When you attach to an ISP using PPP or SLIP, you are assigned an IP number. It can be different every time. That floating number denotes your computer. You know that when you download something, it comes right into your computer. The Internet knows how to do that because you have, while you're attached, an IP number that tells the Internet where to send the information you are downloading. Your computer is literally part of the Web. The number is gone after you log out.

That number you are given acts underneath your server's class A, B, or C IP. You are given a floating IP number like you were a subserver of your main server. That's because you are a subserver while you're attached. You can send and receive files like the main server...sort of. That number is not an assigned IP, but it's not recognized outside your server's domain; thus it is not a true domain. People can't take information from your computer unless you're attached. Because I have my own IP address, I am attached all the time and you can stop in anytime.

You can do what I did to get your own domain—head to your own server head, Webmaster, or technician, and ask if you can purchase space to set aside as a virtual domain. Your current server may not offer you the ability to do this. If you're serious, try another, and another. Sooner or later you'll find a local server that will set the whole thing up for you.

How Much Does It Cost?

That really depends on the cost structure of the server offering the domain. Depending on service, level of equipment, and amount of traffic you are expecting, prices can range widely.

You'll usually pay in two levels: a monthly fee of some sort and a cost for how often your site is visited or downloaded. Oftentimes there is only a monthly fee, but that monthly fee is set higher or lower depending on the traffic you generate.

What Do I Call Myself?

That's up to you. You just need to make sure the name isn't already in use. Head to either a DOS prompt or a Telnet prompt after attaching to your server and type `whois` and your proposed name. If you get an answer that it can't find the name, try entering the name into your browser. If you get a DNS entry error, there's a pretty good chance you're the first to think of it. Try and get it. But, even if it appears that the name doesn't exist, you may still be out of luck. The domain may not be posted, but it still may be owned. There are groups that buy domains that others may want. All the given names are bought: joe.com, bob.com, jane.com, plus other common words. The reason is that if you want the domain bad enough, you might buy it from them. Pretty clever and quite forward thinking if you ask me.

Final Warning

Do yourself a favor when you are deciding on a server to house your virtual domain. Make price the very last option you consider. Yes, I know there are servers out there that offer a domain for little or nothing per month, but what do you get other than the name and a place to store files? Ask a few questions:

- How many other domains will I be sharing the machine with?
- How fast is the server?
- How much memory does the server have? If the answer is not 64MB or better, say no.
- Do I have Telnet, FTP, email, and directory-making capabilities?
- How many email boxes do I get?
- Can I run an FTP server, too?
- What about space? Does it cost more for more space?
- Are you charging me for the space, the download volume, or for the number of hits?
- Can I run each payment method for a month and see which is best for me?
- Can I sign a month-to-month contract?
- What if the server breaks? Does it cost to fix it? The answer should be no because it is not your machine.
- Am I backed up anywhere in case the server hard drive dies?
- Can I talk directly to a service technician? I mean talk—not email and hope to get a response.
- Is someone available 24 hours a day?
- Can I place CGI scripts?
- Do I have access to modification changes?
- Can I buy my own server in the future?
- Can I run advertising off this server?
- Can I run a chat room?
- Has the server paid blanket fees to BMI or ASCAP so that I can play sound recordings from my site?
- Any RealAudio capabilities?

- Who else is using this server? Can I talk to them?
- What does it all cost me? The lowest price may cost the most in service and data. People won't come to your site if they can't get into it.

Enjoy!

How Do I Get Advertisers on My Site?

Note to you: The following is a tutorial that people have been asking me to write for some time now. This consists almost entirely of my opinion; most of the information comes from my slant having gone through the process. There are other ways of doing this. This is my way of doing it. So far, it's worked. The topics discussed are from different emails I have received.

What Do You Have That People Want?

That's a bold question—but it's a pretty good one. I get letters all the time saying they want to advertise on their home page. I say great! How many people are coming in a day? I'm not talking hits mind you, I'm talking visitors. How many? Furthermore, does that warrant someone paying money for your site?

Hits Versus Visitors Versus Impressions

When you are talking to a possible advertiser about the number of people that roll through your site in a day, month, or year, the advertiser usually wants to know about impressions or visitors. Too often this gets confused with the concepts of hits. Here are the differences:

- Hits—A *hit* is a request of the server. Let's say, for example, that you have a page that has five graphics on it. That page is equal to six hits, the page and then the five graphics. Sometimes people report hits to a possible advertiser. This is wrong because it creates an inflated report of site traffic. If I could report hits alone, I could create graphics-filled pages and report numbers well into the millions, no sweat.
- Visitors—*Visitors* are the number of actual people coming into the site. This is a count of actual people.
- Impressions—Also called *page views*. This denotes the number of pages viewed, or more specifically, the number of ad banners viewed. Where this differs from visitors is that one visitor can create multiple impressions by seeing many different pages. A thousand visitors might create thirty-thousand impressions.

What Is the Magic Number?

Ten thousand visitors per month. The question I am asked time and time again is how many people must come through the site for it to be worth selling to an advertiser. When I first was interested in gaining advertisers, the number I kept hearing was 10,000 visitors per month. Not 10,000 hits, but 10,000 visitors. This appears to be the threshold where a serious advertiser will begin to talk to you.

How Much Do I Ask For?

How much do you need? I don't mean that to be clever, either. What does it cost you in both hardware and time each month to run your site? I add time to that list because you must put in time. People want to be able to talk to, or email, a real person. People also want to see change and improvement. It is my opinion that a site must evolve or it will die. I am forever answering email or writing a new tutorial.

Now stop and think how much profit you want to make. Yes, we'd all like to make 500% profit, but that's not always possible. You may price yourself right out of contention.

Finally, be flexible. You know what you want, but maybe an advertiser would like a break in price. You might say okay if they then offer to buy for five months rather than one, or pay up front. There is always a deal to be made.

Flat-Rate CPM, Click-Throughs, or Impressions?

Your choice. I always go with a flat rate per 1,000 impressions, called a *CPM* (cost per thousand). I think it is most fair to the advertiser. As I suggested, I often give more impressions than I offer. That's good for the advertiser and shows good faith on my part. The advertiser also has it easier with flat rate because he can budget easily and forecast whether he can remain on my site next month.

If you go by exact number of impressions, you make the cost a floating number and that makes it harder to forecast dollars. It may lead to the end of an advertiser relationship. Plus, with a floating rate you need to prove exact numbers, which are far more difficult to provide than simply hitting a plateau of visitors.

Selling by click-throughs is another popular method. A *click-through* is when someone clicks the advertiser's banner to see what it links to. I've seen contracts anywhere from .20 cents to $1 per click-through.

The problem with click-through advertising is that you need to be able to keep track of the clicks. I do it with a program I purchased that rotates my advertising banners and records impressions and clicks. The program is from Central Ad Pro (http://www.centralad.com) and cost me around $600. You have to decide if that is worth it to you. If it isn't, how will you track people?

How Much Does HTML Goodies Ask For?

None of your business. Just kidding. I used to have different costs for each of the pages. When I created `htmlgoodies.com`, I asked for $500 if you wanted to be at the top of the main page. Each tutorial was $200. That was for one calendar month.

That meant I could offer 150,000 impressions for $500. Maybe that will help you decide on the amount you want to charge as you're getting off the ground.

As I said, I am now using a CPM rate. I also have someone selling for me. The site has over three million impressions a month. Those are number I can't begin to think about. I actually stay pretty far away from the money side of the site. I believe the rates now run about $30 or better for a thousand impressions, depending on the deal. The site's pretty profitable.

How Do I Get Started?

I would suggest putting together two things, after putting together the Web site, of course:

- A description of the site—Make this detailed. It's a PR-type thing. Say someone asks you to send some information about your site and what it offers. This is the information you would send them.
- A rate card—This is a listing of every page and its price, or how much per 1,000 impressions, or however you are going to do it. You may only be selling the main page. If so, great. List it.

Getting Advertisers

There a couple ways of doing this. I only use one.

- Sell yourself.
- Hire someone to sell for you.

Sell Yourself

Get out there! Press the flesh! Shake a few hands! Slap a few backs! Sell! Sell! Sell!

Not much I can say here but to sell where you might find clients. Head to Internet shows; write to advertisers over the Net; put your pages on every search engine you can find; post a rate card for all to see. I've never really done this, outside of people asking about advertising simply because the site was there. I personally have never solicited for an advertiser outside of a return email now and again.

Hire Someone to Sell for You

This is what I did. I felt I put enough time in working on the site. I'd head to the poor house before I made any contacts, so I hired a company to sell for me. I think it's the best way.

The one downfall is that you don't get to keep all the money. These people won't work for free, you know! There is always a commission involved. In my case, it's 30% of the gross. There is also usually a statement that says you don't get paid until the advertiser pays. You may run a banner for a while, the advertiser doesn't pay, and you lose out. It happens; it's part of doing business.

What About Advertising to Get Advertisers?

I guess you can. The only problem with that is that they want to post a banner, which takes away from space you may sell in the future, it and appears that you have banners already and might not need advertising.

I'm just a big believer in "build a better mousetrap and they will come." Just make a point of registering all your pages so that you are fairly easy to find when someone goes looking for what you offer.

Read my tutorial in this chapter on registering your pages; it describes search engine databases and helps you learn more about getting people to your page with engines' aid.

How Many Advertisers Should Go on One Page?

That depends on you and your advertisers. Some advertisers want to be the only one on the page and will write that directly into a contract. Other advertisers allow themselves to be around other banners if they themselves are at or close to the top. My limit was four when I had the old format of one long page linking everything, two at the top, one in the middle, and one at the bottom. I offered special prices to the one at the bottom.

Now that I use a program to rotate my banners for me, I go a few per page. You'll notice from your surfing that ad banners come in different sizes. Smaller banners allow for more per page and less intrusion. It's always going to boil down to your choice; it's a delicate balance between making money and cluttering your pages.

If you do start selling ad space on your site, let me suggest that you also purchase a program that posts banners to pages on-the-fly. If you assign specific ad banners to specific pages, it tends to make the site look static. The CentralAd program I use works well for posting on-the-fly ads.

Final Thoughts

It is my opinion that undertaking advertising is more than a hobby on the side. You must look at this as a small business. Not only must you offer something nice to attract people, but you need to continually update and add to what you offer. You need to keep balance sheets for tax purposes. It's hard to hide that you're making money on the WWW—everyone can see it.

Most important of all, ask yourself what you have that people want. The purpose should be providing something people will come to see. The advertising will come easily after that.

Finally, I can give no better thought-provoking information than this: This site was up and running for five months before I made a penny in profit. Now that it is getting established, I am making enough for the site to pay for itself, and a dinner out with my wife once a week...and that's about it.

May you become rich! I'm certainly not...not yet, anyway.

Enjoy!

So You Want a Web Ring, Huh?

Like most really good ideas, Web rings are simple and effective. Anyone can set one up on any topic and it doesn't take rocket science brain power to get it up and running. "Me do Web ring good," as I like to say.

Web Ring?

Yup. Easy concept. Let's say you have a Web page that discusses your overt love for collecting foam rubber from couches and sofas produced in the mid 1970s. Let's also say, and this is a long shot, that there are 10 other people out there who have a similar page. One guy does foam rubber from La-Z-Boys. Another guy collects foam rubber from chairs that were sat on by famous Americans. Whatever.

Now you, the main foam rubber guy, decides it would be nice if others who are foam rubber-inclined could just jump from one page to another, all dealing with foam rubber. You set about creating a Web ring.

Web Ring Method One: Linear Rings

A Web ring is just what it is named—it's a series of pages, all with a common theme, that are all linked to one another.

Let's say there are 10 pages in all. One person sets herself up as the "ringmaster" and takes charge. With a little bit of planning, all you really need is a section of the page denoting that the current page is part of a ring. Provide a link to the page preceding you in the ring, and the page following that page in the ring; a user can move in a linear fashion through the ring. Just make sure the last page in the series then links back to the first page. Done: Web ring.

The only hard part about all of this is when a new page joins the ring. It's up to the ringmaster whether she should be added at the end or somewhere in the middle, nearer a page it couples with. Either way, the links have to be kept up-to-date and those in the ring have to be willing to make updates when you ask.

Web Ring Method Two: Generated Rings

This is a better way of setting up and mastering a ring. You have one central location for the ring and those who want to attach simply put a line of code into their page. A JavaScript, or some other type of interface, is contacted every time someone clicks to go to the next page in the ring.

I'm seeing rings now that have options for Previous Page, Next Page, and Random. I guess that's good, but isn't going for a random page sort of killing the whole concept of moving through a ring? It's just my opinion; take it for what it's worth.

 With a little thinking, you can use a myriad of random and linear JavaScripts to set this all up. I went through Java Goodies and found a couple that would do the trick. The one by Qirien Dhaela (`http://www.htmlgoodies.com/javagoodies/webring.html`*) is set up to do just that—be a Web ring. It places three buttons on your page allowing you to choose next, previous, and random. It's slick and can be run on all Web ring pages, or as an external JavaScript so members only have to place a simple* `SCRIPT` *code on their page.*

 If random is your thing, see the links section of Java Goodies (`http://www.htmlgoodies.com/javagoodies/but.html`*) for a number of random links scripts that allow for one-click Web-ring ease. However, going with only a random link generator might mean that the same page comes up twice or three times in a row. It is random, you know.*

Web Ring Method Three: Let Someone Else Handle It!

If you haven't been already, you should head to `http://www.webring.com` if you have any interest in joining or creating a ring. The site provides over 22,000 rings for you to join. If you can actually think of a topic that isn't already covered, they'll let you become your own ringmaster. Gosh!

Now here's the good part. It's free (at least it was at the time of this writing).

In order to go through the process, I signed the online version of this tutorial up with a Web ring. I still write the bulk of my HTML stuff in NotePad, so I attached this page to the "Made with NotePad" ring. Here's what happened:

- I went to `Webring.com` and looked at the full list of available rings, did a search, and ended up wanting to join the Made with NotePad ring.
- The NotePad ring is kept at `http://www.pvideos.demon.co.uk/notepad/`. I got to the page by clicking a link that appeared when I saw the full list of all the sites that are part of the ring.
- I clicked the link that said I wanted to join the ring and got my general issue stuff.

- I was asked to take a banner (you'll see it in a minute) and a few lines of code to put on my Web page. I had to alter the code slightly so that the image was being called for correctly, but that was very minor. I also had to put in my email address.

- Next I filled out a short form giving my page's address, its title, and a few other items, such as a description and keywords.

- You are also asked for a password. Write it down—don't forget it.

- I clicked to submit all this to Webring.com.

- You're registered if you do not get any errors.

- For this particular NotePad Web ring, I had to email the owner and tell him that I had posted the items. He took a look at the page and had the final yes or no as to whether it would become part of the ring. He chose yes.

I can't say that each and every one of the ring-joining experiences will be just like this, but I'll bet they're all pretty close. By the way, here's the exact HTML code I received when I signed up:

```
<!-- Begin NotePad Ring Fragment-->
        <font size=2>
        <center>
                <CENTER>
        <br><IMG SRC="notepad.gif" HEIGHT="50" WIDTH="340"
        border="0" usemap="#notepad.map"><br>
        </CENTER>
<br>
This <a href="http://www.pvideos.demon.co.uk/notepad/"
        target=_top>NotePad Ring</a> site is owned by
        <a href="mailto:jburns@htmlgoodies.com">Joe Burns</a>.<br>
        Click for the [
        <a
        href="http://www.webring.org/cgi-bin/webring?
id=308&ring=notepad&next"
        target=_top>Next Page</a> ¦
        <a
        href="http://www.webring.org/cgi-bin/webring?
id=308&ring=notepad&skip"
        target=_top>Skip It</a> ¦
        <a
        href="http://www.webring.org/cgi-bin/webring?
id=308&ring=notepad&next5"
        target=_top>Next 5</a> ]
        <br>
        Want to join the ring? Click here for
        <a href="http://www.pvideos.demon.co.uk/notepad/"
```

```
target=_top>info</a>.
<br></center></font>
<map name="notepad.map">
<area shape="rect" coords="0, 0, 60, 70" target="_top"
href="http://www.pvideos.demon.co.uk/notepad/">
<area shape="rect" coords="465, 0, 549, 75" target="_top"
href="http://www.webring.org/cgi-bin/webring?
id=308&ring=notepad&next">
</map>
<!-- End Webring Fragment-->
```

Figure 15.1 shows the image and what appeared on they page when I posted that code into a Web page.

Figure 15.1
Web ring code.

And that's that. As you can see, it goes from super simple to pretty involved, depending on if you want to be a member or actually run your own Web ring. But like I said earlier, the best ideas are those that are usually the simplest.

Enjoy!

So You Want a Password-Protected Page?

Ever since word got out that I was working on this tutorial, I have been bombarded with requests to "Hurry up!" Well, here it is; you may not be happy with the answers I give you. Then again, you may. I don't know you.

The answer is that you can't do this with HTML commands alone. Password protection is done at the server level. You see, I was not waiting all this time in order to write a large tutorial, but rather for my Webmaster to arrange a protected directory in my account.

Here's What Happens

First, tell your Webmaster, server tech, or the guy who takes your checks each month that you want to do password-protected pages. He will immediately ask what you have that is so darn important that you require these pages. You say, "None of your business" and ask again.

A protected directory will be created for you after a short time. Not a page-by-page protection, but a directory. Basically, the technical people set aside a whole section of the server hard drive as protected. Every page you put into that directory requires a login and a password.

Some new files are added to that directory. These are the three most common files:

1. `.htpassword`   This is a password file (duh). It contains one password for each login you denote to the server. It should be created initially with a password for you, its "owner." If you start playing around with this file, never delete the initial password; otherwise you can't get in again to make changes.

2. `.htgroup`   This contains the logins you denote. How you change or add logins or passwords depends on how the technician sets up your server. I have to Telnet into my server directly, enter some cryptic UNIX commands, and answer a couple of questions to prove I am who I am. I can then enter logins and passwords to my heart's content.

3. `.auth`   This is a possible third file. Some servers allow you to enter passwords and logins directly to an HTML document. This is that document. It's very easy this way. A nice form page comes up and you just enter it all straight away. I didn't get this. You may not either.

When you enter a login and password, it works for everything you placed in that protected directory. That means that the server won't continue to ask for passwords when a new page is requested.

Do All Servers Work This Way?

My tech informs me that any system can be configured a hundred ways, but no matter what the files are named, what I have just described is what happens. At least two files, one password and one login, are added to your accounts and you configure them to allow only certain people in.

You need to call your Webmaster and ask for the protected directory to get things started, and I'll ask before he does: What exactly do you have that is so important that must be protected? I know. None of my business.

Enjoy!

What Is XML?

The buzzword *XML* is beginning to pop up all over the Net, as well as in the Goodies email box. People are wondering what this new language is and how it's going to effect the way people write. To be honest, I was wondering the same thing until I started looking into it.

You'll find XML mentioned in Appendix A, "Everything You Need to Know about HTML 4.0," and in Chapter 13, "Internet Explorer Tutorials and DHTML." The language is starting to make a few in-roads into the Web and that makes a few people nervous. As one Goodies reader put it, "I just got pretty good with HTML, and now they're bringing out this thing." I feel your pain. It means I need to learn it all first so that I can teach it to you.

Here we go. This first tutorial is an introduction to what the heck this XML thing really is.

What Is It?

You mean in five words or less? That can't be done. XML stands for Extensible Mark-up Language. Seems strange that the first word is Extensible, yet they use the *X* to denote the word. My guess is that XML looked a lot cooler than EML.

Lineage

You may not know this but HTML and XML are brother and sister. Their mother is SGML. SGML (Standard Generalized Mark-up Language) is the overriding language that sprang both XML and HTML.

SGML is not a language per se, but a series of commands that are all understood by another program. JavaScript is a similar example. By itself, there's not much to it, but if you use the JavaScript commands in a particular order and then allow a Web browser to read it, you get some neat effects.

DTD—Document Type Definition

SGML is what is known as a *meta-language*; it allows a programmer to write a DTD (document type definition) that numerous pages can follow. For instance, JavaScript you use a word processor. Say you type the letter *j*. Something inside that word processor must understand what you did and display that letter. That's the DTD. You then alter the letter's size, font, and color. Again, the commands the word processor used were all understood and acted upon by using the DTD as a guide.

HTML uses DTDs. Ever seen one of these at the very top of a page's source code?

```
<!doctype html public "-//w3c//dtd html 4.0//en">
```

That's a *document declaration*. It states that the DTD to be used is HTML 4.0 is English. See that? Where is the DTD actually located? In the browser. Yup, Netscape Navigator, Internet Explorer, Opera, and Mosaic are more than programs that display pretty little pictures—they are actually carrying a DTD so that the browser knows how to handle it when you type a command like <B>, <UL>, or <CENTER>. The browser sees the command <B>; it goes to its DTD to check what that command is supposed to do. It sees that the command makes things bold. The effect is then generated.

The one drawback with a word processor, and HTML, is that you cannot set up your own DTDs. HTML is a very stable mark-up language format; the commands mean the same thing everywhere. The language is easy to learn because, to some extent, it is like playing blocks. The tools you use are never changing. JavaScript is more difficult because you are actually creating the blocks before you play with them.

Actually, that's XML's purpose: to allow you to create your own blocks to play with.

Making Your Own Blocks

Say you want to create a document where a certain type of text is going to bold, italic, red, 25 point, Arial font, and a few other fancy things. And this type of text appears a great many times. In HTML you need to write out the start and end flags every time you made the text, or you can set up a style sheet to do that. That's the general idea here. You set up a giant style sheet type document that acts as "mother" for all the other documents. What's the difference? Style sheets work inside HTML documents. You have to create one to use the other. Creating your own DTD eliminates one whole step in the process—the HTML.

Fine, but What Is XML?

XML is a simplified version of SGML intended to allow people like you and me a pretty good shot at learning it. SGML is wide open. It is a 10,000-piece jigsaw puzzle with double-sided pieces spread all over the floor. XML is the same jigsaw puzzle with big sections already put together.

So What's Wrong with HTML?

My personal opinion is that nothing is wrong with it. It was the first computer language that could be understood and used by the masses. It gave the Web to the common person. Those in the XML know claim that HTML is clunky; they say it's become static. There's not a lot more one can do with it. Supposedly, XML will allow a lot more flexibility in your Web pages. There will also be more flexibility in your HREF links. You'll be able to create cross references, threads, and other fun stuff. At least that's what the brochure says.

HTML is not dead, nor is it breathing funny. HTML will be around for years to come, if not forever. It is still a solid format and too many people know it. I believe I will be able write HTML and post Web pages as long as I live using HTML alone. They just might not be as fancy as other pages.

Two Kinds of XML Pages

The two main types of XML pages are the standalone and those that use a DTD. The *standalone* is just what it says: The page stands alone, relying on the browser to have the XML DTD. In the XML language, the browser is the XML processor. The other type of page offers the DTD to the browser so that it can run the page.

The Standalone

The standalone can be created by simply making some alterations to your current HTML document:

- Lose the current declaration statement and replace it with this one:

    ```
    <?XML version="1.0" standalone="yes"?>
    ```

- Remember that XML is case sensitive. If you use caps to start the command, use caps to end the command.

- This format of caps or no caps must continue fully through the document. If you use IMG first, you must continue to capitalize it the rest of the way through; otherwise the XML DTD will see it as two different commands.

- All tags that do not require end tags (such as <IMG> or <P>) must now be given one.

- All tags that did not require an end tag must also be given a slash before the final >. Like so:

    ```
    <IMG SRC="pic.jpg" /></IMG>
    ```

- Each subcommand must be surrounded by quotation marks, such as TEXT="brown".

- Lose all & commands and ASCII code characters.

- Make sure you are running the page in a browser that supports XML.

If you have followed all these rules, you have created a document that is termed *well-formed*. That means it will run. You see, XML is nowhere near as forgiving as HTML.

Creating the DTD

The second type of page uses a DTD. In XML, you need to set up your own DTD items, which are called *entities* in the business. Each entity allows you to create you own tag in a traditional HTML format. Entities themselves do nothing. They simply block off sections of the page. Any text that happens to be captured inside that space is then affected by the parameters assigned to the entity. Sound familiar? HTML works the same way. For example, say you wanted to create the tag <SUPER> that would make text red and underlined. (As far as I know that one doesn't exist in HTML.) The basic format is given here; please understand that there is a bit more than this, I am just trying to stay basic at first to keep us all on the same page.

- You would create a basic text file with a DTD extension. This file would hold all the entities.

- Create an entity like this one in the DTD file:

```
<!ELEMENT SUPER (#PCDATA¦u¦ff0000)*>
<!-- Tag attribute - red and underlined -->
```

- Now save the DTD text document as joe.dtd.

- Put up a declaration like this one on the XML document you are writing for display in the browser window:

```
<?xml version="1.0"?>
<!DOCTYPE SYSTEM "joe.dtd">
```

  The SYSTEM command denotes that the DTD can be found on the system running the XML document.

- Now you are prepared to add the command to the XML document, like so:

```
<SUPER>this is the effected text</SUPER>
```

- Again, this is a very simplistic offering. If you would like to view an honest and true DTD, try http://www.sil.org/sgml/xmlspec-19980323-dtd.txt. It's frightening, to say the least.

Is There More?

Yupper! In fact, there's much more. I don't know how goofy into this stuff you are, but if this is your bag, XML certainly offers some enjoyable reading before bed. There isn't a lot written on the subject (I mean in a relative fashion, like when compared to the number of pages available on the music group Hanson), but what is written is very thick—very technical. It takes some plowing through, but you'll start to see it all come together after spending the time.

I relied on five main sites when putting this tutorial together:

- W3.org—Extensible Mark-up Language (XML): Part I. Syntax. This is a very technical site.

  http://www.w3.org/TR/WD-xml-lang-970331.html

- XML.com—Fantastic site, very helpful. It takes the technical document from W3.org and explains each section in greater detail.

  http://www.xml.com

460

- Robin Cover's XML Page at `sil.org`.

  `http://www.sil.org/sgml/xml.html`

- Frequently asked questions about Extensible Mark-up Language. This is written a lot like I write; you'll understand it.

  `http://www.ucc.ie/xml/#FAQ-GENERAL`

- What the ?XML? a Fun page on Geocities.

  `http://www.geocities.com/SiliconValley/Peaks/`
  `5957/xml.html`

These authors deserve far more of the credit than I. For a great deal more than is given here, try the Yahoo! XML page: `http://www.yahoo.com/Computers_and_Internet/` `Information_and_Documentation/Data_Formats/XML/`.

So Now What?

Well, nothing really. XML is still in the test stages. The XML Working Group, a body created to set the language somewhat in stone, has not quite arrived upon the golden goose (as of the time of this writing, at least). But they will soon enough.

Netscape plans to put XML into its future browser versions. You can read about the XML inclusion here or mozilla itself at `http://www.mozilla.org`. Those of you who are Explorer fans can read up on their current and future efforts to incorporate XML at `http://` `www.microsoft.com/xml/xmlfaq-f.htm`. I don't know if Opera plans to get into the XML pool.

Gluttons for XML punishment can read about how XML will be used in cooperation with cascading style sheets at `http://webreview.com/wr/pub/97/11/28/xml/index.html`. Those of you advanced enough to know some of the inner workings of Perl programming can visit their XML/Perl site at `Perl.com`. Or have fun learning why Perl and XML might be the best of friends at `http://webreview.com/wr/pub/97/12/05/xml/index.html`.

XML is still a ship on the horizon. We can see it coming, but goodness only knows when it will hit the docks, and yet you can start XML right now if you'd like. Internet Explorer 4 already has some limited capabilities to act as an XML processor when you incorporate its active channels.

My personal plan of action is to hurry up and wait. I am a big fan of watching to see if the new wave of the moment hits hard. Those people who are advanced enough at this game to program a bowling ball and three packs of Bubble gum to play Pac Man will jump on this right off the bat. I want to see if this is the DHTML or the VRML of the future. I can only offer help in case of an XML landslide.

Enjoy!

So You Want to Screen Capture?

Here's a quick tutorial about screen captures, thus the title. If you're not sure what a screen capture is, think about the pages you've seen lately: Maybe some of them have had specific sections of the desktop or a program made into an image. It was almost as if they captured part of the screen as an image.

Well, the person did capture part of the screen—it is a *screen capture.*

Be Careful of Violating Copyright Laws!

What I'm about to show you is going to give you the ability to copy anything your computer displays, like those little Microsoft icons, among other things—but remember that those images are copyrighted. Make sure you either give credit when using the image or ask permission. Yes, you can just copy and post, but that doesn't mean it's legal.

I should say that Windows operating systems allow this type of screen capture by simply pressing the Print Screen button on the keyboard at any time. You can then paste the image you've grabbed into a graphics editor by choosing Edit, Paste—but I suggest following this format. It works with a graphics program open and you can save in multiple formats and edits straight away.

Here's How You Do It

1. Get Paint Shop Pro. That is the program I outline here, so go get it and install it. It is shareware, which means you will be asked to send in your bucks after a month or so. But go grab it for now. The best place to download it is at http://www.shareware.com or http://www.jasc.com.

2. Open the program. You get a screen that says you're starting your 30-day trial. Click **OK**. There should be a screen with a bunch of brightly colored buttons in the upper-left or -right corner. There are also menu items. One of them is **Capture**; click it and choose **Setup**. It should look like Figure 15.2. That brings up the dialog box shown in Figure 15.3.

3. The Capture Setup dialog box allows you to set up how you want your capture to take place. The far-right groupings denote what will be captured. I almost always leave it on Full Screen. The only other one I find helpful is the Area selection. That allows you to draw crop lines around the area you want to capture. Stay with Full Screen for now.

   There are buttons on the other side of the dialog box. Click to include (or exclude) the cursor or to make multiple captures.

   The area in the middle is what you're interested in as far as initiating the capture goes. That is where you set up what key grabs the screen. I have never used the right mouse button. As you can see, I like the F11 button—but feel free to choose. You can also delay it, but I never understood why.

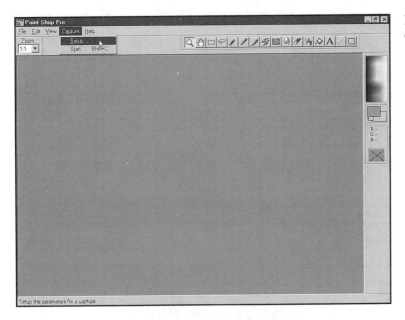

Figure 15.2
Choosing Setup.

Figure 15.3
The Capture Setup dialog box.

Click **OK** to set your wishes in motion.

4. Start the process; now you have the hotkey setup. In order to perform the capture, go back to the **Capture** menu and choose **Start**. It should look like Figure 15.4.

   The Paint Shop Pro program minimizes and becomes a small graphic at the bottom of the screen.

5. Capture! When what you want is on the screen, hit your hotkey or click your right mouse button. Paint Shop Pro becomes full screen again, but now the screen is there as an image. Crop out what you want. Now you have it as an image. Save it as a GIF or JPEG and put it on your page. Figures 15.2, 15.3, and 15.4 were made this way.

That does it. Enjoy and be sure to not break any laws by posting copyrighted stuff without credit or permission. It can really get you into trouble.

Figure 15.4
Starting the capture process.

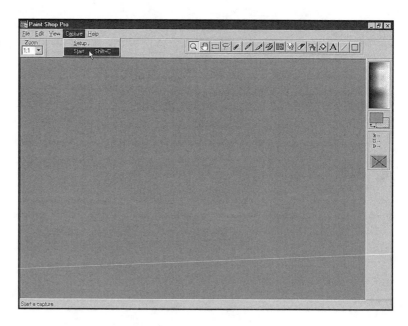

How to Use Telnet

Ever since I posted the three CGI tutorials to the HTML Goodies site, I have been getting mail asking what I mean by "Telnet into your system." I put this quick lesson together to explain in a bit more detail.

Telnet

The term *Telnet* is a mushing together of *telephone* and *network*. The term means to use telephone lines for the purpose of contacting and entering another network computer. For example, let's say I am on joe.net and there is a file I want on fred.com. Once attached to the Internet, I use the Telnet program to work from joe.net on fred.net. It works much like a remote control.

Please note that just because I am discussing Telnet does not mean you are guaranteed Telnet capabilities with your account. You may not be able to connect you own system. It's up to the server people to allow you access.

Even if you can log onto another server from yours, you still may not be able to do all the things I talk about in the CGI tutorials (see Chapter 12, "Common Gateway Interface (CGI)"). Again, it's up to your server people to give you the ability to do anything. Hopefully you will have full access, but if not, contact the people you pay each month and see if your account can be altered to include full access.

Where Will I Find Telnet?

If you are running Windows 95 or Windows 3.*x*, you already have it on your system. Windows 95 people find the program by clicking Start, Programs, Accessories, and choosing Telnet. The icon looks like the one in the heading text. You could also jump right to it by clicking Start, Run, and typing in Telnet. The program pops right up. You can shorten the process by simply typing the name of the server you want to attach to right after the word Telnet; Telnet joe.com, for example.

You should get a Telnet program from the people who act as your service providers if you are running Windows 3.*x*. The operating system doesn't always come with the Telnet program loaded.

Those of you using Macintosh systems need to grab a Telnet program, which are plentiful and small. You'll have no trouble finding one; see either http://www.shareware.com or Yahoo!'s Telnet page. If you want a specific program to shoot for, I suggest NCSA Telnet (http://www.ncsa.uiuc.edu/SDG/Homepage/Platform.html). Telnet programs are usually very small. All they do is make the connection from one server to the next. The two servers do the rest.

How Does It Work?

Well, now I'm into an area that isn't so exact. The programs all work just about the same way, so I'm going to talk in generalities here and use screen captures of my Windows 95 Telnet program to explain.

First off, you have to attach to your server just like you do when you want to surf or get your email. After clicking the Telnet icon to start the program, you get some kind of blank screen where text commands will appear. Mine looks like Figure 15.5.

There is a series of menu items somewhere along the top of the screen. One of them should give you the ability to connect. Your connection command might be under one of the menus; it will be fairly obvious when you run across it. Sometimes it says Connect to Another System or words to that effect. My connect command is right along the top (see Figure 15.6).

After clicking Connect, you are given a way to enter the name of the machine you want to attach to (see Figure 15.7). Usually you'll be good to go by entering the URL without the http://. I can get away with just putting in the domain name. You may also be asked for a port and a terminal type. The settings shown here are the most common; usually they are chosen for you.

Figure 15.5
The Telnet screen.

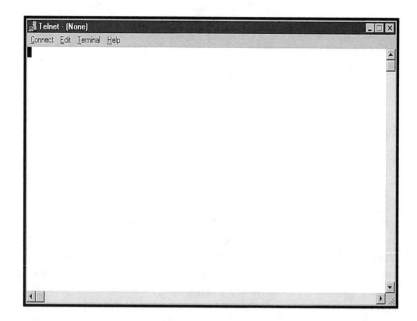

Figure 15.6
The Telnet Connect menu.

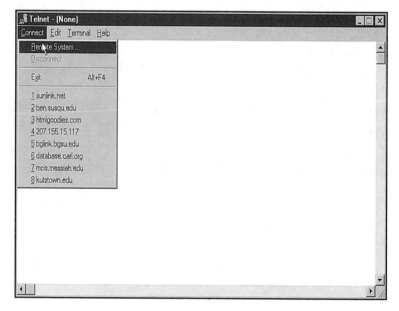

Putting in just the domain gets you to the server's front door. If you are given a longer address including some directories, place them where you enter the attachment directions. They get you right to where you want to go. Click Connect or press Enter to initiate the connection.

Figure 15.7
The Telnet Connect dialog box.

Magic happens, and hopefully a connection is made. You'll know it happened when the screen comes alive and asks for a login and password. Put in the correct pair and you're good to go.

That's about it. Once you're attached, you can make directories and change modifications to your heart's content.

Enjoy!

Appendixes

Everything You Need to Know About HTML 4.0

HTML 4.0 buzzwords are starting to make the mainstream. The email letters asking questions about what is to come are beginning to pile up. I guess if I were to wrap HTML 4.0 up in a nutshell, it would be that there is more user interactivity and more use of style sheets. In fact, style sheets are supposed to rule the roost, but don't sweat it. HTML is completely backward-compatible. You can write pages that never use any of these commands and they display just fine. If you never actually use a style sheet, your pages will look fine. This tutorial is simply to introduce you to new commands, new subcommands, and three dead commands that I bet you've never used, anyway.

Add the commands you like to your arsenal of HTML. Those you dislike, leave for someone else. Here we go...

Readers' Questions Regarding HTML 4.0

I thought I would teach you about the new HTML 4.0 commands by addressing the question I hear most often on my HTML Goodies Web site.

What Is HTML 4.0? Should I Be Concerned About It?

Concerned? As in HTML 4.0 might steal away in the night with your good china? Nah. From everything I've found, it will actually make writing a bit easier for you and on the search engines. The people at the World Wide Web Consortium stepped up to the plate and agreed, in late 1997, that the next version of HTML, version 4.0, should be the accepted version. Now, this *by no means* indicates that it is so. HTML is not fully adopted yet. Even so, remember who you are writing for. Contrary to what many Web-heads believe, the vast majority of Web users are still around the version 2.0 level. Watch the level of your writing. You may be above some heads. Most heads, actually.

I Use Netscape 4 (or Explorer 4). Does That Mean I Should Be Writing in HTML 4.0?

Ah, logic! Man, that sounds like it should be correct, I know. But it ain't. Version numbers of the two main browsers have nothing to do with what version of HTML they use. Now, someone is going to go bonkers at this point and tell me that some elements of HTML 4.0 are available for use in browsers version 4. True—but the manufacturers of the browsers did not wait for their version 4 number to incorporate HTML 4.0. This is one of those strange scientific synchronicities called a coincidence.

With that said, some of these commands can be run using the 4.0 (and some earlier) browsers. When we actually get to the commands, I'll offer some additional examples; then you can see if they actually work for your browser.

On Versions...

Now might be a good time to discuss what all these version numbers mean. There are no hard or fast rules to this, but here's the generally accepted method for giving version numbers to software:

- If there is a major change to the product, step up the number by one.
- If there are tweaks to the product, add a point something (1.1, for example).

With good writing like that, it's a wonder I wasn't hired on at Microsoft years ago, huh?

For instance, say I create a software program that counts the number of times you curse at your computer screen while writing HTML code. I call it Cursor. The first version out of the gate is version 1.0. I offer that version for free over the Net so I can get fine people like you to test it out for free—you are my R&D (research and development) team. This is what companies call a *beta version*. It's something they assume will be replaced by a better version. Kind of like beta video tape. Remember that?

You play with it and find a few bugs. I fix the bugs. Now I have Cursor version 1.1. This is probably the one I sell.

Six months later I decide I hate the *interface* (the look of the screen) and decide to make major changes to my Cursor program. The changes are substantial, so I change the version number. I now have Cursor 2.0. Again with the beta testing. You find a few bugs, I fix them. Ta da! Cursor 2.1. But wait! You suggest an extra function for the program. I add it. We now have Cursor version 2.2. Get it?

What Version of HTML Are We Currently Using?

The last accepted version is HTML 3.2. You can see that HTML has gone through three major overhauls and a couple of tweaks. Have you ever seen one of these?

```
<!DOCTYPE HTML PUBLIC "-//W3C//DTD HTML 3.2//EN">
```

That's a *declaration statement*. It sits at the very top of the page and proclaims to the browser that displays the page that the following page is using HTML 3.2. The *document type declaration* (DTD) is HTML 3.2. When you start to run 4.0, you'll change out the 3.2 with the number 4.0. The EN stands for English.

Who Decided We Should All Go to HTML 4.0?

The World Wide Web Consortium, and they actually don't decide at all. They are the governing body of HTML, among other things. They make suggestions and hopefully the browser-makers follow. But not always. Case in point: The <BLINK> command works in Netscape, but not in Explorer. Go figure.

Every Time I Hear About HTML 4.0, I also Hear About SGML and XML. What Are They?

And you have these conversations with whom? You and your friends are either really, really up on the future of code or you need to get out more.

SGML Stands for Standard Generalized Mark-Up Language

And you already use it. SGML is the mother of HTML. Think of it this way: By using SGML, you have the ability to create your own tags. I want the tag <ZORK> to represent text that is bold, italic, and Arial font. I can set it up with SGML code. HTML is simply a set standard of tags under the huge SGML umbrella.

XML Stands for Extensible Mark-Up Language

XML is a subset of SGML, just as HTML is. The best description of the language comes from Ken Kopf, computer specialist at Susquehanna University. He denotes XML as a very simplified version of SGML. It is a version of the language that people can understand. If SGML is a bear, XML is a kitten. It allows you to set up your own tags and mathematical equations using commands that you can understand. If you'd like to fill your brain cells regarding XML now, see the tutorial earlier in the book.

The concern I see coming out of all of this fancy new stuff is that it might do damage to the Web. You see, HTML was a stunningly easy language that took computer programming out of the hands of men with slide rules and gave it to you and me—the weekend silicon warriors. We understood it. It made some sense.

Introducing SGML and XML, in my mind, is the first real shot the higher-ups have of driving people away. It's something new and most people are comfortable now. Introducing it might stratify the audience or make people drop out altogether.

But not to worry. The full incorporation of these languages is years away. By then there will probably be good, solid, programming software that does most of the XML work for you.

Will You Puh-Leeze Get to HTML 4.0!?

Stop yelling. I'm there. I should say up front that the majority of my research came from the World Wide Web Consortium's pages on HTML 4.0. There are miles of data available. Here's where I attempt to boil it down to the basics.

There are four sections here: "New Commands," "New Subcommands," "Deprecated Commands," and "Dead Commands." After the first two sections, there is an URL to a page containing the commands. Some are actually available today for use. You'll see if your setup does the trick or not with these HTML 4.0 commands.

New Commands

The following 22 commands are "new" and will be incorporated into HTML 4.0:

- `<ABBR>`

  This indicates an abbreviated form of a word. Example:

  ```
  <ABBR TITLE="National Football League">NFL</ABBR>
  ```

  The TITLE command produces a rollover title like the ALT command does on pictures.

- `<ACRONYM>`

  This works the same way as `<ABBR>` except it denotes a acronym. Example:

  ```
  <ACRONYM TITLE="Self-Contained Underwater Breathing Apparatus>
  SCUBA</ACRONYM>
  ```

- `<BDO>`

  This is difficult to explain. Text goes left to right and sometimes right to left. The BDO command denotes to the computer to leave the text in the direction it is currently in. If you write in Hebrew, a language written right to left, using BDO ensures that other elements such as spelling checkers won't be incorporated and flip text around. It is most often used in the `<PRE>` tags. Example:

  ```
  <PRE> <BDO DIR="LTR">hello</BDO> </PRE>
  ```

  LTR means "left to right." Guess what "right to left" is represented by? Yup: RTL.

● <BUTTON>

This becomes standard code for creating link buttons, in a guestbook form for example. Example:

```
<BUTTON name="submit" value="submit" type="submit"></BUTTON>
```

What's more, this format easily allows an image to be placed on the button.

● <COLGROUP>

This command allows for an entire column of data in tables to be affected by one command rather than using a separate command for each cell. Example:

```
<COLGROUP WIDTH="30%"></COLGROUP>
```

● <DEL>

Surrounding something with this command provides a strikethrough over what it deleted. Example:

```
Version <DEL>3</DEL><INS>4</INS>
```

Now you have a jump on what the new command INS does. You'll get to it an a few.

● <FIELDSET>

This allows people to group controls on a page together, like grouping buttons that affect a certain JavaScript so there won't be any interaction between other scripts on the same page or sections of a guestbook. In works in tandem with the LEGEND command. An example is waiting there with that command's explanation.

● <FRAME>

This works the same way as the FRAME command we have today except it has been delegated new powers. These powers include denoting specific traits to each frame cell. It allows for much more capabilities when working with style sheets. This is listed because it will be a specific subset of commands for use with SGML format styles.

● <FRAMESET>

Ditto this one except this deals with larger sections of frame pages. For instance, you have a page with four frame cells. You want only those on the left to have green borders. You use this command to set aside those two vertical frames and assign traits to that section. This is listed because it will be a specific subset of commands for use with SGML format styles.

● <IFRAME>

This again works much the same way as the inline frames we currently use. Again, this is listed because it will be a specific subset of commands for use with SGML format styles.

○ <INS>

You saw earlier how this works. It sets something aside as having been added or "inserted" at a later time. It is denoted via an underline.

○ <LABEL>

This command attaches a label to form commands. Example:

```
<FORM ACTION="--">
<LABEL for="email">Email Address</LABEL>
<INPUT type="text" name="email_address" id="email">
```

○ <LEGEND>

Now we get to the example denoted earlier from the FIELDSET command. FIELDSET groups form items together. LEGEND denotes those sections. Example:

```
<FIELDSET>
<LEGEND>Personal Information</LEGEND> Name: [Input Text Box]
EMAIL: [Input Text Box]
AGE: [Input Text Box]
</FIELDSET>
```

It keeps it all straight for the computer.

○ <NOFRAMES>

This denotes text content that displays whether the user has frame capabilities. It's been around for a while but now is being officially brought into the fold.

○ <NOSCRIPT>

Ditto from <NOFRAMES>.

○ <OBJECT>

This command replaces IMG, ISMAP, APPLET, SCRIPT, and a myriad of other "objects" that appear on the page. This one command represents that something is going to be placed on the page. The computer then decides what kind of object it is due to its extension. Example:

```
<OBJECT data="image.gif" type="image/gif"></OBJECT>
<OBJECT classid="applet.class"></OBJECT>
<OBJECT data="movie.avi" type="application/avi"></OBJECT>
```

○ <OPTGROUP>

How this will be handled is still a little fuzzy, but it appears that it allows multiple groups of information inside pull-down menus, much like the menus produced by the W95 Start button.

- ◯ `<PARAM>`

  This command is used with applets to set parameters. It's already in use, but is now being brought into the fold.

- ◯ `<SPAN>`

  Think of the span element in terms of its being an equal to the `<DIV>` command. It denotes a certain division of the page or span of text that can then be altered to your heart's content. Example:

  ```
  <SPAN CLASS="green">This would be green text</SPAN>
  <TBODY>
  ```

  This command surrounds a block of table cells so that you can affect just that section. Keep reading...

- ◯ `<TFOOT>`

  This allows you to place a footer below each TBODY section of a table. Notice that all the commands are TR rather than TD. Here's an example for both TBODY and TFOOT:

  ```
  <TABLE>
  <TBODY bgcolor="--">
  <TR> text
  <TR> text
  </TBODY>
  <TFOOT>
  <TR>The above cells...
  </TFOOT>
  </TABLE>
  ```

- ◯ `<THREAD>`

  This is header information for a group of cells, used the same way as TFOOT—above the group of cells set apart by the TBODY command. Example:

  ```
  <TABLE>
  <THREAD>
  <TR> The following cells...
  </THREAD>
  <TBODY bgcolor="--">
  <TR> text
  <TR> text
  </TBODY>
  <TFOOT>
  <TR>The above cells...
  </TFOOT>
  </TABLE>
  ```

○ <Q>

The difference between the Q command and the BLOCKQUOTE command is that the Q command is much easier to write. Use them exactly the same way.

Take Them for a Test Drive

I've set up a page online that demonstrates these new commands in action. When you go see it, make sure you're using a version 4.0 browser; otherwise you won't get any of the new effects. Please remember that even through you may have the 4.0 browser, some of the commands are still not supported. You should make a point of looking at the source code. The latest HTML 4.0 declaration statement is used. That said, go to http://www.htmlgoodies.com/newcommands.html.

Some New Subcommands

In my opinion, this is where HTML shines—the subcommands. The subcommands allow a simple table cell to have color and size. It allows an image to have text and set sizes, and there are a few new ones to be concerned with in HTML 4.0. Here you go:

○ <CLASS>

This is already in use in Explorer versions 3 and 4. First you set up a class with a style sheet command. (See my tutorial on classes and IDs for how to do it.) Then you call for the style sheet using the CLASS command. Example:

```
<SPAN CLASS="purple">Affected text</SPAN>
```

○ <DIR>

This was touched on in the BDO command explanation. The DIR subcommand denotes whether the text is to be read LTR (left to right) or RTL (right to left).

○ <ID>

The ID can be used in the same manner as the CLASS subcommand, but in HTML 4.0 it is also being used to denote sections of the page. In short, it acts like a page jump. Example:

```
<A HREF="#sectionone-id">Jump to Section One</A>
```

The command jumps to this:

```
<SPAN ID="sectionone">section One
```

This method is a little better than the page jump because it jumps to a section of text rather than to the page.

○ <LANG>

This is clever because it helps the search engines understand different languages as being different languages rather than just misspelled English. Example:

```
<SPAN LANG="es">Hola! Como esta?</SPAN>
```

Those of you who remember your high school Spanish know that phrase loosely translates to "Hi, how ya doin'?" Contrary to what you might be thinking, the LANG subcommand does not translate. You must still write the text in the native tongue. The LANG command allows the search engines to recognize that section as Spanish text. In case you're wondering, here are some other codes: ar (Arabic), de (German), el (Greek), fr (French), he (Hebrew), hi (Hindi), ja (Japanese), it (Italian), nl (Dutch), pt (Portuguese), ur (Urdu), ru (Russian), sa (Sandskirt), zh (Chinese). Yes, there is also a code set aside if you want to denote a language that doesn't really exist, like Pig Latin or Klingon. Follow the same form as earlier but add x- before the name. Like so: LANG="x-ubbee dubbie". The x indicates that it's an experimental language.

○ <TITLE>

This title command works just the same as the ALT command in an IMG command. It allows you to place a title onto just about anything so that a text box pops up when the mouse remains stationary for a second. Example:

```
<SPAN TITLE="National Football League">NFL</SPAN>
```

Now every time someone places his mouse on that set of initials, the box pops up saying "National Football League." It can be very helpful.

Now Take These for a Test Drive

 Same deal as before: There's a page set up for you to go look at these subcommands in action. Make sure you're using a version 4.0 browser. Remember to look at the source code. Go to http://www.htmlgoodies.com/newcommands.html.

Deprecated Elements

Table A.1 contains commands that are still good, but have better ways of getting the effect. When a command is deprecated, it also means that the next version of HTML might not support it. That means you run a risk of the next-generation browsers not recognizing it.

Table A.1   Deprecated Elements

Deprecated Command	What to Use Instead
`<APPLET>`	`<OBJECT>`
`<BASEFONT>`	Style sheet commands
`<CENTER>`	The `ALIGN="center"` sub command or style sheet commands
`<DIR>`	Create lists through `<UL>`
`<FONT>`	Style sheet commands
`<ISINDEX>`	Create various `<INPUT>` commands to create the text box `ISINDEX` creates
`<MENU>`	Create lists through the `<UL>` command
`<S>`	Create strikethrough text using style sheet commands
`<STRIKE>`	Create strikethrough text using style sheet commands
`<U>`	Create underlined text using style sheet commands

Dead Elements

In with the good, out with the bad. These three puppies are gone for good:

R.I.P	Now What?
`<LISTING>`	`<PRE>`
`<PLAINTEXT>`	`<PRE>`
`<XMP>`	`<PRE>`

That's the Scoop

Now you know far more about HTML 4.0 than I'm sure you cared to know. If I were to put it all into a few simple sentences, I would say that this is not yet something to get all excited or nervous over. It will probably be a while before these commands are all commonplace.

Let me again say that you should be taught the value of understatement in any Web page design class. Just because you have all these fancy commands doesn't mean you have to use them.

Think of your audience. If they are real Web-heads that simply go gah-gah over the newest stuff and have the latest browsers and all the stunning plug-ins, maybe you should get involved with this. If your audience is a mass of people with greatly varying browsers and platforms, maybe you should stay at a lower level. No matter how cool your page is, I can't be impressed by it if I can't display it.

There. I've now put my soap box away.

Enjoy!

Appendix B

Useful Charts

Color Codes

 Table B.1 contains a list of popular colors along with their hex code equivalents. You can see this chart online in full living color at http://www.htmlgoodies.com/colors.html.

Table B.1 Color Codes in Word and Hex Form

Color Code	Hex Code	Color Code	Hex Code	Color Code	Hex Code
Aliceblue	F0F8FF	Darkmagenta	8B008B	Hotpink	FF69B4
Antiquewhite	FAEBD7	Darkolive green	556B2F	Indianred	CD5C5C
Aqua	00FFFF	Darkorange	FF8C00	Indigo	4B0082
Aquamarine	7FFFD4	Darkorchid	9932CC	Ivory	FFFFF0
Azure	F0FFFF	Darkred	8B0000	Khaki	F0E68C
Beige	F5F5DC	Darksalmon	E9967A	Lavender	E6E6FA
Bisque	FFE4C4	Darkseagreen	8FBC8F	Lavenderblush	FFF0F5
Black	000000	Darkslateblue	483D8B	Lawngreen	7CFC00
Blanchedalmond	FFEBCD	Darkslategray	2F4F4F	Lemonchiffon	FFFACD
Blue	0000FF	Darkturquoise	00CED1	Lightblue	ADD8E6
Blueviolet	8A2BE2	Darkviolet	9400D3	Lightcoral	F08080
Brown	A52A2A	Deeppink	FF1493	Lightcyan	E0FFFF
Burlywood	DEB887	Deepskyblue	00BFFF	Lightgoldenrodyellow	FAFAD2
Cadetblue	5F9EA0	Dimgray	696969	Lightgreen	90EE90
Chartreuse	7FFF00	Dodgerblue	1E90FF	Lightgrey	D3D3D3
Chocolate	D2691E	Firebrick	B22222	Lightpink	FFB6C1
Coral	FF7F50	Floralwhite	FFFAF0	Lightsalmon	FFA07A
Cornflowerblue	6495ED	Forestgreen	228B22	Lightseagreen	20B2AA
Cornsilk	FFF8DC	Fuchsia	FF00FF	Lightskyblue	87CEFA
Crimson	DC143C	Gainsboro	DCDCDC	Lightslategray	778899
Cyan	00FFFF	Ghostwhite	F8F8FF	Lightsteelblue	B0C4DE
Darkblue	00008B	Gold	FFD700	Lightyellow	FFFFE0
Darkcyan	008B8B	Goldenrod	DAA520	Lime	00FF00
Darkgoldenrod	B8860B	Gray	808080	Limegreen	32CD32
Darkgray	A9A9A9	Green	008000	Linen	FAF0E6
Darkgreen	006400	Greenyellow	ADFF2F	Magenta	FF00FF
Darkkhaki	BDB76B	Honeydew	F0FFF0	Maroon	800000

Color Code	Hex Code	Color Code	Hex Code	Color Code	Hex Code
Mediumauqamarine	66CDAA	Orchid	DA70D6	Sienna	A0522D
Mediumblue	0000CD	Palegoldenrod	EEE8AA	Silver	C0C0C0
Mediumorchid	BA55D3	Palegreen	98FB98	Skyblue	87CEEB
Mediumpurple	9370D8	Paleturquoise	AFEEEE	Slateblue	6A5ACD
Mediumseagreen	3CB371	Palevioletred	D87093	Slategray	708090
Mediumslateblue	7B68EE	Papayawhip	FFEFD5	Snow	FFFAFA
Mediumspringgreen	00FA9A	Peachpuff	FFDAB9	Springgreen	00FF7F
Mediumturquoise	48D1CC	Peru	CD853F	Steelblue	4682B4
Mediumvioletred	C71585	Pink	FFC0CB	Tan	D2B48C
Midnightblue	191970	Plum	DDA0DD	Teal	008080
Mintcream	F5FFFA	Powderblue	B0E0E6	Thistle	D8BFD8
Mistyrose	FFE4E1	Purple	800080	Tomato	FF6347
Moccasin	FFE4B5	Red	FF0000	Turquoise	40E0D0
Navajowhite	FFDEAD	Rosybrown	BC8F8F	Violet	EE82EE
Navy	000080	Royalblue	4169E1	Wheat	F5DEB3
Oldlace	FDF5E6	Saddlebrown	8B4513	White	FFFFFF
Olive	808000	Salmon	FA8072	Whitesmoke	F5F5F5
Olivedrab	688E23	Sandybrown	F4A460	Yellow	FFFF00
Orange	FFA500	Seagreen	2E8B57	Yellowgreen	9ACD32
Orangered	FF4500	Seashell	FFF5EE		

Non-Dithering Color Chart

As if there isn't enough to be concerned about in terms of colors, here's one more little deal. It's called *non-dithering*. In layman's terms, non-dithering colors look the same when displayed by all browsers with all computer screen resolution settings.

Doesn't that happen with all colors? Nope. Have you ever seen a color created by what appeared to be one solid color and then a few lighter-colored dots laid across the top? It didn't blend at all, but the two colors together sort of created another color. Or have you ever printed something in color, and instead of being one color, it appeared to be a series of different-colored dots? That's called *dithering*, and it's not pretty.

 See this tutorial online, in color, at `http://www.htmlgoodies.com/non_dithering_colors.html`.

Non-dithering colors always give a nice, smooth color on Web pages and in graphics. That's because these are the 216 colors chosen by Windows and Macintosh operating platforms to make up their palettes of colors. The colors that aren't represented here are the colors that these try to make up by dithering. Get it?

The color list comes from a mathematical formula using the shades 00, 33, 66, 99, CC, and FF from hex codes. Using just those six hex combinations—over red, blue, and green hues—gives us a total of 216 colors that render perfectly on your screen. Obviously this isn't going to show up too well in a black and white book, so I suggest you go to the HTML Goodies Web site at `http://www.htmlgoodies.com/non_dithering_colors.html` to get a good look.

An Explanation of Hexadecimal Codes

It's pretty easy to understand the word color codes, but those hex codes are rather strange. Here's a quick explanation.

The three primary colors are red, blue, and yellow. Remember that from high school art? They are called the *primary colors* because there are no two "lesser" colors that make them up. Purple is not a primary color because it can be created through combining equal parts of blue and red.

In the world of mechanical things that make color, like a television or computer screen, color is created through mixing three basic colors. It's a process known as *additive color*.

You would think that the TVs and computer monitors of the world would simply use the three primary color to start with, but nothing in life can be that easy. The three colors used to start additive color mixing are red, green, and blue. Why? Because by starting with one composite color, green, you can still create yellow because it's contained in the green. In addition, now you are actually starting with four colors: red, green, blue, yellow. Stay with me here...

To go on, I need to explain a second process of working with colors—subtractive color. *Subtractive color* is the concept of combining colors to make another, like mixing red and blue paint to get purple. That may sound like additive color, but in reality, colors are made by subtracting a hue from the color scheme by adding more of another. Adding more white to black makes it more silver, subtracting more black as more white is mixed in. Get it?

One other big difference between additive and subtractive color—and this is the key—is what you get when you add them all together.

If you add all the colors together in a subtractive color method, you get black. Why? Because you added them all together and all those colors subtracted from all the others leaves no set color: black.

A computer, on the other hand, works with light, not paint or any other goopy stuff. Mix a computer's additive colors—red, green, and blue—together and you get white.

No kidding, you really do. Shine a white light at a prism or a lead crystal glass. You'll get a rainbow of colors. Actually, that's how a rainbow is created. White light is being shown through water in the air. That separates the white light into the "rainbow" of colors.

Now on to the six-digit representation of color known as the *hex code*.

Basic Hexadecimal Notation

Hex numbers use 16 characters:

0 1 2 3 4 5 6 7 8 9 A B C D E F

Zero (0) is the smallest representations of a color. It's almost the total absence of color. F is 15 times the intensity of the color 0. Combinations of these digits create different shades of a particular color. Double zero, 00, is equal to zero hue; FF is equal to a pure color.

This color representation is done three times, once for red, once for green, and once for blue, in that order. Put the three two-digit codes together and you get a six-digit hex code. The hex code is just a representation of the red, green, and blue intensity, in that order. The computer creates the three intensities, mashes them together, and you get a single shade of color.

For an example, here are the opposite ends of the color scale:

```
FFFFFF
```

The code is equal to white. Why? Notice the three colors are all set to FF. That means the highest level of red, green, and blue. As I said, the combination of all three primary colors creates white in a computer or television. Now here's black:

```
000000
```

This is just the opposite. All three settings of red, green, and blue are set to a total absence of color: black.

Now, here are a few other codes and their breakdown:

FFFF00

Let's start with yellow. This code produces pure yellow. Notice that the red and the green are at full tilt? There is no blue. By mashing the red and green up against each other, the red cancels out the blue and all that is left is the yellow. It's actually a subtractive color method being employed in an additive world. This gets loopy, huh?

DC143C

The code creates a shade of red called crimson. The red setting, DC, is pretty intense. There's not much green. Blue is set a little less than halfway up.

EE82EE

That's violet. The red and the blue are at pretty high levels. The green is there, but at a lower level. Now, this is not purple, but violet. Again, purple is a combination of red and blue alone. The code is 800080. Notice there's no green at all, just an equal amount of red and blue.

FFA500

That's orange. There's lots of red, not quite an equal level of green, and no blue.

That's how the hex codes work. This lesson probably won't make you an expert in color creation, but at least you'll be able to understand the creation of color in a computer.

So, are there more hex code colors that what I showed? Oh, yes. There are thousands upon millions, covering every color in the scale from pure black to pure white. When you set your computer monitor to 16 million colors, you're not kidding. You're setting it to the number of shades available in the computer universe. Every time you change even one of the red, green, or blue levels, you change the color. Most changes are so subtle you'll not recognize it, but it's there.

Enjoy!

Ampersand Commands

Ampersand commands are quite useful, especially to me. I use them all over my HTML tutorials to create the characters not found on the keyboard or to make command characters show up on the page.

Let's say you want a copyright insignia. Well, there isn't any copyright on the keyboard. That means you'll need to either create it as a graphic or use an & command to place it. Have you also noticed a World Wide Web page that shows HTML commands like <HTML>? Don't you find it strange that if I enclose HTML in brackets (< >) that it shouldn't show up on the page? It's done using an & command to create the greater than and less than signs.

Here's How It Works

Your browser reads commands inside greater than and less than brackets. But did you know it also reads commands inside an & and ; (semicolon) insignia?

Those who create the HTML code have created a slew of these commands that sit inside an ampersand and a semicolon. All you need to know is the little three- or four-letter code that goes between the characters and you'll be placing little insignias all over your page.

Figure B.1 shows as many ampersand commands as I could find. Remember that you do not place these codes inside < and > commands. These just sit as they appear in the chart shown here. They always begin with an & and end with a ;.

Each chart cell is set up with the ampersand command, as it should appear on your page, and then what the command created. Remember, capitalization counts here!

® ®	± ±	µ µ	¶ ¶	· ·	¢ ¢
£ £	¥ ¥	¼ ¼	½ ½	¾ ¾	¹ ¹
² ²	³ ³	¿ ¿	° °	¦ ¦	§ §
< <	> >	& &	" "	 (A Space)	&Ccdil; Ç
&ccdil; ç	Ñ Ñ	ñ ñ	Þ Þ	þ þ	Ý Ý
ý ý	ÿ ÿ	ß ß	Æ Æ	Á Á	Â Â
À À	Å Å	Ã Ã	Ä Ä	æ æ	á á
â â	à à	å å	ã ã	ä ä	Ð Ð
É É	Ê Ê	È È	Ë Ë	ð ð	é é
ê ê	è è	ë ë	Í Í	Î Î	Ì Ì

Ï Ï	í í	î î	ì ì	ï ï	Ó Ó
Ô Ô	Ò Ò	Ø Ø	Õ Õ	Ö Ö	ó ó
ô ô	ò ò	ø ø	õ õ	ö ö	Ú Ú
Û Û	Ù Ù	Ü Ü	ú ú	û û	ù ù
ü ü	« «	» »			

Figure B.1
Ampersand commands and the characters they print.

Please note that some of these commands are higher in the HTML realm than others. You may have trouble with the first 10 or so if you are using a lower version browser.

Enjoy!

ASCII Commands

Thank yous go out to Steven Erickson of Optum NewMedia Services for explaining these commands to me.

When writing a Web page you want to have as much flexibility as possible in placing characters. If you have read the preceding ampersand command section, you know you can create characters not found on the normal keyboard using an & and a ;. Well, you can do the same using &# and a ; and a command in between. They are called *ASCII commands* and are very similar to what your computer uses to display the text you type.

What are listed here are the ASCII commands that produce certain characters not readily found on the keyboard (some are though, just to keep the flow of the numbers).

Some are repeats from the ampersand command tutorial. Just follow the format to place any of these on your page. Do not enclose these in the brackets commands; they sit just as they look in the boxes.

Since these are ASCII commands, there must be an equivalent for all the characters already found on the keyboard. There are:

- Numbers 33–47, 58–64, 91–96, and 123–126 are the non-letter and non-numerical characters on the keyboard—things like a $ and an *.
- Numbers 48—57 are the numerals 0 through 9.
- Numbers 65—90 are the capital letters *A* through *Z*.
- Numbers 97—122 are the lowercase letters *a* through *z*.
- 127 is the Delete key entry.
- 128–159 are not in use.
- 160 is the Spacebar.

The other numbers are shown in Figure B.2. You'll see what the command creates in each cell and the command you use to create the symbol below it.

`&#0130;`	*f* `&#0131;`	„ `&#0132;`	… `&#0133;`	† `&#0134;`	‡ `&#0135;`
ˆ `&#0136;`	‰ `&#0137;`	Š `&#0138;`	‹ `&#0139;`	Œ `&#0140;`	‘ `&#0145;`
’ `&#0146;`	“ `&#0147;`	” `&#0148;`	• `&#0149;`	– `&#0150;`	— `&#0151;`

˜ `&#0152;`	™ `&#0153;`	š `&#0154;`	› `&#0155;`	œ `&#0156;`	Ÿ `&#0159;`
`&#0160;`	¡ `&#0161;`	¢ `&#0162;`	£ `&#0163;`	¤ `&#0164;`	¥ `&#0165;`
¦ `&#0166;`	§ `&#0167;`	¨ `&#0168;`	© `&#0169;`	ª `&#0170;`	« `&#0171;`
¬ `&#0172;`	`&#0173;`	® `&#0174;`	¯ `&#0175;`	° `&#0176;`	± `&#0177;`
² `&#0178;`	³ `&#0179;`	´ `&#0180;`	µ `&#0181;`	¶ `&#0182;`	· `&#0183;`
¸ `&#0184;`	¹ `&#0185;`	º `&#0186;`	» `&#0187;`	¼ `&#0188;`	½ `&#0189;`

¾ `&#0190;`	¿ `&#0191;`	À `&#0192;`	Á `&#0193;`	Â `&#0194;`	Ã `&#0195;`
? `&#0196;`	? `&#0197;`	Æ `&#0198;`	Ç `&#0199;`	È `&#0200;`	É `&#0201;`
Ê `&#0202;`	Ë `&#0203;`	Ì `&#0204;`	Í `&#0205;`	Î `&#0206;`	Ï `&#0207;`
Ð `&#0208;`	Ñ `&#0209;`	Ò `&#0210;`	Ó `&#0211;`	Ô `&#0212;`	Õ `&#0213;`
Ö `&#0214;`	× `&#0215;`	Ø `&#0216;`	Ù `&#0217;`	Ú `&#0218;`	Û `&#0219;`
Ü `&#0220;`	Ý `&#0221;`	Þ `&#0222;`	ß `&#0223;`	à `&#0224;`	á `&#0225;`

â `&#0226;`	ã `&#0227;`	ä `&#0228;`	å `&#0229;`	æ `&#0230;`	ç `&#0231;`
è `&#0232;`	é `&#0233;`	ê `&#0234;`	ë `&#0235;`	ì `&#0236;`	í `&#0237;`
î `&#0238;`	ï `&#0239;`	ð `&#0240;`	ñ `&#0241;`	ò `&#0242;`	ó `&#0243;`
ô `&#0244;`	õ `&#0245;`	ö `&#0246;`	÷ `&#0247;`	ø `&#0248;`	ù `&#0249;`
ú `&#0250;`	û `&#0251;`	ü `&#0252;`	ý `&#0253;`	þ `&#0254;`	ÿ `&#0255;`

Figure B.2
ASCII commands and the characters they print.

Valuable Links

Links to Search Engines

This appendix includes a list of some of the more popular search engines, each of which accepts submissions of personal pages. Whether they will post them is another story.

If you do submit your pages, you should check back within a month to see if it has been posted. If not, you will want to resubmit.

Ahoy!

```
http://ahoy.cs.washington.edu:6060/
```

AltaVista

```
http://www.altavista.digital.com/
```

Apollo—The Web's advertising catalog

```
http://apollo.co.uk
```

BizAds Business Locator

```
http://bizads.2cowherd.net/
```

ComFind—A business directory

```
http://comfind.com/
```

EuroSeek

```
http://www.euroseek.net/page?ifl=uk
```

Excite

http://www.excite.com

Galaxy

http://galaxy.einet.net/search-pages.html

Humor Search Comedy Search Engine

http://www.humorsearch.com/

HotBot

http://www.hotbot.com/index.html

Human Search—Real humans do the search for you

http://www.humansearch.com/cgi-bin/limit.pl

InfoSeek

http://www.infoseek.com

Inktomi

http://inktomi.berkeley.edu/query.html

Internet Sleuth

http://www.isleuth.com/

Lycos

http://www.lycos.com

Magellan

http://www.mckinley.com/

MetaSearch

http://www.metasearch.com

MoneySearch—Geared to small business and investment

http://www.moneysearch.com/

Nerd World Media

http://www.nerdworld.com

OpenText

http://www.opentext.com

PedagoNet—Geared to teaching and learning sites

http://www.pedagonet.com/

Planet Search

http://www.planetsearch.com/

Public Safety Search Engine—Geared to police, fire, and public safety sites

> http://www.policeworld.net/search/urlsrch.shtml

Rescue Island

> http://www.rescueisland.com/

SavvySearch—Search multiple search engines at one time

> http://rampal.cs.colostate.edu:2000/

SoftSearch—Geared to finding software programs

> http://www.softsearch.com

Starting Point

> http://www.stpt.com/search.html

Webcrawler

> http://webcrawler.com

WebSeer—Searches for online pictures

> http://webseer.cs.uchicago.edu/

Websurfer

> http://www.io.com/websurfer/

What-U-Seek

> http://www.whatuseek.com/

What's New Too!

> http://newtoo.manifest.com/search.html

WWWomen—Geared to finding sites regarding women's issues

> http://www.wwwomen.com/

WWWW (The World Wide Web Worm)

> http://www.goto.com/

Yahoo!

> http://www.yahoo.com

Search for Search Engines

If you couldn't find what you were looking for, don't fear. There are well over 500 search engines on the World Wide Web covering every imaginable topic. Here are a few links to pages that can help you search for search engines:

Beaucoup's Search Engines—Close to 600 at last count

```
http://www.beaucoup.com/engines.html
```

Dr. Webster's Big Page of Search Engines

```
http://www.drwebster.com/search/search.htm
```

Search.Com—From C-Net Central

```
http://www.search.com
```

Yahoo!'s Search Engine Page—This is the mother lode

```
http://search.yahoo.com/bin/search?p=Search+Engines
```

Registering with Search Engines

In order to get people to your site, you must let them know your site is there. The best way to do that is register your site with search engines. Here are a few sites you might find helpful in your quest for more visitors:

@Submit!

```
http://uswebsites.com/submit/
```

1–2–3–Register Me!

```
http://www.123registerme.com
```

Acclaim Web Services

```
http://www.acclaimweb.com
```

Add Me!

```
http://www.addme.com
```

Add URL

```
http://addurl.com
```

Linkosaurus

```
https://secure.rt66.com/swestart/linkosaurus.html
```

Postmaster

```
http://www.netcreations.com/postmaster/
```

Register-It!

```
http://www.register-it.com/
```

Submit-It!

```
http://www.submit-it.com
```

Sites Offering JavaScripts

Here is a list of sites offering JavaScripts for downloading:

Cool Nerds JavaScript Links

```
http://www.coolnerds.com/linkjava.htm
```

Danny Goodman's JavaScript Pages

```
http://www.dannyg.com/javascript/index.html
```

Gamelan

```
http://www.gamelan.com
```

HotSyte

```
http://www.serve.com/hotsyte/
```

Java Goodies (part of my HTML Goodies site)

```
http://www.htmlgoodies.com/javagoodies
```

JavaScript Authoring Guide

```
http://home.netscape.com/eng/mozilla/Gold/handbook/javascript/index.html
```

JavaScript Connection

```
http://Monroe-Computer.cnchost.com/
```

JavaScript FAQ

```
http://www.freqgrafx.com/411/jsfaq.html
```

JavaScript Forum

```
http://www.geocities.com/ResearchTriangle/1828/index.html
```

JavaScript/Netscape's JavaScript Resources

```
http://home.netscape.com/comprod/products/navigator/version_2.0/script/
script_info/index.html
```

JavaScript Planet

```
http://www.geocities.com/SiliconValley/7116/
```

JavaScript: Simple Little Things to Add to Your Pages

```
http://tanega.com/java/java.html
```

JavaScript World

```
http://www.mydesktop.com/internet/javascript/
```

Live Software: JavaScript Resource Center

```
http://www.livesoftware.com/jrc/index.html
```

Yahoo!'s JavaScript Page

```
http://www.yahoo.com/Computers_and_Internet/Programming_Languages/
```

Pages Offering Java Applets

Here is a list of sites offering Java applets for downloading:

Earthweb Chat—Offers applets for creating chat rooms

```
http://chat.earthweb.com
```

Gamelan

```
http://www.gamelen.com
```

Jars.Com—A massive site with links and reviews

```
http://www.jars.com
```

Java Boutique

```
http://javaboutique.internet.com/
```

Java Centre

```
http://www.java.co.uk/JC/javacentre.html
```

SneakerChat Offers Applets for Creating Chat Rooms

```
http://www.sneakerchat.com
```

The Java Place

```
http://www.thejavaplace.com/
```

Yahoo!'s Applet Page

```
http://www.yahoo.com/Computers_and_Internet/Programming_Languages/Java/
Applets/
```

HTML Helper Applications

Try these sites for HTML assistant programs. Some are free, some are shareware, and some want the money up front.

Globetrotter Web Assistant

```
http://www.akimbo.com/globetrotter/index.html
```

HotDog

```
http://www.sausage.com
```

HoTMetaL

```
http://www.akimbo.com/globetrotter/index.html
```

HTML Assistant

> http://www.brooknorth.com/

HTMLpad

> http://www.intermania.com/htmlpad/index.html

Live Mark-Up

> http://www.mediatec.com/mediatech/

MS FrontPage

> http://www.microsoft.com/frontpage/

Web Director

> http://www.webdirector.com

Yahoo!'s HTML Editors

> http://www.yahoo.com/Business_and_Economy/Companies/Computers/Software/
> Internet/World_Wide_Web/HTML_Editors/

Yahoo!'s HTML Editor Review Page

> http://www.yahoo.com/Computers_and_Internet/Software/Reviews/Titles/
> Internet/Web_Authoring_Tools/HTML_Editors/

Yahoo!'s Window's HTML Editors

> http://www.yahoo.com/Business_and_Economy/Companies/Computers/Software/
> Internet/World_Wide_Web/HTML_Editors/MS_Windows/

Internet Browsers

There are more than one or two browsers out there. There may also be a newer version of the browser you are currently using. You have to know where to find them. Here are the download sites for some of the different World Wide Web browsers:

Cello

> ftp://ftp.law.cornell.edu/pub/LII/Cello/

HotJava—This is a Java-based browser from Sun Microsystems

> http://java.sun.com/products/hotjava/index.html

Lynx—This is a text-only browser

> http://lynx.browser.org/

Microsoft Internet Explorer

> http://www.microsoft.com/ie/

Mosaic for Macintosh

> http://www.ncsa.uiuc.edu/SDG/Software/MacMosaic/MacMosaicHome.html

Mosaic for Windows

> http://www.ncsa.uiuc.edu/SDG/Software/WinMosaic/HomePage.html

NetCruiser

> http://www.netcom.com

Netscape Communicator—This is a suite of programs including the Navigator

> http://home.netscape.com/comprod/products/communicator/index.html

NetTamer—This is a DOS-based browser

> http://people.delphi.com/davidcolston/

Viola!

> http://xcf.berkeley.edu/ht/projects/viola/violaHome.html

Voyager—Made for the Amiga computer

> http://www.vapor.com/voyager/

Web Explorer (IBM)

> http://www.raleigh.ibm.com/WebExplorer

WinWeb

> http://www.einet.net/EINet/WinWeb/WinWebHome.html

Yahoo!'s Browser Page

> http://www.yahoo.com/Computers_and_Internet/Software/Internet/
> World_Wide_Web/Browsers/

Index

504

523

What-U-Seek Web site,
493
What's New Too! Web
site, 493
WIDTH command
applets, 286, 291
browser pop-up win-
dows, 309
images, 96, 103
inline frames, 369
<MULTICOL> flag, 70
scrolling marquees,
353
sideline images, 130
<TD> flag, 160
width definition (style
sheets), 229
<WIDTH> flag, 38
WinWeb Web site, 498
WinZip Web site, 118,
259
word-spacing definition
(style sheets), 227
World Wide Web Con-
sortium Web site, 256
World Wide Web
Consortium's Style Web
site, 231
WWW. *See* Internet
WWWomen Web site,
493
WWWW (World Wide
Web Worm) Web site,
493

X

XML (Extensible Mark-up
Language), 457-458,
461, 473-474
DTD Web pages,
459-460
HTML, compared, 458
Internet Explorer, 461
Netscape, 461
Perl, 461
SGML, compared, 458
standalone Web pages,
459
style sheets, 461
XML and style sheets
Web site, 461
XML.com Web site, 460
<XMP> flag, 58, 480

Y-Z

Yahoo! search code, 217
Yahoo!'s (Web sites), 433,
493
Applet Page, 496
Background Image,
127
Browser Page, 498
copyright search, 422
DHTML Games, 375
HTML Editor Review
Page, 497
HTML Editors, 497
HTML Formats:
DHTML, 375
imagemap links, 138
Java Script Page, 495
Search Engine Page,
494

Transparent Image,
109
Window's HTML
Editors, 497
XML page, 461

z-index definition (style
sheets), 229
zip files, 259